The Child
and the Law

The Child and the Law

Nicholas C. Bala, B.A., LL.B., LL.M.
Faculty of Law, Queen's University

Kenneth L. Clarke, B.A., LL.B.
Barrister and Solicitor

foreword by
Judge George Thomson

Associate Deputy Minister
Ministry of Community and Social Services
Children's and Adults'
Policy and Program Development

McGraw-Hill Ryerson Limited

Toronto Montreal New York St. Louis San Francisco Auckland Bogotá
Guatemala Hamburg Johannesburg Lisbon London Madrid Mexico
New Delhi Panama Paris San Juan São Paulo Singapore Sydney Tokyo

1 2 3 4 5 6 7 8 9 0 H R 0 9 8 7 6 5 4 3 2 1
Printed and bound in Canada
Care has been taken to trace ownership of copyright material contained in this text. The publishers will gladly take any information that will enable them to rectify any reference or credit in subsequent editions.

Canadian Cataloguing in Publication Data

Bala, Nicholas C.
  The child and the law
Includes index.
ISBN 0-07-077868-X
1. Children – Legal status, laws, etc. – Canada.
I. Clarke, Kenneth L., date   II. Title.
KE512.B34   346.7101'35   C80-094690-1

To our parents
and our children

Foreword

This book is a thumb-nail sketch of the laws that affect children — those who run afoul of the law; those on whose behalf the protection authorities must intervene; children caught up in the marriage break-down of their parents; children who strive for recognition and peaceful co-existence within their family unit. It sees those laws imbedded in the context of history, impinging on the present, informing the future. It awakens those laws that have lain dormant, stirs to life those of recent birth, and captures, through case illustration, their elusive quality to not only adjudicate and determine disputes regarding children, but to forge and shape society's attitudes toward them.

And what emerges? An attestation to the law's power to aspire to the improvement of the status of that segment of our population until so recently passed by, an attestation particularly impressive because of the deftness with which the authors disentangle those legal principles from the complexities of their machinery.

This book is intended as a textbook for in-service training of professionals who work with children and their families in disciplines allied to the law — social workers, corrections officers, teachers, psychologists, physicians, nurses — people who encounter the law to an increasing extent in their day-to-day duties, and who want to know, not just what the law is, but why it is there, what it can do and what it cannot. There is much here to answer their questions, and more importantly to lessen the sense of forboding with which they often approach a court-room.

It is a skillful and refreshing presentation, one that will excite the enthusiasm of all those who have passed through the realm of childhood and now strive on behalf of those who have come after.

Judge George Thomson
Associate Deputy Minister
Ministry of Community and Social Services
Children's and Adults'
Policy and Program Development

Preface

This book was written for people who are not lawyers, but who seek insight into the legal problems faced by children in our society. They include child care workers, probation officers, social workers, psychologists, teachers, doctors and nurses.

The book is intended as a reference work for the practising professional, and as a community college textbook; it will also be appropriate for use in some university courses and for in-service training programs. Many members of the public, especially parents, will find the book provides interesting and informative reading.

The first two chapters are introductory in nature, discussing the evolving status of children in society, and how children are affected by the legal system. The third chapter deals primarily with problems which can arise when families break up: custody, access and support. The fourth chapter covers child protection legislation: laws designed to help children who have been neglected or abused, or in some other way are being cared for inadequately by their parents. Chapter 5 is devoted to adoption. Chapter 6 concerns the *Juvenile Delinquents Act*, legislation governing children who violate the criminal law. The seventh chapter deals with the property and the civil rights of children. The last two chapters in the book are designed to assist the professional dealing with children, Chapter 8 by explaining some of the laws of evidence which may be important if the professional is required to testify in court, and Chapter 9 by discussing professional obligations.

A brief appendix, dealing with how to find statutes and cases, and a glossary complete the book.

Space has not permitted detailed consideration of the law of each Canadian province, therefore, we have tended to follow the precedent set in most legal texts, and focused on the law in Ontario. The basic principles, however, are the same in all provinces, and where appropriate, considerable reference has been made to legislation and judicial decisions from other provinces.

Readers seeking detailed information concerning the law in provinces other than Ontario are advised to consult the legislation in question.

The authors must also underline two further caveats. Much of the law concerning children is complex, and while we have attempted to fully discuss all of the relevant legal issues, we have inevitably had to sacrifice some of the law's intricacies for the benefit of the reader without legal education. Further, the law is dynamic and there have been many changes affecting children in recent years. Doubtless the future will bring further reforms and revisions; however, although the details may change, the fundamental principles tend to remain constant. Readers having specific legal problems are urged to obtain appropriate assistance.

We have tended to focus on the law as it exists today. While commenting on some of the inadequacies of our laws and discussing proposed reforms, the book is more expository than polemical. This should not be misunderstood as implying that the authors are prepared to quickly acquiesce to present injustices; rather, we feel it is desirable for our readers to understand the law as it now stands (along with its evolution) before embarking on explorations of various needed reforms.

For ease of exposition, we have followed the general practice of using masculine pronouns and adjectives in cases where gender is uncertain. Doubtless our readers need no reminder that judges, lawyers, doctors, children and others come in both sexes.

We would like to express our thanks to John E. Smith for his initial inspiration, to Steve Hersey and Chris Ho for their research assistance, to Karel Bala for his invaluable comments and suggestions, to Mike Fisher, our editor, for his patience and support, to Mary McCooeye for her tireless work in reviewing the manuscript, to Marlene Hymers who worked long hours typing the manuscript, to Liz Scott who typed, edited and inspired, to Martha Gunn who gave much needed moral support during humid summer days, and to the Faculty of Law at Queen's University for providing us with a place to work and materials to work with.

K.L.C.
N.C.B.

Contents

The Child and the Law

Chapter 1

Childhood

A. IN THE BEGINNING

Childhood. A time of carefree play. A time when every morning awoke to a sun-spilled room and the promise of exhilarating adventure. Hopefully that is the golden memory most adults have of their own lost youth. Such an idyllic existence has not always been the lot of children. Just over a hundred years ago, many children subsisted as little more than beasts of burden, forced to work unimaginably long hours in factories, mines and farms. And the further one retreats into history, the story becomes ever more distressing, ever more despairing. If childhood in the 20th century may be described as a dreamlike existence, then it is not unfair to say that throughout most of history childhood was a nightmare.

In the ancient world, an infant, from the moment of birth, stood precariously on the balance of life. And if a child was female, the odds were weighed in favour of the scales tipping towards death. Infanticide, the killing of new-born children, was a common practice in antiquity. Indeed, any child that was not perfect in shape and size, or cried too little or too much, was exposed to the elements and left to starve on some lonely mountainside. There was even a textbook written by a learned Roman obstetrician entitled, *How to Recognize the Newborn That is Worth Rearing.*[1] It was not only the deformed child that met such a fate. Girls were of little value and, more often than not, were not allowed the right to live. The instructions of a prospective Roman father to his wife in the year 1 B.C. typifies the openness with which decisions were reached, "If, as may well happen, you give birth to a child, if it is a boy, let it live; if it is a girl, expose it."[2]

Child sacrificing was a common feature in both the ancient world and in more recent times as well. It was practised by the ancient Egyptians and Phoenicians and, in later centuries, by the Irish Celts. Thousands of bones of sacrificed children have been dug up by archaeologists, some of them bearing inscriptions identifying the victims as the first born of families of the nobility. This particularly tragic practice extended its insidious tentacles even into the modern era. A German case documented that in the year 1843, children were sealed in the wall of a building because of religious superstition. The sealing of live children in the walls of structures has been with us since time immemorial. Even the walls of Jericho are said to have consumed children in this manner.

The casual dismissal of human life was not only a tragic feature of the ancient world. An English gentleman, Thomas Coram, opened a "foundling" hospital in 1741 because he was unable to bear the sight of dying babies lying in the gutters and rotting on the dung heaps of London.[3]

Selling children into slavery was legal in Babylonian times and was a regular practice among other nations of antiquity. The law's response to such behaviour as infanticide, child sacrifice and child slavery was at first one of simple tolerance. It was not until Christianity gained a secure toe-hold in the fourth century A.D. that the law began to consider such activities as illegal. The active censure of society of such behaviour was not to be mobilized for many centuries. In the seventh century, the Archbishop of Canterbury ruled that a father might not sell his son into slavery after the age of seven. Yet a child, once having reached the age of 13, could sell himself into slavery. In Russia, the practice of child slavery was not outlawed until the 19th century.

Infanticide, child sacrifice and child slavery represent an extreme. However, such practices serve to illustrate (with dramatic and painful force) that society, in the ancient world, afforded almost no protection to its children. It is not that the ancients were "killers" of children as a person who engaged in such behaviour today would be considered. Rather, it was that childhood, as a stage of human development, let alone as a period conferring a certain legal status on young people (with rights and protections), was largely unrecognized until only the most recent times. In other words, childhood as a concept, either legal or social, for the most part, did not exist during much of man's history.

B. HISTORICAL DEVELOPMENT

1. Ancient Rome

In ancient Rome, children were at the mercy of their parents and in particular at the mercy of their father. Indeed, the Roman father held the power of life and death over his offspring. This power was derived from the Roman concept of *patria potestas* which granted autocratic power within a family to the eldest male ancestor (an individual described as the *paterfamilias*). To facilitate a better understanding of the power of the *paterfamilias*, it must be recognized that in ancient Rome, a family's affairs and individual family relationships were laws unto themselves. The word of the *paterfamilias* ruled the day-to-day affairs of the family including the parent–child relationship.

The extent of this power is dramatically described by Dionysius, a Greek historian:[4]

> That the lawgiver of the Romans gave virtually full power to the father over his son, even during his whole life, whether he thought proper to imprison him, scourge him, to put him in chains, keep him at work in fields, or put him to death.

As the Roman Empire progressed through the years before Christ and on into the first and second centuries A.D., the power of the *paterfamilias* gradually diminished. By the time of Emperor Hadrian (117 – 138 A.D.) a father could be punished for misusing his power. Side by side with this loss of power a *quasi-judicial* process evolved in which a magistrate arbitrated a parent–child grievance. As well, a father could not sell his children into slavery and his power to arrange marriages fell away. Horace gives us a rather amusing description of an irate father whose attempts to negotiate a marriage ended in frustration, "The father blazed with wrath when his son, mad on some tart, refused to win a wife with a huge dowry."[5] Such historical developments might be said to represent the inception of a novel concept: the recognition of children's rights — rights independent of and protected from the dictates of the child's father.

Young Romans also came to enjoy a certain legal status within society. In this context, childhood consisted of three legally recognized stages. The first stage, *infantia* (the origin of our word "infant"), was a child under the age of seven. The second stage ended with the onset of puberty, fixed at the age of 14 for boys and 12 for girls. The last stage extended to the age of 25 at which time it could be said the young Roman attained the age of majority. On attaining this age, he could be said to have the legal capacity to sue and be sued, to own and sell property, and perhaps most importantly to a young Roman, he could legally borrow money.

By the time of Justinian I (560 A.D.), the power of the *paterfamilias* had dwindled to a right for reasonable chastisement. The reign of Justinian I might be said to represent the high watermark of children's rights in the latter stages of the Roman Empire. Unfortunately, with the collapse of the Empire, many of the gains made in recognizing the unique status of children also disappeared as the world entered the centuries to be known as the Dark Ages.

2. The Dark Ages

When the Barbarian tribes overran Rome, they brought with them tribal rights to replace the relatively sophisticated legal process evolved by the Roman Emperors. Without question a Barbarian father had absolute control over his children's well-being including, once again, the power of life and death.

In the seventh century, although it was against general ecclesiastical principles, the Church was even compelled to allow that in the case of necessity, an English father might sell his children under the age of seven into slavery. An older child could not be sold without his consent but once he had reached the age of 13 or 14, he could sell himself into slavery. Infanticide, child sacrifice, and child slavery were all common experiences of the Dark Ages.

3. Feudal Times

The Dark Ages are said to have ended, at least in English history, with the Norman Conquest in the 11th century. The Norman Conquest had the effect of uniting many of the fractious tribes and of giving birth to feudalism. Feudal life was structured around the holding of land, most of which was held by a tenant-in-chief directly answerable to the King. The tenant-in-chief in turn parcelled out the land to major tenants who in turn sectioned their holdings to sub-tenants and so it went on down the line to the lowest peasant. The *raison d'être* for most people (including children) in feudal times was to work the land.

It was the land which provided existence and guaranteed livelihood. As a consequence, families and children were essential and it is out of this social structure that the feudal concept of childhood arose. Generally, the child was the possession or chattel of his father. However, he was accorded limited economic and social recognition although a father could still choose a spouse for his child until he reached the age of 21. The child's legal status was also such that he could not exercise direct property control. However, a child could own property through the mechanism of "wardship" (an adult holding property in trust for an infant heir).

Within the family unit the father continued, during the Middle Ages, to have absolute control over the discipline and behaviour of his children. The day-to-day life of the average child during this period in history was one of arduous labour. To be born into the peasant class was to be born but one small step above the very animals a person husbanded for his lord and master. A child born into the nobility enjoyed a somewhat better fate but in the end he, too, remained under the absolute dominion of his father. Existence in the Middle Ages was often subject to wars and such other evils such as famine and the plague. Tenderness, compassion and the capacity to comprehend the needs and emotions of others, particularly expressing such feelings toward children, was difficult to nurture in such times. Life was literally a life and death struggle and to this struggle the rights of children were subordinated. There was little recognition of childhood as a unique status; a child was often regarded simply as an adult in miniature, though an adult without legal status. It was not until the last 100 years that systematic identification and recognition of children's rights (from a social and humanistic point of view) became a public issue and the public's consciousness was raised to the point where special attention was paid to these rights.

4. The 19th Century

In *Oliver Twist*, Charles Dickens created two memorable characters, Fagin and the Artful Dodger. These two rogues organized orphaned or deserted children into gangs of pickpockets and housebreakers. Through their colourful escapades, one can capture the life and times of children born into the lower classes during the early 1800s.

It was during these times that the recognition of children's rights gained enormous momentum. In fact, the children's movement of the 19th century was to enjoy the public spotlight as perhaps no other social phenomena. Many common and blatantly wicked practices involved children. These practices attracted sensational headlines and galvanized reformers into action. Perhaps the most sensational and repugnant of all practices was known as the "white slave market." This involved the sale of young girls into brothels both in England and on the Continent. Prostitution offered an escape into a life of relative ease for girls whose parents existed in the direst poverty. As well, servant girls in Victorian households (a common choice of employment) lived in a form of bondage just short of slavery. Although there were laws concerning prostitution during this period, they existed to protect the clientele, not the girls. On the Continent, many countries officially licensed brothels and these establishments sent recruiters into England to "buy" girls. At the time of Queen Victoria's golden jubilee (1887) the port city of Liverpool had an estimated 9000 prostitutes, 1500 of whom were younger than 15 and 500 younger than 13. This scandalous blight on society resulted in the age of sexual consent being raised from 13 to 16 for females. More importantly, however, it sowed the seeds for what has come to be known as child welfare legislation. Although the legal concept of "child welfare" was in its infancy, the white slave market caused laws to be passed allowing social workers (a new profession) to search brothels and other houses of ill repute in order to determine if under-age girls were engaging in prostitution. Girls so found could be placed under official guardianship until they reached age 21.

There were other common Victorian practices involving children which attracted the attention of reformers. "Baby farming" was a common practice, whereby individuals took into their care large numbers of infants without either proper facilities or any sense of proper care for the children. It was a classic situation of profit margin defeating moral responsibility. Baby farms were outlawed and legislation passed to regulate the placing of infants in certain types of environments.

Although such phenomena as child prostitution and baby farming made good newspaper copy, child labour was the issue which truly drew attention to the plight of children. Indeed, the entire 19th century was punctuated by controversy over the volatile issue of the use of child employees. Factory owners cried "bankruptcy" at any attempts by the government to regulate the number of hours children could work in factories and mines. It was the picturesque profession of the chimney sweep which attracted most public empathy. Given the nature of his work, the chimney sweep had to be small in stature and, as a result, children at a very young age were often employed in this line of work. Unfortunately, they were exploited and worked long back-breaking hours for only pennies.

The chimney sweep was not the only child exploited by greedy and rapacious employers. In the mining industry, children from the age of five were employed for 12 hours a day, often seven days a week, working at the face of a coal seam thousands of feet beneath the ground. These children often never saw "the light of day" and their life expectancy was 30 years of age. Much of this exploitation occurred during the Industrial Revolution. There was a sudden great demand for labour and children were cheap and adept at working in factories and mines. Although laws protected them from working in coal mines, child labour laws continued to allow children to be worked virtually as slaves in industrial factories and on farms. They were paid next to nothing and worked hours which today are unimaginable. However, society in general was becoming increasingly enlightened to the plight of children. Various "save the children" organizations (such as the

National Society for the Prevention of Cruelty to Children) gained immediate public support and were instrumental in forcing reforms on reluctant factory owners and on others who benefitted from the exploitation of children.

Further, childhood as a unique legal status gained growing acceptance as the century passed. Children could not own property (without the assistance of an adult) although in certain circumstances they could contract to buy goods and be protected from the vendor should he attempt to enforce an unfair contract against them. Children could make wills—boys at 14 and girls at 12 (today the testamentary age is usually 18)—and they could serve in the army. In the area of criminal law, a concept known as *doli incapax* won widespread acceptance. The effect of *doli incapax* was to limit a child's criminal responsibility because of his age. This principle is discussed in detail in Chapter 6.

Further, universal public education was becoming very much of a popular phenomenon and, as mentioned earlier, child labour laws offering increasing protection to children became prevalent. The courts were also at work in their own way, expanding the growing notion that children had a unique legal status not only in a civil law sense, but also within the family unit. In a landmark case, *R. v. Gyngall*,[6] an English court wrestled with a concept which had been slowly evolving over many centuries of English common law. This concept known as *parens patriae* is of fundamental importance in the area of children's law. *Parens patriae* may be generally defined as the inherent jurisdiction of a court to look after the best interests of a child. In effect, the court acts as a substitute parent. Under the authority of this doctrine, the courts have the power to interfere with parental rights if it is in the best interests of the child. In the *Gyngall* case (decided in 1893), the mother was attempting to regain custody of her 15-year-old daughter. The mother, a maid and subsequently a dressmaker, through no fault of her own, had to place the child in the care of a foster family. Some years later she attempted to regain custody of the child. The court held that she could not because it would not be in the welfare of the child. The mother's itinerant life-style and uncertain future mitigated against the child being taken out of a secure and loving foster home in which she was very happy and well adjusted. This is a rather remarkable decision in light of the fact that only a few short decades before parental authority over children was almost absolute. In fact, at the time the *Gyngall* case was decided it was virtually unthinkable to deny a parent custody of his child. The *Gyngall* case symbolizes, as perhaps no other case does, the start of a new era in child custody and was the forerunner of very recent cases including the leading case of *Re Moores and Feldstein*[7] in which the Ontario Court of Appeal held that there is generally no distinction between natural parents and non-parents. Briefly, this case (discussed in detail in Chapter 3) held that on examination of the facts of each case, either parents or non-parents could be granted custody regardless of any alleged biological parental right.

5. Canadian Developments

Canadian law has been very much influenced by the trends developed in English courts. Therefore, it is hardly surprising that advances in children's rights in England were quickly transplanted in Canada. The first Children's Aid Society was founded in Toronto in the early 1890s. Subsequently, other provinces enacted child welfare legislation similar to the Ontario laws. The first *Factory Act* in Canada was enacted in 1887. This Act regulated and limited the employment of children in factories.

In Ottawa, the Federal Parliament moved on the criminal law side by providing in 1894 that the children convicted of criminal activity be segregated (while imprisoned) from older prisoners. Prior to 1894, children were treated much the same as adults in the eyes of the criminal law—a rare exception was the *doli incapax* rule—and were not treated any differently within the penal system. In the same year, 1894, children were granted private trials in recognition of the stigma attached to criminal proceedings.

The first separation of children from adults in criminal proceedings probably took place in 1899, in Chicago, with the formation of the first Juvenile Court. The same development occurred in Canada with the enactment of the *Juvenile Delinquents Act, 1908*. This Act underwent extensive revision in 1928 and is in force today almost as it was over 50 years ago. The Act underlines the philosophy that a child brought before the court as an alleged juvenile delinquent is to be treated as a misguided and misdirected child, one needing help and assistance.

In conclusion, the reforms of the 19th century as they pertain to children and the law were profound. By themselves, child prostitution, baby farming and intolerable child labour laws deserved resounding condemnation. Their eradication, without question, was a necessity and an important part in the advancement of children's rights. Yet, it is more the sum of the individual reforms that is important. Together, the reforms led to a general legal and social recognition of a concept which could be described as "childhood." Childhood came to be seen as a *continuum*, from birth at the beginning to adulthood at the end. Laws came to be enacted not just to stamp out individual injustices, but rather to protect and enhance the general quality of life within the *continuum* of childhood. It is this philosophical foundation which has left a lasting mark on the rights of children and which has survived even into the laws of today.

C. THE MODERN ERA

Throughout the early decades of the 20th century, children's rights stagnated. The great reforms of the late 1800s were consolidated but were not expanded upon. It was not until the 1960s that once again children's rights were to be mobilized side-by-side and as part of a general "renaissance" in family law.

Yet, the first half of the 1900s was not without attempts at making the world a better place for children. The League of Nations (formed as a result of the brutalizing shock of World War I) concluded that a more humane society must be built. The building blocks were, of course, to be the children of the world. As a result, in 1924 the General Assembly adopted the Geneva Declaration of the rights of the child. It would seem the Declaration did nothing to alter the status of children in the world and it died a "natural death" with the expiration of the League of Nations at the outbreak of World War II. However, the League's successor, the United Nations, took up the torch and after many, many years of debate and discussion, the General Assembly of the United Nations adopted yet another Great Charter on the rights of the child.

Among other things, the Charter provides that children should be granted special protection and opportunities by law and by other means, to develop physically, mentally, morally, spiritually and socially, in conditions of freedom and dignity. The Charter provides that children should also be protected against all forms of neglect, cruelty and exploitation. Further, children are entitled to love and under-standing in the care and nourishment of parents and to exist in an atmosphere of moral and material security.

The United Nations' campaign to publicize the plight of children culminated in 1979 with the "Year of the Child." Predictably, a member of Parliament jumped on the bandwagon and introduced a Canadian Bill of Rights for Children. This Bill (never passed into law) basically adopted the provisions of the United Nations' Charter on children's rights.

It is, of course, one thing to create principles; it is yet another matter to enact laws which are workable (enforceable) within the family unit and within society at large, for instance, that children are to be given special protection by law to develop mentally, morally and spiritually. The logical extension might be to have laws which prohibit questionable television programming and advertising aimed at children. The law could also mandate that children be guaranteed a nutritionally balanced diet which might be effected through subsidized school lunches. In any event, probably the most important benefit of the Year of the Child is that it has raised public consciousness of the unique status of children. With increased aware-ness, elected officials (under the impetus of the general population) can enact laws motivated by the spirit of such an enlightened philosophy.

Laws inspired by high ideals and principles must, none the less, deal with the realities of life. They must take a "nuts and bolts" approach to implementing children's rights and admittedly the task is not always an easy one. For instance, how does one guarantee a child "love and understanding" or a world of "peace and universal brotherhood"? Obviously, the law can offer no such guarantees. Yet the law, more than any other social resource, has the power to forge and shape new attitudes. In this sense, one might consider the law to be a crucible — that is, a melting pot in which social change can be hammered out according to the principles of natural justice. One cannot bring a parent to Court and accuse him of lacking love according to a legal definition. Yet, the law can nourish the concept that a child is a legal *person*, a person entitled to certain rights and protections. Thus, the law can enhance, conceptually, the idea of the uniqueness of childhood and of the worthiness of endeavours to allow children to explore their full potential as individuals and not as mere extensions of their parents.

The lawmakers must shoulder an extra burden with respect to the creation of laws concerning children. Children cannot vote; they cannot lobby and thus influence legislation. Thus they are, as a group, uniquely handicapped by their inability to participate in a meaningful way with the legislative decision-making process. To make the task even more difficult is the problem of maturity. Judgement and the ability to weigh the pros and cons in one's life come with experience. Children, particularly those in their pre-teen and early teen years, generally have not yet reached that stage in life where the law can attribute maturity to them. As a consequence, the law must create a legal framework and superimpose it on children, the framework being based on what is (hopefully) best for the child.

Many of the advances made in the area of children's rights can be directly attributable to the ever-mushrooming evidence on the emotional and behavioural development of children, and more particularly, the effect on children of the disintegration of the family unit and the effects on a child who is the victim of child abuse or neglect.

The wealth of knowledge on children suddenly inundated society in the 1970s. The results seemed to indict parents, teachers and other officials, such as lawyers and judges, with respect to their handling of matters affecting the lives of children.

An article in *Maclean's Magazine*, entitled "Kids Without Rights,"[8] said it all. Much of the article is based on a report prepared by the Canadian Council on Children and Youth.[9] The conclusion of the report was that Canadians view children as exotic pets and have essentially constructed a society that abuses or discriminates against one-third of the population (those persons under the age of 18). Apparently the basic perception of most individuals in Canadian society is that children are dependent, incompetent possessions, and that they are to be seen and not heard. This view is shared by the Massachusetts Law Reform Commission: "the child's legal status is an amalgam of non-citizen, slave, overprotected pet and valuable chattel."[10]

1. Children's Liberation — The 1970s and 1980s

Children themselves would appear to be aware of their inferior status. In fact, the media in the 1970s made children's rights a *cause célèbre*. In New York, a children's "Defence League" sprang up as did the Children's Rights Incorporated and a Children's Rights Newspaper. One can almost picture children at the barriers. Certainly, if one believes everything that is written with respect to the plight of children, one is forced to conclude that as a group they are struggling under the yoke of oppression. A child born in ancient Rome or even during Victorian England would undoubtedly suffer severe cultural shock if he stepped into the shoes of a child of the 1980s. He would undoubtedly be overwhelmed by freedom. Perhaps we might accurately describe this (the 1980s) as the age of "children's liberation" and accept that we are subject to the normal political rhetoric put forward by most social reform movements.

One such movement, formed in Canada, was the Canadian Foundation for Children and the Law Incorporated. This organization serves as more than a watchdog and, further, is not merely a political organization designed to attract headlines to the plight of children. In fact, the Foundation recently completed a *Brief on Medical Consent of Minors*[11] which has been submitted to the Ontario Minister of Health. This brief focuses on such issues as the age of consent to medical treatment, confidentiality, and the right to refuse treatment. These issues are discussed in Chapter 9.

In spite of the outcries of activists and critics, the decade of the 1970s can be said to contain many advances in the rights of children. Perhaps the greatest change in the law relating to children is the tendency to move away from stereotyped presumptions and traditional rules. For example, at one time it was unthinkable that a person other than the parent should gain custody. But in recent years, relatives and even individuals with no "blood tie" have been granted custody of a child. Perhaps even more dramatically, a number of recent cases have granted custody of children to homosexual parents. There have been many other child–law related changes over the past decade which have usurped many traditional, often moralistic viewpoints. One such change was the abolishment of the concept of the illegitimate child with the passage of the *Children's Law Reform Act* of Ontario in 1978. Before this Act came into force, the bastard child in Ontario (and other provinces), suffered social stigma and also legal handicaps. For instance, he was excluded from a parent's will and even at one time, if the parent died without a will, the child was not entitled to a share in the parent's estate. Other innovations in laws affecting children include a child's right to be present at certain types of legal actions which play an important part in their future (for example, child welfare proceedings), and a further right to have a lawyer appointed to represent the child. This development, perhaps more than any other, demonstrates the increasing attention of the law to the independent legal status of children. The *Child Welfare Act, 1978* of Ontario, for example, allows the judge to direct that the child should have independent legal representation to protect his interests and express his views and wishes. Perhaps to put this development in its proper light, one should compare it to the total absence of any voice whatsoever for children under the iron-fisted rule of the Roman *paterfamilias*.

With respect to a custody dispute between parents and other persons, the child (the "prize" in a custody dispute) has traditionally had no say in the matter. However, the courts are now gradually displaying a greater willingness to recognize a child's active participation in a decision which will, without question, vitally affect its life. This usually involves a judge appointing the lawyer to represent the children at custody trials. The lawyer can then represent fully the child's wishes and even bring evidence to the court's attention to support the position of the child.

These developments are, in fact, the end product of a concept which made its first appearance at the turn of the century. This concept has come to be known as the "best interests of the child test," the forerunner of which was the *Gyngall* case, previously mentioned. As a principle, it seemed to lay dormant for a number of decades and did not really surface again until the 1960s. In assessing situations in which a child's welfare is at stake, briefly, the principle states that it is what is in the best interests of the child which must be the pre-eminent consideration of the court. In other words, the particular circumstances are viewed through the eyes of the child and not through the eyes of the parents. The end result is that a custody placement will not be used to punish a parent guilty of a matrimonial offence, for instance, a parent guilty of adultery. Nor will a parent who has by physical absence ignored a child for a number of years automatically be granted custody if the child has been receiving parenting from other persons. Further, the courts are placing ever-increasing reliance on the findings of experts in the field of child behaviour.[12] These studies have undoubtedly put to rest many ghosts of the common law as they relate to the law of custody. Behavioural principles such as "the continuity of surroundings," "separation anxiety," and the "myth of blood tie" have all found their way into the lawmaking process. Conventional judicial wisdom of yesteryear, often rooted in moralistic concepts, has fallen to the wayside as new social and behavioural findings are reported. The law of custody is canvassed fully in Chapter 3.

2. New Frontiers

The law continues to extend the rights of children beyond legal frontiers never before explored. Parental discipline, a thorn in the flesh of every child, surfaced as a public issue during the Year of the Child as highlighted by a Swedish law forbidding parents the right to spank their children. Prior to this, in the late 1960s and early 1970s, the length of a boy's hair brought many a father–son, and teacher–student relationship to the edge of disaster. Indeed, many schools actually took children to court in order to force them to cut their hair. This may seem absurd, yet litigation over the length of hair (and spankings) illustrates the fragility of the parent–child (and teacher–student) relationship.

More controversial and sensitive issues, such as a physician prescribing contraceptive devices to children without parental consent or treating drug-related problems or a veneral disease without parental knowledge, focus attention on the growing recognition of children's rights and the law's willingness to give teeth to these rights.

Where will such an enlightened atmosphere lead us? This is a question asked by teachers and parents and others faced with the task of either raising or shaping children's lives. The spectre of children challenging their parents before the courts haunts the public mind. As the law expands with respect to children's rights, the tension between parental authority and the State's right to interfere with such authority will almost certainly continue to attract headlines. In the United States, parents have actually been brought to court under the head of "malparenting" suits. In these actions, children who have suffered emotional scarring as a result of parental neglect have attempted to be compensated for the emotional damage suffered. Such legal developments have received legislative sanction in certain Canadian provinces. Ontario, for example, in its *Family Law Reform Act, 1978* specifically grants children the legal right to sue their parents (see p. 39). The average Canadian does not quarrel with the state jumping into cases of child abuse. However, when the State interferes in areas which have traditionally been left to parents — for instance, discipline in the home — then the question is raised, "Is the State not trespassing into the private affairs of the family?" There is no question that the State must ever be on the alert to exercise discretion in its dealings with family relationships. However, the State has the ultimate responsibility to safeguard the rights of children. Sometimes, of necessity, this pits the law against the parent, and in effect child against parent. The law must juggle the rights of three parties (the child, the parent and society) to ensure the best for its children. The dividing lines between these competing rights are often obscure. If, in the past, the law has erred in the direction of the rights of the parent, there are those who say the pendulum has now swung too far in the opposite direction. Still others maintain the pendulum has not yet swung far enough. John Holt is one such critic. Eloquently, he condemns the *institution* of childhood:[13]

> It has made a Great Divide in human life, and made us think that people on opposite sides of this divide, the Children and the Adults, are very different. In short, by the institution of childhood I mean those attitudes and feelings, and also customs and laws that put a great gulf or barrier between the young and their elders, and the world of their elders; that make it difficult or impossible for young people to make contact with the larger society around them, and even more, to play any kind of active, responsible, useful part in it; that lock the young into 18 years or more of subserviancy and dependency, and make of them . . . a mixture of expensive nuisance, fragile treasure, slave and super-pet.

The law is moving (and has moved) to break down the walls of the institution of childhood. It is doing so by elevating the position of children so that they attain the status of *legal* persons — not to the extent of an adult but certainly to a point beyond that of a "super-pet." Perhaps at the root of the problem is the question of image, that is the "institution" of childhood. Unfortunately, the image cast on the legal "retina" is, and has been blurred by uncertainty and inconsistency in laws relating to children. It is something like the "who came first" question; the chicken or the egg? Was it the law that created the institution of childhood or was it society? As always, the answer probably lies somewhere in the middle ground. Certainly the problem has been exacerbated in the past by the law's repressive attitude (albeit unintentional) towards children. The law has smothered the younger members of society under the guise of judicial love and concern (based on the perception of the general emotional, physical and intellectual "inferiority" of a child) and in the process has denied children basic human rights. Society's complicity lies in its inculcation of such overbearing and protective behaviour. The law is attempting to clear the air and create a healthy legal environment for children. Hopefully, this environment will destroy the institution of childhood as it exists today and reconstruct in its place a concept of childhood as a legal and social status conferring a full measure of rights and protections on its members. The following chapters explore the relationship between the child and the law from the perspectives of yesterday, today and tomorrow.

FOOTNOTES

1. See *The History of Childhood*, edited by Lloyd deMause (Psychohistory Press, 1974), at p. 26. See also *Centuries of Childhood*. Phillipe Ames, Alfred A. Knopf (New York, 1962).
2. *Supra*, at p. 26
3. *Supra*, at p. 29
4. See M.C.J. Olmesdahl, ''Paternal Power and Child Abuse: An Historical and Cross-Cultural Study,'' in John Eekelaar *et al.*, *Family Violence* (Toronto, 1978), at p. 255
5. *Supra*, at p. 256
6. [1893] 2 Q.B. 232
7. (1973), 12 R.F.L. 273
8. November 20, 1978, at p. 40
9. See Canadian Council on Children and Youth, *Admittance Restricted: The Child in Canada* (1979). Available from the Canadian Council on Children and Youth, 323 Chapel St., Ottawa, Ontario K1N 7Z2.
10. See *Time Magazine*, ''Children's Rights: The Latest Crusade,'' December 25, 1972, at p. 42
11. See paper published by Justice for Children (Canadian Foundation for Children and the Law Inc., Toronto, Ontario), ''Brief on Medical Consent of Minors,'' February 18, 1980
12. See Goldstein, Solnit and Freud, *Beyond the Best Interests of the Child* (New York, 1973)
13. See Holt, *Escape from Childhood* (New York, 1974), at pp. 25-26

Chapter 2

The Legal System

A. THE NATURE OF LAW

1. General

Before delving into the specifics of children and the law it is necessary to discuss the law as a general body of knowledge; and as the means by which society governs its members.

Let us start with a simple definition. Law can be defined as that body of rules which regulates the conduct of members of society. These laws are recognized and enforced by the various levels of government. In this day and age there are vast numbers of laws addressing themselves to almost everything we do in our day-to-day living. There are laws that say we cannot do certain things. We cannot steal, we cannot abuse our children, we cannot drive our cars too fast; nor can we consume alcohol in a public place or smoke marijuana. On the other hand, there are laws which tell us we must do certain things. We must pay taxes, we must serve on a jury if called upon to do so, and if we are collecting unemployment insurance benefits, we must do all of the things the *Unemployment Insurance Act, 1971* commands of us. It seems that, indeed, we are surrounded by a vertitable forest of laws. Although this may appear to be an age of prolific lawmaking, it has actually been this way since earliest recorded history. For instance, one of the earliest known collections of written law is the *Code of Hammurabi*. Hammurabi, while King of Babylonia (approximately 1800 B.C.) codified approximately 300 laws. These laws were literally carved in stone; one such stone exists today in the Louvre in Paris and remains the earliest example of codified law.

Why do we have laws? To preserve order within society is perhaps the most obvious answer. A world without laws would be a world of anarchy and would cause the destruction of society as we know it.

The law describes our rights, privileges and obligations. It also determines the structure of our government and assigns duties and powers to its various branches. The law further tells us how we may create laws and by whom laws are to be made. The most pre-eminent lawmaking "law" is, of course, the *British North America Act, 1867*. This statute creates our federal system of government, and further, it divides the authority to make law on various subjects between the Federal Parliament in Ottawa and the provincial legislatures. Sometimes this jurisdictional authority appears to overlap. Section 92 of that Act provides that the authority to make laws dealing with children is vested in the provincial legislatures. On the other hand, criminal law is within the jurisdiction of the Federal Parliament. As a result, the

Juvenile Delinquents Act (J.D.A.) is federal legislation with application to all the provinces and territories. This constitutional framework whereby criminal law and hence, the law of juvenile delinquency is a federal responsibility, and the law pertaining to the general welfare of children is vested in provincial legislatures, has led to a requirement that federal lawmakers and provincial lawmakers walk hand in hand when considering laws as they relate to children in trouble with the police. For instance, a juvenile (a person under 16 years of age in most provinces) might rob a variety store. That is against the federal law — the *J.D.A.* As a consequence, he may be sent to one of many training schools which are administered by provincial laws. This issue is further discussed in Chapter 6.

The law is a dynamic force within society. In this context, it may be described as a social resource. In other words, as a society evolves and attitudes towards various behaviours change, the law responds by either sanctioning the particular behaviour or enacting prohibitive legislation to control unwanted types of behaviour. Thus, in recent years, the laws surrounding abortion have undergone dramatic changes. At one time, there was an absolute prohibition against abortion. However, the law, responding to forces within a constantly evolving society sanctioned first the performance of an abortion if a threat to life was occasioned by the pregnancy, and then further liberalized circumstances under which an abortion could be approved. Generally, an abortion can now be authorized by a therapeutic abortion committee if the general health of a woman is jeopardized by pregnancy.

Currently, the lawmakers in Ottawa are wrestling with the issue of the legalization of marijuana. There is a growing campaign, fueled primarily by the energies of younger members of society, to have marijuana taken out of the *Narcotic Control Act*, an Act which is criminal in nature, and have it placed under the *Food and Drugs Act*, an Act which is primarily regulatory in nature. The examples of abortion and marijuana illustrate that the law is ever-changing, ever being shaped by the changing attitudes of society. Perhaps in no other area of the law is this drama more pronounced than in the area of family law; Lesbian mothers being granted custody; children sueing their parents for support; doctors being permitted to prescribe contraceptive devices to children independent of parental knowledge. All of these legal developments reflect the dynamic nature of our laws.

Judicial recognition of the need for the common law to keep pace with contemporary life may be taken from a judgement of an English court:[1]

> . . . that case was decided in the year eighteen eighty-three. It reflects the
> attitude of a Victorian parent towards children. The expected unquestioning
> obedience to his commands. If a son disobeyed, his father would cut
> him off with one shilling. If a daughter had an illegitimate child, he would
> turn her out of the house. His power only ceased when the child became
> twenty-one. I decline to accept a view so much out of date. The common
> law can, and should, keep pace with the times . . .

2. Classes of Law

There are two main classes of law: public law and private law. Public law pertains to rules which govern relations between the various branches of government and between the government and private citizens. Private law, or as it is perhaps more commonly known, civil law, consists of the rules governing the relations between private citizens or groups. The main types of public law are constitutional, administrative, and criminal law. Types of private law include tort, contract, and property law.

Within each class or type of law there are substantive rules and procedural rules. Substantive laws describe our rights and duties and obligations. On the other hand, procedural law defines how substantive law can be enforced. It is a substantive law that a person may obtain a divorce if his spouse is guilty of the matrimonial offense of adultery. It is a matter of procedural law that an action for a divorce must be started with a petition and a notice of petition (which states the grounds relied upon by the party seeking the divorce); these papers must be served on the respondent spouse.

There are two major systems of law in the western world today. One system is described as common law; the other as the civil law system. It should be noted that civil law has two definitions. It may refer to civil or private law as discussed above or it may refer to the system of law which is used by many Continental European countries. Except for Quebec provincial law, which has adopted the civil law system, Canadian law has inherited the common law tradition.

Civil law has its roots in Roman law and more particularly in the law as formulated by Justinian I, a Roman emperor in the sixth century A.D. It was the *Justinian Code* which influenced Napoleon in the 19th century and which led to the *Napoleonic Code*, which in turn is antecedent to the surviving Quebec *Civil Code*.

It is perhaps common knowledge that from approximately 50 B.C. to 400 A.D. England was occupied by the Roman army, and hence was subject to Roman law. However, during the fifth century A.D., various Anglo-Saxon tribes chased the Romans out of England. This historical event had the effect of erasing the influence of Roman law in England. For many centuries, centuries often referred to as the Dark Ages, England was occupied by various tribes who went through life with only infrequent contact with one another and then usually only to make war. Within each tribal community, laws were rules based on the traditions and customs of that particular tribe. At this point in English history it cannot be said that any one body of law existed which could be described as English law. It was not until that date famous in English history, 1066 (when William I, the Duke of Normandy, conquered England), that England could be said to be a unified country. William I set as his first task the setting up of a centralized government for the purpose of effectively controlling his new subjects. A corner-stone to his central government was the creation of a royal court system. Under this system, judges, appointed according to the Royal prerogative, would travel through the countryside holding court in populous areas. Each judge's route was called a circuit and court sittings were known as "assizes." To this day, High Court Judges in Canada still travel to County or District seats (specially designated towns) and hold court sessions described as assizes.

Early judges were in a most difficult position because they did not have a set of rules or a set of laws to which they could refer when presented with a case. This, of course, can be contrasted with Roman law which gave judges recourse to the *Justinian Code* or, jumping several centuries ahead, to French judges who could refer to the *Napoleonic Code* to guide them in their decision-making process. As a result, the earliest English judges were forced to rely on their wits and common sense and base decisions on what appeared to them to be principles of justice and fairness. Gradually, a process evolved whereby judges began discussing among themselves the cases they had heard and the decisions they had made. Eventually, this practice led to judges circulating their decisions and if another judge found himself faced with a case in which similar facts existed, then he would follow the earlier judge's decision. This practice became refined to the point where, rather than relying on his own judgement, the judge would research previously decided cases until he found one in which similar, or at least substantially similar, circumstances were involved. Then he would make his decision based upon the results of the first case. It should be noted that one of the assets of a system of law is that it introduces the element of certainty in an individual's day-to-day contact with legal matters. In other words, an individual can rely on previously decided cases in order to guide his affairs.

This system of following decisions in similar fact situations is often described as the system of precedents. A precedent is defined as a case which is to be followed in future similar circumstances. This principle of precedent law, which is of cardinal importance to our judicial system, was further refined in the 19th century by the development of a rule known as *stare decisis*. A definition of *stare decisis* may be enunciated as follows: lower courts must follow the decisions of higher courts, and courts equal in rank must attempt to follow each other's decisions. The end result of this practice, that is, the practice of following certain decisions in case after case, was that there arose within England (and subsequently Canada), a body of law which applied to all of the people within its borders. Another way of looking at this development was to say that the law was common to all or that it was "common law."

An example of law being created by a judge and becoming part of the common law involves a consideration of the question of custody. At one time, the common law was that the father received custody of his children. Then, as the centuries passed and judges began to accept evidence from such expert areas as child psychology, a principle known as the "tender years doctrine" emerged. This principle held that children of tender years, usually under the age of seven, were better off with their mother. This formed part of the common law until very recent times when the tender years doctrine was eclipsed by the appearance of the "best interests of the child" concept. There is no doubt that the tender years doctrine, that is, that young children are perhaps better off with their mother, is still a consideration (see

Chapter 3, "Custody") but it by no means carries the weight it once did. The tender years doctrine does, however, illustrate how a judge can create law and how at one time it was an almost automatic decision that young children would be placed in the custody of their mother. It further illustrates that the common law is constantly responding to changes within society and to the most recent developments in the social sciences and in the field of behavioural psychology.

Another way to create law is for the government body which has jurisdiction in a particular area to pass a statute or an Act. As noted previously, the primary authority for jurisdictional competence is the *British North America Act, 1867*. There are basically three levels of statute law: federal laws applicable to Canada (the *J.D.A.*); provincial laws applying only to the province (the *Family Law Reform Act, 1978* of Ontario); and municipal laws (laws passed by city councils and other municipal agencies). Perhaps the most common and by far the most unpopular municipal by-law would be one dealing with parking restrictions. However, municipal laws may also affect children, for instance, curfew restrictions.

In Canada, statute law always has priority over common law. In other words, if a conflict exists between a court decision and a statute, the statute must overrule the court decision. This is because the ultimate authority to make law is vested in our elected officials and their word is the last word on the topic albeit that a judge in an earlier decision may have ruled differently.

Statute law does not always conflict with common law and it should be pointed out that statutes often codify common law. That is, if a principle of law becomes enshrined in the common law, that is, if it is repeatedly followed in case after case, a statute may be created encompassing the principle. In this sense, the common law, through the process of legislation, becomes statute law. For instance, the concept of the "best interests of the child" as discussed briefly in Chapter 1 and discussed at length in Chapter 3. This concept has its origins in the common law and was finally codified in s. 35 of the *Family Law Reform Act, 1978* of Ontario (*F.L.R.A.*) which came into force in the spring of 1978.

Further, with the increasing technology of the 20th century and the creation of governmental branches in the administration of almost every endeavour there are many modern topics which have never been dealt with by case-law. But, on the other hand, there are still large areas of law in the form of case-law which have never been the subject-matter of a statute and are still being developed by judges. The law of evidence as discussed in Chapter 8 is an example of rules largely ignored by statutes.

Aside from a judge's lawmaking function, in the sense of reducing certain fact situations to precedent-setting decisions, the judge also has a very important role in the interpretation of statutes. The language of the legislatures and other government agencies frequently require interpretation. These interpretations, of course, become part of the law as subsequent cases will follow these interpretations. It may be asked why these statutes need interpretation. In the first instance, the statutes usually only contain general rules and the question may arise as to how a general rule applies to a given specific situation. As well, the authors of legislation, as do all of us, frequently encounter difficulty in clearly communicating their intent. If ambiguity arises, then it is the responsibility of a judge to decipher the statute and render an interpretation.

A judge's exasperation at attempting to unravel a complicated tangle of conflicting statutes is to be found in the Manitoba case of *Funk v. Funk*:[2]

> Dealing with the statutory arguments first, I confess that once again I have had difficulty understanding certain provisions of a statute too often amended and too seldom revised. I am not at all surprised that counsel have disagreed on the interpretation of certain sections, for these sections are capable of being read and understood in a number of ways. It is not now appropriate to consider all of the unfortunate inconsistencies in the Act . . .

An example of a court's interpretation of a statute is given in a Manitoba case, *R. v. Frost*.[3] In that case, the words "sexual immorality" were interpreted by the judge. Section 2 of the *J.D.A.* defines a "juvenile delinquent" as "any child . . . who is guilty of sexual immorality. . . ." It was necessary for the judge to interpret the meaning of sexual immorality. He introduced the problem as follows:

> One must approach the task of defining the terms morality and immorality with great concern, care and even trepidation. Morality is very much like the weather; everyone talks about it, has an opinion about it and watches with fascination as it changes from time to time. The task of definition is made somewhat easier in that I only have to consider the meaning and definition of the words "sexual immorality" within the limited sense that the words are used in s. 33 of the *Juvenile Delinquents Act*.

He concluded, "sexual immorality connotes sexual behaviour which is not publicly acceptable because it is wrong, bad, vicious or promiscuous." For a further discussion of the definition of juvenile delinquent as it applies to sexual immorality, see Chapter 6.

B. THE ADVERSARIAL SYSTEM

1. General

We have discussed the major function of laws. Now it is necessary to discuss the system by which legal disputes are resolved. This system — much maligned in recent years, particularly with respect to family disputes — is known as the adversary system. The oft-quoted dicta about democracy — as a system of government it's not perfect but it's the best we have — appears to have equal application to the adversarial system. What do we mean when we say "adversarial"? Perhaps the best way of explaining the concept is to contrast it with the inquisitorial system established during the Spanish Inquisition. During this historical period, the Roman Catholic Church established an "inquisition" in order to seek out and destroy heretics. This approach involved questioning or examining the accused, the questioning coming from a person in authority. The chief instrument of the inquisition was the torture chamber. This was the means by which the Church sought the truth. An inquisitorial system (without recourse to torture, of course) is a means by which an authoritarian figure attempts to arrive at the truth by subjecting a person to a rigorous, one-sided examination. The adversarial approach is another truth-seeking system. Unlike the inquisitorial system whereby the authoritarian figure not only decides the issue but also decides the issue based on his own questioning, the adversarial approach emphasizes a non-partisan judge who listens to evidence that is introduced by the participants themselves.

The basic assumption of the adversary system is that there are always two sides to every story. According to carefully constructed rules of evidence, each side places its version of the story before a judge and, based on what the judge hears from both parties, he reaches a decision. Each party is subject to cross-examination by the other side. In other words, each side has the opportunity to "test" the veracity of its opponent's story. Cross-examination has been described over the centuries as the most effective means ever devised for getting at the truth. As an historical sidenote, cross-examination did not actually become a regular feature of judicial procedure in England until approximately 300 years ago. For a full discussion of the laws of evidence see Chapter 8.

2. The Judge's Role

It is important to emphasize the role of the judge as being that of an impartial arbiter. It is not his responsibility to conduct the cases of the litigants (the parties to an action). Indeed, if the judge oversteps this rule, then his decision is subject to being overturned should the losing party decide to appeal. In a recent Ontario case, a Family Court Judge was hearing what is frequently described as a "paternity suit." A paternity suit is one in which an unmarried mother attempts to prove who fathered her child. If she is successful, then the father will usually be ordered to pay support for the child. In the case at hand, the mother was not represented by her own counsel and despite objections from counsel for the alleged father, the judge proceeded to question witnesses and take an actual part in the hearing. At one point, in response to an objection, the judge stated, "When one party is not represented I feel I have to . . . *balance the scales.*" The lawyer representing the alleged father felt his client was being prejudiced because the person asking the questions would also be making the decision. In other words, he felt that the judge had, as it were, "come into the arena" and that this was contrary to the proper functioning of the adversary system. The Ontario Supreme Court, on appeal,[4] made the following observation:

The fundamental principle, as I see it, of litigation, is that it must not even be felt that a judge gets into the arena . . . I feel in this case that the impression of bias could conceivably have been conveyed — certainly not intentionally, because His Honour was most particular in trying in every way to protect the rights of all parties — but it was a difficult position once the questioning began . . . to maintain that strict sense of neutrality which a judge must maintain.

As a result, the Court of Appeal ordered that a new trial take place.

3. The Role of the Lawyer

Few members of any profession are as vilified as the lawyer. Shakespeare once wrote in a play: "Let's kill all the lawyers first!"

In addition to Shakespeare's cutting sentiment, there is a pithy Irish proverb which perhaps most accurately sums up the public's general feeling toward the legal fraternity: "If the horse pulling the hearse is snickering, they must be burying a lawyer!"

At best, lawyers are seen as a necessary evil in the general scheme of our system of justice. Putting aside the general public's criticisms, a lawyer's role is vital to the administration of justice. In the area of family law his role is, in the existent system (albeit frequently controversial), of particular importance. A lawyer is subject to certain guidelines concerning general court-room decorum and various "do's and don'ts" in advancing his client's position.

The Canadian Bar Association, in its *Code of Professional Conduct*, provides guidelines which address themselves to the personal and professional behaviour of the lawyer. In general, the lawyer must behave before the court with courtesy and respect while at the same time representing his client "resolutely, honourably, and within the limits of the law." Unfortunately, what is "within the limits of the law" is somewhat obscure given the nature of the adversary system and abuses occasionally occur. There are a number of procedures prohibited by the Canadian Bar Association in its *Code of Professional Conduct*. A lawyer must not, for example, abuse the process of the court by instituting proceedings which, although legal in themselves, are clearly motivated by malice on the part of his client and are brought solely for the purpose of seeking revenge. Further, a lawyer must not knowingly assist or permit his client to do anything which the lawyer believes is dishonest or dishonourable. In adversarial proceedings, the lawyer's function is openly and necessarily partisan. On the other hand, and perhaps somewhat surprisingly, the lawyer must inform the court of any law which he considers to be directly on point even though that law may weaken his client's case. He is also prohibited from needlessly abusing or harassing a witness although in fact the dynamics of cross-examination are such that it is often difficult to distinguish between aggressive questioning and harassment.

4. Representation of Children

The lawyer's role in the representation of children (a developing trend in the law) is particularly difficult. Does he follow the strict instructions of his client, even if, in his opinion, the child is not acting in his own best interests (as perceived by the lawyer)? Is he less an advocate than a social worker? Underlying both of these pertinent questions is the more fundamental issue of whether or not a child has the legal capacity (right) to instruct his own lawyer. This troublesome issue has apparently been put to rest by both statutory intervention and by recent case-law. For instance, the *Child Welfare Act, 1978* of Ontario (*C.W.A.*) (discussed at length with respect to child protection proceedings in Chapter 4) specifically provides that a judge may direct that a child have independent legal representation to protect his interests and further to express his views and preferences. The question of a child having his own lawyer in custody proceedings has proven to be more difficult for the judiciary. Unfortunately, most provinces (Alberta is an exception) do not provide statutory authority for legal representation for children in custody disputes. On the other hand, although marked by concern, other jurisdictions are allowing the participation of children in custody proceedings through the mechanism of separate representation for children.

An example of conflicting emotions as it relates to separate representation for children in custody disputes may be taken from two Ontario cases, *Rowe v. Rowe* and *More v. Primeau*. In the *Rowe* case, the judge made the following statement:[5]

> Based on my experience in this case, I doubt the desirability of having children represented by counsel or advised by "their own" (the children's term) solicitor as a practice. There may well be cases where in the circumstances a trial judge considers it desirable for the children to have separate representation at trial. If that is so, the office of the official guardian would appear to be available and can be called upon at that point. Earlier involvement of solicitors for children can, I think, cause more harm than good.

On the other hand, in the *More* case the Ontario Court of Appeal commented as follows:[6]

> I also believe that the court must recognize growing public support for the view that children are entitled to independent representation in custody cases, at least where it is clear that their true interests will not be served by an adversarial contest between parents or other parties.

It would appear that the position taken in the *More* case is representative of the prevailing sentiment concerning representation of children.

There are genuine problems in placing too much faith in the views of children. This has much to do with the difficulties faced by the child's advocate in identifying the legal needs of his client. For example, a child who is the object of a custody action may have been unduly influenced by one parent, or he may simply wish to go to the parent whose strong suit is a relaxed attitude towards discipline. In other words, the child is unable to form, or is ignoring, what is perhaps the best solution to his problem. On the other hand, it is most unjust to simply pass over or ignore the views of a person most affected by the proceeding — the child.

The current practice appears to be that if the child is of an age and maturity to appreciate the nature of the proceedings, then his counsel will put forward his client's position as forcefully as if the child were an adult. It goes without saying that the child's advocate has the task of fully evaluating his client's position and advising him accordingly. This responsibility is particularly onerous considering the youth and relative inexperience of the child client, and his need, therefore, for greater reliance on direction and advice from his legal counsel. Child advocacy is a new and unique area of the law. It is still suffering "birth pains" as it wins growing acceptance in the courts of the land. Many provinces recognizing the special problems attached to dealing with children before the courts, not the least of which is understanding or "reading" child behaviour, have instituted special training programs for lawyers representing children.

The issues of legal representation for children in child protection, custody and juvenile proceedings are discussed individually in subsequent chapters.

C. FAMILY LAW IN THE ADVERSARIAL SYSTEM

1. General

As described in Chapter 1, the decade of the 1970s heralded a new dawn for family law. In those 10 years, most provinces enacted Family Law Reform Acts (with the emphasis on the word "reform") which erased antiquated concepts of family relations from the dusty and cumbersome pages of legal and social history. Yet, although much has been reformed in the area of family law, much is still in need of reform. Perhaps the most criticized feature of the existing family law system involves attacks on its adversarial character. Certainly no other area of the law is more prone to adversarial system abuses than that of family law. Indeed, a number of studies have recommended that alternatives to the present system be adopted. This criticism is particularly pertinent when litigation involves children because the issues are not related to a definite past event (for instance, the determination of guilt or innocence in a criminal proceeding), but rather to predicting the best future for the children involved (for instance, which parent should have custody).

The Law Reform Commission of Canada in a 1976 paper entitled "Family Law," made the following comments with respect to children:[7]

> The position of children is even more difficult. Although protected by a system of obligations, they have never had independent legal claims. They have no standing to make their own voices heard in a system that

allows one parent to deprive them of the other because of an instance
of adultery. We do not suggest that they should have such a right but
neither do we suggest the retention of such a system. What we should
have is a process that tries to get to the reality of why one parent would
seriously consider doing this in the first place — the process wherein
children are heard, in which their interests are always important, and at
times dominant, and one in which children do not serve as bargaining
counters or as objects to be kept and used. Many parents in a marriage
breakdown cannot see beyond their own needs. The process for dissolution
of marriage must compensate for this. It is also important for children to
understand, as best they can (and this is often a great deal better than
we assume), what the situation is and what their parents are facing. A new
approach to the problems of children when a marriage breaks down is
essential.

The Law Reform Commission then condemned the adversarial system in more
general terms:[8]

> The philosophy . . . of the law in dealing with the family in difficulty is
> condusive to and reinforces the inception of accusatory and adversary
> stance by each spouse. The traditional way to avoid the grave economic
> and personal injuries that can be suffered under the divorce law has been
> to inflict them on the other spouse. The law provides efficient adversarial
> weapons with which to do this, as well to use the occasion of divorce to
> gain revenge . . . for such things as rejection, accumulated hostility,
> and disappointed expectations. The limitations created by the adversary
> relationship prevent the state from taking any constructive and positive
> approach to husbands and wives with serious matrimonial problems.
> Marriage as the major institutional foundation of our society, is primarily
> supported by laws and legal policies that emphasize the triumph of
> vindication of one spouse rather than a reconciliation of both. This impairs
> the ability of the legal system to deal with family breakdown as a
> continuum in which there could be, with timely and appropriate systems of
> adjustment, viable intermediate alternatives for family survival and
> renewal. The legal system should provide a means to preserve families as
> well as dissolve marriages.

2. Alternatives to the Adversarial System

Adjustments to the adversarial system have been instituted in a number of provincial
jurisdictions. In Ontario, for example, a system of pre-trial conferences has been
successfully instituted by the Supreme Court of that province. At the pre-trial
conference, the judge acts as a mediator or conciliator of litigation which is ready
for trial. The judge's object is to resolve marital disputes already placed before the
court. Generally, the purpose of the pre-trial conference is to avoid delay, eliminate
matrimonial confrontations between the parties, minimize the cost of the court

action and, hopefully, diminish the emotional strife suffered by all concerned. Essentially, the pre-trial conference attempts to play down the aggressive and antagonistic attitudes adopted by opponents already swept up in the adversary system. However, the pre-trial conference is not the only innovative step created to lessen the abuse of the adversarial system within the domain of family law.

3. The Unified Family Court

The concept of a "Unified Family Court" is very much at the centre of what is hoped to be a new legal approach to the problems of families in crisis. Families are not primarily legal institutions (unlike the family unit in ancient Rome). In fact, in the ordinary course of daily existence, nothing is more remote than the use of the law for dealing with the personal, economic or other needs as experienced by a family. However, this is not the situation in critical circumstances when the traditional network of relations and understanding breaks down and personal and community resources are no longer able to relieve pressures. The Law Reform Commission of Canada notes that: "It is at these points that the law is seriously considered as an instrument for ordering a family relationship. It is also at these points that the law in its institutions show their strengths and weaknesses." The Law Reform Commission of Canada goes on to make the following observation:[9]

> Married people with serious family difficulties should have — and do not now have — viable alternatives provided by the legal system for avoiding the adversary process. This means access by spouses to a court that is capable of dealing with social problems without requiring their translation into legal issues before anything can be done about them. The Unified Family Court is a new concept in Courts, offering a broad spectrum of dispute-resolution techniques and having at its disposal a wide range of solutions. These things are not now available to persons whose family problems have been brought into the legal system. The institutional emphasis of the Court should be on the services it makes available to help persons find, if at all possible, consensual solutions to family difficulties rather than on its judicial functions.

Provinces such as Prince Edward Island and Ontario have already instituted pilot Unified Family Courts. Not only do these courts attempt to down play the adversarial approach, but they further gather, under one roof as it were, a judge empowered with the jurisdiction to address himself to all problems encountered in a family law dispute. That is not the case today. In fact, a variety of courts have jurisdiction to hear a number of family law-related matters. For instance, a person interested in pursuing custody in Ontario can end up in at least four different courts under four different statutes. Yet, some of these same courts are not vested with the jurisdiction to hear other matters such as the division of the family property and/or exclusive possession of the matrimonial home. Needless to say, a custody application is often merely one factor to be resolved in a family dispute. There are usually a host of other issues to be dealt with, including what happens to the family home and property and who is to pay support. As well, the procedures to be followed in each particular court are vastly different as are the cost factors involved and the question of how long it takes for the matter to appear before the court. This situation has resulted in considerable confusion both in the law itself and certainly in the public's understanding of the law as it relates to family matters.

This situation, in reality a veritable "smorgasbord" of courts and legislation which address themselves to family law issues, is another area ripe for reform.[10] Table 1 illustrates the various courts and the family law-related issues they are entitled to resolve. The Province of Ontario is used as an example. However, it should be noted that this organization is parallelled in most of the provinces.

At present, in all of the provinces, there exists a hierarchy of courts. At the bottom rung are the Provincial or District Courts usually divided into Criminal and Family Law Divisions. A judge sitting on the Bench of one of these courts is the "low man on the totem-pole" in the judiciary, except for a Justice of the Peace who is really not a judge but a member of the public chosen to hear minor legal disputes (for instance, speeding and parking tickets). It should be noted that although Provincial and District Courts sit on the bottom rung they still play a vital role in the administration of justice. In the family law context they are empowered to hear such important matters as custody of children, and support for children and spouses. The Chief Judge of the Provincial Court (Family Division) for the province of Ontario, H.T.G. Andrews, opened the 1980 session of the Family Courts by commenting on the court's expanded jurisdiction to pursue policies which:[11]

> . . . seek to maintain the family unit in domestic peace and sound collective life on the basis of individual dignity, opportunity, the essential equality of the sexes and the interdependent rights and responsibilities of each of its members. The policy objectives are:
>
> To repair the family unit where there is a breach; to reinforce the remainder of the unit where the breach is irreparable; to strengthen the inadequate; to protect the weak; to guarantee individual rights; to enforce individual responsibilities.
>
> The Family Court is at the fulcrum of these social concerns.

The next level of court is known as County Court; at approximately the same level there is the Surrogate Court. The highest level of court in each province is generally known as the Supreme Court of the particular province (for instance, the Supreme Court of Ontario or the Supreme Court of British Columbia). All of the courts mentioned above are known as "Trial Courts." This means that trials are heard by the judges of these courts. Evidence is called, witnesses are examined and cross-examined, and a decision is then made. There is, however, yet another level of court known as an Appellate Court or Appeal Court. Each province has an Appeal Court (for instance, the Alberta Court of Appeal), and for most matters in the area of family law, an appeal is made to an Appellate Court.

In every trial, there are two main issues which must be determined: the facts surrounding the case and the law which applies to those facts. A person appeals an error made by the trial judge based on either a "question of fact" or a "question of law" or a combination thereof. In other words, he hopes to have the trial decision reversed. For example, a parent found liable to support a child may contest the decision based on the judge's interpretation of the definition of "child" as found in the Act in question. In short, then, Appellate Courts do not hear witnesses. Nor, except in very rare circumstances, do they examine new evidence. Rather, an Appellate Court reviews the decision of the Trial Court for any errors as described above, and, if necessary, substitutes its own conclusions.

There is one court of ultimate appeal and that is, of course, the Supreme Court of Canada which consists of nine judges and hears appeals from all of the provincial Appellate Courts. (See Table 2 for a flow chart of the hierarchy of Trial Division and Appellate Division Courts.)

The above outline is a simplification of the court structure and is by no means intended to be an exhaustive treatise on the organization of the Canadian court system.

It is this tangle of fragmented and overlapping jurisdictions which has pointed reformers to the need of a court structure with jurisdiction to deal with all of the major issues in family law, in other words, a Unified Family Court. Such a court can deal with all of the problems faced by a family in crisis and can allow for a more expeditious and efficient resolution of the problems to be solved.

4. Conciliation Services

The Unified Family Court retains a judicial and adversarial character. However, attached to the court are a number of support agencies. These support services include family counselling which may or may not involve attempts at *reconciliation* — that is, attempt to repair a damaged family relationship. On the other hand, *conciliation* services are available to help make adjustments to a family which will not be getting back together again. The purpose of the support services is to preserve the strength in the family where possible, and where not, to attempt to create a decent and workable atmosphere for inter-spousal communications in the resolution of sensitive issues, including custody and support of the children.

The Ontario Law Reform Commission defined three functions for support services:

(1) To identify the particular problems facing a family in crisis in order to prevent unnecessary resort to judicial determination and to encourage resolution of the problems by supportive therapy (if court action is deemed appropriate, then it is at this stage that legal remedies should be explained and the consequences thereof explored);

TABLE 1

Courts of Original Jurisdiction in Ontario

Justice of the Peace	Provincial Court (Family Division)	County Court	Surrogate Court	Federal Court (Trial Division)	High Court (Supreme Court)
1. Receiving informations under *Criminal Code* and as between family members	1. Children "in need of protection": CWA	1. Divorce: *Jud A*, s. 118(3)	1. Custody, guardianship and access, *Inf A* scheduled for repeal by amendment to *CLRA*	1. Divorce: *Div A*, ss. 2, 5(2)(b)	1. Divorce: *Div A*, s. 2
	2. Juvenile delinquency: *JDA*	2. Support (ancillary to divorce): *Div A*, ss. 10, 11, 12 (LJHC)		2. Support (ancillary to divorce): *Div A*, ss. 10, 11, 12	2. Support (spouses): *Div A*, ss. 10, 11, 12; *Jud A*, s. 2: *FLRA*, ss. 15, 18
	3. Truancy, *Education Act*	3. Custody and access (ancillary to divorce): *Div A*, ss. 10, 11, 12 (LJHC)		3. Custody and support (ancillary to divorce): *Div A*, ss. 10, 11, 12	3. Support (children): *Div A*, ss. 10, 11, 12; *FLRA*, ss. 16, 17, 18
	4. Committal of juvenile to training school: *T Sch A*, s. 9	4. Property disputes between spouses: *FLRA*, ss. 4, 8, 45			4. Custody and access: *Div A*, ss. 10, 11, 12; *FLRA*, s. 35
	5. Support of spouse and children: *FLRA*, ss. 15, 16, 18	5. Appeals from Provincial Court (Family Division) under *CWA* and *FLRA*			5. *JDA* and *T Sch A* appeals
	6. Custody and access: *FLRA*, s. 35				6. Property disputes between spouses: *FLRA*, ss. 4, 40
	7. Criminal offenses between family members (for instance, husband assaulting wife)				7. Establishment of parentage: *CLRA*, s. 3
	8. Enforcement of Supreme Court orders re support and custody: *FLRA*, s. 27				
	9. Adoption: *CWA*				

LEGEND

CWA—Child Welfare Act
CLRA—Children's Law Reform Act, 1977
Div A—Divorce Act
FLRA—Family Law Reform Act, 1978
Inf A—Infants Act
Jud A—Judicature Act
JDA—Juvenile Delinquents Act
LJHC—Local Judge High Court
T Sch A—Training Schools Act

Under Bill 140 (to be in force). "An Act to Amend the Children's Law Reform Act, 1977," the following courts would have jurisdiction over custody, access and guardianship of the children under s. 25: Provincial Court (Family Division), Unified Family Court, County Court, and Supreme Court.

NOTE: The Unified Family Court has original jurisdiction in divorce, custody, support, division of property, child protection, delinquency, and

TABLE 2
Flow-Chart of the Hierarchy of Courts

•·····► ·· Path of Appeal

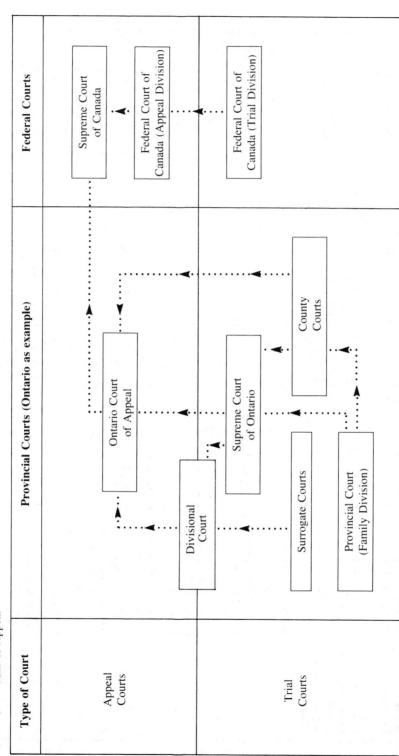

NOTE: The Divisional Court is a unique "trial–appellate" Court. It can conduct both trials and it can also hear certain types of appeals. A Divisional Court decision is appealed to the Ontario Court of Appeal.

(2) To classify the need and select the appropriate support agency for further assistance;

(3) To refer individuals to the appropriate community agency or the appropriate court.

The welfare grants directorate of the Department of Health and Welfare (a federal government agency) funded a study aimed at evaluating the adversarial approach to family law disputes and, more particularly, to evaluate the functioning of viable conciliation and support services designed to lessen the impact of the adversarial stance.

The authors of the study introduced the problem from the following perspective:[12]

> While the judicial process is the necessary ultimate recourse for the resolution of family disputes, there are a significant number of families for whom such procedures are neither appropriate nor helpful. Indeed, the use of the adversary system in the court process frequently has the undesirable effect of entrenching the very attitudes and acrimonious actions which brought the parties to the court. Paradoxically, this defeats the very purpose for which the family court system was created.

> Another problem of the family court system is that it is overloaded by the necessity of rendering judgments on issues which might be amenable to alternative methods of dispute resolution.

> It is therefore paramount that we explore the possibility of offering an alternative to the present family court system that would reduce both the time taken in court to deal with non-legal problems and offer dispute resolutions in order that family relationships could be handled in a more amicable way.

The authors interviewed a number of spouses and parents to gain insight into their perceptions of a conciliation service. Those interviewed felt such a service would be welcome for the following reasons:

(1) to have an impartial person help them reach a fair agreement;

(2) to lessen the negative effect on their children of "messy" and prolonged court actions;

(3) to reduce the unpleasantness experienced by the spouses themselves.

Lawyers and judges favoured conciliation services and stressed the following benefits:

(1) reduction of unnecessary litigation which is costly in both emotional and financial terms;

(2) such a service combines social and legal resources to arrive at fair and workable arrangements for the future welfare of all persons party to a marriage break-up.

The comments of both those who had personally experienced the "court-room forum" (parents and spouses) and those who had worked within the confines of the existing adversarial system emphasized the need for a team approach. Such a team would involve lawyers, judges, family counsellors, psychiatrists and psychologists.

Studies such as that conducted by the Department of Health and Welfare (Canada) demonstrate a growing inter-disciplinary approach to the resolution of family law issues. Many Family Courts already have support services "plugged in" to the decision-making process.

With the advent of conciliation services, a corresponding (and gratifying) reduction in litigation has occurred. As the use of conciliation services grows, so does the use of experts, such as psychiatrists and psychologists in the resolution of difficult issues such as custody. These experts play a role both inside and outside the court-room, hopefully more frequently in the latter setting. However, if a case must be placed before a judge, then a psychiatrist may be called upon to give his opinion on the issues involved. The appearance of such an expert begs a question. Is a person such as psychiatrist (or psychologist) who specializes in child psychiatry perhaps not better qualified than the judge to decide such vital questions as custody and/or access? Does his unique knowledge and immersion in the study of child behaviour not make him a better "judge" of the issues than the person actually cast in that role? Most psychiatrists and other health professionals will tell you they have no ambition to usurp the court of its power to render the ultimate decision.

The responsibility attendant with deciding custody disputes is awesome. There are many complex factors to be considered of which a health professional's opinion is but one. There are also legal questions to be resolved. No matter the approach adopted, it must conform to basic rules such as the right of all parties to be heard. Thus, the law of evidence (discussed in Chapter 8) cannot be disregarded. Further, opinions among psychiatrists and psychologists may differ. Doctor "A" may favour one option; Doctor "B" may endorse yet another. As well, a health professional involved in a custody assessment might be impaired in his primary role as a consultant and/or therapist if, superimposed on this already oncrous and sensitive responsibility, is cast the burden of acting as the decision-maker. Finally, there is the issue of ensuring that all parties perceive that the decision to award custody in favour of one party was reached only after an all-encompassing and formal hearing into the best interests of the child. A judge's decision is thus more "palatable" to the parties involved, particularly to the person losing custody. To quote an old legal maxim, "Justice must not only be done — it must be *seen* to be done."

5. The Adversarial System and Juvenile Justice

Paradoxically, although the adversarial approach is subject to much criticism within the context of custody disputes and other matters related to the disintegration of the family unit, it is, in the juvenile justice system, a much-advocated approach. As a result of the philosophy underlying the *J.D.A.* (a treatment-oriented philosophy where a juvenile is treated as a misguided child and not fully accountable for his actions), the actual court-room hearing and procedures followed therein were all too often in the nature of an informal, almost casual, inquiry into the "delinquency" of the child. The strict adversary approach adopted in adult criminal court was far removed from the "tolerant" atmosphere found in Juvenile Court. This informal approach has been severely criticized and has resulted in a greater emphasis on juvenile rights and a more adversarial process in juvenile matters. This modification has more to do with protection of a young person's rights than it does with punishing, or subjecting the young person to a rigorous trial experience. See Chapter 6 for a full discussion of the juvenile justice system.

6. Constitutional Problems of Reform

In conclusion, a general comment should be made about the dilemma constantly facing (and frustrating) lawmakers in their attempts to reform family law. At first glance it may seem to be a relatively simple matter to change the law. Yet, because of our constitutional framework, nothing could be further from the truth. As noted earlier, the *British North America Act, 1867* divides power between the provincial legislatures and the Federal Parliament. Unfortunately, with respect to laws affecting children, there is considerable overlap. Thus, there is a need for co-operation between both levels of government. To use an example cited earlier, if Ottawa passes laws affecting juvenile delinquents, then, frequently, "companion" legislation must be enacted simultaneously by each of the provinces. Needless to say, given the often controversial nature of "children's law," this co-operation between Ottawa and the provinces is subject to underlying tension and much debate. It is for this reason that reforms in the area of family law are often long overdue and, as in the area of the *J.D.A.* (see Chapter 6), one despairs as to whether the various levels of government will ever get their "act" together and amend the *J.D.A.*

To further illustrate the legislative tension between Ottawa and the provincial capitals, recourse can be made to the law surrounding marriage. The *British North America Act, 1867* provides in s. 91(26) that Parliament is given power to legislate with respect to "marriage and divorce." However, s. 92(12) gives the provincial legislature power to deal with the "Solemnization of Marriage." As a result of this jurisdictional overlap, a number of cases have come before the court to clarify the confusion created by ss. 91 and 92 of the *British North America Act, 1867*. The end product of these cases would indicate that the power to make laws concerning marriage may be divided as follows:

Province can legislate	*Parliament can legislate*
(1) Day-to-day affairs of the family.	(1) The beginning (except solemnization) and the end of marriage through divorce.
(2) Rights and duties of married persons.	
(3) Consent of a parent for children under certain age.	(2) The marriage "relationship."
(4) Issuance of licence.	(3) Personal capacity such as age, impotence, mental capacity and consanguinity.
(5) Registration of officiating clergymen.	

FOOTNOTES

1. *Haver v. Bryant*, [1969] 3 All E.R. 578
2. (1978), 6 R.F.L. (2d) 151 at p. 155
3. (1977), 37 C.C.C. (2d) 65 at pp. 70-71
4. *Smith v. Zeiger* (1978), 2 R.F.L. (2d) 324 at p. 329
5. (1976), 26 R.F.L. 91 at p. 96
6. (1978), 2 R.F.L. (2d) 254 at p. 260. See also Ministry of the Attorney-General of Ontario, "Second Report of the Attorney-General's Committee on the Representation of Children," 7 R.F.L. (2d)1 (1979) at p. 1; J.K. Genden, "Separate Legal Representation for Children: Protecting the Rights and Interests of Minors in Judicial Proceedings,"11 Harvard Civil Rights–Civil Liberties L.R. 565 (1976); and F. Maezko, "Some Problems With Acting for Children," 2 Can. J. Fam. L. (1978) at p. 267.
7. Report on Family Law, Law Reform Commission of Canada (1976), at p. 4. See also Bernard M. Dickens, "Representing the Child in the Courts," in Baxter *et al.*, *The Child and The Courts* (Toronto, 1978), at p. 273, sponsored by the Program on Family Law and Social Welfare (1976), Faculty of Law, University of Toronto; Report by the Ontario Law Reform Commission on Family Law, "Children" (1973).
8. *Supra*, at p. 16
9. *Supra*, at p. 19
10. See O. Stone, "Jurisdictions Over the Custody and Upbringing of Children," 2 Can. J. Fam. L. 365 (1979)
11. *Re W* (1979), 13 R.F.L. (2d) 381
12. See Irving and Gandy, "Family Court Conciliation Project: An Experiment in Support Services," 25 R.F.L. 47 (1976)

Chapter 3

The Child in the Family

A. THE FAMILY

The nuclear family, it has been said, is the basic unit or fabric from which the cloth of society is woven. The concept of what constitutes a family, however, has undergone dramatic change in the past decades. Traditionally, a family unit has been made up of parents (two of them) and their offspring. Further, father "brought home the bacon"; mother cooked it, and rarely left home and hearth. Now the trend is for both parents to work and, as a result, more and more children are cared for by baby-sitters or daycare centres. Of course, parents were once always married; both in the eyes of God and in the eyes of the law. Today they may only be married in the eyes of the law and recognized as common-law spouses — a relationship once considered scandalous by the matrons of polite society. Also, the one-parent family is emerging as a rather common phenomena and other more innovative variations on the family theme are evolving: some parents share their children on an equal basis in what is often described as a joint custody relationship where the children spend one-half of the year with their father; the other half with their mother. Some families exist in even more unorthodox circumstances: the children live in the family home and their separated parents take turns living in, and parenting in the home "month on, month off."

In Chapter 1, we saw that historically the family unit was very much a legal entity — a law unto itself as it were. In ancient Rome under the concept of *patria potestas* the *paterfamilias* exerted full control over the other family members. Children were particularly "under the thumb" of their father and within the family were accorded no legally recognized protections or privileges. The Bible perhaps best sums up what has been considered to be the general scheme of things (within the family hierarchy) for most of history: "Wives submit to your husband . . . children obey your parents" (Colossians).

The women's movement, both at the beginning of this century, and with a resurgence in recent years, has done much to alter conventional role playing within the family. Similarly, the children's movement has reshaped the social and legal view of the child as a family member.

As a result of such varied yet related phenomena as spiralling divorce rates, the working mother, the unmarried parent, and common-law relationships, the traditional family structure has been placed under unparalleled stress.

The law has been slow to respond to many of the above-described changes in society, particularly as they pertain to the legal relationships within the family unit. The Law Reform Commission of Canada passed the following judgement in 1976:[1]

Although Canadians have always considered it self-evident that the family has a special and central place in our society, there have in fact been only a few occasions when the legal basis of the family and the legal relationship of its members have received official attention over the past century. Changes we have experienced socially, as well as changes in the composition, structure, expectations and thwarted hopes of families and their members have at best led to palliative accommodations by the law to social pressures, such as making divorce generally available, but hardly to a re-examination of the image of the family the law reflects. This image may by now be so far removed from reality that the law and its institutions may weaken rather than strengthen family life, especially in crisis situations.

This indictment of the law has been diminished, to a certain extent, by a flood of legislation in the area of family law in the last few years. Although the concept may have appeared dormant, the law has always viewed the family as integral to a well-ordered society. Further, without question the law has always considered the family as the optimal social environment for children to be raised in, and to facilitate achievement of their fullest potential.

The preamble to the *Family Law Reform Act, 1978* of Ontario (*F.L.R.A.*) is an eloquent statement of the law's position on the family in today's society:

WHEREAS, it is desirable to encourage and strengthen the role of the family in society;

AND WHEREAS for that purpose it is necessary to recognize the equal position of spouses as individuals within marriage and to recognize marriage as a form of partnership;

AND WHEREAS in support of such recognition it is necessary to provide in law for the orderly and equitable settlement of the affairs of the spouses upon the breakdown of the partnership; and to provide for other mutual obligations in family relationships, including the equitable sharing by parents of responsibility for their children . . .

However, you might wonder about this preamble. On the one hand it preaches family solidarity — "to encourage and strengthen the role of the family . . ." — yet, almost in the same breath, it speaks (like a prophet of doom) of "the breakdown of the partnership . . ." A superficial reading of the philosophy contained in the preamble would leave one thinking the object of the Act is to acknowledge marriage breakups, in fact to accept such developments as almost inevitable. If the object is to "shore up" the role of the family why not place legal obstacles in the face of those wishing to escape the institution? The answers lie in consideration of the key phrase "to recognize marriage as a form of partnership."

At face value marriage as a partnership may seem a rather ordinary concept. Yet it is an extraordinary development in the law. In the past, marriage, and other family relationships, were less like a partnership than they were dictatorial in character. There was a distinct, and unfortunately, destructive pecking order with the father as the dominant figure. Laws were shaped around this self-perpetuating hierarchy. Husband–wife, parent–child relationships are delicate and intricate organisms. They are dynamic and subject to constant growth and evolution. To flourish they must exist in an environment which recognizes their uniquely fragile yet hopefully enduring nature. Like a garden denied the life-sustaining sun the family will wither and die if its members are regulated by rigid legal attitudes and outdated role-models. Thus the law, by sweeping aside the dusty cobwebs of time and recognizing the principle of equality of family members within the institution of marriage, has in effect strengthened the family and its vital role within society.

B. THE CHILD AS A MEMBER OF THE FAMILY

1. General

How has the parent–child relationship been affected by legal reforms? Illegitimacy as a legal status has been abolished in many provinces. Custody law now focuses attention on the child's best interests, and not on which is the more deserving parent. The definition of a "parent" has been enlarged to include not only biological parents but those who have assumed the role of a parent. Such a person can be compelled to support "his" child. As well, the law surrounding child protection proceedings (see Chapter 4) has been rewritten both to give a child a voice in the proceedings and to strengthen the protection procedures themselves. This is an area in which the state will interfere with the parent–child relationship; if need be taking the extreme step of severing the relationship. The courts are vested with this authority under *parens patriae* and have the power to act in the best interests of the child and thereby override parental authority. But what about the day-to-day decisions in family life? In corporate law there is a principle that the courts will not "pierce the corporate veil," that is pry into the internal working of the corporation. This attitude is replicated in the court's attitude about not intruding upon the privacy of family life (provided parental action does not trespass on such areas as child abuse). Thus issues such as parental discipline and parental rights to direct their children in education, religious training and life-style are largely within the discretion of the child's parent or guardian and are not subject to detailed legal rules and regulations.

The question of parental discipline has recently surfaced as a public issue. Coinciding with the Year of the Child, Sweden enacted legislation which forbids a parent from administering that old-fashioned form of discipline commonly known as "a spanking." The new Swedish law prohibits any act which, "for the purpose of punishing, causes the child . . . pain, even if the disturbance is mild in passing." It is meant to include psychological punishment and one wonders whether confining a child to his room would run afoul of the law. Certainly this law has attracted criticism from many parts of the population, parents being by far the most vocal.

One annoyed Swedish parent (a father of three) summed up his reaction to the law as follows:

> There is a difference between deliberate spanking and what I would call an outburst of temper. I never spanked my kids in cold blood, only on the spur of the moment. I am sure it did not harm but helped them.

One suspects this father's reaction is typical of the general feelings of most Canadian parents. The *Criminal Code* of Canada explicitly sanctions parental discipline in the form of spankings. That section states:

> 43. Every schoolteacher, parent or person standing in the place of a parent is justified in using force by way of correction toward a pupil or child, as the case may be, who is under his care, if the force does not exceed what is reasonable under the circumstances.

The question of corporal punishment is further examined in Chapter 4 on parent–child discipline and Chapter 7 as it relates to teacher–student discipline.

The parent–child relationship in its earliest years is not subject to the tension that inevitably exists with the arrival of the teenage years. The length and style of a son's hair or the amount of make-up applied by a daughter are common sources of friction in a family. The parent has the general power to "direct" the children in these sensitive areas. This is usually effected by threats of "groundings" and allowance reductions. Although these coercive tactics are not calculated to win popularity they are accepted by many people as an essential form of discipline. On the other hand, a child's choice of friends and his choice of vocation and major course of study in high school should ideally be discussed in a democratic manner between parent and child. Unfortunately, the ideal is often not achieved and a major confrontation between parent and child is the result. For instance, assume a child wishes to enrol in a technical course as opposed to entering the academic stream in high school. Suddenly a mother and father who had visions of welcoming a doctor or lawyer into the family see a less socially acceptable future for their child. That is, of course, the parents' perspective and may by no means be in touch with reality. The child's interests and talents should be the deciding factors. In any event, how is the conflict resolved? Can the child override his parents' demands and take the course *he* wants? The answer does not lend itself to precise definition. Theoretically, the parents can enforce their wishes as it is they who have "executive" control over his education. This authority is gleaned from the common law. However, from a practical point of view, it is almost impossible to force-feed parental wishes with respect to education. The roles of the teacher and guidance counsellor are vital in this area and with their assistance what is best for the child should become clear.

An American case considered the issue of parental authority to direct the choice of education for a child and in the same context discussed the issue of parental control over the religious upbringing of offspring. The question of parental authority over education is further discussed in Chapter 7. The case at hand, *Wisconsin v. Yoder*,[2] involved an Amish parent who had withdrawn his child from the public school system after the child had completed grade 8. The parent was critical of the liberal attitudes of a conventional high school education and further felt it would threaten his child's religious upbringing. The state argued it had a responsibility to enforce the child's attendance to ensure the child was adequately prepared to participate in the mainstream of society. In the majority decision the United States Supreme Court found in favour of the Amish parents and the child was removed from the public school system and was taught within the Amish community. However, the dissenting opinion written by the late Mr. Justice Douglas made pertinent observations with respect to the shortcomings of the majority decision:

> The Court's analysis assumes that the only interests at stake in the case are those of the Amish parents on the one hand, and those of the State on the other. The difficulty with this approach is that, despite the Court's claim, the parents are seeking to vindicate not only their own free exercise claims, but also those of their high-school-age children.

> If the parents in this case are allowed a religious exemption, the inevitable effect is to impose the parents' notions of religious duty upon their children. Where the child is mature enough to express potentially conflicting desires, it would be an invasion of the child's rights to permit such an imposition without canvassing his views.

> Religion is an individual experience. . . . Crucial . . . are the views of the child . . .

> While the parents, absent dissent, normally speak for the entire family, the education of the child is a matter on which the child will often have decided views. He may want to be a pianist or an astronaut, or an oceanographer. To do so he will have to break from the Amish tradition.

This dissenting opinion can be considered as somewhat enlightened as it attempts to incorporate the child's "voice" in something as vital to his future as his choice of academic training. Unfortunately, the dissent in the *Yoder* case has not carried much weight in either Canadian or American courts.

The issues of parental control can be further complicated if one parent has one expectation for the child and the other has another. For instance, with respect to religious upbringing, various statutory guide-lines would appear to vest authority in the father. This parental prejudice has its roots in the common law, in which, of course, the father occupies the most prominent role. The law rarely intervenes in such controversies leaving the conciliation process up to the parents themselves. The *F.L.R.A.* of Ontario allows for parents to contractually agree to various aspects of child raising as part of a domestic contract; this would include an agreement concerning religious upbringing.

A new development in the area of family roles involves contracts between parents and their children. These contracts specify areas of responsibility and often detail the child's chores. For instance, in return for taking out the garbage, mowing the lawn and washing the car, the child's allowance would be stipulated. If the chores were not completed, the child would have breached the contract and the allowance would be forfeited. On the other hand, the child may negotiate a curfew and should he break curfew, he may be subject to an agreed-upon penalty. These contracts may, on the face of it, seem rather out of the ordinary; however, they may lessen the tension in the family because they give the child a voice in the running of day-to-day family life. It should be noted that these contracts are not enforceable in a court of law.

2. Child v. Parent

It was noted in Chapter 1 that children in certain jurisdictions have the legal right to sue their parents. Such a right would appear to strike at the very heart of the family relationship. The thought of a child facing his parent in a court-room armed with all of the adversarial weapons found in the judicial arsenal is repugnant to most people. Yet the situation envisioned by the legislature apparently is one in which the parents, through negligence, have injured their children. The Supreme Court of Canada made the following statement involving the claim of a five-year-old child who was seriously injured when his father negligently backed his car over him: "However repugnant it may seem that a child should sue his own father, it would probably be equally repugnant that a child injured by his father's negligent act should have no redress for the damage suffered."

Several American courts[3] have dealt with the issue of parental negligence and a doctrine based on immunity of the family has emerged. Briefly, the doctrine underlines the fear in certain American courts that sanctioning parent–child litigation impairs efforts to reunite the family. It is important to note that the doctrine of immunity of the family has thus far been restricted to circumstances in which the child has suffered emotional or psychological injury as a result of parental neglect. Claims by children for physical injuries resulting from beatings, rapes (incest), and auto accidents have been approved by the American judiciary. Apparently the doctrine of immunity will apply only in the limited circumstances where a family's chances of being reunited are adversely affected by the child taking his parents to court. As yet no cases have surfaced in Canada with respect to the issue of parental neglect and, therefore, it is perhaps too early to consider the impact of the doctrine of immunity of the family in the Canadian judicial process. However, s. 67 of the *F.L.R.A.* of Ontario reads as follows:

> 67. No person shall be disentitled from recovering damages in respect of injuries incurred for the reason only that the injuries were incurred before his birth.

This provision would apparently be applicable in a situation in which a pregnant woman, due to drug addiction or even alcohol or nicotine addiction, gives birth to an unhealthy child. Once again, no cases have as yet considered this issue. But, it would appear that a child injured *in utero* because of maternal neglect has legislative sanction to sue. A logical extension of s. 67 would indicate that if a child in the womb is entitled to sue because of parental neglect any child whether *in utero* or not is probably possessed of the same legal right.

C. THE FAMILY IN CRISIS — DIVORCE AND SEPARATION

Unfortunately many marriages fail. The effects (both emotional and legal) of such an event on all concerned are profound. It is necessary to briefly consider what can happen upon the disintegration of a family, beginning first with divorce. "What God hath joined together, let no man put asunder." This biblical reference outlines society's once-conventional attitude towards the institution of marriage. However, in today's society, divorce no longer carries the stigma it once did, and divorcées are no longer the pariahs of respectable society. A measurement of this trend is a statistic which indicates that, in Canada, one in every three marriages is destined to end in divorce.

Divorce is a matter of federal legislative concern and in 1968, the Federal Parliament enacted the *Divorce Act* which has equal application to every citizen of Canada. Termination of marriage is granted only by authority of the grounds and procedures outlined in the *Divorce Act*. This Act specifies the conduct commonly described as "grounds for divorce" and the petitioning spouse must in many circumstances be able to prove the other guilty of such conduct, frequently described as a matrimonial offence. This matrimonial offence approach is rooted in the adversarial nature of judicial proceedings and is thus a frequent target of criticism by those advocating reform of the Canadian *Divorce Act*. In Germany, the concept of "no-fault" or, as it is described in Germany, "no-guilt" divorce is now available. Prior to the passage of the new laws (in 1978), German law paralleled our own law by employing the same concept of a matrimonial offence as grounds for divorce. Under the new German law, the sole criterion for divorce is the breakdown of the marriage. If both parties consent, then a one-year separation is sufficient for divorce. If, on the other hand, only one party wishes divorce, then a three-year wait must occur. Various authorities, including the Law Reform Commission of Canada, have advocated a similar amendment occur in our divorce laws in the near future. The Law Reform Commission proposes:[4]

> We propose that the only basis for dissolution of marriage should be the failure of the personal relationship between a husband and wife. We refer hereafter to such a failure as "marriage breakdown". The doctrines of "matrimonial offence", "matrimonial fault", "collusion" and "connivance" should be wholly inapplicable in all future marriage breakdown cases.

The grounds provided for in the *Divorce Act* for dissolution of marriage include adultery, cruelty (mental or physical), and desertion. There are, however, other grounds infrequently resorted to; these include bigamy, bestiality, sodomy and homosexual behaviour. Also included as grounds are imprisonment and gross addiction to drugs or alcohol. In addition, non-consummation (no sexual intercourse) of the marriage is sufficient reason to have the marriage terminated.

It should be noted that the concept of matrimonial offence, although still a very prominent part of our divorce laws, was diminished in importance by the 1968 *Divorce Act*. Prior to the passage of this Act, a matrimonial offence was the only ground for divorce. It should be noted from the above-listed grounds that certain sexual practices and other types of behaviour such as alcoholism are not matrimonial offences or at least within the literal legal interpretation of this phrase. At present the most popular ground for divorce is colloquially described as "desertion." In fact, the more accurate way of viewing this ground is to describe it as a permanent breakdown of the marriage resulting in the spouses living "separate and apart." If two spouses consent to living separate and apart (for instance, through the medium of the separation agreement) then at the end of three years either spouse may petition for divorce. On the other hand, if one spouse departs the family home (for instance, the husband runs off with another woman without the consent of the wife) then the husband would have to wait five years before he could petition for divorce. His wife, on the other hand, could use the second most popular ground for divorce, adultery, in order to launch a petition, or she could wait three years and petition her husband at the end of that period.

A person who has committed adultery cannot use his or her own act to secure a divorce. He is at the mercy, so to speak, of his spouse unless, of course, the spouse engages in his or her own act of adultery. Two parties cannot engage in collusion (a fraudulent and secret understanding between the spouses) in order to secure a divorce. Further, a person having condoned a matrimonial offence such as adultery, that is, having forgiven an act of adultery, cannot later use the act to secure a divorce. Basically, any agreement between the parties in which they connive at arranging a divorce may be a bar to such a divorce being granted, unless the judge hearing the matter decides it is in the best interests of the public that the divorce go through.

A divorce is granted in two stages: the decree *nisi* stage and the decree absolute stage. A decree *nisi* is granted at the termination of the actual court-room hearing. This is an interim decree of divorce and does not entitle the spouses to remarry. A three-month waiting period must occur at which time, if no appeal to the decree *nisi* has been filed, the parties may apply for a decree absolute. Upon the granting of the decree absolute, the parties are free to remarry.

With respect to spouses who are also parents the *Divorce Act* provides that an official known as the Official Guardian must be notified when divorce proceedings are instituted. The Official Guardian is employed by the provincial government and acts as a legal agent for children (and others incapable of looking after their own affairs). He is not an ombudsman for children. His role is more like that of a surrogate parent or legal "watchdog" who becomes involved when a child's interest in a legal situation (parents divorcing) appears before the courts. With respect to divorce it is the duty of the Official Guardian to determine if any problems exist with respect to custody and if so advise to the court. This is generally accomplished by a social worker conducting an investigation into the custody arrangements and submitting a report on behalf of the Official Guardian's office.

Divorce is the only means by which a marriage may be terminated (excluding annulment). Along with the decree of divorce issues related to the breakup of a marriage, for instance, the granting of custody, the payment of support and the division of the matrimonial property may also be decided by the court. However, judicial intervention may decide these other issues independent of a proceeding for divorce. For instance, if a wife has no grounds for divorce she may still proceed in Family Court for custody and support for herself and her children. As well, spouses may decide for themselves how these matters are to be resolved in the form of a separation agreement. With respect to children a court will not be bound to give effect to provisions which are not in the best interests of the child.

Issues such as division of matrimonial property have occupied the minds of the judiciary in recent years and a brief note on these developments may be helpful. In the past, at least prior to the passage of Acts such as the *F.L.R.A.* of Ontario, each spouse owned separately property that belonged to them before the marriage. As well, property purchased during the marriage belonged to the person who actually made payment. This system of separate property was viewed as being very unfair in that it failed to recognize the contribution of the spouse who did not actually invest money in the purchase of family property. Traditionally, the husband was the "bread-winner" and the wife cared for the children and performed the household chores. As a consequence, she rarely contributed in financial terms to the purchase of family property and thus was deprived of an interest therein if the marriage foundered. This inequity has been remedied by legislation in most provinces. As well, in all of the provinces, a court may order that, regardless of the "paper" ownership of the matrimonial home, one of the spouses and the children may have exclusive possession of the family home.

The preceding overview of divorce and marriage breakdown may be described as only a thumb-nail sketch. The actual legal machinery for dealing with divorce and separation is very complicated and outside the focus of this book. Issues that go hand in hand with marriage breakdown such as custody, child kidnapping and support for children will now be discussed individually.

D. CUSTODY

1. An Historical Perspective

A. Custody — Who Gets the Children?

This question is being asked at an ever-increasing rate as the incidence of divorce and matrimonial separation escalate. To ask the question is to involve oneself in an emotional tug-of-war. Anyone who has had experience, personal or professional, in a contested custody situation, can testify to the almost superhuman difficulty faced in arriving at a just solution. It has been said that if ever the wisdom of Solomon was needed, it is in a contested custody case.

Chapter 2 noted that the present system for resolving questions of custody is very much adversarial in character. Unfortunately, the children are often viewed as the prize to be won by the successful litigant. This sentiment underlines an attitude which seems to indicate that children are merely pawns in a contest and, like pieces on a chess-board, are to be manoeuvred and sacrificed according to the dictates of bitter and revengeful parents. To say that the law has experienced considerable difficulty in dealing with such a sensitive issue is to make an understatement. Indeed, the evolution of laws surrounding custody matters parallels the painfully slow growth and recognition of children's rights in general as discussed in Chapter 1. Historically, custody decisions had less to do with what was good for the child than what was best for the parent — particularly the father. In feudal times, working the land was the heartbeat of an agrarian society. Families and children were essential to this way of life and healthy heirs (preferably male) ensured the continuation of the line. As a consequence, the earliest common law decisions with respect to custody demonstrated a marked reluctance to take the children away from their father. It was not until the general recognition and acceptance of both women's and children's rights — after the middle of the 19th century — that consideration was given to maternal custody. This development had its roots in a concept known as the "tender years doctrine." Briefly stated, this doctrine provided (and still provides) that young children were considered better off with their mother. It was mother who provided the stimulation and emotional nourishment so critical to the healthy development of a young child. However, this doctrine remained an exception to the general rule — that the father had a pre-eminent custody right — until relatively recent times when statutory intervention replaced common law principles. The basic statutory premise today is that until otherwise agreed, custody is vested equally in both parents.

2. Definition

It must be said that the law surrounding custody remains unsettled at present. Varying statutory terminology and uncertain juridical interpretation of that terminology have fuelled the problem. There is an abundance of statutory law, both federal and provincial, which addresses itself to the topic of custody. However, it must be remembered that parents can agree to a custody arrangement without judicial — and hence statutory — supervision. Most often these private arrangements are spelled out in a separation agreement although, once again, if the arrangement may subject the child to harm a court may disregard it.

The concept of custody does not lend itself to precise definition. It is perhaps easiest to understand the concept involved by looking at it as if it has both a narrow and a broad meaning. At its narrowest, custody refers to the actual physical care and control of the child; in other words, the responsibility for day-to-day decisions concerning the child's well-being. Custody in its widest sense was defined in the following way by an Ontario Family Court Judge:[5] "Custody encompasses . . . the full responsibility and control in providing physical nurture as well as mental and emotional nurture of children — for providing physical care, educational training and guidance in all matters that are considered of importance in the healthy rearing of a child." In the case under consideration the mother had legal custody of the children of the marriage. She was raising them as Roman Catholics. However, the father, who had access rights, was preaching the beliefs of the Jehovah's Witnesses when he visited the children. A court order forbade him to engage in such activity as the right to direct the children in their religious upbringing was vested in the custodial parent — in this instance the mother. The father, as access parent, had no say in the matter.

Another way of considering custody in this broad sense is to recognize that the custodial parent has the authority to make decisions which will have a permanent effect on the life and development of the child (for instance, under what Church affiliation is the child to be raised and what sort of schooling is the child to receive).

An understanding of the narrow and broad senses of custody is of particular importance when one considers the alternatives available to the court in deciding custody. In general, there are three choices: sole custody (by far the most popular choice), split custody, and joint custody; the latter types of custody orders being considered somewhat unique. In any event, it should be stated that the most common judicial perspective with respect to custody is to take it in its broadest sense.

As a general rule, one person is granted custody with the non-custodial party given access (visitation) privileges. In other words, one parent has *sole* custody — in its widest sense — with reasonable or specified access available to the other. It is important to note that the effect of a sole custody order is to preclude the access parent from having any legally enforceable control over the upbringing of the child.

A *split* custody order results in the granting of legal custody to one parent and the actual care and control — physical possession — to the other parent. For example, a father may be given custody, and, therefore, the right to supervise the educational, religious, and general upbringing of the children but the mother may have the actual day-to-day care of the children. Of course the father usually enjoys reasonable access while the children are in the mother's physical possession.

The most recent type of order is an order for *joint* custody. The acceptance of this arrangement has been greeted by scepticism by both the courts and child care professionals. As a concept, a joint custody order grants full legal custody to both spouses. Usually each parent has physical care and control for a designated period of time. Needless to say, having an equal say in the children's lives presupposes parental co-operation at its fullest. As a result, a joint custody order is somewhat rare. Split custody and joint custody are discussed at greater length on p. 61.

3. Jurisdiction

Most provinces have a number of different courts empowered to grant custody. Generally, each of these courts derives its custody jurisdiction from a different statute. For instance, in the Province of Ontario, custody disputes may be decided by judges sitting on the Benches of the Supreme, County, Surrogate and Family Courts. The statutes which address themselves to custody are also plentiful: the *F.L.R.A.*, the *Infants Act* (scheduled to be repealed by an amendment to the *Children's Law Reform Act, 1977 (C.L.R.A.)*), and the *Divorce Act* (see Table 1 on p. 28).

The Supreme Courts of most provinces also have the inherent jurisdiction to grant custody outside of the above-described family law statutes. This jurisdiction is derived from a special statute often referred to as a Judicature Act. In most provinces this statute assigns judicial responsibilities and procedures to the various levels of the courts. It is primarily a civil law statute and does not deal with criminal matters which are, of course, a matter of federal concern. In any event, most Judicature Acts enshrine the concept of *parens patriae* (discussed in Chapter 1 briefly, and in Chapter 6 in greater detail). *Parens patriae* refers to the responsibility of the government to look after those persons (including infants) who are unable (in a legal sense) to manage their own affairs.

As most of the provinces and territories have a hierarchy of courts and statutory authorities, similar to that found in Ontario, that province's custody jurisdiction will be used to illustrate in what court and by whom a custody action may be initiated.

The Supreme Court of Ontario has jurisdiction under the *Infants Act*. At the time of writing, an Act to amend the *C.L.R.A.* of Ontario will have the effect of repealing the *Infants Act*. The amending Act does not restrict the right to bring an application for custody to parents only. The existing *Infants Act* provides that applications can be brought only by the mother or father of the child. As an aside, it should be mentioned that dissension in the case-law as to whether a mother or a father under this Act includes unmarried parents has been put to rest by the *C.L.R.A.* which abolished the historical distinction between legitimate and illegitimate children. However, although only a mother or father may make application under the *Infants Act*, custody may still be given to a third non-applicant party.

The Supreme Court of Ontario also has custody jurisdiction under the *F.L.R.A.* Such action may be started by any party and custody orders are not restricted to parents. Any party may also proceed in the Supreme Court by way of writ of summons, and statement of claim. This is a formal and, relative to other custody applications, a cumbersome, time-consuming and expensive procedure. Hence, custody disputes are rarely resolved by this method. However, it should be noted that until the passage of statutes such as the *F.L.R.A.* of Ontario (March, 1978), a person other than a parent (for instance, grandparents) often had no option but to proceed by way of writ.

The Supreme Court of Ontario (and the Supreme Courts of the other provinces and territories), also has jurisdiction under the *Divorce Act* to make a custody order. However, an important point to remember is that a custody order alone cannot be made under the *Divorce Act*. The parties must be married and seeking a divorce; custody will then be granted corollary to (as part of) a decree of divorce. An exception to this rule involves an interim custody order pending the ultimate determination of the petition for divorce.

The Surrogate Court of the county in which the child resides may also make a custody order pursuant to an Act such as the *Infants Act* of Ontario. Only the parents may make application. The County Courts and Provincial Courts (Family Division) are also vested with the authority to resolve custody disputes under jurisdiction of provincial statutes such as the *F.L.R.A.* of Ontario.

The confusion surrounding which courts to use (and the parties who may appear therein) in a custody dispute is greatly relieved by the Unified Family Court concept as discussed in Chapter 2.

As was mentioned on p. 43, custody may be determined without reference to any of the judicial proceedings described above. In such circumstances, custody is decided privately by the parents in a separation agreement. Usually custody is given to one of the parents although it would appear that parents may agree to vest custody in a mutually agreed third party. However, as mentioned earlier, a court may disregard such provision in a separation agreement if it is not in the best interests of the child. The "best interests of the child" concept is crucial to an understanding of custody law and is examined at length on p. 47.

In the absence of a court order or a valid separation agreement, pursuant to s. 2(1) of the *Infants Act* of Ontario, "the father and mother of an infant are joint guardians and are equally entitled to the custody, control and education of the infant." The amendments proposed to the *C.L.R.A.* of Ontario continue the arrangement whereby the father and the mother of the child are equally entitled to custody prior to agreement or intervention by a court order.

In the course of a normal marriage breakup, there is an interval between the couple physically separating and custody being resolved by one of the methods outlined above. In such circumstances, one parent generally assumes *de facto* custody. This is a custody arrangement in fact and not in law — in other words, not pursuant to a court order. This does not mean *de facto* custody is unrecognized by the judicial process. As a general rule, the law recognizes a *de facto* custody arrangement and will maintain it with an interim custody order pending the final resolution of the matter. *De facto* situations are often fraught with difficulty. At this stage parents are still adjusting to the marriage breakup and are susceptible to erratic and unstable emotional behaviour. As has been noted earlier, most custody statutes state that custody is vested jointly in both parents. What is to prevent the non-custodial parent from kidnapping his own children? The simple truth, in a legal sense, is that nothing can really be done. However, the courts frown, and understandably so, upon such behaviour. The question of kidnapping one's own offspring is discussed on p. 72.

4. Factors in Contested Custody Cases

A. The Best Interests Test

The *Divorce Act*, and provincial legislation such as the *F.L.R.A.* of Ontario provide criteria or guidelines that the courts are to take into account when they are deciding custody. The guidelines differ according to the Act being followed. However, regardless of the particular Act, one concept is of overriding importance in the area of custody law. This concept is described as the *best interests of the child* doctrine, or more simply put, "the best interests test." In short, this concept means that the paramount consideration in making a custody order is that custody be awarded to that person in whose care the welfare of the child will be maximized.

The *F.L.R.A.* of Ontario provides that the only basis for deciding custody is "the best interests of the child" (s. 35). Historically, this has not always been the case. In fact, the *Divorce Act* and various provincial Infants Acts, while noting the best interests of the child as the most paramount consideration, make mention of other relevant criteria. Specific reference is made to the conduct of parents (sexual or otherwise). For many years, prior to the passage of Acts such as the *F.L.R.A.* of Ontario, the best interests test existed only in the common law. The *Divorce Act*, in fact, makes no specific mention of the best interests test. However, the case-law (judicial interpretation of the *Divorce Act* included) is well settled: the best interests of the child is the paramount consideration in any custody dispute.

What do we really mean when we say the "best interests test"? It is without question a general statement of law, and within its ambit the courts take a number of factors into account. The proposed amendment to the *C.L.R.A.* of Ontario notes that in determining the best interests of the child a court shall consider all of the circumstances including a number of specifically described factors:

(1) The emotional ties between the child and the person or persons having custody.
(2) The views and preferences of the child (where such views and preferences can be reasonably ascertained).
(3) The life and time the child has lived in a stable home environment.
(4) The ability of each person applying for custody to provide guidance and education, the necessities of life and any special needs of the child who is the object of the custody action.
(5) Any plans proposed for the care and upbringing of the child.
(6) The permanence and stability of any proposed custodial home as a family unit.
(7) The relationship by blood (blood type and tie) between the child and each person who is a party to the application for custody.

This Act specifically notes that the past conduct of a person is not relevant to a determination unless one can relate that past conduct to the person's fitness to parent.

The factors described above are in fact derived from the case-law and represent the sort of issues which have been influencing judges deciding custody disputes for a considerable period of time.

B. Conduct

It must be stressed that most statutes, including the *Divorce Act*, do not provide specific criteria and, therefore, factors such as conduct are still of considerable importance in the resolution of custody disputes. In any event, conduct will become an issue if it can be related to the overall picture of an individual's ability to parent.

A number of cases have discussed conduct which may adversely affect an individual's chances of obtaining custody. At one time, adultery often provided an almost insurmountable obstacle for a parent to overcome in a custody action. The rationale for this rule was based on the belief that adultery was immoral and any person who engaged in such conduct would be a corrupting moral influence on children. It must be recognized that this policy had a punitive element; adultery was not socially acceptable and individuals found to have committed this act would be penalized. As social attitudes changed, adherence to the rule began to erode. Today if a person has committed adultery, yet on the basis of other factors is the most fit parent, then he, or she, will nevertheless be awarded custody.

A more worrisome issue than adulterous conduct is that in which one of the spouses has unilaterally decided to break up the family unit. Conduct of this sort is viewed seriously by the law and has been considered in a number of recent decisions. In *Talsky v. Talsky* the husband was a successful dentist. The wife managed a well-organized home for her husband and children. As in most marriages, during the first years, everything seemed rosy; then, abruptly, the wife decided she had made a mistake and "wanted out." The Ontario Court of Appeal[6] felt that the wife's conduct of arbitrarily pulling out of the family brought "into grave question her fitness [to mother] since for selfish reasons she . . . destroyed the children's home and deprived them of a loving father." Since in other respects the welfare of the children would be equally served either in the father's or the mother's custody, substantial weight was given to the wife's desertion. In fact, it tipped the scales in the father's favour and he was awarded custody of the children.

Another case, *MacDonald v. MacDonald*,[7] went all the way to the Supreme Court of Canada. The situation in the *MacDonald* case was not unlike that in the *Talsky* case and a similar decision was reached. The Supreme Court of Canada made the following statement:[8]

> . . . the conduct of the parties must be considered in the assessment of the relative fitness of the contesting parties to have the care and custody of the infant children of the marriage and . . . the conduct of a spouse who has deliberately acted in such a fashion as to make impossible continuation of life of infant children in a two-parent family is relevant to the fitness of that person to be the custodian of the said infant children.

C. The Common-Law Relationship

The question of common-law relationships has increasingly occupied the minds of those deciding custody disputes. Although common-law relationships are gaining growing acceptance in society, they are still viewed with what might be described as a jaundiced eye by the judiciary. In a Saskatchewan case, *Friday v. Friday*,[9] matrimonial strife adversely affected the health of Mrs. Friday to the point where she left the family home. She took one of her three children with her, the two remaining with their father. A short time after leaving, she discovered that her husband was living (in the family home) in a common-law relationship with a Mrs. Forsyth. Mrs. Forsyth was divorced, had two children, and was pregnant with a child of whom Mr. Friday was not the father. Mr. Friday and Mrs. Forsyth lived openly as if they were man and wife. The court exhaustively examined all the factors relevant to the determination of whether it would be in the best interests of the Friday children to be in the custody of their father. Except for one telling point, the court felt that the children would be equally well off in either the care of the mother or father. The decision hinged on Mr. Friday's adulterous relationship with Mrs. Forsyth. The court was concerned that the children, if left with Mr. Friday, would grow up believing that such a relationship was quite proper and normal and one which they could and should emulate. The court stated:[10]

> [Thus, although] being fully cognizant of today's changed mores, I am of the opinion that the long-range welfare of the three boys presently with their father would best be served by their being given an opportunity to grow up in a home where such irregular behaviour and conduct did not prevail.

As a result, the mother was awarded custody.

An earlier Ontario case, *Hill v. Hill*,[11] is an example of a case where custody was awarded to a parent (the mother) living in a common-law relationship. It was held by the court that the existence of such a union was undoubtedly a factor and an important one in determining what was in the best interests of the child. However, it was held the mother's common-law relationship was merely one factor to be considered in the context of the whole picture. In this case, since among other things, there was no evidence of any act of immorality in the presence of the children, by word or deed, "the adulterous relationship of the mother was insufficient to tip the scales in favour of the father."

In both the *Friday* and *Hill* cases, the common-law relationships were examined only in the context of how they reflected upon the adulterous spouse's ability to be a good parent; in other words, conduct was examined within the context of the children's best interests.

The case-law would indicate that the bad "spouse" must be distinguished from the bad "parent." It does not necessarily follow that a bad spouse is a bad parent, at least relative to the parenting skills of the other person engaged in the custody dispute. Conduct (it would appear) in and by itself, as distinct from conduct as it reflects on the child's best interests, has been whittled to a position of relative unimportance in deciding custody disputes. This fact is reflected in the words of the Supreme Court of Canada:[12]

> . . . the conduct of the parents should not be considered in an attempt to

make any award of custody punitive to the person whose conduct the court found to be improper. Such a course would be exactly contrary to . . . the paramount consideration, that is, the welfare of the children, and would be using the children as a whip to beat the misdoer.

D. Sexual Orientation: The Homosexual Parent

In recent years homosexuals have been advocating equal rights. This includes the right to parent either singly or in pairs. Not surprisingly they have carried their case into the court-room and into the area of custody disputes. In *Case v. Case*,[13] another decision from a Saskatchewan court, the mother was a lesbian. She separated from her husband and managed to buy a small house in Saskatoon. She had established a homosexual relationship with another woman. The two women occupied the same bedroom and slept in the same bed. The two children of the marriage lived with their mother and her lesbian partner. During the trial, Mrs. Case admitted to having homosexual tendencies since childhood. She had had a number of affairs with other women during her marriage. She frequented homosexual clubs in Regina and Saskatoon and was the vice-president of the lesbian section of the Saskatoon Homophile Club. She frequently invited members of the club to her home in couples or singly. The court held, properly, that Mrs. Case's homosexual conduct was only one factor, albeit an important one, among all others to be considered in determining the children's best interests. Homosexuality is not a bar in and of itself to a parent's right to custody. Nevertheless, the court weighed all of the factors pertinent to the children's best interests and, particularly expressing the fear, "that if these children are raised by the mother they will be too much in contact with people of abnormal tastes and proclivities," awarded custody to the father.

By way of contrast, in *K. v. K.*[14] the parents lived in Alberta. In this case, custody of a child was awarded to a lesbian mother. The *Case* decision was considered in *K. v. K.*, but it was distinguished on the facts. The court was particularly impressed with the fact that: "Mrs. K. is not a missionary about to convert heterosexuals to her present way of life."

The following passage from the *K.* case illustrates the importance the court places on the best interests test and the relative unimportance attributed to a sexual orientation which, on the face of it, could have automatically excluded a person from being given the care and control of a child a short time ago. The judgement is quoted at length because it fully discusses not only the question of homosexuality but in a larger sense focuses attention on viewing custody placements from the perspective of what is best for the child:[15]

Cheryl Malmo, a psychologist having done her master's thesis in the field of feminine psychology, is in private practice at the present in Edmonton. She performed on Mrs. K. a personality assessment and on all 12 scales of the test Mrs. K. was within the normal range. She scored high in the area of self-regard and lowest in her handling of anger and aggression on the part of other people.

She observed Mrs. K. and Sheryl together and noticed a close relationship between mother and child, claiming this to be one of the best mother-child interactions she had seen in her professional practice. Sheryl appeared to be happy and well-adjusted and an interview with the teachers at the school confirmed this, together with a favourable report on Sheryl's school work.

Ms. Malmo also related in her evidence some of the recent research on homosexuality and filed with the Court a paper she had prepared on the subject containing numerous references to well-known resource material in the field of psychology and psychiatry. The tenor of the report was that homosexual women are no more neurotic than female heterosexuals and that homosexuality is not a disease that is capable of nor should it be attempted to be corrected. The opinion of Ms. Malmo, supported by research which supported her opinion, was that the manner in which one fulfills one's sexual needs does not relate to the abilities of being a good parent. Ms. Malmo also testified that homosexuality is much more common than once thought and that the incidence may be one in seven persons. That statistic is, in my view, suspect but is not relevant to the ultimate issue of this case.

Dr. Brown, a psychiatrist employed with Mental Health Services, examined Mrs. K. on 29th August 1975 and found her to be alert, pleasant, with no major problems and found her to be vitally concerned for the welfare of her daughter. Dr. Brown, in fact, felt the homosexual relationship between Mrs. K. and Mrs. O. could be a factor but that it depended mostly on the manner in which it was handled. For example, if sexual contact between Mrs. K. and Mrs. O. was overt and if Mrs. K. encouraged her daughter to shun male companionship and, in effect, preached the joys of lesbianism, problems could arise. He feels, however, that Mrs. K. is not a crusader and had until her meeting with Mrs. O. spent her life as a heterosexual. She may, in the future, return to a heterosexual relationship. Dr. Brown testified that the American Psychiatric Association no longer regarded homosexuality as a disease or a mental illness. The research available tends to indicate that homosexuality is often the result of a distant and cold relationship with a parent of the same sex. Dr. Brown did feel that separate accommodation, or, at least, separate bedrooms by Mrs. K. and Mrs. O. would be a better situation.

Miss Jean P., a graduate student at the University of Alberta, Edmonton, with a bachelor of education degree and three years' teaching experience, is a lesbian. She testified that she has been living with a woman for the past five years and that her 11-year-old daughter has lived with her and her partner and that she feels her daughter is a normal, well-adjusted child. On cross-examination Miss P. said she did not care if her daughter formed a relationship in adulthood with a man or a woman so long as it was one that satisfied her needs.

. . . . .

One must guard against magnifying the issue of homosexuality as it applies to the capacity for performing the duties of a parent. Heterosexuals produce children who become homosexual and the evidence of the psychiatrist and psychologist in this case did not indicate the odds of becoming or being a homosexual would increase solely by reason of being reared by a homosexual parent. Mrs. K. is a good mother, capable of caring for the physical and emotional needs of her child. She would be physically present on a continual basis. Having had the opportunity to observe her in the course of her testimony together with that of Mrs. O., I am satisfied that their relationship will be discreet and will not be flaunted to the children or to the community at large. I considered the potential effect on the child of negative reaction emanating from the other children at school and from the community should the exact relationship of Mrs. K. and Mrs. O. become well known. I considered also the fact that community standards in Mrs. K.'s town might be less sophisticated than that of Edmonton or Toronto with respect to homosexuality and am of the view that such differences, if they exist, are not material. A heterosexual living with a partner of the opposite sex but of a different race would be equally likely to suffer from negative community reaction and this would in turn be visited upon the children.

The *Case* and *K.* decisions demonstrate that what is important is not the conduct and sexual habits of the parent in an abstract sense but, rather, the effect of such conduct or habit upon the child. So long as it can be said that the parent has the ability to inculcate in his or her children the basic social values of the community as a whole, sexual preferences of the parent are not determining factors in reaching a custody decision. The fact that homosexuality is contrary to the norm is not in and by itself a sufficient reason for depriving a homosexual parent of custody.

A case illustrating perhaps the extreme of judicial tolerance with respect to sexual orientation is the American case of *Christian v. Randall*.[16] In that case, in which the participants lived in the State of Colorado, the mother was awarded the custody of four girls, and thereafter underwent a transsexual change from female to male. Under these circumstances, the father was unsuccessful in getting a variation in the original custody order, the court holding that the "mother" was providing an excellent environment for the girls and that the girls were not being adversely affected by their "mother's" transsexual operations.

E. The "Psychological" Parent

Decisions such as *K. v. K.* and *Case* illustrate a radical departure from the old common-law rule wherein the father had a pre-eminent legal right to the custody of his children. The evolution of the best interests test has, like a breath of fresh air, cleared custody laws of antiquated attitudes and stereotypes. Much of the impetus for such change came from clinical studies which examined the effects on the behavioural development of children as a result of the loss of a parent through divorce or separation. An influential but controversial authority in this area, *Beyond the Best Interests of the Child*, by Goldstein *et al.*, was footnoted in Chapter 1.

One of the most important and influential finds arising out of their studies concerns the question of continuity of surroundings and relationships. The following passage succinctly states the "continuity principle":[17]

> Relationships, surroundings and environmental influence are essential for a child's normal development . . . physical, emotional, intellectual, social and moral growth does not happen without causing the child inevitable internal difficulties. The instability of all mental processes during the period of development needs to be offset by stability and uninterrupted support from external sources. Smooth growth is arrested or disrupted when upheavals and changes in the external world are added to the internal ones.

Out of the continuity principle the legal definition of the model parent has arisen, like a phoenix arising from the ashes of the common law. He is known as the psychological parent and is distinguished from the biological parent — a child's natural mother or father. Ideally, of course, a biological and psychological parent is one and the same person. However, in the course of a marriage breakup, indeed, depending upon the relationship between the child and his parents, biological and psychological parenthood frequently do not coincide.

Goldstein *et al.* define the psychological parent:[18]

> [For] the child, the physical realities of his conception and birth are not the direct cause of his emotional attachment. This attachment results from day-to-day attention to his needs for physical care, nourishment, comfort, affection, and stimulation. Only a parent who provides for these things . . . will become his "psychological parent" in whose care the child can feel valued and "wanted". An absent biological parent will remain, or tend to become, a stranger."

Disruptions in continuity have different effects for different age groups. Thus when infants and toddlers are separated from their parents, according to Goldstein *et al.*, they,

> . . . not only suffer separation, distress and anxiety, but also set-backs in the quality of their next attachments, which will be less trustful. Where continuity of such relationships is interrupted more than once, and perhaps due to multiple placements in earlier years, the children's emotional attachments become increasingly shallow and indiscriminate. They tend to grow up as persons who lack warmth with their contacts with fellow human beings.

This view is reflected in the relatively old and prescient Ontario Court of Appeal decision, *Re Duffell*.[19] In that case, Mr. Justice Laidlaw said:

> . . . I am deeply conscious of the fact that the child cannot be removed from the custody of the respondents, after the great care and devotion

given to it for more than 20 months, without much hardship to the child by reason of the change with perhaps much disturbance to its affections. Such a change of custody should not be made lightly. I think that before it is made by order of the Court, the person who asks for the order should show to the satisfaction of the Court that the proposed removal will enure to the welfare of the child.

The traditional approach, prior to *Re Duffell* and the appearance of the continuity of surroundings principle, was expressed in *Re Thain*, a 1926 case. The court made the following statement:[20]

It is said that the little girl will be greatly distressed and upset at parting from Mr. and Mrs. Jones [the couple in whose care she had been virtually since birth]. I quite understand it may be so, but, at her tender age, one knows from experience how mercifully transient are the effects of parting and other sorrows, and how soon the novelty of fresh surroundings and associations effaces the recollection of former days and kind friends, and I cannot attach much weight to this aspect of the case.

Re Thain puts into perspective the conventional wisdom of yesteryear as compared to the prevailing and enlightened approach of today.

In an article entitled, "An Empirical Study of the Attitudes of the Judges of the Supreme Court of Ontario Regarding the Workings of the Present Child Custody Adjudication Laws," by Professor Adrian Bradbrook,[21] it was ascertained that all but one of 13 judges canvassed would seldom upset the *pre-trial* (temporary) arrangement as to a child's custody unless in consideration of the child's best interests there was exceptional evidence suggesting possible harm to the child. This presumption of continuance also depends upon the length of time that the pre-trial arrangement has been in operation. Possession of a child for less than six months appeared to carry little weight in the minds of the majority of the judges.

There are other traditional factors considered by the court in assessing custody actions; these factors are discussed below. However, they pale in comparison with the importance of principles such as that of "continuity of surroundings."

F. Financial Position

At one time in the history of custody law, the question of financial position was an important factor in arriving at a just custody arrangement. This importance has been eroded in recent years and the relative financial position of the parties vying for custody is taken into account as merely one of the many factors to be considered. In the *Talsky* case referred to on p. 48, the point was made that the courts are swayed not only by the fact that one party has greater financial resources than another (for example, a better house and a better neighbourhood) but also by the fact that that party has a carefully conceived and workable plan for the proper care and upbringing of the children. This thoughtful approach is compared with one which is haphazard and pays little attention to how that care and upbringing can be properly accomplished. In short, the courts look both for significant financial superiority and for an organized financial plan for the future rather than merely balancing the financial worth of both spouses at the time of trial. It is not uncommon for a parent living on public assistance to be awarded custody.

G. Tender Years Doctrine

According to this doctrine, children under the age of seven will be given to the custody of their mother in the absence of exceptional circumstances dictating otherwise. The classic statement of the doctrine is described in *Bell v. Bell*:[22]

> No father, no matter how well-intentioned or how solicitous for the welfare of [the] child, can take the full place of the mother. Instinctively, a little child, particularly a little girl, turns to her mother in her troubles, her doubts and her fears. In that respect nature seems to assert itself. The feminine touch means so much to a little girl; the frills and the flounces and the ribbons in the matter of dress; the whispered consultations and confidences on matters which to the child's mind should only be discussed with Mother; the tender care, the soothing voice; all these things have a tremendous effect on the emotions of the child. This is nothing new; it is as old as human nature and has been recognized time after time through the decisions of our Courts.

This decision was written approximately 25 years ago and perhaps, one might say, it was written from the perspective of a different generation. Certainly, such notions are not in vogue in these days of single parenting. The popular press and movies such as "Kramer v. Kramer," supported by a body of behavioural and other psychological evidence, suggests there is no inherent magic in a child being better off with mother vis-à-vis father. As long as the father is performing the role of a psychological parent, then it appears he is equipped to give the child the love and attention it requires. The *Bell* case is therefore considered to be an antiquated precedent.

However, it should be mentioned that some studies lend support to the tender years doctrine. Much attention has been focused on the issue of maternal deprivation. Studies which analyze this phenomenon indicate that children deprived of a mother's care are retarded in their intellectual and social growth. More particularly, they manifest an inability to function normally in social relations, and later in life suffer from an incapacity to act as effective parents. However, these studies on maternal deprivation have been criticized because they ignore the results of paternal deprivation; the results of the studies, therefore, really depict *parental* deprivation in general rather than maternal deprivation in particular.[23]

H. Wishes of the Child

About the only voice that is not heard in the court-room during a contested custody dispute is that of the person who is the very object of the proceedings. A mother and father, with the able assistance of their lawyers, get to have their say. But what of the child? When is his voice heard? In an article on child representation in custody proceedings,[24] the author, an Ontario judge, quoted a letter from a young boy whose parents were involved in an acrimonious custody battle. The letter rather eloquently makes the point that many children wish to have their say when their parents are fighting over custody. This is not perhaps an unreasonable desire considering that it is the child's "life" hinging on the outcome of the court proceedings. The letter reads:

> Today is my birthday, so I decided to give not only myself but my brother and sister who feel the same way, a treat. We wish to speak our minds about the Judge's decision. I feel this judgement was poorly made and is unfair to my brother, my sister and myself. I feel all three of us have suffered and continue to suffer until something is done about where we are living now. We all feel as if we are being held against our own will . . . either the Judge was blind or some of this information was not made available. My sister and I can hardly see the need for sending a social worker if we cannot speak in more detail about our true feelings about our custodial parent.

This letter is certainly a *cri de coeur*; one can sense the voice crying in the wilderness. The issue of child representation was discussed in Chapter 2. There is a growing trend towards a child having his own lawyer to advance his *own* wishes in custody dispute though this is still relatively rare.

Are a child's wishes relevant? Yes, and the older the child the greater the importance attached to the wish. Younger children are deemed not to have the emotional maturity to be able to decide what is in their own best interests. The child may be attracted to a parent in whom discipline is lacking or who buys affection. Judicial concern for this type of behaviour was expressed in *Re S.*,[25] an English case:

> There are occasions when the wishes expressed by a boy of thirteen and a half may count for very little. In many cases it is unfortunately plain that they are reflections of the wishes of one of the parents which have been assiduously instilled into the ward and are not anything which could be called an independent exercise of his own will. Sometimes again the ward's wishes, although genuinely his own, are so plainly contrary to his long term interest that the court may feel justified in disregarding them.

In reality, the other parent may be best for the child, and further, many children simply do not wish to be forced into a situation where they have to pick and choose which parent they wish to live with. Indeed, many children simply will not make a selection at the risk of hurting one or both of the parents and will defer the decision to the wisdom of the court.

With respect to older children, an Ontario case, *Sharpe v. Sharpe*,[26] made the following common sense point:

In practice it is recognized that there is no point in making custody orders when children get to be about 15 or 16 because they will simply make their own choice and obviously courts cannot supervise these custody orders in the case of older children, with any real degree of effectiveness.

The question is often asked as to how best to put a child's wishes and feelings before the courts. Until recently, the judge often interviewed the child privately in his chambers (office). This procedure has been severely criticized by a number of experts. Barbara Chisholm, a social worker with a great deal of experience in working with children involved in custody disputes, has made the following comments:[27]

> My concern . . . about the device of the judge's interview is that I worry that it can realize its goal. This is in no way meant to be or sound like a put-down of the capacity of our judges to read character or personality, any more than it is meant to be a reverse suggestion that social workers, for example, could do it better. But I am suggesting that since the children . . . are those caught in contested custody situations, they are children already exposed to some considerable parental warfare, perhaps of some duration. Such children are scarred in their ready capacity to trust adults; they have been burned. A single interview, no matter how avuncular, can rarely break through the *real* mistrust of the adult, no matter how superficially pleasant. All sorts of professionals have learned this lesson to their cost, of the "successful" first interview, where the child was "really talking," seducing the interviewer into a sense of competence similar to that . . . of the judges who were sure they "knew" when the child was repeating what he had been told to say and when he was not.

Should the child take the stand, as it were, in his own defence? Only on the most rare of occasions is a child called as a witness to give evidence during a custody dispute. The courts do not wish to drag a child into the arena and subject him to the trauma of a tension-filled court-room. Undoubtedly, he is already emotionally scarred from the parental battling that frequently accompanies custody actions.

How then is a child to put his wishes before the court? If he is separately represented then his lawyer can assume that responsibility. Another mechanism is through the use of expert testimony. Frequently, in custodial disputes (as discussed in Chapter 2) a family is referred for professional assessment and a psychologist or child psychiatrist can elicit, in a meaningful sense, the child's true wishes and have them placed before the court and explained in a meaningful way.

I. Miscellaneous Facts

The courts are loath to separate brothers and sisters. Unless the most unusual circumstances exist siblings are kept together in order for family solidarity and affection to develop and so that bonds which have already been developed will not be broken.

Same-sex placements (mother–daughter; father–son) are seriously considered. The tender years doctrine, although somewhat displaced by the best interests test, fades in importance as the child passes the age of seven. Thus, the older the child is the more likely the court will pay attention to matching boy–father and girl–mother.

The list of factors delineated in the previous sections are not exhaustive. However, they are traditionally the most visible criteria referred to in custody decisions. A composite picture of the criteria focuses attention on the pre-eminent consideration in custody law: the best interests of the child "test".

Although the best interests test is the current philosophy underlying custody placements, it, too, is not without its critics. In *Beyond the Best Interests of the Child* the authors advocate a new statement of the principle. Rather than looking at custody arrangements from the point of view of maximizing what is best for the child, Goldstein *et al.* suggest that a more realistic approach is to look at the least detrimental of the placement choices available. The following passage summarizes their rationale:[28]

> Whether the problem arises in separation, divorce, adoption, neglecting parent, foster care, or even juvenile delinquency proceedings, the overall guideline for decision which we propose is to select "that placement which is the least detrimental among available alternatives for the child". To use "detrimental" rather than "best interest" should enable legislatures, courts, and child care agencies to acknowledge and respond to the inherent detriments in any procedure for child placement as well as in each child placement decision itself. It should serve to remind decisionmakers that their task is to salvage as much as possible out of an unsatisfactory situation. It should reduce the likelihood of their becoming enmeshed in the hope and magic associated with "best", which often mistakenly leads them into believing that they have greater power for doing "good" than "bad".
>
> The concept of "available alternatives" should press into focus how limited is the capacity of decisionmakers to make valid predictions and how limited are the choices generally open to them for helping a child in trouble. If the choice, as it may often be in separation and divorce proceedings, is between two psychological parents and if each parent is equally suitable in terms of the child's most immediate predictable developmental needs, the least detrimental standard would dictate a quick, final, and unconditional disposition to either of the competing parents.
>
> The proposed standard is less awesome and grandiose, more realistic, and thus more amenable to relevant data-gathering than "best interest". It should facilitate weighing the advantages and the disadvantages of the actual options.

Judicial support for this approach has been slow in coming. However, there are signs of growing awareness. In a recent case before the Ontario Court of Appeal[29] the dissenting judge made this observation:

It is perhaps timely for Courts in Canada to shed their "healthy cynicism" and reflect in their orders a greater appreciation of the hurt inflicted upon a child by the severance of its relationship with one of its parents. Our Courts have tended, while purporting to award custody on the basis of a child's best interests, to overlook that in some circumstances it may be in the child's best interests not to choose between the parents but to do everything possible to maintain the child's relationship with both parents. We accept now, I believe, that men and women who fall short as spouses may nevertheless excel as parents. We have also become increasingly aware over the last number of years that the context of a divorce action is the worst possible context in which to form an assessment of the spouses as people let alone as parents. The adversarial process by its nature requires each spouse to attack the other in order to protect his or her economic interests. This has caused an undue emphasis to be placed at trial on the deterioration of the husband-and-wife relationship and not enough on the parent-and-child relationship.

E. RIGHTS OF NON-PARENTS TO CUSTODY

At one time, giving custody of a child to persons other than natural parents was unthinkable. However, with the advent of the best interest test and the evolution of the idea of a psychological parent (see p. 51) a number of cases have been decided in which it was felt that the children were better off with a non-biological parent. Much of the reluctance to place a child with a non-biological parent was rooted in the concept of "blood tie." It was as if a sacred biological bond was formed between child and natural parent. There is much psychiatric evidence which weakens such a bonding theory. Goldstein *et al.* note:[30]

> Unlike adults, children have no psychological conception of relationship by blood-tie until quite late in their development. For the biological parent, the facts of having engendered . . . or given birth to a child produce an understandable sense of preparedness for proprietorship and possessiveness. These considerations carry no weight with children who are emotionally unaware of the events pertaining to their birth. What registers in their minds are the day to day interchanges with the adults who take care of them and who, on the strength of these, become the parent figures to whom they are attached.

On the other hand, the question of blood tie is not irrelevant but is a factor to be considered in determining what is in the best interests of the child. If the child would benefit from the blood tie, then it is in that parent's favour.

Although not the first case to award custody in favour of a non-parent, the celebrated American case, *Painter v. Bannister*,[31] drew public attention to the issues involved. In the *Painter* case, the father and the maternal grandparents (the child's mother had died in a car accident) were vying for custody of the child. The court found the father had a "Bohemian approach to finances and life in general." His main ambition was to be a free lance writer and photographer; he wished to settle in the artists' colony of Sausilito in San Francisco; he was "either an agnostic or atheist and has no concern for formal religious training. He has read a lot of Zen Buddhism and has been very much influenced by it." On the other hand, the parents of the deceased mother were able to provide the child with a "stable, dependable, conventional, middle-class, middlewest background and an opportunity for a college education and profession if [the child] desires it. It provides a solid foundation and secure atmosphere." The court did not overtly criticize the father's way of life since "An individual is free to choose his own values, within bounds, which are not exceeded here." Indeed, the court said that if the child lived with the father, his life would be more intellectually stimulating. Nevertheless, the court was of the opinion that the child's best interests would be best served if he lived with the parents of the mother and, therefore, custody was awarded to them.

The *Painter* case was decided 15 years ago during the height of the hippy movement (Mr. Painter's "Bohemian" life-style), and although the court supposedly used a "best interests test," it appeared more reliance was placed on a good, solid, middle-class American upbringing (a class bias) than on Mr. Painter's parenting skills. It is questionable whether the same decision would be reached today.

The leading Canadian case on topic is *Re Moores and Feldstein*.[32] The Moores, originally from Newfoundland, moved to Toronto. In 1968, they separated because of Mr. Moores' chronic drinking problem. In fact, Mr. Moores was admitted to the Donwood Clinic in Toronto to receive treatment for alcohol addiction. A year after separation, the Moores attempted a reconciliation and resumed cohabitation but, shortly thereafter, Mrs. Moores learned that she was pregnant and that her husband was not the father. Her husband refused to consent to a therapeutic abortion (his consent being a requirement at the time). Mr. Moores agreed to a last attempt at reconciliation but on the condition she deliver the child to a foster home. In fact, the child was turned over to a Mr. and Mrs. Feldstein. Unfortunately, the Moores' last efforts to make their marriage work failed and, shortly after the child was placed with the Feldsteins, they parted ways once and for all. Some four years later and with almost no prior contact with her child, a little girl, Mrs. Moores attempted to gain custody. The Feldsteins contested Mrs. Moores' application and during the course of the trial it was demonstrated that they had given excellent physical and emotional care for the child for the almost four years that she had been in their care.

In its decision, the court first made reference to the continuity of surroundings principle:[33]

> Serious harm may be occasioned by removing this bright, alert little girl from her present surroundings and placing her in the custody and care of some one who would now likely be quite a stranger to her.

The court then referred to the question of blood tie:[34]

In my view, since the evidence does not show that the child will benefit by the mere fact of its blood relationship with its mother, it cannot be said that the welfare of the child in its broadest sense will best be served by its being returned to her. In its present surroundings, it will have the loving care of a father and a mother who will be able to devote her full time to her in her formative years. There will be no risk of the uprooting of the child from its present happy surroundings having a serious effect on her.

In a case comment[35] about the decision in *Re Moores and Feldstein* it was noted that:

Although legal tradition has given the biological parents considerable power over their child, this has not been based on a consideration of the needs or interests of the child. There is no scientific basis for an assertion that any weight should be given to the blood tie in assessing the child's interests in the kind of situation under discussion. In a consideration of the needs of a child, the parent is the person understood by the child to be fulfilling the parental role, irrespective of biological relationship. The effect on a child of separation from the person to whom such an attachment has been formed is no less catastrophic than the removal of any child from his intact family.

If we consider with due seriousness the settlement of custody disputes in the best interests of the child, then we must give lower priority to the blood tie. It is unwarranted to promote the fallacy that the biological parent will be better than a foster parent or an adoptive parent.

F. NOVEL CUSTODY ORDERS

It was mentioned on p. 44 that there are basically three types of custody orders: sole custody, split custody and an order for joint custody.

Sole custody is relatively straightforward. One parent is granted custody and is therefore given full care and control of the child. Split custody, on the other hand, involves custody being granted to one parent and the actual physical possession to the other parent. When custody is used in this sense, it means that the parent having custody retains the rights of supervising the children, religious training and general upbringing of the children, and making decisions which have a permanent effect on their lives and development. In a split custody order, the custodial parent has all the powers inherent in custody except actual physical care and control which is the responsibility of the other parent.

A split custody order was made by a Saskatchewan Court in *Huber v. Huber*.[36] In this case, the parents separated in 1974 but only after Mrs. Huber tried "conscientiously and desperately to save the marriage . . ." Notes made by Mrs. Huber when the marriage was faltering bear poignant testimony of her concern:

My goal . . . to save our marriage . . . to appreciate my family more . . . my husband works hard and had a good job to provide for me and my children. Learning to open up and talk with Larry [the husband] about everything would really help . . . that takes time . . . learning to appreciate my kids a little more . . . they are human beings too.

Unfortunately, the relationship could not be salvaged and the Hubers separated.

After separation, the children lived with their father, a teacher, in the matrimonial home. While Mr. Huber worked the children attended a daycare centre. Meanwhile, Mrs. Huber started a training course financed by Canada Manpower. She obtained an apartment with adequate accommodation for the children and then commenced an action for custody.

The court, in deciding on the split custody order, made the following observations:[37]

> . . . the paramount consideration is the welfare and happiness of the children. . . . My duty is to dispose of the children here so that this paramount consideration is realized. The children are mere infants about four and one-half and two and one-half years respectively. That they need the care of a mother is beyond question and that the mother can, although she takes training or employment, give this care is also clear. She, of course, will have to make use of day care facilities in either event, just as the father has done since she left. On the other hand, the father is not only capable of but is very much interested in the rearing and training of his children. His concern in this area is amply demonstrated by the extreme caution and care he exercised in selecting a day care centre where the children are placed while he is at his school work. . . . The attitude of the husband, his concern for the children, his interest in their welfare, his ability to guide and his maturity persuade me that he should be involved actively with the education, training and general upbringing of the children in the future. This father should have the authority to be involved in the making of important decisions in matters having a permanent effect on the life and development of his children.

The *Huber* case demonstrates that a split custody order is, as its name implies, simply a partition of all the rights and obligations of a typical custody order between two parents. Split custody orders, as a general rule, will only be granted in situations where the parents are sensible and indicate a spirit of close co-operation where the welfare of the children is concerned. It might be said that the custodial parent is the one who demonstrates the most intelligent and mature response to major decisions affecting the children's lives, while, on the other hand, the "care and control" and perhaps less trustworthy (in the sense of assuming the role of the major decision-maker) parent is responsible for the day-to-day care and nourishment of the child. Certainly the custodial parent is granted generous access (visiting privileges with the children).

Another type of order is the joint custody order and it is the object of much controversy at the present time. Conceptually, a joint custody order confers full legal custody to both parents. In other words, each parent has an equal say in the child's education, upbringing, and general welfare. In such arrangements, usually one parent is also given the care and control of the child, while the other parent is granted liberal access.

A recent case involving a joint custody order, as distinct from a split custody order, is *Baker v. Baker*.[38] The Bakers were married in Toronto in 1964 and a son was born to them in 1970. The child was born by caesarean section and developed early health problems requiring surgery. There was considerable financial diffi-culties at the time and Mrs. Baker developed physical and emotional problems. As a result of these difficulties, the marriage rapidly deteriorated, the husband blaming it on the wife's inability to cope with ordinary domestic responsibilities and her excessive use of alcohol which led to bizarre behaviour, and the wife blaming the matrimonial problems on her husband's insensitive and domineering attitude and his disregard of her proper role within the family. A last-ditch effort was made to save the marriage with the assistance of family counselling but proved unsuccessful and, in 1975, Mrs. Baker left with her son to live with her sister.

Both parents sought legal custody thereafter. In deciding to grant an order for joint custody, the trial judge made the following statement:[39]

> Parents with joint custody have the right to continue to act as parents, as well as the responsibility of sharing in such important decisions as the child's health, education and spiritual and general welfare. Such an order retains for both parents participation and influence in the child's life, which does not occur when one parent has custody and the other has access, as the granting of even the most liberal access does not confer the right to participate in the upbringing of the child. Joint custody should be considered in cases where there are two parents who are well qualified to give affection and guidance to the child and where it can be reasonably contemplated that they are capable of co-operating with each other in the best interests of the child.

The trial judge went on to comment that the laws surrounding custody must respond to changes within society. She observed:[40]

> Courts must be responsive to the winds of change. In today's society, the breakdown of the traditional family is increasingly common, and new ways of defining post-divorce family structures are desperately needed. It is apparent that the traditional award of custody to the mother and access to the father is the cause of many of the problems and most of the tensions between parents and children and between the parents themselves. Our courts see many cases in which the father has been deprived of access. Gradually he loses interest or finds he cannot afford to continue his court battles, and as a result the child is deprived of the love, influence and financial support of its father. Joint custody would seem to be the ideal solution to present challenges and past experiences.

The trial judge's decision to grant joint custody was appealed and the Ontario

Court of Appeal,[41] while not necessarily disputing the need for custody laws to keep pace with the changes in the family structure, criticized the decision to award joint custody. Basically, the Court of Appeal attacked the decision to award joint custody on the basis of a lack of co-operation between the parents. Indeed, during the marriage the parents proved they were incompatible and unable to agree on the upbringing of their child and the post-trial proceedings demonstrated a continuing inability to co-operate. The Appellate Court pointed out that the very crux of a joint custody order is that both parents be capable of co-operating with each other and that they must be relatively stable and amicable parents. An award of joint custody placed on already embittered parents can only enhance familial chaos and would not be in the best interests of the child. As a result, rather than awarding custody to either parent, a new hearing was ordered.

It would appear from an analysis of the *Baker* case that joint custody will not be ordered unless both parents are willing and able to co-operate with each other in the proper upbringing of their child. A conclusion to be drawn from the *Baker* case is that few orders for joint custody will be made because they presuppose that both parents, if they are motivated by a spirit of co-operation with the child's best interests pre-eminent, would not require a court to decide the matter. Rather, they would make such an arrangement through the mechanism of a separate agreement. Indeed, private joint custody arrangements have become increasingly in vogue with enlightened parents.

The benefits of joint custody are many. A psychiatrist, Dr. Edward J. Rosen, in an article entitled, "Joint Custody: In the Best Interests of the Child and Parents,"[42] made the following general observations:

1. The child develops strong emotional bonds to both the mother and the father, who have both given loving care.

2. The practice of giving sole custody to one parent has the effect of breaking the bond between the child and the non-custodial parent. The emotional consequence is equal to a loss as great as the death of a parent with the additional stress of knowing that the lost one is still alive and potentially available.

3. The great majority of parents can reach a mutually co-operative understanding about their parental decisions regarding the health, education and welfare of their child.

4. Some parents may require the help of conciliatory services of psychiatrists or court counsellors.

5. Joint custody in most cases is in the best interests of the child and the parents following a divorce.

G. ACCESS

Access refers to the visiting privileges of the non-custodial parent. Once again, it must be remembered that the non-custodial parent has no legally enforceable say in the decisions relating to the upbringing of the child. Rather, access exists to allow exposure of the non-custodial parent to the child and, of course, allows the parent–child relationship to be maintained. Different considerations apply to the question of access as distinct from the question of custody although the test continues to be the best interests of the child.

An Ontario case, *Stokes v. Stokes*,[43] illustrates that the court will deny access only with the greatest reluctance. The Stokes separated as a consequence of the husband becoming a patient of a psychiatric hospital, his condition being diagnosed as schizophrenia. Mr. Stokes believed that he was reincarnated as Jesus Christ and exhibited violent behaviour to both his wife and child. He threw tables and other objects, including the family cat, during fits of temper and frequently struck his "petrified" child. Mr. Stokes, needless to say, underwent preventive psychiatric therapy. At trial, a psychiatrist testified as follows:

> I believe this lad has the potential for further disorganization, but with a combination of appropriate drug therapy and control over the amount of stress he experiences he should be able to remain stabilized and free of psychotic [behaviour]. Nevertheless, with the [diagnosis] of schizophrenia [from the] onset there is a strong likelihood of recurrence at sometime in the future if the stresses are excessive.

Based on these facts, the court denied access to Mr. Stokes, but only for the immediate future. The court went on to state:[44]

> I think that if the present treatment is reasonably successful and the father is reasonably able to re-establish himself . . . free from the threat of the exacerbations of his ailment, and if this has proceeded well, the Court might then consider . . . whether access should be granted subject to conditions in the hope that there might then develop a relationship between the father and the son.

Another case, *O. v. O.*,[45] demonstrates that access will be granted unless such exposure to a child will be harmful and disturbing. In *O. v. O.*, the mother, who was seeking access, had actually killed three of her children and had attempted to kill another. She had a long history of psychiatric treatment and was diagnosed as a manic-depressive and a schizophrenic. After her release from a psychiatric hospital she gave birth (over a period of years) to three more children and when she and her husband separated, the children were granted into the custody of their father.

The court made the following observation:[46]

> While Mrs. O. has been physically separated from her children for the biggest portion of their lives it is very apparent she has not lost her love for them and that M. and G. have a substantial attachment to her. They, to the extent possible in the circumstances, treat her as their mother and in my view it will be in their best interest to permit them to continue that relationship provided it can continue without risk of harm to them.

No one can give an absolute guarantee that a parent, any parent, will not harm or kill his or her child. Where a parent has the misfortune to be psychotic and has already killed three of her children, the only way to make certain that parent will not harm another child is to detain that parent in hospital or prison . . .

Even if access were denied Mrs. O., as long as she remains at large there would be no guarantee that she will not harm her children. Whether supervised access is given or denied then, no guarantee will exist as to the safety of the children. The real issue then is will the children, M. and G., suffer any appreciable risk of harm if Mrs. O. is permitted supervised access to them?

The obvious answer is that if the supervision is strict enough risk of injury because of access can be almost eliminated.

Accordingly, the court ordered supervised access, supervision including authorization to search the person and clothing of the mother.

The *Stokes* case and *O. v. O.* demonstrate that provided access is in the best interests of the child, it will almost always be granted.

A perhaps more thoughtful and sensitive approach to access resulted in a mother being denied access although on the facts her behaviour was less "offending" than either of the parents granted access in *Stokes* and *O. v. O.* An excerpt from the decision of a Manitoba court follows:[47]

Here, I look at Jacqueline Gwen, who is six years old. She has been with her father almost exclusively for more than four years. She has made excellent progress in Kindergarten and is now in Grade 1 at school. She is adjusting well to her new mother, Sylvia.

I understand the feelings of the natural mother, Judith, who is asking for access to her child, but would it be psychologically good for Jacqueline? I find the following remarks from Dr. Loadman's report of 12th September 1975 to be very appropriate:

"From the information I have received and from the results of today's examination and interviews I feel that the natural mother's desire to reinstate visits is inadvisable at this time. Jacqueline's relationship with Mrs. Podolsky as her father's wife and as her mother is in its early stages and should be allowed to continue until it has been consolidated. I feel that visits with the natural mother at this point would be most confusing for Jacqueline.

"In addition Jacqueline needs time to think about the idea that she has a natural mother for her father seemingly in all good faith, had been unaware of the importance of talking freely about this until recently. It is quite conceivable that she will discuss this quite voluntarily with him at some future date and it would be at this time that it might be appropriate to reconsider the advisability of visits.

"During my interview with the former Mrs. Podolsky today, I told her that in my opinion visits with Jacqueline should be postponed for a year at which time the whole matter could be reconsidered. I believe this approach to be in Jacqueline's best interests. I plan to interview Mr. Podolsky and his wife again, to reassure them, that in the future, such visits might be helpful to Jacqueline as long as they are undertaken with the child's approval and consent.''

Access privileges are not restricted to parents. The *F.L.R.A.* (Ontario) provides that access may be granted to third parties. For instance, a child's grandparents may have had custody and sometime later returned the child to a parent. In such cases the grandparents could be granted access.

Before leaving the topics of custody and access one last point must be made: custody and access orders are never final. The best interests test, when applied to custody and access, dictates that a change in circumstances may require that a re-evaluation be made of what is best for the child, and if need be that a change be made. However, it almost goes without saying that the change in circumstances must amount to something more than the desire of a frustrated non-custodial parent hoping the court will have a change of heart.

H. GUARDIANSHIP

The term "guardianship" is often heard in the context of custody matters. Guardianship and custody are not, contrary to popular knowledge, different legal "titles" conferring identical powers on individuals. The mechanism of guardianship is designed to fulfil a distinct need for a child who finds himself in particular circumstances. A custodian of a child has the all-encompassing powers of parenthood at his disposal. A guardian is usually only charged with the care and management of the property of a child. On occasion, the responsibilities of guardianship and custody overlap. Perhaps the best way of explaining the distinction is through example. Assume the parents of a child or the child himself wish him to attend school in another province. It is agreed that relatives of the child will take him in and give him room and board. As often as not, the province to which the child is going will require that a guardian be appointed to look after the property of the child. The "parenting" of the child remains vested in his mother and father, although the day-to-day care is in the hands of the relatives. As well, a child may live at home with his parents and, if the child inherits substantial property, a guardian may be appointed to look after this property until such time as the child attains the status of adulthood. In such circumstances, the guardians usually appointed are the child's parents.

I. THE CHILD BORN OUT OF WEDLOCK

Perhaps no other aspect of family law reform has enjoyed more public support than the abolishment of the concept of the illegitimate child. This reform has swept most of the provinces and is indeed a most welcome change. Under Ontario's new laws, for instance (as contained in the *C.L.R.A.*), a child's rights to financial support from his or her father are dependent only on the parent–child blood relationship. In most instances, the question of parenthood is obvious. However, if a child is born out of wedlock it is difficult to prove on occasion that a particular individual fathered the child. As a result of this potential difficulty, the *C.L.R.A.* of Ontario identifies a number of circumstances to assist a judge in arriving at a decision as to paternity. These circumstances or, as they have come to be known, these "presumptions of paternity," may be summarized as follows:

1. The man was married to the mother of the child upon the child's birth;
2. The man was married to the mother of the child within 300 days (to encompass the term of pregnancy) before the child was born;
3. The man married the mother subsequent to the child's birth and acknowledged fatherhood;
4. The man was living with the mother in a common-law relationship of some permanence when the child was born or the child was born within 300 days after they ceased living together;
5. The man and mother of the child registered the child on records such as hospital records and the man registered therein identified himself as the father.

The issue of blood tests usually arises if there is some doubt as to whether a person is indeed the father of the child. However, there is an important limitation with respect to the use of blood tests and that is that such a test can only prove that a man is *not* the father. The tests can never conclusively prove who the father is. Further, the taking of blood samples requires the consent of the person who may or may not be wrongly accused of fathering the child. A court cannot force a person to submit to a blood test. On the other hand, if a person refuses a court's request for a blood test, an adverse inference may be drawn from the person's refusal. Incidentally, an alleged father may request that the mother undergo the same testing.

There are more sophisticated tests which can be conducted to determine paternity. These include "tissue typing" but they are rarely employed because of expense and because of the relatively complicated nature of conducting the tests.

The issue of children being born out of wedlock introduces the concept of the common-law relationship. Persons who live together as husband and wife (without the benefit of holy matrimony or a civil ceremony) are, of course, referred to as common-law spouses although the term is more often than not taken from the language of the day and does not appear in statute. The common-law family is one which is enjoying growing legal recognition as the incidence of such relationships increases. However, the mere formation of a common-law union does not bring the law into operation. For instance, under the *F.L.R.A.* of Ontario, legal rights are not created until a couple have lived in a relationship with some permanence and have had a child of the union, or are childless and have lived together continuously for five years.

The issue of children born out of wedlock gives rise to another unique circumstance. Prior to the passage of the *C.L.R.A.* of Ontario that province's law basically gave the natural father no right to have any say in the raising of his child. Although he could be ordered to pay support, the mother retained full custody of the child including the right to have the child placed for adoption. Today, it is not uncommon for a putative (biological) father to seek custody of his child if the mother does not wish to keep her offspring. Under the best interests of the child test, a father may pursue custody and a liberal reading of the law would indicate that even if the mother wished custody she could lose such custody to the father if he were the more fit parent as there is no longer a property right in children. A case which canvasses such issues is the Ontario decision of *Frank v. Hainey and Children's Aid Society of London and Middlesex County*.[48] In that case, an official referee was brought in. Such a person is empowered to hear evidence on specific issues and report back to the court. The reason for employing such a person is to expedite and simplify the disposition of defended matrimonial matters.

In the *Frank* case, the unmarried father of a child wished custody. However, his former girl-friend, the mother of the child, wished to have it placed for adoption. The official referee's report is extensively reproduced. This report offers a succinct review of the issues.[49]

This is an application brought by Peter Frank under *The Infants Act . . .* for custody of Kelly Anne Hainey. The issues of custody and costs have been referred to me for inquiry and report.

On September 28, 1977, Pauline Hainey gave birth to Kelly Anne. It is undisputed that Peter Frank is the father of the child. Upon the request of the [mother], Kelly Anne was admitted to the care of The Children's Aid Society of London and the County of Middlesex on October 7, 1977 and was subsequently made and still remains a temporary ward of the Society. The [mother] is requesting that the [father] be denied custody of Kelly Anne in order that she might be placed for adoption.

The [mother] is presently 18 years old and is residing with her parents. She is attending Grade 12 at Wexford Collegiate and is planning to continue her education. She met the [father] at a summer camp in the summer of 1976 and continued to see him regularly until she discovered in May, 1977 that she was pregnant with his child. Shortly thereafter she ceased all communication with the [father].

The [father] is 18 years old and is enrolled in Grade 12 at East York Collegiate. The [father] anticipates that he will graduate from Grade 12 in January, 1979. The [father's] ambition is to become either a policeman or a fireman. The [father] has not ascertained the nature of the requirements for entry into either of these professions nor has he assessed the likelihood of his ability to meet these requirements.

The [father] resides with his mother, Mrs. Lotte Frank, and his younger brother in a three-bedroom townhouse owned and operated by Ontario Housing. Mrs. Frank, who is 49 years old, receives $390.00 per month by way of Mothers' Allowance and supplements her income by caring for children in her home, for which she is paid $165.00 every two weeks. Mrs. Frank has been separated from her husband for sixteen years.

The [father] is extensively involved in school athletic activities and often does not return home before 5:30 p.m. In addition, he is presently coaching a baseball team on Monday and Wednesday evenings from 6:30 p.m. to 8:30 p.m. The [father] has obtained part-time employment with a furniture moving and repair company and works Friday evenings, all day Saturday and Sunday. He hopes to spend the summer working for United Van Lines.

If custody of Kelly Anne should be awarded to the [father], the primary responsibility for the infant's care would rest with Mrs. Frank, who has indicated her willingness to assume such responsibility. At this time the [father] anticipates that his mother will care for Kelly Anne until the age of five or six years, at which time he will assume responsibility for her. The child would sleep in the same bedroom as Mrs. Frank and the [father] would continue to assist his mother financially from his part-time and summer employment earnings.

If the [father] were denied custody, then Kelly Anne would be placed in a two-parent home for adoption.

. . . . .

The welfare and best interests of the child are the paramount consideration in determining the issue of custody. I have given consideration to the biological tie that exists between the [father] and Kelly Anne, but in the circumstances I have not been satisfied that placing the child in the [father's] custody would be in her best interests. Neither the [father] nor Mrs. Frank have ever seen or established contact with Kelly Anne, who consequently has not developed any emotional ties to them. It was initially Mrs. Frank's idea that the [father] seek custody and she has encouraged him to continue with the application.

The [father's] plans for his own future are understandably rather vague and indefinite at this time. It would be contrary to Kelly Anne's best interests to place her in the [father's] custody and thereby deprive her of an opportunity to be adopted by a two-parent family who would be able to provide her with the long term stability, both financial and otherwise, essential to a child's healthy emotional and psychological development.

In summary I recommend:

(1) The [father] be denied custody of the infant, Kelly Anne Hainey.

(2) Each party bears his own costs.

J. CHILD SUPPORT

Before discussing the issue of child support it would be appropriate to discuss the definition of "child" in this context.

The *Divorce Act* defines a child as: any person to whom the husband and wife stand *in loco parentis* and any person of whom either of the husband or the wife is a "natural" parent and to whom the other spouse stands *in loco parentis*. At the provincial level, the *F.L.R.A.* of Ontario defines a child as someone who is born within or outside marriage and includes a person to whom a person has demonstrated a settled intention to treat as part of his or her family.

In loco parentis refers to a person who has essentially stepped into the shoes of the role as father or mother of the child. In other words, to be *in loco parentis* the husband or wife must intend to place himself in the position (towards the child) ordinarily occupied by the "natural" father or mother. In an Ontario case, *Re O'Neil and Rideout*,[50] the court provided various criteria for the establishment of such a relationship:

1. Did the person provide financial support to assist in the children's maintenance?
2. Did the person intend to "step into the father's (mother's) shoes"?
3. Was the relationship between the person and the child one with a degree of permanency? (Was it a continuing one?)

A husband or wife would probably not stand *in loco parentis* where the natural parent is paying support and in general continues to exercise all of his or her paternal or maternal rights. For instance, the natural parent maintains a close and active involvement in the child's life through access privileges.

On the provincial level, the *F.L.R.A.* of Ontario provides that "a person who has demonstrated a settled intention to treat a child as a child of his or her family . . ." may be liable for support. This broad definition of "parent" applies not only to support obligations, but also to a range of other matters including custody, access, dependant's relief after the death of the person supporting the dependant, and as will be discussed in Chapter 4, adoption and child protection proceedings. The definition of child in s. 2(*a*) "includes a person whom the parent has demonstrated a settled intention to treat as a child of his or her family . . ." The Ontario provincial definition extends or broadens the concept of parent as defined by *in loco parentis* in the *Divorce Act*. For instance, it has been held that a child is not a "child" as defined in the *Divorce Act* where a husband subsequently discovers that a child whom he thought throughout the marriage was legitimate is, in fact, illegitimate, for instance, a child born as a result of undisclosed adultery.[51] The provincial Act would not exclude such a child from being entitled to support. The essential difference between *in loco parentis* and "a settled intention" is that the latter emphasizes the treatment of the child as a member of the family as opposed to requiring a specific intention to "step into the absent parent's shoes." In the example of the child born of undisclosed adultery, there can be no intention if the husband had no knowledge of the existence of "another" father. Although the distinction may appear somewhat subtle, it is none the less distinguishable in the eyes of the law. It is entirely possible for a court to "bless" a child with multiple "fathers" or "mothers." A natural father may be ordered to pay support; if the mother of the child forms a relationship with another individual and he forms a settled intention to treat that child as a member of the family, he, too, may be ordered to pay support; should the mother move on, yet a third "father" could be acquired.

Support and access often go hand in hand. However, access cannot be denied if support payments cease. The converse is equally true; a parent denied access cannot terminate support payments.

A child assumes the mantle of adulthood, as a general rule, upon attaining the age of 18. Under the *Divorce Act*, however, a parent can be compelled to support a child beyond the age of 18 if the child is enrolled in an educational institution or is developmentally handicapped. However, support of this nature is only awarded payable as part of a divorce decree and, therefore, in order for the support to be payable, the children's parents must be legally married. Provincially, the situation is somewhat different. Under legislation such as the *F.L.R.A.* of Ontario, a parent need only pay support until such time as the child reaches the age of 16. Should the child remain in full-time attendance at a school and not withdraw from parental control then he is eligible for support until the age of 18. For a further discussion of the consequences attendant upon a child leaving home, see Chapter 7. Incidentally, a child who marries after the age of 16 is no longer entitled to parental support. A little-known fact within the general knowledge of the public is that a parent can claim support from his or her children if the parent is unable to meet his or her own needs. The child, however, will not be ordered to pay parental support until such time as the child attains the age of 18 — an age at which a person legally ceases to be a "child."

With respect to support after death of a parent, most provincial laws provide that a child is entitled to such support. This issue is further discussed on p. 222.

K. CHILD KIDNAPPING

Apart from the legal consequences, the removal of a child by a non-custodial parent (often referred to as child kidnapping or "child stealing") can have a devastating effect on the emotional well-being of a child. Depending on the age of a child, he may be unable to understand what is going on. The abrupt removal from the secure home violates principles enunciated in the psychology–custody literature such as the continuity of relationships as defined on p. 53. Such behaviour on the part of a parent calls into grave question whether he or she really has the best interests of the child at heart. As a result, the courts tend to treat such behaviour with the utmost gravity and will usually order the child returned to the custodial parent.

It should be stressed that a parent has no immunity from criminal liability, that is prosecution under the provisions of the *Criminal Code* of Canada if he removes the child from the care of the custodial parent. Section 250 of the *Criminal Code* provides that:

> 250(1) Every one who, with intent to deprive a parent or guardian or
> any other person who has lawful care or charge of a child under the age of
> fourteen years of the possession of that child . . . is liable to imprisonment
> for 10 years.

This same section goes on to provide that such a sanction does not apply "to a person who, claiming in good faith a right to possession of a child, obtains possession of the child." An example of a parent who escaped criminal liability because he believed he had a right to have custody involved a father who removed his child to British Columbia from Ontario.[52] In fact, his wife was granted a court order in Ontario vesting her with custody. However, the father was unaware that the custody order in Ontario had legal force in the Province of British Columbia and was, therefore, acquitted of a charge of kidnapping his child.

It should be noted that authorities such as police and child welfare workers are reluctant to involve the criminal law as a means of dealing with the problem. Incidentally, it should be noted that most statutes empowered to grant custody have a mechanism whereby a person contravening a custody order of the particular court may be cited for contempt of court. For instance, s. 37 of the *F.L.R.A.* of Ontario provides:

> 37(1) . . . every provincial court (family division) may punish by fine or imprisonment, or by both, any wilful contempt of or resistance to its process, rules or orders under this Act, but the fine shall not in any case exceed $1,000 nor shall the imprisonment exceed ninety days.

What are the practical options available to a custodial parent who returns home one day to find the baby-sitter has let the children go off into the hands of the non-custodial parent? As indicated above, the police are reluctant to lay charges in such circumstances. However, if the custody order or a separation agreement is shown to police officials, they will often attempt to locate the children, provided they are still within the jurisdictional area for the particular police force involved. If the custodial parent does not have a court order granting custody, or a separation agreement providing for custody (a *de facto* custody arrangement) the situation is even more difficult. Certainly the authorities will not act without a court order (often not even in the face of a separation agreement) and as a consequence removal of children in *de facto* custody circumstances will require the "custodial" parent to apply before a court for an order for interim custody, and custody. Having obtained an interim custody order (a final custody order is usually not granted until after a formal hearing), that person is still faced with the frustrating task of having it enforced.

What can be done if the children have been removed from the jurisdiction? Unfortunately, an immediate return of the children is often impossible and many a parent has despaired when they learn that a relatively cumbersome legal procedure must be started. The *Extra-Provincial Custody Order Enforcement Act* basically, allows one province to legally enforce the custody order of another. Unfortunately, this Act has not yet been endorsed by all of the provinces. However, it is certainly a step forward in dealing with the issue of the removal of children from the custodial parent's province. The Act requires enacting provinces to recognize and enforce extra-provincial custody orders unless they are satisfied that at the time the custody order was originally made, the child did not have a real and substantial connection with the jurisdiction in which the order was made. For instance, a parent obtaining a custody order from a country in which the child has lived for only a short time. In other words a country (or province) in which *the child* has no real roots or ties.

One of the problems the *Extra-Provincial Custody Orders Enforcement Act* is attempting to defeat is that of multiple custody orders pertaining to the same child or children. For instance, in the case described above in which the father removed the child to British Columbia, even though there was an outstanding Ontario custody order, the father attempted to convince a court in British Columbia to grant him custody. In the past, this actually happened and the consequences were enormously confusing to all of the parties concerned.

The Ontario government has proposed that a court in that province shall not make an order for custody of a child that would have the effect of superseding an order made by a court outside of Ontario unless there has been a material change of circumstances which affects or is likely to affect the best interests of the child. Further, an Ontario court will be prohibited from making a custody order unless the child is: (1) habitually resident in Ontario; (2) the child is physically in Ontario and the court is satisfied that the child has suffered or is in imminent danger of serious harm from the person lawfully entitled to custody of the child; (3) the child has a more real and substantial connection with another jurisdiction and there is no application for custody in the jurisdiction in which the child is habitually resident. This proposed statutory intervention will clarify a complicated and confused area of the law; it is designed to combat the kidnapping parent, who has lost a custody fight in one province, from moving to another province in an attempt to have the issue heard again in another jurisdiction. Most of the provinces are considering enacting similar legislation.

Judicial interpretation of the phrase "real and substantial connection" is found in the Saskatchewan case of *Gergely v. Gergely*.[53] In that case, the father removed his two daughters from the Province of Saskatchewan to British Columbia. Subsequently, and after a court in British Columbia had made an interim order for custody in favour of the father, the mother returned the children to Saskatchewan. In effect, the mother "re-kidnapped" the children. The Saskatchewan court was faced with the task of deciding whether to obey the existing interim custody order or to decide custody itself. The test to be met was whether the two children could be said to have a real and substantial connection to the Province of Saskatchewan. The court considered the following points: the children lived in Saskatchewan from the time of their parents' marriage until the parents separated; the mother continued to reside in the family residence and a number of family relatives resided in the province. On the other hand, the Saskatchewan court found that the children's connection with British Columbia was tenuous at best. The children had no roots in that province and, indeed, the father himself was attempting to start a new life as opposed to having already established a "home." The court made the following comment:[54]

I see no fault with the courts of British Columbia coming to grips with the problem before it, but under the circumstances, to find that there was a real and substantial connection with that province could have the effect of making British Columbia a haven for "civil kidnappers" . . . it would give encouragement to "quick removal" of children followed by an application to confirm the results of such quick removal.

I am satisfied . . . the children did not have a real and substantial connection with the province of British Columbia.

It is important to note that in the *Gergely* case that the judge was concerned with a jurisdictional question, to wit: did the court have authority to decide the question of custody? Having answered that question in the affirmative, the court then faced the task of deciding to whom custody should be awarded — the mother or the father.

The Toronto Star, May 5, 1979, issue provided a rather heart-rending insight into the anguish suffered by a mother who had her two sons surreptitiously removed by their father. The mother did not have a custody order, nor was there a separation agreement in existence. Three months after the parents separated, the mother arrived home to find the children gone. The children had, in fact, been removed to Florida by their father. The mother went to Family Court in Ontario and was granted legal custody of the two boys. By this time, a period of months had passed and she was still uncertain of the exact location of the children in Florida. Finally, approximately a year after the children had disappeared and after a month of searching in that state, she found her sons. The children were taken into custody by welfare officials in the State of Florida and a Florida judge (ignoring the Ontario court order) awarded the father temporary custody. A month later the American court awarded permanent custody to the mother. The entire process cost the mother thousands of dollars and untold hours of anguish, not to mention the emotional damage suffered by the boys.

The situation described above illustrates that the problem of child kidnapping has international connotations. The Hague Conference on private international law hopes to produce a draft treaty in which an international reciprocal enforcement of Custody Orders Acts will be subscribed to by most of the world's countries. It is also interesting to note that in America the House of Representatives is considering passing legislation similar to the *Extra-Provincial Custody Enforcement Act*, although it should be noted that many states already possess reciprocal custody enforcement statutes.

FOOTNOTES

1. Report on Family Law, Law Reform Commission of Canada (1976) at p. 1. See also Katz, *When Parents Fail: The Law's Response to Family Breakdown* (Boston, 1971)
2. (1972), 406 U.S. 205 at pp. 241-44

3. See *Chaffin v. Chaffin* (1964), 397 P. 2d 771; and *Hoffman v. Tracy* (1965), 406 P. 2d 323
4. *Supra*, at p. 19
5. *Benoit v. Benoit* (1972), 6 R.F.L. 180 at pp. 181-82
6. (1973), 11 R.F.L. 226 at p. 231
7. (1975), 21 R.F.L. 42
8. *Supra*, at p. 43
9. (1975), 20 R.F.L. 202
10. *Supra*, at p. 204
11. (1975), 19 R.F.L. 119
12. *Talsky v. Talsky* (1975), 21 R.F.L. 27 at p. 38
13. (1974), 18 R.F.L. 132
14. [1976] 2 W.W.R. 462
15. *Supra*, at pp. 466-68
16. (1973), 516 P. 2d 132
17. Goldstein, Solnit and Freud, *Beyond the Best Interests of the Child* (New York, 1973). See also Bradbrook, "The Relevance of Psychological and Psychiatric Studies to the Future Development of the Law Governing the Settlement of Inter-Parental Child Custody Disputes," 11 J. Fam. L. 55 (1972).
18. *Supra*, at p. 17
19. [1950] 1 D.L.R. 694 at p. 698
20. [1926] Ch. 676 at p. 684
21. 49 Can. Bar Rev. 557 (1971)
22. [1955] O.W.N. 341 at p. 344
23. See Rosen, "Children of Divorce: An Evaluation of Two Common Assumptions," 2 Can. J. Fam. L. 403 (1979)
24. See "Representation of Minors in Proceedings Relating to Their Wardship and Custody," by Mr. Justice Galligan, Reference Material, Family Law Week, July 26–30, 1976, Department of Continuing Education, Law Society of Upper Canada. See also Bates, "The Relevance of Children's Wishes in Contested Custody Cases: An Analysis of Recent Developments in Canada and Australia," 2 Fam. L. Rev. 83 (1979).
25. [1967] 1 All E.R. 202 at p. 210
26. (1974), 14 R.F.L. 151 at p. 151
27. "Obtaining and Weighing the Children's Wishes: Private Interviews With a Judge or Assessment by an Expert and Report," 23 R.F.L. 1 at pp. 6-7
28. *Beyond the Best Interests of the Child* (Free Press, Paperback, MacMillan Publishing Co., New York, New York, 1973), at pp. 62-63
29. *Kruger v. Kruger* (1979), 25 O.R. (2d) 673 at p. 694
30. *Beyond the Best Interests of the Child* (Free Press, Paperback, MacMillan Publishing Co., New York, New York, 1973), at pp. 12-13
31. (1966), 140 N.W. 2d 152
32. [1973] 3 O.R. 921
33. *Supra*, at p. 929

34. *Supra*, at p. 934
35. Weiler and Berman, "Re Moores and Feldstein — A Case Comment and Discussion of Custody Principles," (1974), 12 R.F.L. 294 at p. 305
36. (1975), 18 R.F.L. 378
37. *Supra*, at pp. 380-81
38. (1978), 3 R.F.L. (2d) 193
39. *Supra*, at p. 197
40. *Supra*, at p. 197
41. (1979), 8 R.F.L. 236
42. 1 R.F.L. (2d) 116 at pp. 122-23. See also Fineberg, "Joint Custody of Infants: Breakthrough or Fad?" 2 Can. J. Fam. L. 417 (1979)
43. (1974), 19 R.F.L. 326
44. *Supra*, at p. 331
45. (1977), 28 R.F.L. 389
46. *Supra*, at pp. 396-97
47. *Podolsky v. Podolsky* (1975), 26 R.F.L. 321 at pp. 322-23
48. (1979), 6 R.F.L. (2d) 223
49. *Supra*, at pp. 224-26
50. (1975), 22 R.F.L. 107
51. See *Aksugyuk v. Aksugyuk* (1974), 17 R.F.L. 224
52. *R. v. Austin* (1957), 120 C.C.C. 118
53. (1978), 5 R.F.L. (2d) 365
54. *Supra*, at pp. 369-70

Chapter 4

The Child Protected from the Family

A. INTRODUCTION

It is an accepted and fundamental principle of Canadian society that parents have a right to raise their children in the way they see fit. In our society, there is considerable controversy about how parents should treat their children. Experts disagree about matters of nutrition, medical care, education, physical activity and moral training. Parents are left to choose the best way to raise their children, according to their own beliefs and values. It is accepted that parents are human, and far from perfect. Parents may be unable or unwilling to do what is best for their children, assuming they know what this is. It is fundamental to our way of life that government interference in family life be kept to a minimum. There are, however, situations in which the care a child receives in his home falls below a minimum standard, and interference by the state is justified to protect the child from his own family.

The obligation of the state to protect children from their families has not always been accepted. As described in Chapter 1, many of the civilizations of antiquity gave parents a totally unfettered right to treat their children in the way they saw fit. With the spread of Christian influences, the harshest aspects of Roman law came to be tempered, and by the sixth century A.D. the right of the father was limited to the right to "reasonably chastise" his offspring.[1]

In England, and later in Canada, the right of the parent to "reasonably chastise" his children continued to be the dominant response to the societal protection of children until the 19th century. While provision was made for the care of orphans, first by religious bodies and later by various municipal institutions, very little was done to protect children who lived with their families. The criminal law made it an offence to kill or maim a child, and it was a criminal offence to fail to provide one's child with the necessities of life. It was, however, quite acceptable for children to be severely beaten by parents and to be made to work long hours under terrible conditions in mines and factories.

The 19th century was marked by major social reform efforts, efforts which brought increasing enfranchisement of voters and the introduction of mass compulsory education. In 1893, Ontario enacted the *Child Protection Act* [2] providing for the formation of Children's Aid Societies and giving the courts the mandate to commit neglected children to the care of these societies. This legislation allowed for the active involvement of the state in the protection of children from their families, and for the first time created a tool which was much more subtle than the blunt instrument of the criminal law.

In Canada there are two basic types of legislation which protect children. One type is criminal law, which primarily serves to protect children from physical and sexual abuse, though there are also offences relating to the corruption of the morality of children. This legislation provides for the punishment of people who fail to treat children in an adequate manner. This type of response to the problem of inadequate parental care is more fully discussed at the end of this chapter. The other type of legislation focuses upon children who are abused or neglected and provides for the involvement of the state in their lives; this is generally known as child protection legislation.

In Ontario, the *Child Welfare Act, 1978* (*C.W.A.*) is the primary piece of legislation in this area. Part I of the Act deals with Children's Aid Societies; Part II with the protection and care of children; and Part III with adoption. In this chapter, the primary focus will be upon the Ontario legislation, though there is similar legislation in all of the other provinces, and where appropriate some comparisons and contrasts will be made to other provinces.[3] Section 19 of the Act provides a rather lengthy, but somewhat vague, definition of a "child in need of protection." An understanding of the concept of the child in need of protection is crucial for an appreciation of this area of law. Often a great deal of effort is expended in deciding whether or not a particular child is in need of protection. The various legislative provisions for intervention in the life of a child and his parents only come into operation if a child is in need of protection.

The definition contained in s. 19 includes a child being a person under the age of 16, whose parents are dead, or have deserted him, or do not want the child. It includes a child who is living in an "unfit or improper place," or associating with an "unfit or improper person." A child will be in need of protection where the person in whose charge he is "is unable to control the child," or refuses or neglects to provide adequate medical treatment. A child will be in need of protection if his "emotional or mental development is endangered because of emotional rejection or deprivation of affection," or if his "life, health or morals may be endangered by the conduct of the person in whose charge the child is." Finally, a child will be in need of protection if he is "found begging or receiving charity in a public place," or if he is "without sufficient cause . . . habitually absent from home or school."

On paper the definition seems to be very broad. It includes not only children who are physically or sexually abused, or malnourished or not receiving adequate medical care, but also a more amorphous group of children having various emotional and behavioural problems. Though the definition could conceivably include virtually any child, it has in fact been interpreted quite narrowly by the courts, There is a great deal of respect for the rights of parents and their tendency to limit interference in family life. The Supreme Court of Canada pointed out in *Re Baby Duffell*[4] that parents are not to be deprived of the custody of their children "merely because on a nice balancing of material and social advantages the Court is of opinion that others, who wish to do so, could provide more advantageously for its upbringing and future.''

Clearly, the courts have expressed a bias towards preserving the family unit. This is partially a result of the notion that all people have a right to the minimum amount of state intervention in their lives. It also recognizes the fact that intervention can often be most disruptive, particularly if it involves the removal of a child from his home. For a child, the experience of being separated from his family and all that he has known and loved, can be a most traumatic experience, even if the home life is not very satisfactory. There is a corresponding recognition of the fact that for many children the experience of being in the care of the Children's Aid Society may not be an entirely satisfactory experience, with frequent moves from one placement to another and regular changes in social workers. Influenced by these factors, the courts are frequently slow to make a finding that a child is "in need of protection." This approach does have certain advantages, but one can certainly question whether it sometimes leaves a child in a very unhappy, sometimes dangerous, and occasionally even fatal situation. In *Re Chrysler*,[5] a case involving allegations of abuse, the judge remarked:

> It seems to me that in such a situation the potential for real and immediate abuse must be made clear before the state should be permitted to intervene by removing the child from her parents. If it were otherwise, it would allow a C.A.S. to be the final arbitrator in a so-called child abuse case and would leave the parents and the child with no real recourse to a really independent and impartial court. In adopting this principle, I realize that there is always the danger that some real and even irreparable harm may be inflicted upon the child if the parents are really potential child abusers, but the C.A.S has not been able to prove that fact because of the unavailability of witnesses who can testify to the alleged abuse and therefore has not been able to meet the standard of proof required by the court.
>
> I think that this risk must still give way to the greater risk of irreparable harm that can be inflicted upon a child and the danger to society of the serious undermining of the parents and the family if a C.A.S. is permitted to act in an arbitrary way, even though its intentions are motivated by the highest ideals and concerns.

When considering the concept of the "child in need of protection," it is important to realize that many different types of children can fit within this definition. The newborn child of an unwed mother who does not want to raise the child is a child in need of protection. Young infants who are the subject of physical and sexual abuse are children in need of protection. The adolescent child who is having behavioural problems and whose parents cannot control him is a child in need of protection. The sexually promiscuous child, particularly if female, is apt to be treated as a child in need of protection.

It is difficult to obtain accurate statistics on the number of children in Canada who are in need of protection, but in June, 1975, there were approximately 68 000 children in the care of child protection authorities, and these authorities were working in the home with another 96 000 children, in 42 000 families.[6] One important point to realize is that although the physical abuse of children is an extremely serious problem, and one which has recently received a considerable amount of public attention, the percentage of cases involving physical abuse is not high. In 1973–74, there were only 1 085 reported cases of child abuse and battering in Canada. It is well known that most cases of child abuse are not reported, and that the actual number of battered children is estimated at from 3 000 to 12 000. Problems with reporting child abuse and neglect will be discussed a little later in the chapter. It is certainly safe to say that the child protection agencies are not aware of all the cases involving children who could fit within the legal definition of a "child in need of protection."

B. CHILD PROTECTION AUTHORITIES

In each province there is a government-sanctioned authority which is charged with the responsibility for enforcing child welfare legislation. This authority will have the duty to investigate cases where it is suspected that there is a child in need of protection, and, if necessary, provide services to the child and his family. It is also responsible for most adoptions, though as we shall see in the next chapter, some adoptions are not carried under its auspices. This authority will often provide a range of other services, for example, both to families and unwed mothers requiring counselling or emergency assistance.

In most Canadian provinces, the authority vested with the responsibility for carrying out these tasks is a government department. In Ontario and most parts of Manitoba and Nova Scotia, there are agencies known as Children's Aid Societies (C.A.S.) which have this responsibility. These agencies are not strictly a part of the government, though the government provides the bulk of their funding and exercises a considerable degree of control over their operations; the degree of financial support and amount of control is hardly surprising when it is considered that these agencies are, in effect, exercising a governmental function.

The first Children's Aid Society in Canada was established in 1891 in Toronto, by a group of public-minded citizens. The organization initially did not have legal authority to intervene in situations in which parents were not prepared to voluntarily accept help. Two years later legislation was enacted giving these organizations a certain amount of public financial support and the legal authority to intervene to protect children.

Children's Aid Societies are organized on a geographic, and sometimes religious, basis. Each Society is a non-profit corporation, operated by a board of directors. The directors are citizens elected by the membership; generally any citizen who has an interest may become a member of the Society. Invariably the board is composed of middle class people, and though membership on the board is usually considered a recognition of status and prestige, many board members are acclaimed. The board sets the tone and policy for the C.A.S, though many of its powers are delegated to an executive committee, and in particular to a salaried local director, who administers the staff and operations of the Society. Municipal governments have some influence on the local C.A.S. by having the authority to nominate some members of the board and executive committee.[7]

The government of Ontario appoints a provincial director who has a responsibility for advising and supervising the local Societies. The province provides the bulk of the funding for the C.A.S.'s, though municipal governments are required to provide a portion of the support, and some money is generally raised locally from voluntary donations, especially for use in various special projects. Until recently, local Societies tended to have considerable autonomy and the quality of protective services varied greatly from one locale to another. There was little monitoring of the practices of individual Societies, and no effective effort was made to establish province-wide standards. In the last few years, however, the government has shown a great interest in supervising much more closely the work of each C.A.S., both in institutional terms and on an individual case basis. Unfortunately, it seems that much of the political concern has been a result of public pressure arising out of the tragic deaths of a number of young children.[8]

As a part of the effort to improve the quality of care provided to children, the Ontario government has created a new branch of the Ministry of Community and Social Services—the Children's Services Division—which is responsible for co-ordinating a number of services which were formerly provided by different ministries, and rationalizing the delivery of services. To assist in achieving these objectives, there is a program for the establishment of Local Children's Services Committees. These committees will ultimately be responsible for determining local priorities; and planning and co-ordinating social services for children in their area. Though the C.A.S. has primary legal responsibility for the implementation of child protection legislation, other social agencies are often involved. In some communities Child Abuse Committees are formed to co-ordinate activities aimed at the detection and treatment of abused children. These committees are designed to permit a voluntary pooling of resources from various agencies, local hospitals and public health officials.

In attempting to understand the child protection system, it is essential to realize that regardless of how the system is designed, there will be difficulties as there is a basic and unresolvable problem of role conflict. The individual worker who is sent into the family as a representative of the protection authority must inevitably carry out two conflicting roles, and will invariably face difficulties. One role the worker must carry out is that of investigator, and the other is that of therapist; these roles do not fit together easily. The worker has a statutory duty to investigate a home situation, and establish whether a child is in need of protection. Every worker has this duty, and it is a continuing duty. It exists not only during the initial phases of the relationship between a worker and the family, but also later, as the worker continues to monitor the situation. The worker may have the matter brought before the court and, if necessary, have the child removed from the home if, at any time, the worker feels the situation calls for such action. In this role as an investigator, the worker will engender a feeling of distrust, both from the parents and from the child.

The other role which the worker must attempt to play is that of a therapist. The worker must attempt to diagnose the nature of the problem which led to the involvement of the state, and alleviate that problem. Some assistance can often be provided by arranging support from other sources, such as arranging day care to take a child out of the home for a few hours a day, but ultimately the worker must strive to directly assist the parents and child, and this can generally only be done effectively in a relationship based on trust. However, if necessary any confidential remarks made by the parents to the worker will be related to the court, to prove how unfit the parents are.

There are no easy solutions to this problem, and different workers handle the situation in different ways. Some will play down one role or the other. Often, if the case is brought to court and the worker has to testify, there will be a change of workers. Sometimes, an outside therapist, such as a psychiatrist, will be brought in to deal with the underlying problems in a therapeutic manner. As will be discussed in Chapter 8, the psychiatrist may at some point also be placed in the awkward position of having to reveal his confidences in court, but this is another matter. It is important for the present to appreciate the problem, and recognize the difficulties it can cause.

C. REPORTING CHILD ABUSE

Child protection authorities must of necessity rely on members of the community to report cases of children who are suspected of being in need of protection. An investigation can then be commenced and appropriate action be taken.

Until recently, many members of the community have been most reluctant to report cases of suspected abuse or neglect. Many people who come into contact with abused or neglected children cannot bring themselves to accuse the parents of maltreatment, and, hence, ignore obvious signs of ill-treatment. Some who could report, do not do so out of a fear of "becoming involved," and perhaps having to attend court and incur the hostility of the parents involved. Doctors are often in an excellent position to observe abuse or neglect and report their suspicions, but they have tended to be reluctant, because they have felt that their relationship to the parents is confidential. Public attitudes are changing, and in recent years there has been a considerable increase in the number of reports received. The changes have in part reflected a gradual acceptance of the notion that parents do not have the right to treat their children in any way they see fit. There has also been an increased awareness of the symptoms of child abuse and neglect, especially among doctors, nurses and other medical personnel. Strengthened legal obligations to report have also played a role in increasing the amount of reporting.

In Ontario, the C.W.A., s. 49, provides that every person having information of the "abandonment, desertion or need for protection of a child or the infliction of abuse upon a child," shall immediately report this to the C.A.S. For the ordinary citizen there may be little incentive to report as there is no penalty for a failure to report, though in most other provinces there is a penalty. In Ontario there is provision for a fine of up to $1000 for a person who fails to report reasonably suspected abuse, if encountered "in the course of a person's professional or official duties." This should encourage doctors, nurses, teachers and other professionals to report suspected abuse. Abuse is statutorily defined in s. 47 to mean, "physical harm, malnutrition or mental ill-health of a degree that if not immediately remedied could seriously impair growth and development or result in permanent injury or death; or . . . sexual molestation." It should be noted that the concept of an "abused child" is narrower than that of a "child in need of protection." A professional who comes into contact with a child who might be in need of protection, but who is not abused, has the duty of an ordinary citizen to report this, but incurs no penalty for a failure to do so.

The duty to report applies notwithstanding that the information is confidential or that its disclosure would normally be prohibited by law, as for example, is the case with information possessed by doctors. Further, unless the providing of information is done "maliciously or without reasonable grounds," the person giving the information cannot be sued for damages for making a report. The only group which is exempted from providing information is the legal profession, as requiring reporting from lawyers could completely disrupt the legal system. The reason why lawyers have this privileged position is discussed further in Chapter 8.

It should be noted that a professional person who fails to report suspected abuse may incur liability beyond a fine. In *Landeros v. Flood*,[9] the Supreme Court of California held that a doctor who negligently failed to diagnose that a young girl was suffering from the medical condition known as "battered child syndrome," and did not report the situation to the child protection authorities, could be sued for malpractice. He could be required to compensate the child for injuries where, as a result of his negligence, the child was returned to her parents and suffered further injury. "Battered child syndrome" is now an accepted medical diagnosis used to "characterize a clinical condition in young children who have received serious physical abuse,"[10] and is diagnosed by consideration of the type of injury suffered. There have not yet been any Canadian cases where a professional person has been sued for damages as a result of a failure to report child abuse, but it seems that the principle of *Landeros v. Flood* might be applied in this country.

By on the one hand providing immunity for those who report, and on the other hand providing sanctions for those who do not, it is hoped that the C.A.S. will have more information about children who might need their help. Some doctors welcome these provisions as giving them a duty to report suspected abuse, which may remove, or at least reduce, the feelings of betrayal which parents might have. Opponents of compulsory reporting have argued that some abusing parents will fail to get proper treatment for an injured child, knowing that this might lead to discovery of their abusive behaviour. However, studies have indicated that this is not the case. An American expert in the field has commented:[11]

The number of parents who are willing to risk the life of their child by not seeking medical help is likely to be small. Many of those who inflict deliberate injury in moments of tension, high passion, or psychological imbalance will respond to a child's need in later, calmer times.

Ontario, like most other provinces, is now keeping a record of all reports of child abuse in a provincial central registry. As noted earlier, the concept of abuse is narrower than that of the child in need of protection, and hence there are many fewer reports of abuse than there are of children in need of protection. Section 52 of the C.W.A. governs the registry. Reports are not to identify the person who provided the C.A.S. with the information. If a person's name is entered in the registry as one who is alleged to have abused a child, that person shall receive notification of the registration and may request a hearing to have his name removed if the allegations are unfounded. The registry is not open to the public, and access to it is limited to government officials, researchers and, in some cases, medical personnel. The problem of confidentiality is a difficult one since the information is not necessarily confirmed, and certainly not proven in a court; the government's record of keeping information confidential has been far from perfect, and the existence of such records may give rise to some concern.

One of the prime purposes of having a registry is to help keep track of abusing parents who might move around the province to avoid detection, though this has apparently not been much of a problem in the past. The registry can provide very helpful statistical information for researchers trying to understand the phenomenon of child abuse. A central registry could be an effective tool if medical personnel and others who are in a position to suspect abuse in a particular case can have relatively ready access to information which might confirm their suspicions. Hospitals could check to see whether pregnant mothers have a history of abuse and take steps to protect the newborn. At the present time, registries in Canada are not being used nearly as effectively as they could be.[12]

D. THE CHILD PROTECTION PROCEEDING

1. General

When the child welfare authorities receive information about a child believed to be in need of protection, an investigation will be quickly commenced. Generally, one or more workers will contact the person giving the information, the family and the child involved, and representatives of various agencies who have been involved with the family. It may be that the parents admit that there are some problems; they might even have been the ones who contacted the child protection authorities. If the problems do not appear too serious, a voluntary plan might be arranged for the care of the child, either inside or outside the home. Voluntary plans will be considered later in this chapter.

In many cases, a voluntary plan cannot be arranged, either because the parents are not prepared to co-operate, or because the protection worker feels that the situation is too serious to attempt this. For example, if it appears that the child is suffering from physical abuse, the child may be immediately taken into protective custody by the child protection authorities. Sometimes a hospital emergency department will report that a child apparently suffering from physical abuse has just been admitted, and a protection worker will go to the hospital to take custody of the child at once. If the child protection authorities take the child into their care, the child must be brought before the court within a few days. Alternatively, the child may stay at home, but the parents will be required to appear in court with the child in a few days' time. Following either route, the child and his parents will arrive at court for a child protection hearing.

At such a hearing, there will essentially be two questions. The first is whether the child is in need of protection. Does this child fit within the definition of a "child in need of protection"? If the child is not found to be in need of protection, this will end the matter, though the situation may continue to be monitored with assistance provided on a voluntary basis. If the judge finds that the child is in need of protection, he then faces a second question: determining the appropriate disposition. In most provinces he has three options: he can order that the child be returned home, but subject to official supervision by the child protection authorities; the judge can order that the child be temporarily removed from his home and placed in care of the child welfare authority, or he can order that the parental tie should effectively be severed and the child be placed permanently in care perhaps with the goal of eventual adoption. Though the court faces two distinct questions, generally the hearing will not be divided and evidence will be heard on both issues at the same time.

Frequently there will be a series of hearings about a particular child over a long period of time. The judge may initially order supervision in the home, and if this fails the child may be ordered into care for a period of time, and only then, if the situation appears to be hopeless, a permanent order will be made. As we shall see, in most provinces there is a limit to the amount of time a child can be in care on a temporary basis.

One important point to realize is that many child protection hearings are not actively opposed. It is true that frequently the parents, and even the child, may appear with their counsel, and bitterly oppose the making of any order, and it is in this situation that lawyers are most likely to be involved. Often, however, prior to coming to court, the child protection authorities and parents have discussed the case, and agreed on the type of order that is best for the child. In this situation, the parties will generally appear briefly in court and explain the case to the judge. Though he is not technically obliged to accept their agreement, invariably he will do so.

2. The Nature of the Proceeding

A child protection hearing is not a scientific inquiry into what type of environment would be best for the child in question. Rather, it is an adversarial contest, decided by a court of law. The issue is relatively narrow. In *Hansen v. C.A.S. of Hamilton-Wentworth*,[13] the Supreme Court of Ontario overturned a lower court's order, commenting:

> The learned trial judge stated several times in the course of the hearing that his only concern was the welfare of the child . . . I am not sure that it is a proper test in matters of this nature . . . because by that test more children than I care to contemplate would be taken from their parents and placed in foster homes. The question is whether the child is in need of protection and if so to what extent that protection should be imposed.

In the context of this adversarial proceeding, the onus is upon the child protection authority to prove its case. The case is civil in nature, rather than criminal, and so the issue must only be proven on the "balance of probabilities", and not "beyond a reasonable doubt."

What does this mean? The fact that the onus of proof is upon the child protection authority means there is an obligation upon the authority to prove its case, and if it fails to do so, then no order will be made. It also means that if the judge is genuinely uncertain about what to do at the end of the trial, then he will not make any order.

In a civil trial, such as a child protection proceeding, the judge must only make a finding upon "a balance of probabilities," and not "beyond a reasonable doubt." In a civil trial, it may be possible to prove a fact with less evidence than would be required to prove the same fact in a criminal trial. The difference in the standards of proof is conceptually difficult to understand, and some argue that it is more a matter of semantics than anything else. It can, however, be viewed as a matter of practical significance. Thus, in a child protection case, it may be alleged that the parents have been physically abusing the child. Though there are no witnesses who actually saw the abuse occurring, the nature of the observed injuries would lead one to infer that abuse has occurred. A judge in a civil child protection hearing might be prepared to accept this evidence and make a finding that the child was in need of protection. If, however, the parents were charged with the criminal offence of assault, a judge might well not convict the parents, even if he heard exactly the same evidence, as he might not be satisfied "beyond a reasonable doubt" that they committed the act of assault. It should be noted that the issue in these two situations is not identical. In a criminal proceeding, it must be proven that a specific person committed a specific act at a particular time. In a protection hearing, if it is shown that a child living with his parents is not being adequately cared for, it may not be necessary to prove that the parents committed specific acts. In *Re A.M.*,[14] the judge commented:

Neglect hearings do not require proof beyond a reasonable doubt but a balancing of the evidence as indicated in [child welfare] cases.

. . . . .

. . . as indicated before and it runs throughout the case, there is no strict necessity to apply physically observable evidence of circumstances of neglect. It has been proven that while the child was in the care and control of the parents, it had sustained injuries and a condition of malnutrition that are so serious that the Court, without reasonable explanation from the parents, cannot overlook . . . the legal principle or maxim of "res ipsa loquitur" or "the circumstances speak for themselves" can be applied to this case. That is to say, when it is so improbable that an accident or injury or condition would have happened without the negligence of the parents and in the absence of a reasonable explanation by the parents for these circumstances then the child is in a state of neglect and in need of protection.

The sequence of events in a child protection hearing is generally the same as that followed in other civil trials. The witnesses for the child protection agency are heard first, followed by the witnesses for the parents. Each witness in turn will be subject to "examination-in-chief," "cross-examination," and perhaps "re-examination."

Examination-in-chief is questioning by a lawyer for the party who called the witness. It is generally not permissible to ask "leading questions" (questions which suggest answers) during examination-in-chief. This will be followed by cross-examination, which is questioning by the lawyer for the party who did not call the witness. This can be a quite thorough testing of the witness's honesty and perception, and may involve the use of leading questions. After cross-examination, the party who called the witness may re-examine the witness, which involves clarification of points raised in cross-examination. Sometimes the judge will ask the witnesses questions. It is generally considered that in an adversarial system, the judge should limit himself to asking questions to clarify the responses given by witnesses, though in child protection cases where the welfare of a young person is at stake, judges are apt to participate a little more than in other types of cases. After the parents have called their witnesses, the agency may call evidence by way of "reply" which may rebut the evidence of the parents. The lawyers then have an opportunity to make "submissions," which are summaries of the facts and applicable law. The judge will then pronounce "judgement," giving his decision in the case.

It should be noted that there may be more parties involved than simply the child protection agency and the parents. As we will discuss, the law of Ontario allows the child, and in some cases relatives, foster parents, and others to participate in proceedings. If the parents disagree as to what should happen with the child, for example, if they are separated, each may have separate legal representation.

3. Commencing the Proceeding and Apprehension of the Child

There are basically two ways in which a child protection agency can commence a protection proceeding. The first is by obtaining an order requiring the person having care of the child to produce the child in court. The second is to "apprehend" the child, that is to say take the child into care, and the court proceeding is commenced thereafter. The method chosen depends upon the amount of risk which the agency feels the child may be exposed to if left at home prior to the hearing.

The agency will choose to obtain an order to produce the child if it is felt that the child will be safe where he is until the hearing commences and that the order will be complied with. In Ontario, s. 21(1) (*b*) of the *C.W.A.*, allows the C.A.S. to apply to the court for an order to produce the child, if there are "reasonable and probable grounds to believe" that the child is in need of protection. A worker will appear in court with the request, and a sworn, written supporting statement known as an affidavit. There will be no one present to oppose the request for the order to produce the child, so it will invariably be granted. Failure to comply with the order will constitute contempt of court, and may lead to a fine, or imprisonment, and the immediate apprehension of the child.

The police and employees of the C.A.S. have broad powers to take a child believed to be in need of protection into care. Section 21 of the *C.W.A.* authorizes them to enter any premises to search for a child, with or without a warrant. The C.A.S. may obtain a warrant to search for the child, authorizing the entry into premises to search for and detain the child, but it is not essential to obtain a warrant; this will generally only be done if someone is obstructing the apprehension of the child. When a child is apprehended, he is taken to a "place of safety," which includes a home operated by the C.A.S., a hospital, which is likely to be used if the child was apprehended in the hospital, and in some cases an Observation and Detention Home. If it is likely that the child will run away, he may be kept in a "secure" setting.

After a child is apprehended and taken to a place of safety, s. 27 of the Act requires that the child be brought before a judge within five days. The five days exclude the date of apprehension, and if the last day falls on a Sunday, there will be a one-day extension. It is not completely clear what will happen if the child is not brought before a judge within five days. Courts in New Brunswick[15] and Manitoba[16] have held that this will not affect the proceedings, while a court in Saskatchewan[17] held that the proceeding was of no legal effect and had to be recommenced. In any event, a failure to do as required would doubtless be a violation of the law, and produce civil, or even criminal, consequences. On the other hand, it has been held that if the proceeding is of no effect because the statutory requirements have not been met it is sufficient that the child may be returned to his parents for a moment, and immediately "reapprehended," allowing a new application to be brought, effectively preventing the return of the child.[18]

The C.A.S. is given a very broad power to apprehend children. It is a power which is, in many ways, broader than that given the police when seeking criminals.

It is a power which must be exercised with discretion, and which is sometimes abused. In *Ex parte D.*[19] a judge expressed considerable displeasure and apprehension, remarking:

> (b) I think that when children are living in clean, comfortable and settled family homes where conditions are equal to or above the average in the community, strong evidence is required before a child should be taken out of such a home.
> (c) I think that when charges are made of this kind they should be investigated on the spot and with the parents before a warrant is served and not afterwards.
>
> . . . . .
>
> What moves me is the abuse of the super-normal powers entrusted to the Children's Aid Societies solely for the protection of children in need. They are not provided to make the task of the social worker easier, to be twisted to extort consent, to enter law-abiding homes and spirit children away, or to cut the bonds of blood or adoption, but only to protect children against abuse and to cope with the emergencies and challenges which the sufferings of children present to society and which cannot properly be dealt with unless we sacrifice in particular cases our ancient liberties and much that makes the future of children in our society worthwhile.

In 1979, the Ontario government introduced a somewhat novel provision allowing any individual to bring a case before the court. If a person, suspecting that a child is in need of protection, has informed the C.A.S., and the society has refused or failed to bring the matter to court within a reasonable period, that person may apply to the court under s. 22(2) of the *C.W.A.* for an order directing the C.A.S. to apprehend the child, or for an order requiring the person in whose charge the child is to produce the child. The Society will then be required to act and commence a proceeding. Though it does not seem that wide use will be made of it, this provision may be used by interested professionals who disagree with the position taken by the C.A.S. It is also possible that a dissatisfied parent who has lost custody of a child after separation may attempt to use this as a lever to reopen the issue by alleging that the custodial parent is "unfit"; the courts will be sensitive to preventing this type of misuse of the statutory provisions. As we shall see, it is possible for a person who becomes involved in a proceeding in this way, or is otherwise interested in a case, to become a party to the proceeding.

4. Jurisdiction

In most provinces, child protection proceedings are held in one of the lower courts, which is generally referred to as Family Court. In Ontario, jurisdiction rests with what is officially known as the Provincial Court (Family Division), and in the counties where it exists, the Unified Family Court. The *C.W.A.*, s. 19, provides that a hearing will be held in the Family Court of the county where the child was apprehended, or before which a child was ordered to be produced. There is provision for the transfer of a child to the Family Court of another county, if there is a "preponderance of convenience" favouring such a move. For example, a 15-year-old girl from Kingston might go to Toronto and become a prostitute. If apprehended in Toronto by the Metropolitan Toronto C.A.S., she would initially be brought before the Family Court in Toronto, but the case would probably be transferred back to Kingston for a hearing.

If a child from another province or country, already subject to a child protection order from that jurisdiction, runs away to Ontario, s. 58 of the *C.W.A.* provides that the order is valid in Ontario, and the child will be returned to the jurisdiction where the order was made. If a child from another jurisdiction, but who is not the subject of another order, comes to Ontario, perhaps on his own, he may be found to be a child in need of protection in Ontario, and returned to his own province subject to the Ontario order, either to the care of child protection authorities in the other jurisdiction or to his parents. As a practical matter, if a child has run away from home in another jurisdiction, though he may technically be a child in need of protection in Ontario, his parents may simply be contacted to arrange for his return home.

Jurisdictional problems can arise if an order under child protection legislation conflicts with an order made in a custody dispute between parents. It may be that the mother was awarded sole custody by a superior court pursuant to a divorce. Later, the child protection authorities become involved; the matter is brought to court and the child is found to be in need of protection, perhaps because the mother is physically abusing the child. As we shall see, one of the powers which a judge has, if he has found a child to be in need of protection, is to order the child placed with the parent, *or any other person*, subject to supervision by the child protection authorities. Therefore, even though the mother originally had custody pursuant to the divorce, the order may place the child in the care of his father. When attempting to resolve which order takes priority, the factors to be considered will be the sequence in which the orders were made, the levels of court which made the orders, and the types of legislation under which the orders were made.

Most courts have quite consistently[20] held that once a court is concerned with a child under protection legislation, this court has exclusive authority over the child, as long as the child is in need of protection. This procedure is to apply regardless of which level of court made the other order, and regardless of the sequence of the orders, i.e., the protection order takes precedence over prior and subsequent custody orders. This position is based on the view that protection proceedings are quite different from ordinary custody cases, and deal with a special and distinct question, namely, whether the child is in need of protection. Although widely accepted, this view has not met universal acceptance, and the Prince Edward Island Supreme Court (Family Division) held in *Dugay v. Dugay*[21] that a custody order made pursuant to a divorce takes precedence over a protection order. This alternate view is based on the constitutional doctrine of law that an order under divorce legislation, is "paramount" to an order under provincial protection legislation.

It must be acknowledged that this question has not been completely resolved by the courts. *Dugay* is almost certainly limited to a situation where there is an order pursuant to a divorce, and will not apply if the other order is made under provincial legislation, such as the *Family Law Reform Act, 1978 (F.L.R.A.)*. It is suggested here that the view expressed in *Dugay* is wrong, but the matter is not free from doubt, and legal advice should be sought in regard to the current state of the law in each province.

In Ontario, for the purposes of protection, the *C.W.A.*, s. 19(1)(*a*), defines a child as a person "actually or apparently under sixteen years of age." Though the same age limit applies in most other provinces, in some it is higher, for example, under 17 in British Columbia. In each child protection proceeding the judge will make a finding of age, invariably based on actual age, proven by a birth certificate or testimony, or in the rare case, on the basis of apparent age.

Problems can arise if the child is about to reach the age at which he is no longer legally defined as a child. In a British Columbia case,[22] a girl was apprehended four days before her 17th birthday, the applicable age under that statute, but was only brought before the court after her birthday. The judge held that he did not have jurisdiction to proceed. In some cases a hearing may commence before the applicable birthday, and be adjourned until after it, at which time an order is made. In Ontario, the courts have held that the date for determining age is the date when the application is brought and first heard in court, not the date of the order; in Saskatchewan, it is the date on which the order was made that is determinative.[23] The Nova Scotia *Children's Services Act* statutorily adopts the Ontario position.

As we shall see, once an order has been made, there are provisions for extending the order, even though the child has passed the applicable birthday.

5. Adjournments

A contested child protection application will almost never be heard on the date on which the agency, the child and his parents first appear in court. If all concerned agree as to the order which should be made, the judge will invariably deal with the matter immediately. But if there is to be a full hearing with witnesses and legal argument, the matter will doubtless be adjourned. The adjournment may be necessary to give the parties time to get proper legal advice, to prepare for the hearing, or simply because the court does not have time on that initial date for a full hearing. Indeed, there may be several adjournments pending a hearing.

It is recognized that adjournments, which, in effect, keep the child in limbo, can be most unsettling for all concerned, especially the child. This is particularly a problem in larger urban centres where busy court calendars may often result in situations where adjournments of several weeks are not uncommon, and proceedings can drag on for months. The *C.W.A.*, s. 28(13), now provides that each adjournment is limited to a maximum of 30 days, unless the parties consent to a longer adjournment. It is, however, possible for a proceeding to be adjourned several times before a trial is finally held.

The child protection authorities may wish to have the child kept in care during the adjournments if it is felt that there will be a real risk of physical or emotional harm to the child if left at home, or if there is a possibility that the parents might abscond with the child. If this is the position taken by the authorities, there must be a decision made by the judge when the child first appears in court. This will not be a complete hearing of the issues. Section 28(13) also provides that the onus will be upon the C.A.S. to "show cause" why the child should be in the care of the Society pending disposition. If the Society fails to show cause, the child will generally be returned to the charge of his parents, or the person in whose care he was, though the judge has a discretionary authority to make such order as he deems advisable, except that the child may not be kept in a training school or a similar facility. At the hearing regarding custody of the child during an adjournment, the judge may accept such evidence as he "considers credible and trustworthy in the circumstances." This means that the usual rules of evidence, discussed later in this chapter and in Chapter 8, do not apply. If the parents do not really oppose the Society, it will be sufficient to have an affidavit setting out the grounds. (An affidavit is a written statement, sworn to be true.) If the issue is contested, the Society should have some witnesses relate the reasons why they would like the child in care. As the normal rules of evidence are suspended, the witnesses can give "hearsay" evidence, relating what people who are not present — such as doctors, neighbours and others — may have told them, though the judge still has discretion in regard to the admission of evidence. The hearing regarding the temporary care of the child will normally be much shorter than the full hearing, but its outcome should not be regarded as a foregone conclusion, as the judge may order the child returned home.

If the child is placed with the child protection authority pending a full hearing, it will normally be possible for the parents to apply to the court for access privileges, that is, the right to visit their child. This will usually be granted, though if there is cause for concern, these visits may be supervised by the agency, and quite limited in nature.

Any order regarding the care of the child pending a full hearing may be reviewed or terminated, should the circumstances change.

6. Notice of the Proceeding

Since the consequences of a child protection proceeding can be extremely significant, the law requires that all concerned should have adequate notice of the fact that a hearing will occur, to allow them to participate in the hearing. The C.W.A., s. 28(7), provides that the following persons are entitled to notice:

(1) any parent of the child;

(2) any other person having actual custody of the child prior to the hearing;

(3) any foster parent whom the child lived with for a continuous six-month period immediately preceding the hearing; and

(4) the child, generally only if 10 or older, unless the judge orders otherwise.

The Act provides that the case shall not be heard unless each of these has had "reasonable notice of the hearing or . . . reasonable effort has been made" to notify the person.

The term "parent" is defined in child protection legislation to include more than simply biological parents, and includes those persons who have been actual and psychological parents to a child. This is important as it means that a potentially broad group of individuals have a right to notice of a hearing, to participate in the hearing, and to help determine the fate of the child. The *C.W.A.*, s. 19(1)(*e*), defines "parent" to include a person "who within the twelve months preceding the hearing has demonstrated a settled intention to treat the child as a child of the person's family," this being based on the definition in the *F.L.R.A.* and generally includes stepparents. A "parent" is also a guardian, one who, pursuant to a court order or a written agreement, is paying support for the child or exercising custody or access rights in regard to the child, and one who has provided the C.A.S. with a written acknowledgement of parentage; the definition also includes a person who, within the 12 months preceding the the hearing, has acknowledged that he is the father and voluntarily provided support.

Ontario is taking a leading role in recognizing the right of children to participate in protection hearings. This will be discussed further in the next section; suffice to say that any child entitled to participate in the hearing is entitled to notice of the hearing.

The form the notice is to take is provided for in regulations, and in Ontario, the notice must set out the grounds for the application. Section 28(10) of the *C.W.A.* allows the court to hear evidence not based on the grounds in the application, though if the parents are surprised by new evidence, an adjournment may be granted.

In Ontario, the Rules of Procedure of the Family Court specify that unless otherwise ordered by a judge, a Society must serve the notice of the application by leaving a copy of the notice with the persons in question. Judges are usually very concerned to ensure that parents truly have knowledge of an application, as the consequences of the proceedings are so serious. In *Re Pearson*,[24] a British Columbia case, the statute specified that the parents were to have "notification in writing of the hearing." The C.A.S. sent separate notices of the hearing to each parent by "double registered" mail, which meant that each parent had to sign an acknowledgement of receipt of the registered letters. The mother was completely dominated by her husband, and when the notices arrived at their home, the husband took the notices and refused to show them to her. He simply told her to "shut up and sign the cards." Neither parent attended the hearing, and the child was committed to the care of the C.A.S. Several years later, the mother applied to have the order set aside. On this application, the British Columbia Supreme Court ruled that the notice provided the mother was inadequate, and that the Family Court order should be quashed. The judge remarked:[25]

> It is not necessary, in my opinion, to show that the failure of the applicant to receive due notice was in some way caused by the [C.A.S.]. In cases where grave and serious questions involving important individual rights fall to be determined, it is essential that the interested parties have notice of the time and place of the hearing as well as the issues to be determined at the hearing. The mere receipt of notice in the circumstances of this case cannot be deemed to have acquainted the applicant with knowledge of the facts set out in the notice. It would of course be an entirely different matter if the applicant by neglect or indifference had failed to acquaint herself with the [facts set out in] the notice.
>
> . . . . .
>
> If personal service is made the person making the service should advise the parents (separately) of the important nature of the hearing and the results that may flow from it. In this type of case, it will be noted that many parents have limited intelligence and education and it is important that they be made fully aware of the facts referred to above.

There are two situations in which it may not be necessary to serve notice. First, pursuant to s. 28(11) of the *C.W.A.*, the court may dispense with the requirements for service if "prompt service . . . cannot be effected and any delay might endanger the health or safety of the child." This emergency situation will be discussed further below. Second, if a person cannot be located with "reasonable efforts," then the court may order some form of "substituted service," or dispense with the requirements for service altogether. "Substituted service" will be ordered if the parent cannot reasonably be served personally, that is by giving a copy of the notice to him, but it is believed that he can learn of the hearing in some other way, for example, by sending him a registered letter or advertising in newspapers. The judge will dispense with the notice requirements if there is no knowledge of the whereabouts of the parent. In *Re Pearson*,[26] it was suggested that an "exhaustive investigation" should be made to ascertain the whereabouts of the parents, even though the procedure might "cast an onerous burden on the Children's Aid Society, but it must also be realized that the failure to take such precautions may result in enormous expense and suffering."

7. Representation and Participation in the Hearing

A "party" to a court proceeding is a natural person, or corporation, participating in a proceeding with a stake in the outcome. A "party" has the right to call witnesses to testify, to cross-examine the witnesses called by other parties, to make submissions or arguments at the conclusion of the trial, and to be represented by legal counsel. A party will generally be attempting to convince the court that a certain judicial decision is appropriate. A party must be distinguished from a witness. A witness is a person who is called by a party to give testimony under oath and relate facts and opinions to the judge. A witness may state facts and opinions, but he cannot participate in the hearing beyond answering the questions put to him by the parties or the judge. There may be cases in which a witness will try to convince the court that a certain course of action is appropriate, but he still will not be a party. For example, in a protection case, a psychiatrist can be called as a witness and state that, in his professional opinion, the court should return the child to his parents, but the psychiatrist cannot then have other witnesses come and testify to support his position, though the parents may call other witnesses for this purpose. Only a party has the right to call witnesses.

A party may, of course, be a witness, though parties need not be witnesses. It should be noted that when a party is making submissions, or arguments, at the end of the case, the party, or his lawyer, is limited to summarizing or emphasizing the evidence of other witnesses and making legal arguments. The party or lawyer cannot, at that stage, start to give "evidence," that is, he cannot relate his own opinions at that stage. The distinction between "evidence" and "submissions" is discussed further in Chapter 8.

The parents of a child who is the subject of a protection hearing will be parties. It should be remembered that the definition of "parent" is broader than simply the biological parent. When the parents are living together, they will generally be treated as a single party. If, however, the parents are separated, each will have the right to be an independent party and be represented by a different lawyer. It would be improper for a single lawyer to represent parents who have conflicting views as to what is best for the child. At one time parents involved in protection proceedings had difficulty obtaining adequate legal advice; however, in most provinces there is now some form of legal aid scheme which will generally provide some type of legal representation for the parent involved in a protection proceeding.

A child protection authority is not a natural person, but rather is a legal entity, generally some form of corporation or a branch of the government. A legal entity can only act through people, "agents," who are delegated the responsibility for acting on behalf of the legal entity. Thus, the C.A.S. is nominally a party to a protection proceeding, its presence in court is made by a particular person, usually the worker or supervisor responsible for a case. This person will often be a witness, but also has the right to speak for the Society, examine witnesses and make submissions.

The C.A.S. may also have a lawyer who will present its case, examine and cross-examine witnesses and make submissions. The lawyer will be receiving his instructions from the person who has chosen to be the agent for the Society. All too often, the limited budget of a child protection authority does not permit the hiring of a lawyer to represent the authority, and the obligation for presenting the case for the agency rests upon a "court worker" or other person who lacks legal training. This situation is often unsatisfactory. In *Re R.H.M.*,[27] a judge in the Northwest Territories expressed his frustration:

Unfortunately, the evidence of the mother was not, in my respectful view, properly tested in cross-examination, nor was full or any real advantage taken by the applicant [Superintendent of Child Welfare] of his opportunity to elicit admissions and information from the mother while she was on the witness stand. I am surprised that an application of this kind, considering its evident importance if seriously intended, should not have been conducted by counsel on behalf of the applicant, there being some dozen or more competent solicitors available for the purpose at Yellowknife, exclusive of those employed by the Government of the Northwest Territories for its legal work.

The result, in my opinion, is that the application has not been nearly as fully or effectively presented or pursued as the circumstances may perhaps warrant. That this should be so where "the best interest" of a child of 13 months is at stake, is to my mind a shocking commentary on the system of priorities which provides ample legal aid for offenders against the law but none at all apparently for those attempting to protect helpless and wholly innocent children, who appear without benefit of any legal counsel before the court.

It has long been the practice, I am aware, to have these applications brought in person by child welfare workers appearing without counsel, and in my relatively brief experience as a magistrate . . . few problems of any magnitude arise where the applications are unopposed and the proper foundation for an order is provided. But it is altogether a different matter, in my opinion, where the application is contested, as here. I do not think that I can express strongly enough the need for a trained and actively practising advocate to advise and appear in court in matters of such potentially great human and social importance and delicacy, particularly where there is serious contention.

Unfortunately, the situation described in *Re R.H.M.* continues to be a problem in child protection proceedings. Gradually, however, Canadian protection authorities are obtaining proper legal assistance.

The extent to which the child who is the subject of a protection proceeding ought to participate in the proceeding is a subject which has aroused considerable controversy. Issues have included the extent to which the court should consider the express wishes of the child, legal representation for the children, and whether the child should be present at the protection hearing. Some have taken quite a conservative view, arguing that a child will invariably express a desire to remain in the familiar surroundings of his family home, regardless of how unsatisfactory these surroundings might be. A child may also tend to state a preference for a return to his home out of fear of reprisal. The Supreme Court of Canada has noted that the interests of the child should not be confused with his wishes:[28]

Nothing, in fact, seems to us less satisfactory than trying to decide as to the interest of a child in accordance with its caprice of the moment especially to deduce them from the more or less uncertain statements which it may make in Court. . . . The odds in favour of a preference for those with whom they have been accustomed to live, are overwhelming.

Similarly, many have felt that it is quite inappropriate for a child to have independent legal representation. In 1977, the Ontario Supreme Court held, in *Re Helmes*, that a judge in a protection proceeding did not have the authority to appoint the Official Guardian to act on behalf of an infant child. The court remarked:[29]

> It is further our view that the children's aid society is a society appointed by the community to act in matters to protect the interest of children. To consider the appointment in this particular case of the Official Guardian to act on behalf of the child it seems to us, that we would in effect have two parties acting on behalf of the child.

In a time of rising concern about the rights of children, these conservative views have been opposed with increasing frequency and fervency. The definition of the "best interests of the child," as contained in s. 1 of Ontario's *C.W.A.*, specifically includes as a constituent element "the views and preferences of the child, where such views and preferences can reasonably be ascertained." Although not all provinces recognize the right of children to be parties and have representation, a number of provinces, including Alberta, British Columbia, Manitoba, Nova Scotia, and Quebec have some provisions for the representation of children. In 1979, Ontario began an ambitious program of representation for children in protection proceedings. Section 20 of *C.W.A.*, imposes a duty upon a judge to determine whether legal representation for a child is appropriate, and if it is to direct that a lawyer be appointed for the child. Factors which the court will consider in determining whether representation is appropriate include whether there is an allegation of child abuse, whether the parents are not present at the hearing, and, if the child is to be removed from his home, whether the child's views differ from those expressed by the C.A.S. or his parents.

There is always some difficulty in deciding whether a child should be present at a hearing. Clearly, if a child is too young to understand the proceedings, his presence would make little sense. Further, the nature of the evidence presented might well upset the child. It is recognized, however, that as the one most intimately affected by the proceedings, the child should generally be present. Further, it is unlikely that there will be much evidence presented that the child was not aware of. Section 33 of the Act gives the judge who is hearing a case discretion to exclude a child from all, or part, of a hearing. There is a presumption that a child of 10 or more years shall be present, unless the court is satisfied that his attendance "would be injurious to the emotional health of the child." If, however, the child is under 10 years of age, there is a presumption that he should not be present unless the judge is satisfied that the proceedings would be understandable to the child and not injurious to his emotional health.

It should be understood that the questions of representation and presence at a hearing are quite distinct. A child may be present, and not represented by a lawyer; in this situation the child would simply observe the proceedings and perhaps have an opportunity to express his views to the court. It is also possible for a child to be absent and still be represented. Indeed, s. 20 of the Act suggests one factor the judge should consider in deciding whether to appoint a lawyer for a child is if he has made an order under s. 33 excluding a child over 10. In this situation, the lawyer would at least be expected to make the views of the absent child known to the court, and explain the proceedings to the child.

It must not be imagined that merely providing for the presence of the child and for legal representation resolves all of the problems concerning the participation of the child in the proceeding. On the contrary, more problems may be created than solved. It is frequently difficult for a lawyer representing a child to know what role he should adopt. Should the lawyer simply treat the child as an adult, take instructions from the child, and call evidence to support the views expressed by the child? There are problems with children who are manipulative, or who may not say what they really feel, but rather say what they expect the lawyer, or their parents, may want to hear. If the lawyer is to represent the child's interests, rather than simply his wishes, how is the lawyer to determine the child's best interest? The role of counsel for a child in a protection proceeding is still evolving and many issues remain to be resolved.

Two Ontario decisions, *Re W*[30] and *Re C*,[31] reveal the conflicting judicial attitudes towards the proper role for counsel appointed pursuant to s. 20 of the *C.W.A.*[32] In *Re W*, Judge Abella took the view that the role of the lawyer representing a child is "no different from the lawyer for any other party: He or she is there to represent a client by protecting the client's interests and carrying out the client's instructions."[33] Judge Abella discussed the problems which could arise in the context of a protection proceeding:[34]

> There must undoubtedly be a degree of flexibility in a child's lawyer's role as articulator of his or her client's wishes. The child may be unable to instruct counsel. Or the child may be, as in this case, ambivalent about her wishes. Or the child may be too young. Although there should be no minimum age below which a child's wishes should be ignored — so long as the child is old enough to express them, they should be considered — I feel that where a child does not or cannot express wishes, the role of the child's lawyer should be to protect the client/child's interests. In the absence of clear instructions, protecting the client's interests can clearly involve presenting the lawyer's perception of what would best protect the child's interests. In this latter role of promulgating the infant client's best interests, the lawyer would attempt to guarantee that all the evidence the court needs to make a disposition which accommodates the child's best interests is before the court, is complete and accurate. There could in this kind of role be no inconsistency between what is perceived by the lawyer to be the child's best interests and the child's instructions. Where there is such conflict, the wishes of the child should prevail in guiding the lawyer.
>
> In the case of a child who is capable of coherent expression the lawyer's role in representing the child's wishes does not preclude the lawyer from exploring with the child the merits or realities of the case, evaluating the practicalities of the child's position and even offering, where appropriate,

suggestions about possible reasonable resolutions to the case. Offering
advice is part of the lawyer's obligation to protect the client's interests.
Obviously, however, given the vulnerability of most children to authority
in general and given the shattered sensibilities in family disputes in
particular, great sensitivity should be exercised during these exploratory
sessions. The lawyer should be constantly conscious of his or her posture
being an honest but not an overwhelming one.

In *Re C*, Judge Karswick expressed a very different view of the role counsel for
a child was expected to play. The judge stressed that the lawyer must communicate
the views and preferences to the court, and to adduce appropriate evidence, through
examination and cross-examination of witnesses, to establish a basis for the child's
views. He noted:[35]

> . . . a real difficulty arises where counsel feels that the child's instructions
> or expressed views and preferences are not in accord with the child's
> best interest. In those circumstances does counsel have an obligation to
> advocate the child's stated position or does he have the obligation to also
> state his own views of what is in the best interest of the child, discuss
> the evidence in support of that position and adduce all evidence which
> bears on the issue of the best interest of the child, even though it may be
> unfavourable to the child's views, preferences or instructions?

The judge took the position that the lawyer was not simply to act on the basis of
the child's wishes:[36]

> It can be acknowledged that the views and preferences of a child are not
> necessarily the determining factor in deciding the issue of custody but
> simply one important element among a number of others that have to be
> considered in resolving the crucial issue. When one considers the fundamental
> importance of this issue of custody for both the family and the community
> I do not think that the court can, nor should it, direct the child's counsel
> to take a strict adversarial role and act as a "mouthpiece", blindly advocating
> a view, preference or instructions which confound or shock his professional
> opinion of what is in the best interest of the child. It makes eminently
> good sense to have counsel takes an active, real and positive role in the
> social context of the family court and, as officers of this court, assume the
> obligation to adduce all relevant and material evidence on the issue of
> what is in the best interest of the child and, when called upon, to express
> a professional and responsible view of what that disposition should be.

Judge Karswick went on to express his views about the role of all of the lawyers
in a protection proceeding, and these views must be regarded as being, at the least,
controversial:[37]

> Considering the special role of the Family Court in the community and its
> special social objectives. I do not think that the community will accept

counsel who vigorously, insensitively and haughtily project the traditional adversarial role of a "mouthpiece" for some narrow interest. I think that such an adversarial posture by counsel would be detrimental and undermining to the family court in attempting to achieve its social and community objectives. The parents' counsel have the same role and responsibility as does counsel for the Official Guardian [representing the child] and counsel for the children's aid societies. All counsel have the duty of advocating and expressing the instructions, views and preferences of their clients, be they parents, children or societies, but they also have the professional and social duty of ensuring that all relevant evidence is adduced, that no such evidence is suppressed and, further, to be prepared to give an honest and professional statement of what they feel is in the best interest of the child and the reasons for that position.

By expressing the view that all counsel, and not simply counsel for the child, must somehow be "above the fray" Judge Karswick did more than disagree with Judge Abella. He expressed a view quite at odds with the traditional view of the role of lawyers in Family Courts. While his views about the roles of counsel for the parents and the C.A.S. may be considered enlightened and progressive by some, they are clearly minority views, and if adopted would require change in present practices.

It seems clear that the nature of the role will vary with the nature of the issues facing the court, and with the age of the child, and his capacity to instruct counsel.[38] It is also clear that to do an effective job in representing children, lawyers will need greater access to various support services and to specialized training to deal with young clients. It is encouraging to note that the legal profession in Canada is beginning to respond to these demands through the introduction of legal texts, law school courses and continuing legal education seminars concerning the legal problems of children.[39]

There may be others besides parents, child protection authorities, and children who have an interest in the outcome of a child welfare hearing. In Re E.W.Z.[40] the grandparents of the child appeared and wished to be treated as parties. The judge noted that other relatives or friends with whom the child may have lived, or professionals who were involved with the child might also wish to become parties to the hearing. He held Ontario's legislation allowed the judge a discretion to allow participation by whomever he felt appropriate. It is not clear whether this decision will be followed in other provinces, or even whether, due to amendments in the province's child protection legislation, it is still the law in Ontario, but it certainly marks an encouraging start in the effort to provide the court with as much information as possible before a child's life is vitally affected.[41] As we shall see, in Ontario the court may order that a child in need of protection be placed with a person other than a parent, for example, with a grandparent, and so the possibility of participating and being able to advocate such a placement in a protection hearing may be very significant.

Many of the children who are found to be in need of protection are placed with foster parents under the auspices of child protection authorities. Often a child stays with a single set of foster parents for years, in some cases eventually being adopted by the foster parents. On applications to determine whether a child should continue to be in the care of child welfare authorities, foster parents are frequently called as witnesses to describe the progress and condition of the child, or to relate state-ments made by the child, but they have had no particular legal status. Section 28(9) of the *C.W.A.*, now gives some status to a foster parent who has cared for the child for a continuous period of at least six months immediately before the hearing. Such a foster parent is entitled to notice of the hearing and may appear, if desired with a lawyer, give evidence, and make representations. Unless there are unusual circumstances, the judge will not allow the foster parent to have the full status of a party, with the right to call other witnesses or cross-examine witnesses. It is heartening that the people who, in many cases, have had the closest contact with a child have at least a limited right to participate in a hearing, though since foster parents are under the supervision of the C.A.S., there will probably be many situations in which their positions will not vary significantly from those of the Society.

8. Preparation for the Hearing

After the child protection authorities decide to bring a matter to court, they have to begin the process of preparing for court. If it appears likely that the case will result in a contested hearing, there will have to be more preparation. If a lawyer will be representing the authority, he will be contacted and the case will be dis-cussed. The file will be reviewed, the potential witnesses contacted and interviewed. Similarly, the lawyer for the parents will be preparing his case.

It is recognized that the adversarial system can only operate effectively if each side knows the type of case it must present, and the type of case the other side will be presenting. The adversarial system is, in a sense, a contest, but it is not a contest which should be won by surprising an opponent with evidence which he had no reason to expect. The opposing parties will usually discuss a case before court, narrow the issues and agree to certain facts which are not in dispute. It is generally accepted that there should be some disclosure of the type of evidence which each party intends to rely upon, and that in particular the child protection authorities, who after all are agents of the state, have a duty to disclose information about the nature of their case. After a protection hearing which lasted eight days, the judge in *Re Jamie*[42] remarked: "the length of time required to complete this trial points out the need for some type of pre-trial conferencing, disclosure and negotiation in these matters. It would be hard to measure the strain on the mother that such a protracted hearing causes."

Some provinces, such as Manitoba and Ontario, have formal "discovery" pro-cedures which provide each party with an opportunity to gain information about the case of the other party. This includes the right to conduct an examination of the other party under oath. This "examination for discovery" is not conducted in a court, but simply in the presence of the lawyers and a stenographer. The parents personally may be subject to examination, and the C.A.S. will be represented by an agent, usually the worker or supervisor handling the case. If necessary, a transcript of the examination can be prepared; a witness will be subject to searching cross-examination at trial if there is a significant discrepancy between the statements made at discovery and those offered at the hearing. Section 50(1) of Ontario's *C.W.A.* gives the C.A.S. the authority to apply to the court for an order allowing inspection of any records, writings or documents "relevant to an investigation to determine whether abuse has been or is likely to be inflicted on [a] child." This applies notwithstanding the fact that these documents may be otherwise confidential, and should assist the C.A.S. in obtaining medical and other evidence. This power can be used both to assist in preparing for trial and for investigating a case when considering whether a child should be apprehended.

9. Privacy of the Hearing

Most courts are open to the public. It is an accepted tenet of our democratic society that justice must not only be done, it must be seen to be done. Many trials involve the intimate aspects of the lives of the participants, including cases concerning matrimonial disputes and sex offences; yet generally these trials are open to the public and may be widely broadcast through the media. It is felt that citizens in a democracy have a right to know what is happening in the courts, and the dangers of secret trials are well known. Against this must be balanced a recognition of the highly personal nature of matters dealt with in protection proceedings, the potentially traumatizing effects on a child of testifying in a court, particularly if open to the public, and the adverse effects on parents and child which would result from public knowledge of involvement in such a proceeding. As a result, access to protection hearings is limited, but there is some scope for the public obtaining information about the proceedings.

Section 57(1) of the *C.W.A.* specifies that proceedings under the Act are to be held in a special building (Family Court), or in the private office of a judge, and shall not be held in premises ordinarily used for adult criminal trials. Generally only the parties involved, their legal representatives, and various court and government officials may be present in court. The witnesses will usually only be present while they are testifying. The judge has a discretion to allow other persons to be present, having regard to the wishes and interests of the parties, and whether the presence of such people would be injurious to the emotional health of the child. The judge would probably exercise his discretion to allow the presence of a person who might be supportive of the child, for example, an aunt, or to allow a social work student to attend to further his education. Neighbours and the simply curious would, however, doubtless be excluded. Section 57 (4) provides that representatives of the media may attend a hearing, subject to judicial discretion to exclude them if their presence or the reporting "would be injurious to the emotional health of any child before the court." It is an offence to publish or make public any information which might identify any of the participants or witnesses in a protection proceeding. Thus, the privacy of the individuals concerned may be protected, while at the same time the public may be informed of the general nature of the protection proceedings.

10. Evidence in a Protection Hearing

As was discussed, there are two basic issues in a protection hearing. Is the child in need of protection? And if so, what type of order should be made to promote the child's best interests? Usually evidence will be heard on both issues at once, and the same type of evidence is relevant to both issues. The factors which influence a decision as to what type of order will be made are considered in the next section. Generally, the more detrimental a situation appears to be to the safety or well-being of a child, the more likely that the child will be found to be in need of protection, and removed from the deleterious home environment.

The nature of the evidence which will influence the court depends very much on the facts of a particular case. Different evidence will be significant depending upon whether the case involves physical, mental or emotional deprivation, or some form of neglect, or it involves abandonment or desertion of the child. Frequently, a child protection case may be like a jigsaw puzzle with evidence being given of several different but related problems. Each witness may shed light on these problems from a different angle. A neighbour may testify about seeing the parent strike the child, about the apparent lack of affection shown towards the child. A doctor and a psychologist might then testify about the consequences of these incidents from their perspectives.

Evidence is usually presented in court by means of oral testimony of witnesses, though use may also be made of "affidavits," which are written, signed statements sworn to be true, and of other documents. The presentation of evidence and the laws of evidence are more fully discussed in Chapter 8.

Witnesses for the child protection authority will invariably include the protection workers who have been involved with a family, and frequently there may be people who have had direct contact with the children, such as foster parents. Representatives of various agencies and institutions in the community may also be called to testify. They might include teachers, policemen, and probation officers. Lay people who have had contact with the family, such as friends, relatives and neighbours, may be witnesses. Finally, the child protection authority might wish to rely on the testimony of various "experts," such as doctors, psychiatrists or psychologists. As we shall consider in Chapter 8, courts frequently place considerable reliance on the opinions of expert witnesses when attempting to make a decision about a child's future. The total number of witnesses heard in a case will depend on the complexity of the issues and the number of persons the family has had contact with. It can range from one to over 20. Though it is difficult to generalize, in most contested cases there will be fewer than 10 witnesses.

As was discussed earlier in this chapter, there is an onus upon the child protection authority to prove its case, and this may not be an easy onus to overcome. In the words of the judge in *Re Brown*:[43]

> . . . the community ought not interfere merely because our institutions may be able to offer a greater opportunity to the children to achieve their potential. Society's interference in the natural family is only justified when the level of care of the children falls below that which no child in this country should be subjected to.

It is often very difficult for the court to determine what is the minimum standard of care which every child in the country is entitled to receive. It is recognized that the implicit formulation of such a standard are social and cultural values, and the courts are reluctant to impose the views and values of the middle-class majority on others. These difficulties can be illustrated by considering a few cases.

In *Re Warren*,[44] the C.A.S. was seeking Crown wardship of three children aged four, six and 12. The witnesses for the Society included three police officers, a teacher, a public health nurse, a psychologist, a city welfare worker and three protection workers from the C.A.S. The mother had an intelligence level at the upper end of the mentally defective range, and had a "primitively organized personality, basically hostile and defensive."Her husband was of near normal intelligence, but had "complex personality needs." The parents had a history of alcoholism and continuous fighting, fighting which often resulted in the intervention of the police. The family's income level was low, and apparently augmented by defrauding the welfare authorities. The children had emotional problems and lagging intellectual development. They had not suffered from deliberate ill-treatment at the hands of their parents, but the parents had often ignored their physical needs. They had inadequate diets and were often clothed in a poor way. The oldest child, a girl, had a poor school attendance record, with "minimal" academic progress, and had "overwhelming affectional needs" which were evidenced by her sexual activity. The children had been in the care of the C.A.S. for over a year preceding the hearing. At the hearing in question, the issue was whether the children should become Crown wards, effectively severing the parental tie. The oldest child took the witness-stand to testify that she loved her parents and wished to return home. The judge ordered that the children be made Crown wards. He found the decision a difficult one to make, remarking:[45]

> In a hearing such as this there is danger in over-reliance upon any group of witnesses selfconscious respecting their professionalization. I resolved not to fall victim to this specific bias of the profession, the group psychology of the social workers . . . The conclusions which follow have been reached painfully by me after a painstaking consideration of the evidence in its totality and after a conscientious attempt to weigh that evidence. . . .
>
> It was manifest from the opening that this was a contest between the right of a subsocio-economic family to subsist together and the right of the public, represented by the Children's Aid Society, to insist upon higher

standards of parental care than the couple in question were capable of offering. Many witnesses called for the Society were persons of superior education with post-graduate degrees in social work or some other related specialty. One could not listen to their testimony with all the somber implications of this application without resolving that this Court must not be persuaded to impose unrealistic or unfair middle class standards of child care upon a poor family of extremely limited potential.

In *C.A.S. of Kingston v. Reeves*,[46] the Society sought to take a two-and-one-half-year-old girl into care on a Crown wardship application, with a view to placing the child for adoption. The parents, who had been living in a common-law relationship, were of quite low intelligence, and had "difficulty providing consistent care and attention to the child." Their relationship was characterized by recurrent instability, and they were separated at the time of hearing. The parents were separately represented at the hearing, each lawyer taking the position that the child should be returned to his client under supervision. The little girl had been subject to a supervision order for a year preceding the Crown wardship application, and the family had received considerable support from various community agencies in the areas of daycare, housing, budget counselling, and home-making. The parents, and in particular the father, made considerable progress while the child was subject to a supervisory order. The judge decided that the child should not be removed from parental care, and ordered that she be placed with her father, subject to C.A.S. supervision. The judge expressed concern that it seemed that the father might place reconciliation with his wife before caring for the child, and that the care of the child tended to deteriorate when the parents were together. The judge had some interesting comments on the difficulties facing a judge who must decide whether a child should remain with parents of low intelligence:[47]

> As we enter the age of genetic engineering, it is ironic and yet also comforting to know that we have become increasingly uncertain about the skills and characteristics necessary to perform the role of parent in an adequate fashion. Throughout the child protection and delinquency fields, there is constant questioning of the values and moral principles which underlie the decision to remove children from their parents. Being poor, or unwed or espousing other than middle-class values and beliefs no longer induces the somewhat automatic response it may have in the past. Perhaps the most important recent development in the child-care field has been the growing commitment to prevention work, to family rehabilitation rather than removal from the home. It is recognized that children should be permanently removed from the home only when the factors which have produced an environment of risk to the physical or mental health of the child cannot be ameliorated by help given to that child and those who care for him or her. . . .
> The issue of parenthood and the mentally retarded has been a difficult one for several decades. We have progressed from an earlier attitude which rested heavily upon isolation, institutionalization and compulsory

sterilization as the means of dealing with the question. . . . Now the trend
is away from the use of institutions . . . and away from broad resort to
the power to sterilize. . . . At the same time, it is recognized "that mentally
retarded persons who experience severe difficulties in the management
of their affairs make inadequate parents, not from any lack of affection for
their children, but because they are unable to cope with the pressures of
parenthood" . . . Concern for the rights of persons with low intelligence
must be accompanied by an equal concern for the dangers, both physical
and mental, to children raised by parents who are unequal to the task.
Needless to say, it has been difficult to find the proper balance between
these sometimes competing principles . . .

. . . the fact of low parental intelligence should not be taken as determinative
in itself of the child's need for protection. Rather, the question should be
one of deciding whether, in the light of their individual capabilities, these
parents are able to meet their parental responsibilities. If the answer to
this question is no, then the judge should decide whether, given the proper
assistance and intervention, the parents can be provided with the tools
necessary to care adequately for their child. This issue should not be resolved
by simply noting the difficulties involved in securing the needed help
when the child remains within the home. The actions of the persons involved
in this case show that, with a co-ordinated effort, extensive assistance
can be given to parents such as the Reeves. Only if it is felt that the risk
to the child is too great, even with outside help, should the court remove
the child from the home. . . . I think that it should also be noted that
the risk to the child need not be physical; it would seem to be understandable
that if a child lives in an environment which is grossly deficient in
stimulation and emotional involvement, he or she may be damaged or at
least may fail to develop to the extent to which he or she is capable. It
is difficult to apply this known fact to individual cases but clearly the
court's perspective should be broader than a simple examination of the
child's physical health. It may be that the child's intelligence and capabilities,
if known, would be relevant information when deciding whether the
parents are able to care adequately care for the child. If, even with outside
help, it appears to the judge that they are not able to perform the task,
an order removing the child would be indicated.

. . . . .

. . . the Society has quite rightly argued that it should not be necessary to
wait until serious harm has been done before the child is removed, if
the evidence points to real risk of that harm taking place.

There continues to be disagreement among experts about virtually every aspect
of child care, for example, toilet-training, nutrition, and education. It is hardly
surprising that judges tend to take a conservative approach when considering
whether the parents' conduct is so unacceptable that their child ought to be removed
from their care. One area of considerable controversy is that of discipline. All
experts agree that it is important to set limits for children and exercise control over

their activities. It is clearly inappropriate to permanently maim or injure a child in the course of disciplining the child, but it is not clear how far parents ought to be allowed to go in using physical force to control their children. This issue will be considered at the end of this chapter in terms of possible criminal sanctions for the abusing parent, and will be discussed here in terms of the protection proceeding.

In *Re O.*,[48] the court was concerned with three children, a girl in her early teens and two younger siblings. They lived with their mother, and her common-law husband. The "parents" had subjected the children to "stern physical discipline," including striking the children on the buttocks and upper rear thigh with a belt, wooden spoon, or open hand, and "cuffing" them with an open hand on the head and shoulders for minor breaches of rules. These incidents were accompanied by a discussion of the problem precipitating the discipline. The judge found that this treatment was not a sufficient basis for a finding that the children were in need of protection, though for other reasons the oldest girl was taken into care. On the issue of parental discipline, the judge commented:[49]

> The test to be applied by this court is one of reasonableness of the degree of physical discipline applied. Physical punishment was inflicted on the three children by parents who were concerned for their well-being and motivated to discipline only. There is some repugnance in the image of a fully grown, physically capable adult inflicting physical punishment on a child; however, the court cannot impose its own subjective standards but must impose a reasonable objective standard in determining the degree of physical punishment to be allowed by the general standards of the community. . . . While I question the use of implements in physical discipline and "cuffing" about the head, I find such physical discipline was imposed in a manner that was meaningful, intermittent and within the bounds of reasonable parental discretion.

In *Re O.*, the judge did not consider what various experts had to say about parental discipline, though clearly the parties might have chosen to call psychologists or others to give testimony on this issue. Rather, the judge relied upon his own knowledge of the "general standards of the community" to determine whether the conduct of the parents was such that the children should be found to be in need of protection. Arguably, there are dangers in selecting such a standard. It may be that in certain small and isolated communities, the general community standard is unacceptable, and so a broad definition of "community" may be required. Perhaps more seriously, there may be cause for concern if all parents are expected in all matters to conform to the "general standards of the community." This might infringe upon the freedom to raise one's child as one sees fit, especially for various social, ethnic or religious minorities.

In *Re M.*,[50] the Alberta child protection authorities had apprehended two children found in the care of their father. At the time of their birth, both parents had been members of the Alpha and Omega Order, a religious cult allegedly based on humanitarian principles and a belief in Christ. The Order had denied the mother contact with her children for three years; she then left the cult, and made efforts to be reunited with her children. The children had been legally in the custody of their father for several years, though in fact most of the care was provided through various communal arrangements. The cult had an authoritarian structure and strict rules about most aspects of life, including child rearing. Contact and emotional attachments between natural parents and their children were strongly discouraged. Discipline was strict, including very early toilet-training, severe reprimands by groups of adults yelling at a child in the centre of a human circle, and spanking, though there was no serious physical abuse. For religious reasons the children were not immunized or innoculated. Psychologists testified that the children were "emotionally blunted," apparently as a result of "harsh, authoritarian types of upbringing." The court found that the children were in need of protection, and made the children legal wards of the protection authorities, but with a recommendation that they be returned to their mother. The judge found that the children had suffered "emotional abuse" while in the care of their father, stating:[51] "From my research it appears that legal experts lag behind child development specialists who for years have been structuring a psychological nomenclature and gathering empirical data on emotional neglect and abuse." The judge had to deal with the argument that the state ought not to interfere in the father's personal and religious affairs. The judge commented:[52]

> I do not in any way reject the right of religion with respect to these movements. Freedom of religion is well protected in the province of Alberta through its Alberta Bill of Rights . . . which is almost identical to s. 1 of the Canadian Bill of Rights. . . . Freedom does not, however, include absolute freedom, especially when it comes to the rights of children, their best interests or welfare. Certainly the religious concern of each person is a personal matter, but the concern for children's upbringing is society's major concern . . . The Alpha and Omega Order has a right to an untrammelled religious belief, but it steps over its bounds when it creates an atmosphere which is not conducive to allowing a child to reach his potential on an individual basis. It cannot be stated too often that it is the child's interests that are at stake, and it should be remembered by members of the legal profession that the rule in neglect cases must be utilized as a protection of the child and not necessarily as a bulwark for the rights of parenthood.

From a consideration of these few cases, it can be seen that the type of evidence which the child protection authorities will have to bring to the court to prove their case will depend very much on the basis of their case.

Thus far we have been discussing the types of evidence which the child welfare authorities will adduce to show that a child is in need of protection. Brief consideration will now be given to the type of evidence which the parents may wish to present to the court, though it should be noted that there is no legal obligation upon the parents to bring evidence to the court. Frequently, much of the parents' case will involve challenging the testimony of the witnesses put forward by the child protection authority. The accuracy of the witnesses' memory or perception may be questioned. Incidents which appear inconsistent with the views of these witnesses may be used to confront them. The honesty or sincerity of the witnesses may be challenged, especially if they are neighbours or relatives who may have a personal interest in the outcome of the proceedings.

The parents may also call their own witnesses to support the view that they are good parents. Often these will be lay people, such as friends, neighbours or relatives, though they may also be people with some professional background, such as a family doctor, a priest or minister, or a teacher.

Lawyers who represent parents in protection proceedings are starting to make use of their own expert witnesses, witnesses who may challenge the views put forward by experts who are suggesting that the child is in need of protection. Experts in the same field can have quite different views of the same case. The parents may present a psychiatric or psychological assessment of their child to contrast with an assessment done by an expert retained by the child protection authorities. It must be remembered, however, that the evidence adduced by the parents need not show that they are model or even average parents. Rather, it must simply demonstrate that the situation is not so unsatisfactory that the child should be found to be in need of protection.

11. Types of Orders

After hearing the evidence, the judge must determine whether the child is in need of protection. The judge may determine that the child is not in any danger at home, simply dismiss the application, and have the child returned to the person in whose care he was prior to the hearing. If the judge finds that the child is in need of protection, he faces three basic options in most provinces: keeping the child under official supervision, but not in the actual care of the child protection authority; temporarily removing the child from parental care and placing the child in the care of the child welfare authorities; and, finally, effectively severing the parental tie and placing the child permanently in care, perhaps for eventual adoption. Ontario's C.W.A sets out these alternatives in s. 30(1). Before examining the factors which influence the choice of which of these different orders will be made, the nature of these different orders will be considered.

The "supervision order" is the least serious order which can be made. The child remains at home and the disruption of his life is minimal. A protection worker will have the right to visit the home as often as seems necessary, ranging from once a month to every day. On these visits, the worker will monitor the home situation, ensuring the risks the child faces are minimized. The worker may also provide material supports, such as assistance in obtaining housing or medical care, and will generally provide some form of counselling to assist the parents in dealing with the problems which led to the child being found to be in need of protection. The worker will also provide some assistance in improving child care practices. The judge may impose various conditions on the placement of the child in the home, for example, that the child attend daycare, or the parents attend a child care course. Section 30(1) of the Act provides that the child may be "placed with or returned to the child's parent or other person." Thus, it is possible in Ontario, though not in most other provinces, for a judge to use a protection order to take a child out of his home, but not place him directly in the care of the C.A.S. Such an order may be made to place a child with a grandparent, or to take a child, who is subject to a custody order, and place him with the non-custodial parent.

In Ontario, legislation provides that the initial length of a supervision order will be from six to 12 months, though there are provisions for the early termination of such an order, and for its renewal.

Under a "temporary wardship order," legal custody and guardianship over a child is transferred from the parents to a child protection authority. The authority may then exercise most of the rights which are usually exercised by parents, for example, having the right to consent to medical treatment for the child, and the right to decide where the child will reside. We will consider the way in which a child in care is treated a little later; suffice to say that most children are in foster homes, homes where families agree to take in one or more children in need of protection in return for a small daily payment, and in group homes, which are houses where a small group of children, usually numbering five to 10, live under the care of a full-time paid staff. Some children in care are kept in larger institutions. It is also possible for a temporary ward to be placed back in his own home, and still remain a ward. This situation is superficially similar to that arranged by a supervision order, except that under a supervision order, if the protection authority feels that the situation has deteriorated and the child should be taken into care, there must then be a full hearing. On the other hand, if a temporary ward is placed back with his family, then legal guardianship continues to rest with the protection authority, and the child may be moved at any time without a further court order.

The parental tie may be effectively severed by having an order made that the child be permanently placed in the care of protection authorities. In a number of provinces this is referred to as "Crown wardship." A Crown ward will reside in a foster home, a group home, or an institutional setting. A Crown wardship order may be terminated by court order, and terminates in any event when a child becomes an adult, in Ontario at age 18.

The issues of whether a child is in need of protection and what is the appropriate disposition are theoretically distinct. Though evidence is usually heard about both issues simultaneously, it is possible for a judge to make a finding that a child is in need of protection, and then adjourn the application for further evidence to be heard on the question of disposition.[53] Such an adjournment will be likely if the judge would like to hear evidence which was not available at the initial hearing. Section 29(1) of Ontario's *C.W.A.* provides that once a child has been found to be in need of protection, the court may order an assessment to be made of the child, or his parent(s), or any other person in whose care the child has been or may be. This may be a medical, emotional, developmental, psychological, or social assessment. The assessment is to be carried out by a person designated by the court, and may be used by the court as a basis for its decision, though subject to rebuttal by the parties.

Once the presumption of parental fitness has been overcome and a child has been found to be in need of protection, a judge will make a decision as to what type of order is appropriate by determining what is in the child's "best interests." The term "best interests of the child" has already been discussed in Chapter 3 in the context of custody disputes between parents, and as noted there, is a vague expression, with a meaning that varies according to the circumstances. In Ontario, for the purposes of the C.W.A., s. 1(b) provides that "in addition to all other relevant considerations," a court shall consider the following:

(i)   the mental, emotional and physical needs of the child and the appropriate care or treatment . . . to meet such needs,

(ii) the child's opportunity to enjoy a parent–child relationship and to be a wanted and needed member within a family structure,

(iii) the child's mental, emotional and physical stages of development,

(iv) the effect upon the child of any disruption of the child's sense of continuity,

(v)   the merits of any plan proposed by the agency . . . compared with the merits of the child returning to or remaining with his or her parent,

(vi) the views and preferences of the child, where such views and preferences can reasonably be ascertained,

(vii) the effect upon the child of any delay in the final disposition in the proceedings,

(viii) any risk to the child of returning the child to or allowing the child to remain in the care of his or her parent.

Though most other provinces do not have a statutorily articulated definition of "best interests," it seems likely that these factors would be considered by any court when deciding what disposition is appropriate for a child found to be in need of protection.

The tremendous advantage of a supervision order is that the child is kept in his home, and his life is not totally disrupted. If a child is removed from his home, it may be difficult to reintegrate him at a later date. Further, as long as the child is at home, the protection worker will inevitably be working closely with the family as a unit, whereas if the child is removed from the home, there is a tendency to be less involved with the family, and to focus upon the child in care. As suggested in the passage quoted from *C.A.S. of Kingston v. Reeves*, unless there is a clear risk to a child, there will be an initial tendency to keep the child in the home, and attempt to resolve the problems of the family as a functioning unit. Section 30(5) of the *C.W.A.* provides that in deciding what type of order to make, the judge shall investigate what efforts have been made to assist the child in his home; if greater efforts could be reasonably expected, a supervision order will be made unless there is a danger in having the child at home.

Notwithstanding the disruption which removal from the home can cause the child, sometimes this is necessary. There may be a real risk of physical or emotional abuse if a child remains with his parents. The parents may be unable to cope with the child at the time, and a period of separation will provide needed "breathing space." If the judge decides to remove the child from the home, he must decide whether this arrangement will be permanent, or whether it should be temporary. This decision will be based upon an assessment of whether the situation at home can be improved, and if so, how long will it take. There is a tendency to give parents a chance to improve, and to try a temporary order before permanently severing the parent–child relationship. Each case must, however, be decided on its facts. In *Minister of Social Services v. Geiger*,[54] the judge commented:

> The evidence leads me to the conclusion that the parents of these two girls were not able, are not able, and will not be able, to provide for these two girls so that they will not be in need of protection . . . I am satisfied that no satisfactory improvement of home conditions is possible. While the easier course would be to agree with the temporary committal, I think that temporary committal would simply keep the matter in abeyance without any real hope of improvement.

In *C.A.S. of Winnipeg v. Forth*,[55] the judge remarked:

> It seems to me that in every case where a permanent order is being considered there are certain basic factors that the court must consider. They include:
> (a) The age of the child.
> (b) A permanent order separates a child from siblings permanently. Are there siblings at home?
> (c) Will the child's chances for adoption be *significantly* reduced by the delay of a temporary order?
> (d) Do the child's *long-term* needs require particular and/or special attention that will *always* be unavailable to him in his home?
> (e) What care will be available to the child during the currency of a temporary order?
> (f) Is there a *real* likelihood that the factors justifying the granting of a temporary order will change?
> (g) Has the apprehending authority taken every *reasonable* step to re-unite parent and child?

The question of whether the situation is likely to change is often difficult to resolve. Invariably the parents will testify that they are prepared to do virtually anything to keep their child, but the judge must decide whether they really have the capacity to change.

An important consideration in determining whether the tie with the natural parents should be severed is whether the child is likely to be adopted. If adoption is probable, a permanent order is more likely, as this will facilitate the efforts of the child protection authority in finding a new home in which the child can re-establish familial ties. Adoption is most likely if the child is very young and has not had time to establish close ties with his natural family. Adoption is also more likely to occur if the child is not suffering from physical or emotional problems.

12. Appeals

If a party to an action is dissatisfied with the decision of the trial judge who initially heard the case, then the party may seek to appeal the decision. In most civil and criminal cases, an appeal will not constitute a new trial, with witnesses being called to testify again and a completely new decision being made. Rather an appeal is argued on the basis of the "transcript," a written record of the original proceedings, and of the various documents filed at the trial. The appellate judge is only concerned with determining whether the trial judge misapplied a legal principle, took into account an irrelevant factor, or failed to take into account a material one. The appellate court will generally be reluctant to interfere with an exercise of discretion by the trial judge, especially in cases involving the care of infants. In *McKee v. McKee*, a custody dispute between parents, the court enunciated the general principle in these terms:[56]

> . . . the question of custody of an infant is a matter which peculiarly lies
> within the discretion of the learned Judge, who hears the case and has
> the opportunity generally denied to an appellate tribunal of seeing the parties
> and investigating the infant's circumstances, and . . . his decision should
> not be disturbed unless he has clearly acted on some wrong priciple or
> disregarded material evidence.

Ontario has a statutory provision which may give a judge hearing an appeal in a protection case a greater opportunity to promote the welfare of the child; in other provinces Appellate Courts have similar discretionary powers. Section 43(8) of the C.W.A. allows the judge hearing an appeal, in addition to relying on the written record of the trial, to receive "further evidence relating to matters both preceding and subsequent to the . . . decision being appealed." Making use of this provision can cause some difficulties as the appellate judge may have to compare information received from a somewhat dry, written record with that forcefully presented by a witness in court. As a result, there is some reluctance to make extensive use of this unique provision, however, it will be invoked to facilitate a full inquiry because it is recognized that circumstances may drastically change between the times of trial and appeal in a protection proceeding.

An appellate judge has the authority to make a decision as to the matters at issue, and in a protection appeal this is what is usually done in the interests of expendiency. Alternatively, the case may be referred back to the original court for a new hearing, with directions in regard to the error made at the initial hearing.

In Ontario, appeals are governed by s. 43 of the Act, which provides that a party wishing to appeal has 30 days from the date of the order appealed to file the necessary documents. The time-limit may be extended, but no extension may be granted if the child has been placed for adoption by the C.A.S. In the past there were difficulties in determining what should happen to the child while the appeal procedure was going on; the appeal process can be quite slow, and it was generally several months before an appeal was completed. If a child was apprehended by the C.A.S. and the trial judge did not make an order placing the child with the Society, it was not clear whether the child should be returned to the parents pending the hearing of the appeal.[57] Section 43 now provides that where an appeal is launched to the County Court, there may be a speedy hearing before the County Court Judge to determine what provisions for the temporary care of the child will be best for the child. Thus, even if the C.A.S. failed to satisfy the trial judge of the dangers inherent in a home situation, it may still be possible to keep the child from the home pending an appeal.

E. THE CHILD IN CARE

1. The Legal Status of a Ward

Once a child is placed in the care of a protection authority, most of the legal incidents of parenthood are exercised by the authority, though as we shall see the natural parents may retain certain rights, such as visiting rights, and certain responsibilities, such as the obligation to pay support. Sections 40 and 41 of the C.W.A. provide that legal guardianship over a ward rests in the C.A.S., though in the case of Crown wards this guardianship may be exercised by some other agency, such as a mental health facility. The Society having guardianship will exercise various parental functions, such as deciding about the child's education, medical treatment and residence. Once a child is in the care of the C.A.S., parental involvement in the child's life may be quite limited. Section 46 is directed towards minimizing interference with wards. Except as permitted by the C.A.S. or by a court order, it is an offence to visit, write to, telephone or communicate with a child in care, or to interfere with the activities of a foster parent. It is also an offence to induce, or attempt to induce, a child to leave the care of the Society, or to remove, or attempt to remove, a child from the Society's care. Section 46 is clearly directed at parents who might wish to sabotage the efforts of the C.A.S., and violations are punishable by a fine up to $1000, or imprisonment of up to one year, or both.

An initial temporary wardship order may be for a period of up to 12 months. Section 37 provides that the C.A.S. may bring the case back to court for a review at any time, and in any event, must do so before the initial order expires. The parents, and child, if 12 or older, have a right to have the matter brought back to court for review every six months. At a review hearing the judge may extend the temporary wardship, order Crown wardship, send the child home under a supervision order, or terminate official involvement. Though a review hearing is, in many ways, similar to an initial application, essentially being an inquiry into the suitability of the child's home environment, there tends to be a different focus of concern. The courts[58] have consistently focused their attention on developments since the initial order was made. The issue of whether the child is in need of protection has already been decided and is not to be relitigated. Rather, the court will make a decision based upon an assessment of the "best interests" of the child, without ignoring the parents' rights.

There is one very significant limitation upon a judge's powers at a review hearing. No child in Ontario may be in care for more than 24 successive months without being made a Crown ward. The time in care includes periods under voluntary care agreements and pending adjournments, as well as the time spent as a temporary ward. Thus a series of temporary wardship orders may be made at successive review hearings, but they cannot provide for more than a total of 24 months in care. The rationale for this limitation is that this form of care is seen as temporary, and should only be provided pending some improvement in the home situation which will allow the child to return home. A child should not be left in these indefinite and uncertain circumstances for more than two years. Both the parents and the C.A.S. have a definite time frame within which improvements must be made, or the child must be made a Crown ward and permanent arrangements made.

Legislation in other provinces also provides for a review of temporary wardship orders, though the law concerning the number of renewals varies from province to province. For example, the law in British Columbia and Prince Edward Island is the same as that in Ontario; in Alberta and Saskatchewan, an individual order cannot exceed 12 months, but there is no limit on the number of renewals; in Newfoundland, the total continuous time in care before a permanent order is made cannot exceed 36 months. The law of Ontario is generally much more liberal than that of other provinces concerning the right of children to participate in protection proceedings, giving children the right to seek a review of temporary or permanent wardship orders.

Besides legislation expressly providing for a judicial review of wardship, some provinces are expressly giving children in care the right to be consulted about measures which will affect their lives while a ward. Quebec's *Youth Protection Act*, provides in s. 7 that a child who is in care, and is capable of understanding, must be consulted about any transfer from one residence to another. Ontario has proposed a Bill of Rights for children in licensed children's residences, which would include the right "to have his or her opinions heard and to be included, to the greatest extent possible, when decisions are being made affecting his or her life."

In most provinces Crown wardship terminates when a child reaches the age of 18 or at the time of marriage if this occurs before the 18th birthday. Section 42 of the *C.W.A.* provides that if a child is a full-time student, or is suffering from some disability, the C.A.S. may continue to provide support for the ward until he reaches the age of 21. Generally, after a child reaches the age of 16, the C.A.S. will begin to make provisions for moving the child into the community, perhaps moving an older child into an apartment with another ward. If a child still needs support after reaching the age of 21, arrangements are generally made to continue assistance through the appropriate government agency.

A Crown wardship may be reviewed by a court pursuant to s. 38 of the Act. An application for review may be initiated by the C.A.S. at any time, by the parents, or the child, if 12 or older, every six months. At a review hearing the judge may terminate the order, or send the child home under a supervision order. In *Roulette v. C.A.S. of Central Manitoba*,[59] a mother applied for the termination of a permanent wardship order made a year earlier for her three-year-old daughter. The mother was present when the order was initially made, but she was not represented by a lawyer. At that time she had separated from the child's father and was having difficulty supporting herself and caring for the girl. When the application was made to terminate, the mother was living in a stable common-law relationship, and had completed a training course improving her prospects for obtaining remunerative employment. She had better accommodations and could support the child. Under these circumstances, the judge terminated the wardship order and the child was returned to her mother.

Section 38(7) of the *C.W.A.* places an important limitation on the right of a parent or child to apply for termination of a Crown wardship, in that if a child who is a Crown ward is placed in a home for the purpose of adoption, then the wardship order may not be terminated. This provision of the Act is designed to prevent the disruption of the adoption process, a process which generally takes a minimum of six months from the initial placement to the final adoption order, and which is discussed in the next chapter. This provision was first enacted in December, 1969, after a celebrated series of court battles between Sylvia Mugford and the Ottawa Children's Aid Society,[60] concerning custody of her son David. At the age of 18, Sylvia became an unwed mother. Shortly after the child's birth, with her consent, the Society obtained an order making the child a Crown ward. The mother did not then believe that she could raise the child. When the boy was three months old she indicated to the C.A.S. that she wanted him back, though she changed her mind again after a month. At the age of five months the child was placed for adoption. Shortly thereafter, Sylvia's parents learned the facts for the first time and expressed their willingness to have their daughter and her child live with them. Miss Mugford contacted the C.A.S. when the child was five months old, and when the C.A.S. refused to disrupt the placement, court proceedings were commenced. These concluded after 18 months with an order from the Supreme Court of Canada stating that the child should be returned to his mother. The courts faced a difficult decision in a case where a natural mother who wanted her child, and who had apparently given up custody without having been adequately counselled as to the various alternatives, was competing against adoptive parents who were, in a psychological sense, the only parents the child knew. The final decision of the courts heavily stressed the rights of natural parents. Upon learning of the decision, the proposed adoptive parents declared: "We lost a son. It was like a death in the family."[61] After this decision, the Ontario legislature decided to increase the protection afforded adoptive parents.

Once a child is made a Crown ward, the child welfare authorities have a duty

to develop a plan of care for that child. Often an effort is made to have a ward
adopted, and s. 68 of the *C.W.A.* stipulates that the C.A.S. "shall endeavour to
secure the adoption of Crown wards, having regard to the best interest of each
Crown ward." There are many people who are eager to adopt healthy young infants
and such children are easily placed for adoption, but with many older children who
remember their biological parents and may have quite severe emotional problems,
adoption is often an unrealistic alternative. There has been a tendency for some
Crown wards to drift from one placement to another, Therefore, pursuant to s. 39
of the *C.W.A.*, and to encourage long-term planning for each Crown ward, there
is to be an annual administrative review, carried out by a reviewer who is not a
C.A.S. employee, but directly responsible to the government.

2. Parental Rights and Responsibilities

Though a wardship order transfers many of the rights and responsibilities of parenthood to the child protection authorities, the natural parents continue to have a
role to play. Consideration will be given here to two of the most important aspects
of this role: visiting rights and financial support.

The right of a parent to have access, or visiting rights, to a child in care, can
often be the source of considerable tension and resentment. The parent quite naturally feels that the child is his own flesh and blood, and he should have a right
to see the child. On the other hand, the protection workers, foster parents and
others, may feel that the parent has already done considerable harm to the child,
and feel that further contact with the parent is undesirable.

Problems in regard to access are likely to be particularly severe in the case of
Crown wards, especially if the children are older and have developed emotional
attachments to the parents. In a temporary wardship situation, it is expected that
the child will return home, and the child protection authorities and parents will
generally want all contacts to be maintained to facilitate reintegration into the
family. There may be very different views when a permanent order is made.

One difficult issue is determining the duration and nature of the visits. If the
parents are trusted by welfare authorities, there may be extensive visits, with the
parents taking the child for a day or week-end. However, if the parents are not
trusted, visits may be very closely supervised. Supervision of the visits can serve
to protect the child, but also to observe and "collect evidence" which can be used
in later hearings. Though the court can determine the duration and nature, as well
as the frequency, of visits, if the Society requests supervised visits, this will usually
be granted. In *Plante v. Catholic C.A.S.*,[62] the judge described supervised visits
in the following way:

> In the presentation of the society's case, some emphasis was laid on the
> claim that the parents and particularly the father had shown little
> interest . . . with David since [Judge Beaulieu] made him a permanent
> ward of the society . . . This made me inquire as to the mechanics of such

visits, when the ward had been placed by the society in the home of foster parents. I gathered from the evidence . . . that the procedure was as follows:

(1) The parents communicate with the staff members assigned to the case, stating that they would like to have a visit with the child;

(2) The staff member calls the foster parents to inquire whether the proposed time and date suits them;

(3) If the time and date are acceptable the foster parents are instructed to bring the child to the visiting room at the society's office;

(4) The staff worker informs the natural parent or parents to attend at the society's office at the time and date specified;

(5) Assuming no hitches, the right of access is exercised for whatever period of time the staff worker allows and under rather bleak circumstances . . .

(6) The parents depart and the child is transported back to the foster parents' home.

Even if relations between the staff worker and the natural parents are good, this is quite a cumbersome procedure and might well inhibit natural parents from seeking access very often . . . If the relations between the staff member and parents are hostile, then the situation becomes very much worse, with predictable results.

There are two other possible causes of friction . . . The first concerns who controls the length of the visit, and the second would occur if the parents and child were kept under surveillance during the visit. I do not claim to be able to propose a better system, but it is a situation that a judge must take into consideration when deciding how much significance to attach to the allegation that the parent or parents have no affection or interest because they have not made many requests to exercise their right of access.

The terms under which access is to be arranged may be simply based upon an informal arrangement between the protection authorities and the parent, or it may be as a result of a court order. Section 35 of the *C.W.A.* governs the making of access orders by a judge. An order governing access may be made at the time an order is made placing the child in care, or there may later be a separate hearing to decide that issue. The access order may be varied at any time if circumstances should change.

The judge will base his decision regarding access on an assessment of the child's best interests. As indicated earlier, serious conflicts over access are most likely to occur where there has been a permanent wardship order. In this situation, an important consideration will be whether the child is likely to be adopted. If adoption is likely, it may be considered best to sever the relationship with the natural parents as quickly as possible.

In *C.A.S. of Huron County v. Bunn*,[63] a Canadian Indian mother applied for an access order to allow her to see her four children, aged three to 10, who were Crown wards. Witnesses for the Society expressed concern that visits with the natural mother would make adoption more difficult as prospective adoptive parents would be reluctant to have a child who would still have a close relationship with its natural mother. The judge assessed the situation as follows:[64]

> I appreciate fully that the mechanics and procedures of the children's aid society may be hampered by permitting this mother to have access to her children, but the paramount consideration is the welfare of the children and not the welfare of the children's aid society. . . . This woman has shown a constant interest in her children, although she may be incapable of caring for them properly. . . . She has been persistent in her fight for access, she has endeavoured to amend her lifestyle . . . She is an Indian and her children are part Indian and they have the right to learn from her something of her racial culture. The children have the right . . . to know that they have a mother. In short, I am not convinced that, by allowing her access in that period prior to the children being placed for adoption, it would be against their welfare.
>
> I am conscious, however, that it would not be fair to the children to allow them to spend their entire minority in the limbo of a foster home, and I feel that the children's aid society should use its best endeavours to find an adoption home, hampered though it may be by my permitting access to the mother.

In the result, the judge allowed the mother access with the proviso that such access was to terminate as soon as the children were placed in the home of the persons who had given written notice of their intention to adopt them.

An important factor in the *Bunn* case seems to be the age of the children; all were old enough to remember their mother. Generally, in cases where adoption seems likely, it will be difficult for the parents to get access, though for an older child, who is not likely to be adopted, access may continue for years since it is recognized that links with natural parents and family can provide a child with emotional stability.

As well as having rights, parents have responsibilities, and one of their prime responsibilities is the obligation to financially support their children. As discussed in Chapter 3, this obligation exists regardless of whether a child resides with his parent. Section 31 of the *C.W.A.* allows a court to order support payments from a parent, or, if deceased, from the estate of the parent. These payments are made to the Society caring for the child, and if a parent defaults payments may be enforced in the same way as other support orders, for example, by garnishing wages. With increasing financial restraints, child protection authorities are looking more frequently to parents for support payments, though most of the parents of children in care are poor and can contribute nothing to the support of a child in care. The amount the court will order a parent to pay is based on the parent's financial position.

3. The Child Care System

The child care system in Canada consists of literally thousands of components. Some accommodate only one or two children, others several hundred. A detailed examination of this system is clearly beyond the scope of this book, but a few of the salient features of the system can be considered.

Though there are many different types of facilities, they can be classified as fitting into three categories, foster homes, group homes, and large institutions. Before considering each type of facility, a few general characteristics should be mentioned.

The child care system as a whole tends to suffer from a chronic lack of funds, and this is reflected in the qualtiy of care provided. In many localities there is a real shortage of facilities. The people who are caring for the children, children who are often suffering from various emotional and behavioural problems, frequently have little or no training.

When a child initially enters the system he is assigned to a child care or social worker, who has primary responsibility for that child. Some kind of assessment of the child's needs is made, and the child is sent to the most suitable facility which has a vacancy. The nature of the assessment will depend upon the nature of the child's problems and his age, the duration of the wardship order, the facilities available, and the budget of the protection authority. The assessment may range from a conversation between a worker and a supervisor, lasting a few minutes, to a stay of several weeks in an assessment facility with a battery of physical and psychological tests.

The experience of the child, once in care, tends to be characterized by considerable instability, something which is undesirable for any child, especially one who has a background which is unhappy and has been characterized by an unstable relationship with parents. In one study, it was discovered that on the average, a child in long-term care had four different placements and 12 different social workers.[65] Placements may break down because the child cannot adjust, or because the people offering the placement find that a child is unmanageable, or the facility is closing. The failings of the child care system should not necessarily be blamed upon the people who operate the system. They are largely people who are dedicated and hard working. Given the virtually intractable nature of the problems of some of the children in the system and the lack of resources, there will inevitably be serious shortcomings. Judges, however, when considering removing a child from the home, are always aware of the fact that committal to care is not a magic solution to the problems of a child, and this influences the decisions they make.

The backbone of the child care system is the foster home. There are more children in this type of facility than all of the others combined. A foster home is simply an ordinary home in which people have agreed to take children who have been committed to the care of protection authorities. Foster parents are recruited by the protection authorities and go through a screening process which may consist of one or more interviews, but very rarely includes any form of psychological testing. Foster parents are not required to have any specialized education or training, and only recently have any efforts been made to offer even rudimentary training courses.[66] Foster parents receive a minimal sum for each foster child they have, generally from $5 to $10 a day, an amount which barely covers the cost of feeding the child. Clearly, this is the least expensive form of care which can be provided, as foster parents are virtually in a volunteer status, taking in children out of a sense of love. Many foster parents have children of their own, as well as taking in one or more foster children, and they generally are people who care about children. In recent years it has become increasingly difficult to recruit people to serve as foster parents.

Many foster home placements work out very successfully, especially when younger children are involved. A child may stay many years in the same home, eventually being adopted by the foster parents. Unfortunately, with older children, particularly if they have problems, foster placements are frequently less successful. Foster parents tend to be members of the white Canadian middle class, and this can create adjustment problems for children with a different social and cultural background, and unfortunately most children in care do have a different background. Children from low-income and native families tend to be disproportionately represented among children in care. Breakdowns in foster home placements are very common, and incidents of physical, and even sexual, abuse occur with disturbing regularity.[67]

Group homes are facilities operated by a paid staff for the express purpose of caring for children. There are generally five to 10 children in each group home, though there may be fewer, or more. The amount of training and education of the staff varies quite a bit, but given the generally low salaries, the staff tends to be lacking in formal qualifications, and frequently has high turnover rates. There are many different types of group homes. Some have a particular philosophical or psychological approach and tend to have more structured programs than foster homes. Some are operated by a husband and wife and are known as group foster homes, while others have staffs which are on rotating shifts. The staffs are more professionally oriented than ordinary foster parents which is hardly surprising in view of the pay differentials. It costs the protection authorities much more to keep a child in a group home than in a foster home, but it is possible to place older and difficult children in these homes. Group homes may be operated directly by the child welfare authorities, though most are privately owned and take children on a contractual basis; many are operated by non-profit corporations, though for some this can be quite a lucrative operation.[68]

Both foster homes and group homes are located in the community, and an effort is made to integrate children into the community, for example, by having them attend local schools.

There are a number of large institutions which are used by child welfare authorities. In many provinces a child in need of protection may be sent to a training school. Training schools are institutions where children who commit serious crimes are sent. Their programs are very structured, and the children are under close supervision. Training schools are more fully discussed in Chapter 6; suffice to say that a child who has been found to be in need of protection and is sent to a training school may, with some justification, view himself as somehow being punished for his parents' failure to care for him adequately. Ontario's legislation has now been amended so that a child who has been found to be in need of protection cannot be detained in a training school. Various institutional settings are often used for children who have very serious problems that may require considerable supervision and care, and perhaps medical or psychiatric care. These facilities include mental health centres.

F. MEDICAL TREATMENT

Most child protection cases involve parents who are, for some reason, unable or unwilling to care adequately for their child. There are, however, certain cases which arise not when parents are uncaring, but, on the contrary, when the parents are acting according to certain religious or ideological principles. In this situation, there may be a bitter contest between the child protection authorities, representing the views of the state regarding appropriate child care practices, and the parents, who are putting forward a clearly articulated position based on firmly held beliefs. Earlier in this chapter, we considered the Alberta case of *Re M.*, where child care and discipline practices, based upon the beliefs of a religious cult, were held to be so inadequate that the children concerned were found to be in need of protection. Special problems arise in situations where parents refuse medical treatment for their children on the basis of religious beliefs. In particular, there is often a situation of some urgency, and special legal procedures have been developed for expediting hearings when there is a medical emergency and the parents refuse to obtain medical treatment. The child is made a temporary ward until the emergency has passed, and the wardship is then terminated.

Jehovah's Witnesses are probably the most prominent group involved in this situation, though there have been cases involving other groups. Jehovah's Witnesses believe that any form of consumption of blood, including the administration of blood transfusions, is in defiance of divine ordinance. They devoutly believe that their refusal to allow a transfusion promotes the best interests of their children, as consenting to a transfusion will endanger the child's hope for eternal life. All provinces, except Quebec, have included in the definition of a child in need of protection, a description similar to that found in s. 19(1) of the *C.W.A.*:

> (ix) a child where the person in whose charge the child is neglects or refuses to provide or obtain proper medical, surgical or other recognized remedial care or treatment necessary for the child's health or well-being, or refuses to permit such care or treatment to be supplied to the child when it is recommended by a legally qualified medical practitioner . . .

In *Forsyth v. C.A.S. of Kingston*,[69] the Society invoked this definition to have the new-born child of a Jehovah's Witness couple declared to be in need of protection. The child needed a transfusion to cure a condition known to be caused by problems with the Rh factor in the child's blood.

The parents adamantly refused to allow a transfusion. Though doctors may treat a child without parental consent in an emergency situation, for example, if a parent cannot be located, this is not the same as treating a child in the face of express parental objection. The medical authorities would only act if the child was made a temporary ward of the C.A.S., giving the Society authorization to consent to medical treatment. In the *Forsyth* case, a hearing was held in the hospital at 10:30 p.m., with the mother attending on a stretcher. The father and a Jehovah's Witness minister were present, but the parents had been given little notice of the fact that a hearing would be held. Though an order was made, a transfusion given, and the child's life saved, the parents sought to have the order quashed by a higher court. Due to the procedural irregularities, the order was quashed and, though it did not affect the child in question, a precedent for future hearings was established. In quashing the order, it was held that in this situation the parents must have a real opportunity to cross-examine witnesses and call witnesses of their own.

In 1962, when the *Forsyth* case occurred, the legislation required that parents had to receive "reasonable notice of the hearing," and the failure to satisfy this proviso was a further ground for quashing the order. As a result of that case, s. 28(11) of the *C.W.A.* was enacted, allowing the judge to dispense with the requirement of serving notice of a hearing upon the parents, if "prompt service . . . cannot be effected and any delay might endanger the health or safety of the child." Thus, in such a situation, a hearing might be held without the parents being informed and present, and a wardship order made for up to 30 days. In situations of urgency, a hearing may be held at any place, for example, in a hospital, at any time of day or night, and with very little prior planning. It seems clear, however, that some effort must be made to inform the parents that a hearing will occur, and that they have a right to attend and participate in the hearing.

An adult has the right to determine what medical treatment he will undergo, and for religious or other reasons may refuse certain types of treatment. As we have seen, the legislature has given the child welfare authorities the duty of intervening to protect a child whose parents may refuse to provide medical care. In a series of cases the courts have indicated that they are prepared to protect children even in cases not specifically provided for in legislation. In *Raleigh Fitkin-Paul Morgan Memorial Hospital v. Anderson*,[70] an American case, a mother was about to give birth and upon entering the hospital informed her doctors that she did not wish a blood transfusion, as she was a Jehovah's Witness. The doctors believed that in the final stages of pregnancy severe haemorrhaging was likely and that both the mother and the unborn child would be endangered. The court appointed a special guardian for the unborn child and ordered that blood transfusions could be administered to save the life of the child or mother. It is not clear that Canadian courts would go this far, but as discussed in Chapter 7, our courts are showing increasing willingness to protect the unborn infant.

In *Pentland v. Pentland*,[71] the Ontario Supreme Court was faced with a 17-year-old boy who had been seriously injured in a motor-cycle accident. He was in an intensive care unit, but still conscious. Both the boy, and his mother who had been granted custody in a divorce proceeding nine years earlier, refused to consent to blood transfusions as they were Jehovah's Witnesses, even though it appeared that this might well be essential to save the boy's life. As he was no longer under 16, an application could not be made to have him made a ward of the C.A.S. Instead, the court put the boy in the custody of his grandmother, who was prepared to consent to the transfusions. The judge commented that:[72]

> . . . every child has the right to life and to the continuation of life so long as is humanly possible. I further hold that every child has the fundamental right to the best medical care available in his community. To the extent that such medical care is wilfully withheld by a parent or guardian, then the child is being neglected . . . In these circumstances I accept it as my duty to remove the custody of the child from that parent or guardian and to place the custody of the child in a person who will not deny to the child what I deem to be his fundamental rights.

It is not clear how far the courts are prepared to go in extending the definition of "health and well-being" so as to bring different situations within the definition of a child who is in need of protection. Situations including blood transfusions are generally simple to resolve, as there is agreement among medical experts that the failure to provide a transfusion might well be fatal. In other situations, it may be difficult for the court to decide whether state intervention in the form of a protection order is appropriate, as can be seen by contrasting the two following American decisions.[73]

Re Sampson,[74] involved a 15-year-old boy who was a victim of Von Recklinghausen's disease, which was manifested by severe deformities of the face and neck. The condition posed no immediate threat to his life or physical health. The disfigurement was "so gross" that it caused the boy difficulties at school, and would doubtless cause employment problems. Although the boy did not suffer any serious personality disorders, he had an extremely dependent personality and a poor self-image. Doctors recommended corrective surgery to help the boy lead a normal life. As with other types of surgery, there were risks associated with the procedure, and blood transfusions would be required. The mother, a Jehovah's Witness, refused to consent to the transfusions. The New York Court of Appeal agreed with a finding the boy was neglected and that the corrective surgery should be undertaken while the child was a ward of the state. The court held that though there was no risk to the boy's life or health, since he was suffering from "psychological impairment," the order was appropriate.

The Supreme Court of Pennsylvania took quite a different approach in Re Green.[75] In this case, a boy was a victim of poliomyelitis which caused curvature of the spine, and made it impossible for him to walk. The doctors recommended a spinal fusion. Though recognizing the dangers inherent in such surgery, it was felt that this was the only way to prevent him from being confined to a bed for the rest of his life. As in Re Sampson, parental consent to the operation was forthcoming, but blood transfusions would not be allowed due to adherence to the beliefs of the

Jehovah's Witnesses. The court did not find that the boy was neglected, felt that the approach taken in *Re Sampson* would create endless problems, and that unless the courts restricted themselves to situations where life was imperiled, they would steer towards a "medical and philosophical morass." The court expressed the opinion "that as between a parent and the state, the state does not have an interest of sufficient magnitude outweighing a parent's religious beliefs when the child's life is not immediately imperiled by his physical condition." The wording of Ontario's legislation might lead courts to adopt the approach of *Re Sampson*, though the issue has not been resolved in this country.

G. ALTERNATIVES TO THE PROTECTION PROCEEDING

Thus far our focus of concern has been situations in which the child welfare authorities and the parents disagree as to whether the child is in need of protection, or disagree as to the nature of assistance which should be provided for the child. In fact, in many situations the parents and the authority will agree about what is best for the child, and be able to implement some kind of plan which the parents can follow on a voluntary basis. One way for this to occur is for the child to be brought before the court on a "consent" basis. There will be a prior agreement between the parents and the authority about the terms of a supervision or wardship order; if the child is old enough he, too, may have been consulted. All concerned will appear briefly in court, the judge will be informed of the facts of the case and the terms of the agreement. He may ask a few questions, and theoretically might refuse to make the order requested, but invariably he will simply make the order with the agreed terms. If the judge has any doubts about the wisdom of the order, it now seems appropriate, at least in Ontario, for a lawyer to be appointed to represent the child.

There are a number of ways in which a child, who might otherwise be considered to be in need of protection, can be taken from the care of his parents, without the commencement of child protection proceedings. These attempts to help the child involve a co-operative effort between the parents and the child welfare authorities. One way is for the parents and the authority to enter into a voluntary agreement that the protection authority will care for the child. For children suffering from severe behavioural or emotional problems, it may be possible for the child to be committed directly to a mental health centre, without formal involvement by the protection authority. Finally, in some provinces, though not Ontario, it is possible for a child to be declared unmanageable and committed to a training school.

Before considering the specific nature of these various alternatives to the protection proceeding, the relative merits of a non-adversarial approach should be examined. Parents are frequently prepared to co-operate because they honestly realize that they require help in promoting the welfare of their child. They turn to the agency which is designated by society as providing assistance in these circumstances. A significant number of cases in which child protection authorities are involved result from parents contacting the authority. Parents are most likely to seek help when a child is older and behavioural problems are encountered, though they may even seek help if they are abusing their child.

The protection authority will generally prefer to avoid the adversarial forum in order to promote a co-operative relationship; this is essential if there is to be a realistic chance of accomplishing therapeutic work with the family. A court appearance can be traumatic and time consuming for all concerned, and an effort is generally made to avoid court. There may be a desire to avoid court because it would be difficult to satisfy certain technical requirements of the statute; for example, a voluntary care agreement might be preferred to an apprehension as there is no need to appear in court within five days.

A party may wish to reach some kind of settlement after it is realized that a case may not be as strong as initially believed. Often the adversarial process is only halted after the parties have obtained legal advice and have realistically appraised their chances of success.

Avoidance of the adversarial process is not always an unmixed blessing. One problem is that there is a tendency for children who are in care on a voluntary basis to "drift," and be in care longer than they would be if subject to a court order. Busy social workers will inevitably tend to devote more of their time to cases with fixed court dates, and parental pressures for the return of a child. Further, though it may seem to a parent that a voluntary agreement may be avoiding court intervention, such agreements can still be the first step to an eventual permanent wardship order.[76]

In a situation in which a voluntary plan is being arranged, it is important that the parents and child are truly making a decision based on an exercise of free will. Too often, there have been cases where an overly zealous child welfare worker may, in effect, coerce a parent, or child, into accepting a voluntary plan, holding up the threat of court proceedings as an incentive to obtain the agreement of a person unaccustomed to dealing with a figure of authority, such as a protection worker.[77]

It is quite common for child protection authorities to be involved with families on a voluntary basis. This involvement may consist of visiting the family in the home, and arranging for various supports for the family, such as daycare. The protection worker may simply be fulfilling the role which relatives or friends played when society was less urbanized and impersonal. In some situations, the voluntary help may extend to take one or more children into care. In Ontario, the taking of children into care on a voluntary basis is strictly regulated by legislation. Section 25 of the *C.W.A.* provides for two types of care by agreement. One involves circumstances of a temporary nature, making it impossible for a parent to adequately care for a child; the other may be used when the special needs of a child may require that the child be placed in care.

A "temporary care agreement" can be made for an initial period of up to six months, and may be extended one or more times. Circumstances which call for such an agreement might include a marital crisis, illness, or loss of housing. Section 25(5) provides that no agreement shall be made until the C.A.S. has considered whether assistance in the home is a suitable alternative to removal of the child. The agreement must be in writing, and if the child involved is 12 or older, the child must also consent. The agreement may be ended on 21 days' notice by any of the parties, though the C.A.S. may decide to apprehend the child rather than return him, in which case the matter must be brought before the court within five days. If there is a situation of temporary crisis a home-maker might be placed in the home as an alternative.

To attempt to alleviate the problem of children in care "drifting," and to promote a realization by all concerned that the period in care is to be temporary, and a period in which efforts must be made to ameliorate the home situation, the total time in care under such agreements is limited to 12 months. Further, no child is to be in care longer than 24 months under a combination of temporary care agreements and temporary wardship orders; after this period the child must be returned home or made a Crown ward.

The terms of such an agreement are relatively standardized, though the duration is negotiable. The C.A.S. agrees to care for the child, and limits visits by parents. The parents are expected to give the Society an authorization to consent to emergency medical treatment, and may be required to contribute to the financial support of the child, if their resources permit this. Though parents cannot enter into an agreement concerning a child who is over 16, s. 25(11) allows a child between 16 and 18 to enter into an agreement on his own.

A "special needs agreement" may be entered into where the parents are unable to provide for their child due to a physical, mental, emotional, behavioural, or other handicap. Unlike a temporary care agreement, there are no time-limits on the duration of a special needs agreement, except that it cannot extend past a child's 18th birthday. Such agreements are often expected to continue indefinitely. Under the agreement, the Society may arrange for the provision of services in the home, which the parents could not otherwise afford, or the child may be removed from the home, usually to be placed in a special facility. This type of agreement is subject to termination on 21 days' notice, and may require financial contribution by the parents.

Child welfare authorities, acting as legal guardians, may place a child who is a ward in a mental health facility. Parents may also place a child directly in such a facility. Children who are disturbed or retarded may be placed in a mental health facility. Admittance to such a facility may be on an involuntary or a voluntary basis. An involuntary committal involves an initial decision by medical authorities, with a possibility of review by a board, and ultimately the courts. Such a procedure is almost never used in connection with children; they are admitted as voluntary patients. For an adult suffering from a mental disorder a voluntary committal is made with the consent of the patient, subject to the recommendation of a physician. As we shall see in Chapter 9, medical treatment, including psychiatric care, for a child, requires not the consent of the child, but that of the parent. Thus, without the possibility of any review, a child may be committed to a mental health facility on the instructions of his parents, generally with the approval of a single physician. This is how the vast majority of children are committed to these facilities. The parental decision to seek commitment is frequently made on the advice of a doctor, though it may also be a social worker or child welfare worker who first suggests this course of action. In most cases little injustice is done by the whole procedure, though there may well be cases where real injustice is done and children who are quite sane are sent to mental health facilities.[78]

The definition of a child in need of protection in Ontario, as in most other provinces, includes "a child who is beyond the control of his or her parents." This portion of the definition is likely to be used in cases involving older children, especially females whose sexual activities may provoke societal disapproval. In this type of case, parents are likely to actively co-operate with the authorities. If it is felt by the parents, or child welfare authorities, that the measures which can be provided under child protection laws are inadequate, legislation in British Columbia, Nova Scotia, New Brunswick and Newfoundland provides that an application can be made to have the child sent to training school. This legislation provides for committal to a training school when a judge is satisfied that the child cannot be controlled outside a training school. As was mentioned earlier, and will be discussed more fully in Chapter 6, a training school is a very structured environment which children are physically restrained from leaving. This represents a fairly severe alternative for a child. Section 8 of the *Training Schools Act*, a similar legislative provision in Ontario, came under considerable criticism as creating an inappropriate alternative to protection legislation, and was repealed as of January 1, 1977.

H. THE ABUSING PARENT

Child abuse is a phenomenon which involves not only children, but also parents. When considering an appropriate societal response, it should be remembered that not only must the child be helped, but something must be done with the parents. If the home situation can be ameliorated, perhaps an effort should be made in this direction so that the child can be returned to his family. If the abuse has been very serious, it may be that the parent should be exposed to some form of penal sanction, at least as an indication of societal disapproval.

The term "child abuse" is defined in s. 47(1) of the *C.W.A.* to include physical harm, sexual molestation, and conditions of malnutrition and mental ill-health. As we have discussed, though some children who are in need of protection have suffered from abuse, most have not. Rather, they are, for example, children who are to be placed for adoption after being born of unwed mothers, or older children who are not abused, but whose relationship with their parents is such that placement outside of the home seems desirable. Nevertheless, child abuse is a significant problem in Canada.

There are many theories to explain why parents abuse their children, and they are difficult to summarize briefly.[79] It seems clear that parents who have themselves suffered from abuse as children are likely to abuse their own children. Mothers are more likely to abuse children than fathers, and this is especially likely to occur if the mother and child could not develop a close bond at birth, for example, if the child was premature and had to be separated from his mother. A baby who is difficult to handle because of problems with feeding, colic or vomiting, is more likely to suffer abuse, and it is not uncommon for one child out of several to be singled out as a victim of abuse. If there are environmental problems causing frustration to parents, such as marital strife, financial difficulties, or unemployment, these may precipitate abuse. The young unwed mother, facing life alone with a child, may be prone to abuse her child. The most common pattern of sexual abuse involves an incestuous relationship between a father and his daughter, and is likely to be a symptom of severe marital difficulties.

Though there is a wide variety of methods for dealing with the abusing parent, they can be classified as being either therapeutic or punitive in nature. The therapeutic approach tends to view the abusing parent as someone who is sick, and who can be treated. There is a belief that any form of punishment of the abusing parent in effect punishes the child victim; if the parent is imprisoned, the child loses the only source of love and support he has known, and may have tremendous guilt feelings. The punitive approach views the abusing parent as a criminal, who must be punished, both to correct his own behaviour patterns and to serve as a deterrent to others. Imprisonment of the parent is viewed as the best means of ensuring the safety of a child.

Whether a therapeutic or a punitive approach is taken depends upon a number of factors. The nature and consequences of the abuse are likely to be very important; a distinction must be made as to whether it is the child's *health* which is endangered, or his *life*. For example, if abuse leads to a fractured arm, this is much less likely to result in the adoption of a punitive approach than if exactly the same acts of abuse should accidentally result in the death of a child. The types of community resources available to deal with abusing parents and the particular agencies involved may be crucial. Child welfare authorities and social agencies tend to take a more therapeutic approach than the police. Legal responses to the abusing parent can be either therapeutic or punitive. Child protection legislation tends to take a therapeutic approach; for example, parents may be ordered to undergo psychiatric assessment or treatment under this legislation. On the other hand, we shall also see that the *Criminal Code* and other penal legislation may be invoked to deal with the abusing parent.

Except for the most serious cases of abuse, the tendency in Canada in recent years has been to take a therapeutic approach. This appears to reflect a growing social acceptance of the notion that the abusing parent is a sick person, who is to be pitied and helped rather than persecuted, and because it is felt that if the parents can in fact be helped, then this is best for all concerned, including the child. Further, Crown attorneys, who must prosecute criminal charges, recognize that it is generally much more difficult to prove a criminal charge than to show that a child is in need of protection. As was discussed earlier in the chapter, a criminal charge must be proven beyond a reasonable doubt, whereas in a protection proceeding, a case must merely be proven on the balance of probabilities. Further, to sustain a criminal conviction, it must be proven that a specific person committed a specific act, whereas this is not necessary in a protection proceeding. For example, if a child is brought into a hospital suffering from injuries which are medically diagnosed as resulting from physical abuse, and each parent accuses the other of abusing the child, this will be enough to have the child found to be in need of protection since the child is clearly at risk in his home. It will not, however, be sufficient to sustain a criminal conviction as there is no evidence of which parent committed the assault, unless there is independent evidence, or one parent seems more credible than the other. As evidence of these trends, one can consider that in the period from 1970 to 1975, there were 3 249 reports of child abuse in Ontario, resulting in 348 charges being laid and only 78 convictions.[80]

Though the present emphasis in Canada is upon a therapeutic approach, a punitive approach is taken in some cases. The *Criminal Code*, which makes it a crime for one adult to kill, maim, or assault another, applies equally to attacks upon children. Thus parents may be charged with murder, homicide, criminal negligence causing death, assault, and various related offences, as a result of child abuse. There is, however, one important defence which an adult charged with assaulting a child may raise, but which does not apply to assaults upon another adult. The *Criminal Code* provides:

> 43. Every schoolteacher, parent or person standing in the place of a parent is justified in using force by way of correction toward a pupil or child, as the case may be, who is under his care, if the force does not exceed [that which] is reasonable under the circumstances.

Section 43 permits the use of "reasonable force" to effect the correction of a child. What constitutes reasonable force will depend on the circumstances. Causing bruises or welts has generally been held to be reasonable, but causing permanent injury is not.

In *R. v. Haberstock*,[81] the Saskatchewan Court of Appeal held that s. 43 applied and acquitted a school teacher who had slapped a boy in the face and chipped his tooth, believing that the child was one of three boys who had verbally abused him during the preceding week. Although the teacher was apparently wrong in his belief, it was held that he had reasonable grounds for taking the action which he did, and that the degree of force used was also reasonable. *Haberstock* has been criticized, and in *R. v. Sarwer-Foner*,[82] the judge suggested that "s. 43 should not be an available defence to an assault charge where any kind of measurable injury, whether physical or mental, is shown to result from corporal punishment."

Various forms of sexual abuse are dealt with by different sections of the *Criminal Code*. Incest, the most common form of sexual abuse, is an offence contrary to s. 150 of the *Code*; s. 150(3) provides that a female who commits incest under duress or fear may be exempt from punishment. In fact, charges are never laid against a girl involved in an incestuous relationship with her father, though she will often feel tremendous guilt when the relationship is discovered. Other sexual offences which might be committed by a parent, or other adult, in connection with involvement with a young child include rape, indecent assault, intercourse with a female under 14 (sometimes colloquially referred to as "statutory rape"), and intercourse with a female between the ages of 14 and 16 who was of "previously chaste character." It is an offence for an adult to be involved in homosexual acts with a child.

In addition to these specific sex offences, s. 33 of the *Juvenile Delinquents Act*, a federal law which applies throughout Canada, makes it a crime for any person to do any act "promoting . . . or contributing to a child's being or becoming a juvenile delinquent or likely to make any child a juvenile delinquent." The concept of delinquency will be discussed in detail in Chapter 6; suffice to say for the present that s. 33 serves to protect the morals of a child in many situations, making it an offence for an adult to supply drugs or liquor to a child, or to have sexual relations with a child.

Section 168(1) of the *Criminal Code* deals with the offence of endangering the morals of a child, and s. 166 makes it an offence for a parent or guardian to "procure the defilement" of his child.

In s. 197(1), the *Criminal Code* imposes a duty upon a parent or guardian to provide a child under 16 with the "necessaries of life." This section is sometimes used to prosecute parents whose children die of malnutrition. Section 200 makes it an offence for an adult in whose care a child is to abandon or expose a child under 10 years of age, so that its life or health are ended, or are likely to be endangered.

Various provincial laws create offences regarding the duty of adults to care for children. All of the provinces have legislation making it an offence to supply liquor to a minor. Section 47(2) of Ontario's *C.W.A.*, makes it an offence for a person having the care of a child, to "abandon or desert the child or inflict abuse upon the child or permit the child to suffer abuse."

As this description indicates, there are a number of overlapping offences of which an adult who abuses a child may be convicted. Naturally, a person can only be convicted of a single offence as a result of a single act, even though technically two different offences may have been committed. The sentence imposed will vary with the nature of the offence and seriousness of the consequences of the abuse. Though it is difficult to generalize, there seems to be considerable judicial sympathy[83] for the parent who abuses a child, recognizing that the parent generally has a great sense of guilt and is suffering from some type of personality deficiency.

In addition to the prospect of criminal charges, it is theoretically possible for an abusing parent to face a civil suit. That is, if a child is maimed by his parent, the child, or a person acting on the child's behalf, may sue the parent for monetary compensation. Such a suit is only realistic if the child has been removed from the home, as otherwise all money awarded the child, even if kept in trust until the child becomes an adult, will impoverish the whole family, including the child. Such an action would generally have to be carried out by a legal guardian for the child, and it should be noted that limitation statutes require the action to be commenced within a few years of the acts of abuse; hence a child cannot wait until adulthood to commence an action on his own.[84]

FOOTNOTES

1. See M.C.J. Olmesdahl, "Paternal Power and Child Abuse: An Historical and Cross-Cultural Study," in John Eekelaar *et al.*, *Family Violence* (Toronto, 1978), at p. 255
2. See Jeffrey S. Leon, "The Development of Canadian Juvenile Justice: A Background for Reform," 15 Osgoode Hall L.J. 71 (1977) at p. 87
3. A comparison of much Canadian child welfare legislation is found in Bernard M. Dickens, "Legal Responses to Child Abuse in Canada," 1 Can. J. Fam. L. 87 (1978). Since the article was written, however, there have been substantial changes in the Ontario legislation.
4. [1950] S.C.R. 737 at p. 746
5. (1978), 5 R.F.L. (2d) 50 at pp. 58-59
6. Statistics from Report of Standing Committee on Health, Welfare and Social Affairs, to Canadian House of Commons, "Child Abuse and Neglect" (1976)
7. See Peter Silverman, *Who Speaks for the Children? The Plight of the Battered Child* (Toronto, 1978), especially Chapter 6. Also Ontario, *Child Welfare in Ontario: Past, Present and Future* (Toronto, 1979)
8. See Ontario, Report of the Task Force on Child Abuse (1978)
9. (1976), 551 P. 2d 389
10. See "Child Abuse: A Special Report," [1978] Ontario Medical Rev. 12
11. Monrad Paulsen, "The Law and Abused Children," in Ray Hefler *et al.*, eds., *The Battered Child* (Chicago, 1968), at p. 185
12. See Peter Silverman, *Who Speaks for the Children? The Plight of the Battered Child* (Toronto, 1978), Chapter 9
13. (1976), 27 R.F.L. 289 at p. 292
14. (1968), 22 R.F.L. 78 at pp. 79 and 80
15. See *Re G.* (1976), 30 R.F.L. 224
16. *Re Kowaliuk; C.A.S. of Winnipeg v. Brooklands Village*, [1934] 1 D.L.R. 678
17. *Candlish v. Minister of Social Services* (1978), 5 R.F.L. (2d) 166
18. *Warnock v. Grarrigan* (1978), 6 R.F.L. (2d) 181
19. (1970), 5 R.F.L. 119 at pp. 126 and 128
20. See, for example, *Re J.D.* (1978), 1 Can. J. Fam. L. 583
21. (1978), 5 R.F.L. (2d) 33
22. *R. v. Allcock* (1975), 25 R.F.L. 84

23. See *Re R.* (1976), 30 R.F.L. 221; and *Lakeman v. Andreychuk P.M.* (1978), 6 R.F.L. 389; but *contra, Re Moe* (1979), 13 R.F.L. (2d) 369
24. [1973] 4 W.W.R. 274
25. *Supra*, at pp. 282 and 284
26. *Supra,* at p. 285
27. (1972), 10 R.F.L. 160 at pp. 168-69
28. *Stevenson v. Florant*, [1925] 4 D.L.R. 530 at p. 544
29. (1976), 28 R.F.L. 380 at pp. 380-81
30. (1979), 13 R.F.L. (2d) 381
31. (1980), 14 R.F.L. (2d) 21
32. See also Jeffrey S. Leon, "Recent Developments in Legal Representation of Children: A Growing Concern With the Concept of Capacity," 1 Can. J. Fam. L. 375 (1978)
33. *Re W* (1979), 13 R.F.L. (2d) 381 at p. 382
34. *Supra*, at pp. 384-85
35. *Re C* (1980), 14 R.F.L. (2d) 21 at p. 24
36. *Supra*, at pp. 25-26
37. *Supra*, at pp. 26-27
38. See Jeffrey S. Leon, "Recent Developments in Legal Representation of Children: A Growing Concern With the Concept of Capacity," 1 Can. J. Fam. L. 375 (1978)
39. For example, Ian Baxter *et al., The Child and the Courts* (Toronto, 1978); Jeffrey Wilson, *Children and the Law* (Toronto, 1978); most Canadian law schools now offer courses on children and the law or an equivalent family practice course; it is mandatory for lawyers representing children in protection proceedings in Ontario to have completed a course sponsored by the Ministry of the Attorney-General.
40. (1975), 23 R.F.L. 82
41. At the time of *Re E.W.Z.*, the statute read that "the judge may hear any person on behalf of the child"; it now reads that "the court may hear any person with evidence relevant to the hearing." This change in wording may not affect the validity of *Re E.W.Z.*, but its value as a precedent must be questioned.
42. (1978), unreported decision, Judge Nasmith (Ont. Prov. Ct. (Fam. Div.))
43. (1975), 21 R.F.L. 315 at p. 319
44. (1973), 13 R.F.L. 51
45. *Supra*, at pp. 52-53
46. (1975), 23 R.F.L. 391
47. *Supra*, at pp. 393-96
48. [1978] 3 W.W.R. 1. See a case comment by Bernard M. Dickens, "Parental Discipline," 1 Can. J. Fam. L. 601 (1978).
49. *Supra*, at pp. 7-8
50. (1978), 6 R.F.L. (2d) 297
51. *Supra*, at p. 317
52. *Supra*, at p. 321

53. *St. Pierre v. Roman Catholic C.A.S. of Essex County* (1976), 27 R.F.L. 266
54. (1976), 30 R.F.L. 83
55. (1978), 1 R.F.L. (2d) 46 at p. 61
56. [1951] 2 D.L.R. 657 at p. 661
57. The child was ordered returned to the parent in *Kewakindo v. C.A.S. of District of Parry Sound* (1973), 11 R.F.L. 371, and *Bailey v. C.A.S. of Parry Sound* (1978), 9 R.F.L. (2d) 188, but not in *Paquette v. C.A.S. of Ottawa* (1979, Ont. S.C.), reported in *The Globe & Mail*, February 7, 1979.
58. See *Re G.M. and R.M.* (1978), 20 O.R. (2d) 378; and *C.A.S. of Winnipeg v. Frohnen* (1974), 17 R.F.L. 47
59. (1973), 10 R.F.L. 277
60. The various court decisions are discussed by Bernard Green, in "Re Mugford — A Case Study in the Interaction of Child-Care Agency, Court and Legislature," 1 R.F.L. 1 (1971)
61. *The Toronto Star*, December 13, 1969, at p. 1
62. (1978), 3 R.F.L. (2d) 248 at pp. 253-54
63. (1975), 24 R.F.L. 187
64. *Supra*, at p. 195
65. See Peter Silverman, *Who Speaks for the Children? The Plight of the Battered Child* (Toronto, 1978), at p. 156
66. See "Norton to Announce Plan for Better Foster Care," *The Globe & Mail*, July 12, 1979, at p. 4
67. See "C.A.S. May Defy Court Orders After Reported Rape of Ward," *The Globe & Mail*, June 20, 1979, at p. 2; "C.A.S. Says Judge Wrongly Criticized; Agency Had Sought Custody of Girl," *The Globe & Mail*, June 21, 1979, at p. 1; and Bernard M. Dickens, "Legal Responses to Child Abuse in Canada," 1 Can. J. Fam. L. 87 (1978) at p. 112
68. See Peter Silverman, *Who Speaks for the Children? The Plight of the Battered Child* (Toronto, 1978), at p. 164
69. [1963] 1 O.R. 49
70. (1964), 201 A. 2d 537
71. (1978), 5 R.F.L. (2d) 65
72. *Supra*, at p. 71
73. These and other cases are discussed by Myles F. McLellan in "Jehovah's Witnesses and Child Protection Legislation: The Right to Refuse Medical Consent," 1 L.M.Q. 37 (1977)
74. (1972), 278 N.E. 2d 918m
75. (1972), 292 A. 2d 387
76. See British Columbia Royal Commission Report on the Protection of Children, Part V (March, 1975), at p. 15; and Tombs, "The Fate of the Crown Ward," 7 C.A.S. Jo. 7
77. A discussion of this troublesome issue will be found at p. 89. See also *Ex parte D.* (1970), 5 R.F.L. 119
78. For a critique of the relative readiness of psychiatrists to commit people,

especially females, see Raj Anand, "Involuntary Civil Commitment in Ontario: The Need to Curtail the Abuses of Psychiatry," 57 Can. Bar Rev. 250

79. For a good survey of various issues in child abuse, see John Eekelaar *et al.*, eds., *Family Violence* (Toronto, 1978), especially Part III, Violence Against Children: What and Why?" and Part IV, "Societal Responses to Violence Against Children." See also Kempe and Kempe, *Child Abuse* (Cambridge, Mass., 1978).

80. Ross Dawson, "Current Issues in Child Abuse," 9 Journal of the Ontario Association of Children's Aid Society 3

81. (1970), 1 C.C.C. (2d) 433

82. (1979), 8 R.F.L. (2d) 342

83. See *R. v. Motuz*, [1964] 2 C.C.C. 162

84. For a discussion of innovative approaches to and the philosophies of methods of responding to the problems of children in need of protection see Goldstein, Solnit and Freud, *Before the Best Interests of the Child* (New York, 1979)

Chapter 5

Adoption

A. INTRODUCTION

Adoption is the creation, by court order, of the legal relationship of parent and child between persons who were not previously so related by blood, and at the same time the termination of all of the legal rights and obligations between the child and his biological parents.

The concept of adoption has existed in different forms in various societies. North American Indians had native customs providing for the care of children whose parents could not do so, whether due to death, or for other reasons. The concept of adoption was well recognized in the laws of ancient Greece and Rome, but it was primarily a device for ensuring the continuity of the male line in a particular family. Adoption was unknown to the English common law, partly as it was viewed as a threat to the continuity of family lines and estates. The first Canadian legislation providing for adoption was enacted in New Brunswick in 1873, but most provinces only enacted adoption statutes in the years following WWI, when unprecedented numbers of children were left homeless as a result of illegitimate birth and parental mortality. Unlike the laws of antiquity which were designed to deal with problems of lineage and succession, Canadian adoption laws are designed to promote the welfare of children without parents, and, for example, the laws in Ontario governing adoption are to be found as part of a comprehensive scheme for child care in the *Child Welfare Act, 1978* (*C.W.A.*).

An adoption proceeding is civil in nature, as opposed to criminal, but it is somewhat different from most other types of court proceedings. Usually a court is concerned with trying to resolve a dispute between two parties, one of which may be the state. This type of dispute is known as an action *in personam* (involving a person) and the judgement which is obtained is only binding against persons who are parties to the dispute. An adoption is an action *in rem* (involving a thing or condition). A judgement *in rem* is binding against "the whole world" and involves the status of a person. A judgement in a custody dispute is *in personam* and only the parties to it are bound by it; as we saw in Chapter 3, a third person can claim custody of the child without being bound by a custody order in favour of one of the parents. An adoption is legally binding upon everyone, and a third person cannot challenge its validity at some later date. In an adoption, as in a divorce, there is a change of legal status, and the court in granting an adoption is not simply acting as a state-appointed arbitrator resolving a dispute, but, rather, it is also an official agency of the state, in a sense giving official sanction to the change of status. In an adoption, the court has an independent duty to ensure that the statutory requirements are satisfied, and unlike the situation in an action *in personam*, the parties cannot mutually agree to waive the provisions of the applicable law.

Though each Canadian province has its own legislation governing adoption, the basic statutory framework is very similar throughout the country. The legislation restricts who may adopt a child, and who may be adopted. Throughout North America concern exists about a practice sometimes known as "baby farming," the unscrupulous placement of babies for adoption by operators motivated by a desire for profit and invariably acting without regard for the suitability of the placement. As a result, legislation restricts who may arrange adoptions, and how they are to be arranged; in particular, there are restrictions about receiving payment for placing a child or doing other work in connection with an adoption. In Ontario, any person, other than a parent, who places a child for adoption must be licensed by the government and is subject to government control. There are provisions for obtaining the consent of the natural parents, and sometimes other persons to an adoption; if these consents are not given, the court may dispense with the requirements for consent under certain circumstances. The legislation governs the holding of an adoption hearing, who may participate in the hearing, and the type of orders which can be made. Generally, there will be some provision for an independent assessment of the suitability of the proposed adoptive home with a report being made to the court, and for a probationary period during which the child lives in the adoptive home prior to the making of a final order. The statute will specify what are the effects of an adoption order; generally all legal ties with the original biological parents will be severed and replaced by ties with the adoptive parents, though as we shall see, there are some important exceptions to this rule.

The statutory scheme in each province constitutes a complete framework for adoption as the courts have no common-law concepts on which to rely when dealing with adoption. As the statutory framework marks a departure from the common law and an infringement of parental rights, adoption statutes have generally been construed quite strictly, and the courts have tended to uphold the position of the natural parents unless there is clearly a contrary legislative intent.[1]

There are three different situations in which adoptions may occur. An adoption may involve a permanent ward of a child welfare authority and be arranged and carried out by the authority. Other adoptions are carried out by various intermediaries, but do not involve permanent wards, in which case more parental involvement is required. Finally, an adoption may be directly arranged by the parents of the child.

In each province, there is a child welfare authority responsible for the protection and care of children whose parents are unable or unwilling to care adequately for them. As we discussed in Chapter 4, this authority has a statutory duty to intervene in the family situation, and when necessary, have a child made a permanent or Crown ward with an effective termination of parental rights. Such a termination of parental rights occurs only by court order, often only after a bitter hearing. The child welfare authority will generally try to place a permanent ward for adoption, especially if the child is young. Children who are permanent wards may be born of single mothers unable to fulfil their obligations, orphans, or children whose relations with their parents have deteriorated for one reason or another.

In Ontario, the Children's Aid Society (C.A.S.) is responsible for the apprehension and care of Crown wards. The Society recruits and screens people who wish to adopt children, and this is the agency contacted by most people who want to adopt children. Section 69 of the *C.W.A.* specifies that an adoption order for a Crown ward may be made without parental consent, and without the parents even being informed that an adoption order has been made.

There are a number of different intermediaries who may arrange adoptions for parents who are consenting to the adoption of their child. Often such children are born out of wedlock and placed for adoption virtually at birth. Often child welfare authorities will arrange such consensual adoptions, and over half of all adoptions in Canada involve child welfare authorities.[2] In Ontario, the C.A.S. tends to make Crown wards of all those children which it places for adoption, thereby giving the Society considerable flexibility in arranging adoptions, and minimizing difficulties should the natural parents change their minds about the adoption. In other provinces, child welfare authorities tend to arrange consensual adoptions without having the children made wards. There are various private agencies which are involved in placing children for adoption, for example, arranging for adoptions within a particular religious group, or for orphans from various underdeveloped countries. In many provinces, doctors, lawyers and ministers may be involved in arranging adoptions. In Ontario, agencies involved in arranging adoptions must be non-profit organizations and licensed for this purpose; there are strict limitations on individuals who wish to become involved in placing children for adoption.

Adoptions which child welfare authorities arrange are sometimes referred to as "public adoptions," with others called "private adoptions." The two sets of parents never meet prior to a public adoption, and rarely meet in the case of an adoption arranged through some other intermediary.

Parents may place their own children for adoption by others, though there are legislative restrictions upon this. In Ontario, no payment may be received for such a placement, and it may only be a placement with a relative, being defined as an aunt, uncle or grandparent of the child. Further, the adoption is to be made only with the consent of the court. By far the most common type of adoption arranged by a parent involves adoption by a stepparent. For example, spouses may divorce with the wife obtaining custody of the children. The wife may later remarry and the children lose touch with their natural father. The new husband might then wish to adopt the children so that he and the natural mother are the legal parents. This is known as a "stepparent" adoption and accounts for up to one-third of all adoptions.[3]

The vast majority of adoption applications do not in fact result in contested hearings. These applications are heard unopposed, and, provided the appropriate procedure has been followed, the judge will usually, though not always, make the order requested. In a public adoption, if the child is made a Crown ward and the child welfare authorities have selected an appropriate home, there is rarely much at issue for the courts to decide. Child welfare authorities will generally either obtain the necessary parental consents or have the child made a permanent ward; they will not become involved in a contest over attempting to dispense with parental consent to the adoption. In the case of private adoptions, particularly stepparent adoptions, there may be a contest if there has been difficulty in obtaining the consent of the parent who will be losing connection with the child, and the contest over the issue of dispensing with the consent of this parent may be very bitter.

B. THE ADOPTION PROCEDURE

1. Eligibility

There are statutory requirements as to age, marital status and residence, which govern the capacity to adopt, and to be adopted. These standards exist to ensure the probability of a successful adoption, which can be supervised by the court, though as we shall see, they are only minimal legislative standards and the courts may expect quite a lot more before making an adoption order.

The *C.W.A.*, s. 74(1), specifies that an adoptive parent must be at least 18 years of age, and a married person residing with his or her spouse, unless the court "is satisfied that there are special circumstances that justify the making of an order." It would seem most unlikely that a person under the age of 18 would be allowed to adopt a child, and adoptions by single persons are rare. In *Re Barnett*,[4] it was suggested that a woman living in a common-law relationship should not be permitted to adopt a child as the relationship lacked the necessary stability. Courts are especially reluctant to allow a single person to adopt a child of the opposite sex. An Australian court,[5] however, held that a single woman of good character and adequate material resources should not be denied the opportunity to adopt a male child solely because of the possible lack of male influence in the child's upbringing. Circumstances in which a single person might be allowed to adopt include those where there is a blood relationship or where the child lives with the proposed adoptive parent for a number of years. Recently, the Roman Catholic Archbishop of Ottawa adopted a 17-year-old refugee boy from South-East Asia.

An adoption application may be made jointly by two spouses living together, or by only one spouse provided that the other consents. If only one spouse adopts, the other becomes a stepparent by adoption.

Section 74 of the *C.W.A.* specifies that unless there are "special circumstances" the child being adopted must be under the age of 18 and have never been married. Special circumstances might include a situation in which the child was in fact living with the adoptive parents as a minor for a number of years before the application was made.

It is stated in s. 72 of the *C.W.A.* that at the time an adoption application is made, both the child and the adoptive parents must be "resident" in Ontario. Difficulties arise when trying to define the word "resident." The *Immigration*

Regulations[6] allow a Canadian citizen to sponsor as a landed immigrant a child under 13 whom he intends to adopt, provided that the child is genuinely without parents who can care for him, for example, if he is orphaned or abandoned by his parents. Thus children from outside the country can be brought into Canada, become residents as landed immigrants, and be adopted.

There have been a number of cases in which people have wished to adopt children already in Canada, but who are not landed immigrants. Particular problems arise when determining whether a child here on a visitor's visa or Minister's permit is a resident. In some cases the courts have held that a child who is attending school and actually living in Ontario is a resident,[7] but in others the courts have described such a child as a "sojourner . . . a visitor or tourist,"[8] and found the child was not a resident.

Problems may arise if the adopting parents and the child relocate after the initial application is made, but before there is a final order of adoption, particularly as there is generally a probationary period of six months or more before a final order is made. Section 82(4) of the *C.W.A.* allows the court to make an adoption order in this situation, provided certain procedures are followed.

2. Placement

The process of selecting adoptive parents, actually placing the child to live with them, and monitoring the situation prior to the making of a court order is generally known as "placement". As discussed earlier, placement may be the responsibility of a public agency, private intermediary, or the natural parents. The authority to place children for adoption is governed by legislation, with perhaps the strictest controls in Canada being found in Ontario. The rationale for establishing these controls is not simply to prevent unscrupulous individuals from financially exploiting the situation. It is also to ensure that the best possible placement is made for the child and the adoptive parents.

Public agencies tend to investigate the background of the natural parents, the child, and the adoptive parents more thoroughly than is the case for private adoptions. In Ontario, prior to the placement of a child in a prospective adoptive home, s. 65 of the *C.W.A.* requires the C.A.S. to carry out a formal "home-study" report, indicating that the home is suitable. There is also a requirement that the child reside with the prospective parents for at least six months prior to the adoption, though this requirement may be waived. This provision applies both to public adoptions and to those carried out through intermediaries, though not to adoptions by relatives and stepparents. Public agencies protect the anonymity of all concerned, prevent possible later interference by the natural parents, and provide counselling and other support if difficulties are encountered. Further, it is believed that the dispassionate supervision provided by trained individuals is likely to promote the child's welfare. Studies which have been done comparing public and private adoptions are somewhat inconclusive[9] on the question of which type of placement is best, and some observers are quite critical of Ontario's provisions, regarding them as going too far in restricting private adoptions.[10]

It is recognized that the public and private agencies exercise tremendous discretion in deciding whether people are suitable as prospective adoptive parents. At present there are many more people who wish to adopt children, or at least healthy young infants, than there are children who are available for adoption. Officials responsible for the placement of children have been criticized as being arbitrary in their selection of adoptive parents, for example, the case of the Wisconsin couple who were initially rejected by social workers as adoptive parents as they were "too fat," the wife weighing 210 lbs., and the husband 215 lbs. Thus, ss. 65 and 66 of Ontario's *C.W.A.* now allow people who have been rejected as prospective adoptive parents, either by the C.A.S., or by an adoption agency, to have an impartial administrative review of this decision.

3. The Adoption Proceeding

In Ontario, adoption proceedings are conducted in the Provincial Court (Family Division), though in some other provinces jurisdiction over adoption rests in the higher courts. Adoption hearings are generally held *in camera*, that is to say that they are not open to the public, and the various documents and records used are not publicly available.

At the hearing, the court may hear testimony from various witnesses, though frequent use is made of written affidavit evidence, especially if there are no issues which are being contested.

The course of the proceedings depends on the type of adoption, and varies somewhat from province to province. In all Canadian jurisdictions there is a requirement that the child be placed in the proposed adoptive home for a probationary period prior to the application. This period is six months in most provinces, though in some such as Manitoba and Alberta it is one year. The purpose of the probationary period is to ensure that the placement will be satisfactory. This may be a difficult period for all concerned as there may be some uncertainty as to whether a favourable order will finally be made. There is a provision for dispensing with the probationary period if the circumstances should so warrant.

Most provinces require that prior to the holding of an adoption hearing there be an investigation of the adoptive home, and usually some kind of report is made to the court. Ontario's requirements in this regard are somewhat stricter than those in most other jurisdictions, with s. 75 of the *C.W.A.* requiring a formal written report, setting out the background of the case and including a recommendation as to whether an adoption order should be made. This report is influential, though it should not, in any sense, be viewed as binding on the court.

In Ontario, there are different provisions for a probationary period and home investigation if the proposed adoption is to be by a relative or stepparent. It was found that in these situations, the child had invariably been living in the home where he was to be adopted for a considerable period of time and that conditions were satisfactory. Further, adoption is generally the only viable course of action in these situations, except to the extent that a parent not involved in the adoption may be affected, and as we shall see such persons have ample right to participate in the adoption process. There are, however, in the case of such private adoptions provisions allowing the court to order an independent assessment and a postponement of the making of an order for a period of up to one year, while the child resides in the proposed adoptive home.

In an adoption proceeding, there are generally only two issues which are likely to be hotly contested. One is whether the court ought to dispense with the usual requirement of parental consent to the adoption, and the other is whether the adoption is in the child's best interests. Before considering these two issues in some detail, a few procedural matters about such hearings should be understood. Since the adoption proceeding is an action *in rem*, the court will ensure that the procedural requirements are satisfied, and the parties cannot waive them.

One very important procedural requirement for any type of proceeding is that everyone who is likely to be affected by it must be given adequate notice of the fact that there will be a hearing, so that they may prepare to participate. As a general rule, every person whose consent is required for the adoption must have notice of the proceeding. In Ontario, for any adoption not involving a Crown ward, this means that every person who is a parent, or has lawful custody of the child, must be given notice of the fact that an application for adoption is to be made, and if applicable, that an application will be made to dispense with the consent of that person. The definition of "parent" is almost identical for the purposes of adoption as the definition for the purposes of a child protection proceeding. Under s. 69 the definition of "parent" is extended beyond known biological parents to include a guardian and a person who has, within the preceding 12 months, "demonstrated a settled intention to treat a child as a child of the person's family." It also includes a person recognized as having parental rights or responsibilities pursuant to a court order, written agreement or written acknowledgement, a person who has, in writing, informed the adoption agency of his parentage and a person who, within the preceding 12 months, has "acknowledged a parental relationship to a child and has voluntarily provided for the child's care and support." There are men, however, who are in fact biological fathers but do not fall within the definition of "parent"; thus, if a rape victim has a child the father would not be a parent. Such men need not be served and have no right to participate in the hearing.

It should be noted that Ontario's legislation provides a broad definition of "parent," effectively eliminating distinctions between children born in and out of wedlock. In other provinces, the definition of "parent" for the purposes of consenting to an adoption and receiving notice of the adoption application does not even extend to all who are the natural parents of a child. For example, Prince Edward Island's *Adoption Act* requires the consent of only the custodial parent if the parents are separated or divorced, and if the child is illegitimate, generally only the consent of the mother is necessary. The definition of "parent" for the purposes of adoption was considerably extended in Ontario in 1979.

The applicant in a private adoption must ensure that every person who is included in the definition of "parent" receives notice of the application, unless that person has already consented to the adoption. If the judge is satisfied that a "reasonable effort" has been made to serve notice of the proceeding on a person who cannot be located, he may dispense with the requirement of giving notice to that person. The requirements in regard to serving notice are most likely to cause difficulties in the case of a child born out of wedlock. As long as the parties are acting in good faith when attempting to locate a parent, a valid adoption order will be granted if the court dispenses with the notice requirements, but it seems that if the whereabouts of a parent are known and this fact is hidden from the court, then the adoption order may later be quashed.[11]

In the case of a public adoption, s. 69(5) of the C.W.A. specifies that parental consent is not required for the adoption of a Crown ward and the parents will not receive notice of the hearing.

The child who is the subject of an adoption application has a right to participate in the hearing which will so intimately affect his life. All Canadian jurisdictions require the consent of the child to the adoption, though the age at which consent is required varies from seven in Ontario to 14 in Alberta. In most provinces some flexibility is provided by allowing the judge to dispense with the requirement for the child's consent. Section 71(6) of Ontario's C.W.A. provides for the appointment of a guardian "if in the opinion of the court such appointment is required to protect the legal interests of the child." The guardian may be a lawyer, though this is not essential. The role of this guardian *ad litem* is not to simply express the child's wishes to the court, but to promote the child's interests. The English Court of Appeal in *Re G. (T.J.)* noted the need for such a guardian:[12]

> It is essential to have some such system to protect the interests of the child,
> because a proposed adoption desired by the intending adopter and by
> the natural parent or parents might nevertheless not be in the best interests
> of the child.

In addition to the requirement for a child's consent to an adoption, subject to judicial dispensation, the C.W.A. provides in s. 77 that "the court shall inquire into the capacity of the child to appreciate the nature of the application and shall, where practicable, hear the child." The extent to which a court should be swayed by a child's views is problematic. Young children often have difficulty expressing their true feelings, and may not adequately appreciate the significance of the adoption process. It seems likely that the court would be more likely to be influenced by a child who opposed an adoption, than by one who desired it, as refusing an adoption simply preserves the *status quo* and allows a new application to be made later, whereas making the order permanently and radically alters the situation. In *Re G. (T.J.)*, a 12-year-old boy expressed a desire to be adopted by his stepmother. The natural parents separated when the boy was three, and the child had lived with his father and stepmother since the age of four. The father died when the boy was nine and he continued to reside with the stepmother. Until the age of 11, the boy believed his stepmother was his biological mother. The natural mother would not consent to the adoption, though she had apparently shown little interest in the boy. The court would not dispense with the natural mother's consent and the adoption order was not made. It was felt that the boy would benefit from contact with his natural mother, and that the refusal to grant the adoption would make little difference to the boy's actual living arrangements.

4. Parental Consent

Adoption represents the severing of the links between a child and his parent(s), and generally will effectively terminate any future contact between them. It is hardly surprising that there must be parental consent to such a radical alteration in the relationship, and that efforts are made to ensure that such a consent is given freely, and only after a carefully considered decision. If there is to be an adoption without parental consent, this will only be after the parent has shown himself to be clearly unfit and the child is made a Crown ward, or as the result of a carefully considered court order, one which will only be made "for the most serious reasons."[13]

A valid parental consent for an adoption must be freely given, and with a clear understanding of its significance. In Ontario, the signing of a consent to an adoption must be witnessed by an employee of the C.A.S.[14] Further, if the parent of the child is a minor, then a representative from the office of the Official Guardian must confirm that the consent "reflects the true informed wishes" of the parent.[15] The Official Guardian is a government-appointed lawyer who personally acts on behalf of those persons who cannot adequately represent their own interests, such as minors and mentally incapacitated persons. Further, s. 76 of the *C.W.A.* requires that before making an adoption order, the judge must be satisfied that every person who has given a consent "understands the nature and effect of the adoption order."

A consent must be a true and informed consent. If a consent is obtained by fraud, duress, or trickery, it is not a valid consent, and it seems that an adoption based on such an invalid consent may be set aside at a later date. In one British Columbia case,[16] the paternal grandparents of a child were seeking to adopt him. The mother was 16, and the father 18. The child was born less than three months after the marriage, and when he was four months old, the parents separated, placing him with the paternal grandparents, who then made the adoption application. The grandfather and father sought to pressure the reluctant mother into signing the consent for the adoption. They led her to believe that doing so would assist in the reconciliation of the couple, that she and her husband would regain the child upon reconciliation, and that in any event she could see the child at any time. The husband, in fact, found married life distasteful and restrictive, and had no intention of resuming cohabitation. The consent was signed in the presence of a lawyer, about whom the judge remarked:[17]

> While I am not prepared to find that the solicitor wholly failed in his duty I do find that he was mistaken in the opinions expressed in . . . his

affidavit appended to the form of consent, that it "appeared to be signed freely and voluntarily," and that the mother "appeared to understand fully the effect of her consent and of adoption."

The mother's consent was set aside, and the adoption effectively blocked. The judge stated:[18]

> A consent, induced as this one was by fraud and undue influence, is neither free nor voluntary and is not binding. It is no consent at all. Equally it is plain that the mother, in the induced belief that the adoption of the child would not hinder her right to see the child at will or to regain the child upon reconciliation with her husband, had little or no understanding of the effect of adoption and of her consent thereto.
> It is true that the misrepresentation of the husband was as to his intention but it was nevertheless a representation that the alleged intention did indeed exist and, as it was untrue, there was a clear misrepresentation . . . The misrepresentation was clearly intended to and did in fact cause the mother to sign the form of consent. It brought about in her mind a misunderstanding which induced her to act as she did. The misrepresentation was clearly fraudulent as there was, admittedly, a complete absence of honest belief in the husband's mind that there was any possibility of reconciliation or of regaining the child in a united home.

One of the significant factors in this British Columbia case is that the proposed adoptive parents were actively involved in the deception of the mother, and in other cases where this element was absent the courts have shown considerable reluctance to allow a parent argue that a consent which appeared to have been freely given was invalid. In an Arizona case,[19] a mother argued that her consent was invalid due to duress and mistake. She was physically weakened and emotionally depressed by having recently given birth. The mother was apparently under a mistaken belief that she could revoke her consent for up to six months after giving it, though this belief was not fostered by the adoptive parents or their attorneys. The court held the consent was valid, and sought support from the following comments in *Acedo v. State, Department of Public Welfare*:[20]

> To allow the efforts and expectations produced by, and flowing from, the petitioner's conduct [the mother's consent] to be destroyed by her unexpressed misconception, which was neither the result of actions by the adoption agency nor the adoptive parents, would be contrary to the public policy manifested by our adoption statutes. The continued integrity of the adoption procedure demands that a consentor be held to the natural consequences of his or her actions, absent the presence of highly important countervailing policy considerations . . .

In a number of provinces legislation has been enacted providing that a parent cannot give a valid adoption consent until the child in question has been alive for a certain period of time, ranging from four days in the Northwest Territories, to seven in Ontario, and 14 in Prince Edward Island. This is to ensure that a mother has recovered from the effects of giving birth to adequately consider such a serious decision, though it can be argued that these periods are not sufficiently long.

Sometimes a parent who has voluntarily given a proper consent will have a change of heart and wish to revoke the consent. This can create an extremely difficult situation for all concerned. For the natural parent, the decision to revoke the consent may not be based on a realistic assessment of the situation, but if the parent is not allowed to revoke the consent there may be a permanent sense of loss, and further, the child will be denied the opportunity of living with his own flesh and blood. If revocation is permitted and the child returned from a prospective adoptive home to his natural parents the child may be seriously damaged by the abrupt change in environment while the prospective adoptive parents who may have made a great emotional and financial investment in the adoption will doubtless suffer. Allowing revocation of a consent can severely disrupt the entire adoption process and discourage prospective adopters.

The nature of the parental right to revoke a consent to adoption varies from province to province. In a series of decisions in the 1950s, the Supreme Court of Canada made it clear that, in the absense of specific legislative provisions to the contrary, a parent has a presumptive right to revoke an adoption consent at any time before a final adoption order is made, and this right of revocation is only to be lost "[for] 'very serious and important' reasons."[21] The doctrine of "parental rights" seemed to take precedence over the idea of promoting the child's best interests. Based on a view that a child's welfare lies "first, within the warmth and security . . . provided by his parents,"[22] it was held that unless a natural parent was clearly unfit or had abandoned the child, there was a right of revocation. In *Re Agar; McNeilly v. Agar*, the Supreme Court was faced with a case involving a child who was three years of age and had resided since the age of seven days with his prospective adoptive parents, who intended to adopt the child. The mother, who sought to revoke her consent, was a single woman in her 30s who would have had to leave the child with a baby-sitter while she worked. The Supreme Court of Canada stated:[23]

> I have examined with care the evidence given in this case and, while of
> the opinion that the child would be more likely to have a successful and
> happy life if left in the custody of the appellants [the prospective adoptive
> parents] I have come, with regret, to the conclusion that, applying the
> rule as stated in the decisions of this Court . . . it has not been shown that
> the mother should be refused custody.

In most provinces, including Ontario, legislation has been enacted to limit the right of revocation. In Ontario, s. 69(2) of the *C.W.A.* gives a parent the unconditional right to revoke a consent to adoption within 21 days of giving it, but s. 69(9) provides that after this period of time has elapsed, the consent may be withdrawn only if "having regard to all the circumstances of the case . . . it is in the best interests of the child.'' In *Re Kilmer and Resney*[24] the court was faced with an application by the natural parents to revoke their consents to the adoption of their daughter, aged 21 months. For all but the first days of her life she had resided with the proposed adoptive parents. The natural parents initially placed the child for adoption because they were having marital difficulties and had not intended to conceive the child; at the time of the application to allow revocation they had effected a reconciliation. The judge refused to allow a revocation, commenting that:[25]

> The statute now prevents capricious and arbitrary evasion of a consent.
> The section demands exploration whether the best interests of the child
> require the court to give leave to withdraw the consent. A child is no
> longer a prize to be awarded for the vacillations and changes of mind of a
> natural parent. The inquiry by the court is not to be hampered by the
> regrets and changing whims of the natural parents.

After *Kilmer* the *C.W.A.* was amended and s. 69(10) now provides that a consent to an adoption cannot be revoked once a child has been placed for adoption by an adoption agency or licensee.

An adoption order may be made without the consent of a natural parent, if there is a court order dispensing with such consent. In the case of the adoption of a permanent ward, there is no need for parental consent in most jurisdictions and so dispensing with parental consent is not at issue. Generally, adoption agencies will only become involved if the natural parents are willing participants in the adoption. Problems in dispensing with parental consent are mostly likely to arise in an adoption arranged by one of the parents, especially in the case of stepparent adoptions. It must not, however, be imagined that in most adoptions arranged by parents there is a bitter dispute over dispensing with parental consent. Frequently, the necessary consents will be forthcoming. It is also common for there to be difficulty in locating a parent, and an application will then be made to dispense with the requirement of locating the parent and obtaining a consent. Further, often a parent is located and served with notice of the application for adoption, and while not actually signing a consent to the adoption, the parent does not take any steps to actively oppose the adoption, in which case it is generally not too difficult to persuade a judge to dispense with the required consent if the natural parent has had little contact with the child. Still, there is a considerable amount of litigation concerning dispensing with parental consent.

All Canadian jurisdictions have statutory provisions allowing a court to dispense with the consent of a parent to adoption. In Ontario, s. 69(7) of the *C.W.A.* allows the court to do so if, ''having regard to all of the circumstances of the case, the court is satisfied that it is in the best interests of the child'' that the consent be dispensed with. This particular ''best interests'' test is somewhat different from that which is applied in other situations, particularly custody cases. It is recognized that adoption is permanent, unlike custody which can always be varied. In the case of private adoptions, especially stepparent adoptions, the question of the child's living arrangements is quite separate from adoption, and the principal effect of adoption is the permanent severing of a link with a natural parent, a severance which it is often difficult to characterize as being in the child's best interests.

In Ontario, the courts have consistently held that they will not dispense with parental consent unless there are very serious and important reasons. The courts will consider the nature of the relationship between the child and the non-consenting parent, and the wishes of the child. If there is a likelihood of positive benefits from a continuing relationship, the consent will not be dispensed with. The courts are likely to be concerned about the stability of the proposed adoptive home, particularly if there is a stepparent adoption, as dispensing with the consent and allowing the adoption will deprive the child of the possibility of financial and emotional support from the natural parent, support which may be necessary if the new home should prove unstable.

In *Smith v. Harvey*,[26] the parents of a boy and a girl separated in 1967, when the children were aged one and four respectively. The divorce took place in 1971, with the mother getting custody of the children without access to the father. She remarried in 1972 and the stepfather sought to become the adoptive father in 1973. The natural father refused to consent to the adoption, though at the time of the separation and divorce, he agreed he would not oppose adoption proceedings if the mother remarried. The natural father provided financial support for the children until the wife's remarriage, and though he had not been allowed to visit, he continued to express an interest in the children, sending them Christmas and birthday gifts. The children continued to maintain a relationship with their paternal grandparents. The older child expressed a desire to be adopted, while the younger really did not understand the proceedings. At school, the children were already using the name of their stepfather. The judge would not dispense with the consent of the father, hence preventing the adoption. He commented:[27]

> My own personal feeling is that where an effective end has been put to a relationship between a father and his children and his place has been taken by another it is desirable that the new relationship be confirmed by adoption. I should add, however, that this view would be stronger if the second marriage of the mother had lasted for a substantially longer period of time.
>
> At all events, it seems clear that before a court may grant the order [dispensing with consent] there must be the most serious reasons. I conclude from the authorities that before doing so a judge must conclude that the parent has abandoned his (or her) child or has misconducted himself (or herself) in such a manner that the applicants should be permitted to adopt the child without the parent's consent. In the instant case there is no evidence to support a contention that this is the situation. Mr Harvey [the natural father] has attempted to see his children from time to time in recent years. He has retained counsel to oppose these applications and came from Montreal [to Thunder Bay] to attend the hearings. By his conduct he has indicated that he [has] a very real interest in the children and it may

very well be that, at some future time, he may establish a very real
relationship with them.

A dispensation for the requirement of parental consent will only be given if there
has been a real lack of contact between parent and child for a number of years. It
is an issue which the judge who sees and hears the witnesses will decide on the
basis of judicial discretion. In *Waldron v. Adams*,[28] a stepmother wanted to become
a parent by adoption, and the natural mother refused to consent to the adoption.
The natural parents had separated four and one-half years earlier, with the mother
initially having custody, but giving the father custody after a year, when the two
children were three and one and one-half years old respectively. The mother saw
the children only three times after she gave up custody as she lived in Edmonton
and the children were in Victoria, British Columbia. The natural mother was
satisfied with the care they were receiving, but wished to maintain contact and visit
the children. The court dispensed with the natural mother's consent, saying this
about the stepmother, the respondent in the action:[29]

> I think that the children should go through their formative years with the
> belief that the respondent is their mother and that she, in turn, should have
> the security of knowing that she is, in law, the mother of the children,
> which will induce her to give all the love and affection that a mother can
> give.

5. Making the Adoption Order: The Best Interests of the Child

After satisfying himself that all of the statutory requirements for jurisdiction, notice,
consent and so on have been fulfilled, the judge must decide whether the adoption
order should be made. The making of the order is not automatic. There is no
absolute right to adopt a child, simply because the various specific statutory requirements have been satisfied. Legislation such as s. 76 of Ontario's *C.W.A.* also
requires the judge to independently assure himself that the adoption is in the best
interests of the child. In making this determination, the court will consider all of
the circumstances of the case, often alerted to any potential problems as a result
of the official social investigation of the proposed adoption. If the report is favourable and no one appears to oppose the adoption, invariably there is little
difficulty in obtaining the order. If difficulties do appear to be present, the court
may be faced by a number of complex and interrelated issues when making the
decision, a decision which must not simply promote the child's interests in the
short term, but which must be regarded as creating a permanent environment for
promoting the child's best interests.

Although the court must decide whether a proposed adoption is in the best
interests of a child, this assessment must be made on a realistic basis. The applicant
parents must be assessed on their own merits and deficiencies, and not be compared
to some potentially ideal parents. An Australian court expressed the test in this
way:[30]

It is, in our opinion, irrelevant that other applicants, if they applied, might promote the interests and welfare of the child to a greater degree or that there might be persons who, if they applied for the particular child, might make a better case than the applicants. The Court, in deciding applications such as this, is not required to decide what is best for the child in any combination of circumstances which may reasonably be seen as a possibility, but is required to make the order if it is satisfied that . . . the welfare and interests of the child would be promoted.

In *Re Lamb*, a Protestant couple wished to adopt a four-year-old infant who had resided with them virtually since its birth. The child had been born of a Roman Catholic mother and had been baptized as a Roman Catholic. In making the adoption order, the judge stated:[31]

As there is no statutory bar to the making of an adoption order on the basis of religion, is there any logical reason why religion should be an obstacle? In my view there is not. This does not mean that the spiritual welfare of the child must not be considered. It should be weighed together with his physical, social, intellectual well being. Evidence before a Court that applicants to adopt a child were atheists, agnostics or did not practice the religion which they professed, might well be considered in determining if it would be in the best interests of the child to be adopted by such applicants. But that is not the situation here. The Lambs are both professing and practicing members of their church. To deprive a child of the advantages which adoption would give him simply because the applicants, though Christian are of a different denomination would, in my view, be a denial of natural justice. If that were the law it would mean that children would be denied the permanent values, which a normal family life can provide, simply because the natural parent who, as in this case, was found to have neglected the child, was of a different religion from those seeking to adopt the child. This would be neither common sense nor justice and in my view was neither contemplated nor intended when the Act was passed.

Though a child should ideally be adopted by persons of the same religious faith, *Re Lamb* points out that this factor may not be determinative, particularly where the child is too young to have formed his own beliefs.

Beliefs other than religious ones may also be important. In *Re Grainor*[32] the prospective adoptive parents were firm and active believers in "natural health," and indicated that they would not immunize the child for contagious and other diseases. The judge characterized this as a failure to carry out "one of their obligations and duties in this society" and refused to make the adoption order, unless the prospective adoptive parents satisfied him that they would provide all medically required immunizations and treatment for the child, regardless of their personal beliefs.

The effect of an adoption is to legally create a parental relationship, and in assessing applications the courts have considered the relative ages and previous relationship of the prospective adoptive parents and child, to ensure that it is possible for such a relationship to exist in a real sense. The difficulties of genuinely establishing such a relationship have led to the refusal of a number of applications where a primary motivation in seeking the adoption appeared to be the regularizing of immigrant status, though the difficulty might arise in other situations.

In *Re Khan,* a 26-year-old man and his wife applied to adopt the man's 16-year-old brother. The applicants were landed immigrants, but the boy was only in Canada on a visitor's permit. The Ontario Court of Appeal upheld the decision of the trial judge, refusing the application, pointing out that:[33]

> . . . the adoption of one brother by another with a 10-year age difference . . . appears to us to be inconsistent with the intent of . . . the *Child Welfare Act.* It has the appearance of an accommodation adoption to get around the stringencies or requirements of the *Immigration Act* . . . and the Court and the provincial legislation should not be used as a means to achieve that end.

In *Re A.B.,* an English case, the grandparents of a child who was born out of wedlock applied for adoption of the child. The mother of the child was 15 years old. The judge granted the order, but expressed some concern about the situation:[34]

> Normally an adoption presupposes a complete and final separation between the child and its natural parents. The child looks thenceforth to the adopters as its parents, and the natural parents, relinquishing all their parental rights and duties, step, as it were, forever out of the picture of the child's life. In the present case, on the other hand, the child and its natural parent must inevitably remain in association to a greater or lesser degree, and it is impossible to exclude the risk of grave psychological strain and the emotional disturbance arising therefrom in the future, with consequences to them both which might be quite serious. The ostensible relationship of sisters between those who are, in fact, mother and child is unnatural, and its creation might sow the seeds of grievous unhappiness for them both, and indeed for the adopters themselves.

Though adoptions by grandparents are not uncommon, the factors suggested by the court in *Re A.B.* may always influence the court to reject such an adoption application.

6. The Adoption Order

At the end of the adoption hearing, the judge will usually either grant the adoption order, or dismiss the application. There are, however, other possibilities which include making an interim, or a conditional, order.

The legislation in Ontario and some of the other provinces allows the court to postpone making a decision about the adoption, while leaving the child in the adoptive home. Section 82 of the *C.W.A.* permits an interim custody order to be made for a "probationary period" of up to one year. Generally, it is desirable to avoid delay and have a final decision made as quickly as possible. An English judge warned:[35]

> The question of who is to have care and control of a child, and *a fortiori* in contested adoption cases, who is to be a parent of a child, should be decided as quickly as possible. Any uncertainty as to its future must be bad for the child if the child is old enough to know what is going on, and the longer the status quo, whatever it may be, is maintained, the harder it becomes to change it, even though on other grounds a change may be desirable. Again, as delay tends to favour the side which has possession of the child, if the practice of the court lends itself to delay, that side is easily tempted to spin out the proceedings, and even if it is not in fact doing so, the other side may easily come to suspect that it is.

Notwithstanding the desirability of quickly resolving a matter, there may be situations where such a probationary period is desirable, especially if, as in the case of a parental placement adoption in Ontario, there is ordinarily no statutory requirement of a probationary period before a hearing. This may give all concerned an opportunity to clarify their feelings about a situation, or to demonstrate their intentions by adopting a certain course of conduct. For example, in a stepparent adoption, there might be an interim order where a non-consenting parent who has not seen his child for a number of years has an opportunity to exercise access rights.[36]

At present, no Canadian province has legislation allowing the court to impose a condition to an adoption, and the usual rule is that the order is made with the adoptive parent assuming all of the rights and responsibilities of a natural parent. In rare circumstances the courts have indicated that they are prepared to impose conditions upon adoptive parents, as, for example, in the case of *Re Grainor*, which was discussed earlier. In that case the adoptive parents indicated that on account of their beliefs they would not provide certain types of medical treatment for the child, and the judge required an undertaking from them to provide any necessary medical treatment, before making the order. If conditions are imposed, and later not satisfied, it is not at all clear what will happen, and it does not seem that the adoption order itself would be revoked, or otherwise affected, though there might be some sanction for contempt of court.

As will be discussed a little later, there have been circumstances in which a court will order that a natural parent, or other person, have access to a child after adoption. This is most likely to occur in the case of a stepparent adoption.

Sometimes a parent will give a consent to a child's adoption which is conditional.

For example, a parent may stipulate that the child is only to be adopted by a Roman Catholic family, and brought up in that faith. In this case, a court would probably not make an adoption order unless that condition were satisfied,[37] but once the order is made, the adoption would not be nullified if the situation changed. In the example cited, if the adoptive parents left the faith after the adoption, it would not affect the validity of the order.

7. Appeals and Annulment

In most Canadian provinces there is a statutorily provided right of appeal. For example, s. 84 of Ontario's *C.W.A.* specifically grants the right to appeal a decision granting or refusing an adoption order. The appeal is to the County Court and then to the Ontario Court of Appeal. As with most other types of appeals, there is not an actual rehearing of the case, but instead a review of the transcript of the original hearing, with a view to correcting any errors of law. The Appellate Court will be most reluctant to overturn the decision of a trial judge who had the opportunity of seeing all of the participants in person, and will only overturn the decision if there clearly was an error.

Due to the desirability of having the adoption order finalized, Ontario legislation provides that an appeal must be launched within 30 days.

In addition to the possibility of appealing a decision in regard to adoption, it may be possible to obtain an annulment, or revocation, of the original order. An annulment is a declaration from a court that the original order is invalid because there was a fatal defect in the making of the original order. Arguably, in some situations an application for annulment can be made at any time, though some statutes specifically limit the time for making such an application.[38] Some provinces, such as Alberta and Nova Scotia, have legislation specifically dealing with an-nulment of an order.

In other provinces, it appears that there might be an inherent power in the courts to grant an annulment, for example, if parental consent to an adoption was obtained by fraud or duress. In the American case of *Re Doe's Adoption*,[39] the adoptive parents failed to disclose that they were experiencing marital difficulties when being investigated and supervised by the agency responsible. A new-born child was placed with the couple for over a year before the final adoption order was made. During this time, the couple's marital problems increased and a month after the adoption was made the couple separated. The court learned nothing of these problems at the time of the adoption hearing. Seven months after the initial adoption order was made, the court ordered it set aside as the order had been based upon fraud and misrepresentation. Though it is not clear that this case would be followed in Canada, it might well be accepted as a precedent, indicating that parties presenting adoption applications to the court should take care to be open and honest.[40]

It should be noted that unless there are grounds for an appeal or annulment, an adoption order, once made, cannot be rescinded. In *Re Chappell*,[41] a young man, aged 22, sought to have an adoption order made when he was four, some 18 years earlier, rescinded. The adoption placement was not very successful, and at the age of 10 he moved out of his adoptive home and began a series of placements in the care of the child welfare authorities and in training schools. Finally, at the age of 20 he located his natural mother, resumed a relationship with her, and adopted her surname. The young man, the natural mother, the adoptive parents, and the child welfare authorities all agreed that it would be in the young man's best interests to rescind the initial order, but the court simply found that it lacked the jurisdiction to do so.

8. Subsidies

Some children are especially difficult to place for adoption, and special resources have been developed to assist in the process of finding these children good, stable, permanent adoptive homes. The child may be difficult to place because of a physical or mental disability, emotional disturbance, age, ethnic background, or other factors. Various provincial and national schemes exist to attempt to locate homes for such children. Ontario's *C.W.A.*, s. 88, now allows the government to make subsidy payments to adoptive parents. This is not done frequently, and it is recognized that adoption should not be undertaken for financial reward, nor should the independence of adoptive parents be threatened by giving them government grants. It is recognized, however, that in rare cases subsidies may be necessary to secure a home for a child, either because the adoptive parents cannot afford to raise the child, or because there are special expenses associated with caring for the particular child. Subsidies are likely to be used when foster parents, who have had a child for a period of time, decide to adopt the child, especially if the child has some special physical, mental or emotional handicap.

C. THE EFFECT OF ADOPTION

As a general rule, the effect of adoption is to legally place an adopted child in exactly the same position as he would have been if he had been the biological child of his adopted parents, and terminates all of the legal ties which arose as a result of the relationship with the natural parents. As we shall see, there are some exceptions to this rule, and not all Canadian jurisdictions approach the situation in exactly the same way.

Section 86 of Ontario's *C.W.A.* provides that the adopted child acquires a relationship to all persons as if he were a biological child, thus acquiring new siblings, uncles, aunts, grandparents, and so on. Further, in any will or other document, a reference to a person, or group of persons, shall be deemed to include a person who has acquired status by adoption, unless such an inference is expressly excluded. Thus, if a man in his will leaves his estate "to my nephews," this includes the adopted son of the man's brother. Also, an adopted child acquires all of the rights to inherit property upon "intestacy" (if a person dies without a will), which he would have if he were a biologically related child. In some other provinces, the law is somewhat different. For example, New Brunswick's *Adoption Act* provides that only some of the closest kindred relationships will be legally created by adoption, such as brother and sister, but others, such as nephew and grandchild, will not be created. In New Brunswick, an adopted child may inherit upon intestacy from both his natural and his adopted parents. The laws regarding the passage of property at death are complex, and full of exceptions; a person faced with a problem should obtain adequate legal advice.

In all Canadian jurisdictions, it is usual for an adopted child to acquire the surname of the adoptive parents, and a court order is made to this effect at the time of the adoption. The court also has a discretion not to change the surname, and, for example, in Ontario, s. 78(3) of the *C.W.A.* provides that the child's consent is required if he is 14 or older. In all provinces, except Manitoba, the court may also order that the given name or names of the child be changed when an adoption is made.

It is interesting to note that in cases where a woman with children has remarried and the stepfather does not want to adopt the children, or cannot adopt them, the children will sometimes take their stepfather's last name. Such a change of name may be the result of a formal, legal change of name as a result of following a legislative scheme for a change of name, or it may simply be the result of the informal use of the stepfather's surname, for example, when registering for school. The effect of such a change of name is to present to the community the impression that the stepfather is the legal father of the child, either as a result of adoption or from birth. The attitude of the courts to such a change of name, effecting the appearance of a change in status, is somewhat mixed. Though sometimes an injunction is granted to prevent a change of name, particularly if the husband continues to see the children and contribute to their support, the courts have often been prepared to allow such a change of name.[42]

Though for most purposes adoption results in the creation of a completely new status, for a few purposes it does not. Section 86(5) of the *C.W.A.* provides that in regard to the laws governing incest and prohibitions regarding marriage due to familial relationships, adoption is to be ignored. An Indian child who is adopted by non-Indian parents does not lose his Indian status, even though he has no Indian relatives.[43]

It is accepted that the effect of an adoption order is to terminate both the natural parents' rights to custody of their child and their duty to support their child, while at the same time giving the adoptive parents the right of custody and the responsibility of support. A more difficult question arises when attempting to resolve the issue of whether a natural parent should have the right to visit a child who has been adopted. When a child has been adopted by persons unknown to the natural parents, for example, in an adoption arranged by an agency, it is easy to appreciate that allowing the natural parents access could be most disruptive. On the other hand, in the case of adoption by a stepparent or relative, allowing a natural parent access might sometimes be appropriate.

When deciding the issue of access rights, the courts have had to resolve two questions: (1) whether as a matter of law there is jurisdiction to allow access; (2) whether on the facts of the case it is appropriate to grant access.

The issue of whether a court has jurisdiction to allow access to a natural parent after adoption is complex, and it is hardly surprising the courts have not been unanimous in their resolution of the issue. One important factor is the legislation under which a parent is applying. It has been held that in a situation where a child who was the subject of an access order under the federal *Divorce Act* and then becomes subject to an adoption, generally by a stepparent, the access order under the *Divorce Act* takes precedence over any limitation of access resulting from an adoption order made pursuant to provincial adoption legislation.[44] This argument rests on the constitutional doctrine of the paramountcy of federal legislation. If the child was made a permanent ward, effectively terminating parental rights, it has been argued that access cannot be granted except under child protection legislation.[45] On the other hand, some courts have held that provincial legislation, such as s. 35 of Ontario's *Family Law Reform Act, 1978*, allows any person to apply for access to a child, including a natural parent who has lost all parental rights due to an adoption order.[46] While the situation is far from clear, it seems that the courts in most provinces are prepared to accept that they have jurisdiction to grant access, at least if the application is made under appropriate legislation. In 1979, Manitoba's *Child Welfare Act* was amended so that s. 100 now expressly allows a biological father to seek a court order giving him access to his child if it should be adopted by its stepfather.

Although it would appear that the courts have the authority to grant a natural parent access to his child, access is likely to be granted only "in the most exceptional cases."[47] In *Re C.A.S. of Metropolitan Toronto and CB*,[48] the judge stated:

> . . . with the ordinary situation of adoption by a couple who are strangers
> to the natural parents . . . ordinarily it is clear that it is neither in the
> interests of the child who has an opportunity . . . to be adopted, nor in the
> interests of the adopting parents to have anything short of a clear outright
> adoption without sharing custody or access. Some cases . . . indeed show
> unusual circumstances such as adoption by a divorced mother and her
> new spouse, of a child, with consent of the father of that child, with
> continued access to him.

In *Sobel v. Fogler*,[49] one of the rare cases in which a court was prepared to grant a natural parent access to his child after adoption, the judge relied heavily on the testimony of a psychologist who was of the opinion that the child would need to know about his real father and that a right of access would be of real value to the child, showing that his real father cared about him. The *Sobel* case involved the granting of access to the father of a child born out of wedlock. The father lived with the mother during the first year of the child's life, and was granted access for three hours a week. Even in cases involving adoption by a stepparent, visiting rights would rarely be granted to the natural parent since an adoption order would not have been made to begin with if a close bond already existed between the child and its natural parent.

One of the most controversial issues in the adoption field is whether an adopted child should have the right to know the identity of his natural parents, and to meet them. The two sides of this question were addressed in *Lyttle v. C.A.S. of Metropolitan Toronto:*[50]

> There can surely be no doubt but that any child, knowing he has been adopted, will be curious about his origins . . . there is more than mere curiosity but a basic, if sometimes unexpressed, need for a child, who knows he has been adopted, to get in touch with his natural parents. This need becomes most apparent during early adolescence. To know who his real parents are gives a child a sense of identity, an assurance of belonging, and an awareness that he has not come from nowhere, but has his own place in history as the child of known parents. . . .
>
> On the other hand, the sense of security of the child in his new home ought not to be disturbed [lightly]. He must continue to know that this is indeed his home; that he is entitled to demand the loyalty of his new parents and that he is obliged to give them his loyalty in return. That sense of security and loyalty would be diminished if the adopting parents felt that a natural parent could interfere with the affection of the child, or their authority over him. They might feel that they were mere custodians of the child, with less than ordinary parental rights and responsibilities. Another factor, of general public policy, which I think is almost conclusive with children's aid societies, is that prospective adopting parents would be more difficult to find if they were generally aware that natural parents might be permitted to regain contact with adopted children.

Though a child might have a genuine desire to know who his "real" parents are, it may not always be in his best interests to make this discovery. This point was poignantly made in a letter to the "Dear Abby" newspaper advice column:[51]

DEAR ABBY: I can understand the adopted child's desire to know who his "real" parents were. I'm sure that almost every person who sets out to find his "real" parents imagines that he or she is the product of a beautiful, impetuous love affair between a couple who were forced by circumstances to part.

Such is not always the case. A child can be born as a result of lust, greed, fear, intimidation, blackmail, rape and a number of other ugly situations. Abortions were not always possible, and if they were, many would have refused.

Before a person starts searching for his "roots," I suggest he or she ask this question: Would I be more or less happy if my real mother were to say to me, "I don't know who your father was. You were conceived in a brothel and he had 15."

Who would want to be the product of an affair between the Jewish girl in Holocaust and the prison guard who promised to keep her young Jewish husband alive in return for her favors?

I think someone should point out that these mothers might well be protecting their illegitimate children from further pain by disclosing the circumstances of their conception.

SPEAKING FOR MYSELF

The proposal to allow disclosure of information concerning natural parents has caused considerable political controversy, and most governments have not been quick to introduce legislation to deal with the problem. In 1976, a scheme providing adopted children with information about their natural parents was introduced in Britain. In a close vote, a similar scheme was adopted by the Ontario Legislature in 1979. The Ontario scheme is created by s. 81 of the *C.W.A.* It allows an adopted child who is 18 or older, and a natural parent whose child was adopted, to apply to a central Voluntary Disclosure Registry. If both make application, the government contacts the child, the natural parents, and the adoptive parents, if living. If all confirm their consent to the disclosure in writing, the information will be released to the child and natural parents. The C.A.S. will generally be involved in the process, and will provide counselling as required.

The *Child Welfare Act* of Manitoba, in s. 94, provides that application may be made to a County Court for the release of confidential information concerning the granting of an adoption. In a recent case, *Re A*,[52] a Manitoba court ruled that such disclosure would only be made in the case of strong and compelling reasons.

FOOTNOTES

---

1. See, for example, *Re Baby Duffell; Martin v. Duffell,* [1950] S.C.R. 737
2. See Simon Fodden, ed., *Canadian Family Law* (Toronto, 1977), at p. G-38
3. See Alastair Bissett-Johnson, "Step-Parent Adoptions in English and Canadian Law," in Ian Baxter *et al., The Child and the Courts* (Toronto, 1978), at p. 335
4. [1978] 3 A.C.W.S. 43
5. *Re M.J.W. and the Child Welfare Act,* [1964] N.S.W.R. 1108
6. *Immigration Regulations,* s. 4(g)
7. *Re S.* (1978), 6 R.F.L. (2d) 229
8. *Re Khan* (1978), 21 O.R. (2d) 748. See also *Re Raghbeer* (1977), 3 R.F.L. (2d) 42
9. See Daniel G. Grove, "Independent Adoption: The Case for the Gray Market," 13 Vil. Law Rev. 116 (1967)
10. See Ontario Law Reform Commission, Report on Family Law: Children, Part III (1973), at p. 53
11. See *C.A.S. of Metropolitan Toronto v. Lyttle* (1973), 34 D.L.R. (3d) 127; and *Re Winsor* (1966), 59 D.L.R. (2d) 42

12. [1963] 1 All E.R. 20 at p. 29
13. *Re Liffiton and Campbell* (1972), 7 R.F.L. 353
14. Rules of the Provincial Court (Family Division), Rule 63
15. The *Child Welfare Act, 1978*, s. 69(13)
16. *Re Adoption No. 71-09-013131* (1972), 9 R.F.L. 196
17. *Supra*, at p. 199
18. *Supra*, at p. 200
19. *Anonymous v. Anonymous* (1975), 530 P. 2d 896. See also *McKeever v. C.A.S. of Metropolitan Toronto* (1975), 22 R.F.L. 346
20. (1973), 513 P. 2d 1350 at p. 1354. See also *Re J.* (1979), 9 R.F.L. (2d) 281
21. *Re Baby Duffell; Martin v. Duffell*, [1950] S.C.R. 737 at p. 746
22. *Hepton v. Maat*, [1957] S.C.R. 606 at p. 607
23. [1958] S.C.R. 52 at pp. 55-56
24. (1973), 11 R.F.L. 375
25. *Supra*, at p. 382
26. (1974), 19 R.F.L. at p. 368
27. *Supra*, at pp. 372-73
28. (1978), 2 R.F.L. (2d) 220
29. *Supra*, at p. 228
30. *Ex parte H* (1963), 63 S.R. 407 at p. 410
31. [1961] O.W.N. 356 at p. 359
32. (1975), 23 R.F.L. 348
33. (1978), 21 O.R. (2d) 748 at p. 249, but see *Re S* (1978), 20 O.R. (2d) 767
34. [1949] 1 All E.R. 709 at p. 710
35. *Re W. (Infants)*, [1965] 3 All E.R. 231 at p. 248
36. *Re Shymr*, [1976] W.W.D. 36
37. See *Re An Infant M*, [1968] 1 N.S.W.R. 770; and *Re J.A.D.*, [1968] 1 N.S.W.R. 781
38. See *Re Hadder* (1976), 12 N. & P.E.I.R. 418
39. (1964), 197 A. 2d 469
40. See *C.A.S. of Metropolitan Toronto v. Lyttle* (1973), 34 D.L.R. (3d) 127 at p. 138; and *Re M.J.C.* (1972), 5 N.B.R. (2d) 28
41. (1977), 4 R.F.L. (2d) 3
42. See Frank Bates, "Changing Children's Names Unilaterally," 10 R.F.L. (2d) 263 (1979); *Zumpano v. Zumpano* (1979), 7 R.F.L. (2d) 263; and *Re Newman* (1976), 29 R.F.L. 172
43. *Natural Parents v. Superintendant of Child Welfare* (1976), 21 R.F.L. 267
44. *North v. North*, [1978] 6 W.W.R. 75; *Re S* (1979), 6 R.F.L. (2d) 48
45. *Cox v. C.A.S. of Metropolitan Toronto* (1979), 8 R.F.L. (2d) 391
46. *Re Cromwell and C.A.S. of County of Kent* (1979), 1 F.L.R.R. 101
47. *Re S* (1974), 20 R.F.L. 233 at p. 236

48. (1977), 1 Fam. L. Rev. 152 at pp. 152-53
49. (1972), 8 R.F.L. 128
50. *Lyttle v. C.A.S. of Metropolitan Toronto* (1976), 24 R.F.L. 134 at pp. 136-37
51. "Dear Abby" column of July 26, 1979, *The Kingston Whig Standard*. Copyright, 1979, Universal Press Syndicate. All rights reserved.
52. (1980), 2 A.C.W.S. (2d) 472

Chapter 6

The Child in Conflict with the Law: The Juvenile Delinquents Act

A. INTRODUCTION

1. Criminal Law

Criminal laws are made to protect society and its members from the actions of certain individuals. Children, just as adults, are capable of committing acts which are a danger to others, or to themselves. It is recognized, however, that children are quite different from adults and have a limited ability to appreciate the nature of their acts. If punished, they will respond quite differently from adults. As a result, special laws have been developed to deal with children who have violated the criminal law and have committed acts which would be met with the full force of the law if they were adults. Most of these laws are at present to be found in the *Juvenile Delinquents Act (J.D.A.)*, which like other federal legislation applies throughout Canada.

A crime may be defined as a wrongful act, the doing of which will subject the perpetrator to penal sanctions, such as a fine, imprisonment, or in countries other than Canada, sometimes even the death penalty. Criminal laws are made by the ruling political authority in a particular jurisdiction. Laws vary from one society to another, though both geographically and historically there is surprising uniformity of laws protecting people and property from harm. Criminal laws exist not only to protect individuals and property, but also to preserve social order and protect individuals from harming themselves. As a result we have laws concerning prostitution and the use of drugs, as well as laws restricting physical assaults. In Canada, the *J.D.A.*, s. 2(1), provides that a child who is guilty of "sexual immorality or any similar form of vice" is guilty of a criminal offense; the purpose of this law is to protect the sexually immoral child—the offender is also the victim. Many of these "victimless" crimes are quite controversial, and they will be further discussed as they relate to children.

When a person is apprehended after violating the criminal law, he is subject to some form of punishment. The rationales for punishing an offender include deterrence, retribution and rehabilitation. It is believed that the threat of suffering some form of penalty will deter others from committing the proscribed act, and deter the individual from committing the act again. Retribution is the notion that the commission of certain acts is inherently worthy of punishment as a means of demonstrating societal disapproval. The aim of rehabilitation is the reform of the offender, the improvement of his character so that he does not want to commit crime again. It has been generally accepted that these goals may not apply equally to children as to adults. Children often have a limited concept of the future, and are less impressed by the threat of future punishment. There seems to be less moral value in seeking retribution against children, who have a less highly developed moral sense than adults. It is, however, the concept of rehabilitation that most fully sets apart our present treatment of child offenders. It is believed that the young offender is much more likely to respond to treatment and be inclined to reform. As a reflection of these beliefs, the *J.D.A.* specifies, in s. 3, that the child who has committed a crime is to be dealt with "not as an offender, but as one requiring . . . help, and guidance and proper supervision."

2. The History and Philosophy of the Juvenile Delinquents Act

From the Middle Ages, if not earlier, the English common law recognized that children had a limited ability to understand and appreciate the wrongfulness of their acts, and hence ought to have diminished criminal responsibility. This recognition came to be embodied in the common-law defense of *doli incapax* (an incapacity to form an intention to do wrong). There was an irrefutable presumption, in effect a rule of law, that a child under seven years of age lacked the capacity to commit a crime. For children from seven to 13, it was presumed that there was an incapacity to commit a crime, but this was a presumption which could be rebutted by evidence that the child did in fact have sufficient intelligence and experience to know that what he was doing was wrong. The defense of *doli incapax* still exists, and is discussed more fully later in this chapter. Although the special defense of *doli incapax* was available to children who were charged with criminal offenses, there was no provision for different treatment until late in the 19th century. Until that time, in both England and Canada, children charged with criminal offenses were tried in the same public court as adults, and if convicted, were subject to the same penalties, such as hanging or incarceration in a penitentiary. Young children were imprisoned in the old Kingston Penitentiary in the same cells and subject to the same rules as adult offenders.

In the latter half of the 19th century, there was a strong reform movement which was concerned with the treatment of children. This movement produced new laws and special facilities in Britain, the United States and Canada. The reformers stated their objectives to include the protection and reclamation of "destitute youths, exposed either by death or neglect of their parents, to evil influences and the acquisition of evil habits, which in too many cases lead to the commission of crime."[1] Many modern social historians have been critical of this movement, and its members have come to be described as "child savers." There is no doubt that by modern standards there was a tremendous "class bias" in the movement; its members were very paternalistic and patronizing, not only towards children, but also towards the poor, and at that time vast sections of the population lived in large urban slums. It is true that the reformers often did not make much of a distinction between neglected and criminal children. This was simply viewed as a distinction between the potentially and the actually criminal. One of the draughtsmen of the Canadian delinquency legislation stated that "there should be no hard and fast distinction between neglected and delinquent children, but that all should be . . . dealt with with a view to serving the best interests of the child."[2] It must be recognized that great improvements were effected by these reformers. First reformatories, and then industrial, or training, schools were opened so that young offenders were no longer incarcerated with adults; though the programs at these facilities were rudimentary and harsh by modern standards, emphasis was placed upon the rehabilitation of children. There was also emphasis placed on keeping children in their homes under the supervision of a probation officer, rather than taking them to an institution. Provision was made to have trials for children separately from adult trials and without publicity.

In 1908, the reformers' efforts culminated in the passage of the *J.D.A.* by the Parliament of Canada. This Act consolidated many of the reforms previously achieved, and broke some new ground. With a few minor amendments, the Act as originally passed is still in force. As indicated above, the primary focus of the Act, and the various institutions created to carry out its aims, is not the punishment of children who violate the criminal law, but rather their rehabilitation. The philosophy of the reformers who pressed for the adoption of the Act was expressed in 1906 in the following way:[3]

> Children should never be treated or spoken of as criminals, but should be studied and dealt with in exactly the same way that a sick or defective child is handled. Wherever there is an offence there is a cause behind it and our children's court and probation system should be able to reach that cause and by some means or other remove it for the safety and protection of the children in the home.

This philosophy is clearly expressed in the Act. Section 38 states:

> 38. This Act shall be liberally construed in order that its purpose may be carried out, namely, that the care and custody and discipline of a juvenile delinquent shall approximate as nearly as may be that which should be given by his parents, and that as far as practicable every juvenile delinquent shall be treated, not as a criminal, but as a misdirected and misguided child, and one needing aid, encouragement, help and assistance.

The Supreme Court of Canada has had occasion to consider the purpose of the Act in upholding its constitutional validity as a valid exercise of the federal government's "criminal law" power. The purpose of the *J.D.A.* is not simply to deal with crime, but to eradicate the human and social conditions which produce crime. The Supreme

Court has stated that the provisions of the Act "are primarily prospective in nature. And in essence, they are intended to prevent these juveniles to become [*sic*] prospective criminals and to assist them to be law-abiding citizens."[4]

The philosophy of the *J.D.A.* may be questioned, and indeed many current observers are most critical of the approach taken. Some alternatives to the present approach will be considered at the end of this chapter. It is important, however, to recognize and appreciate the existing philosophy in order to understand the way in which our juvenile justice system operates.

3. Criminal Law and the Juvenile Delinquents Act

The *J.D.A.* governs the prosecution of all criminal offenses committed by children. For the purposes of the *J.D.A.*, children, in most provinces, are defined as persons under the age of 16, though in some provinces the age limit is 17 or 18. The Act governs procedures, pre-trial confinement and certain evidentiary matters. It deals with the dispositions which can be made after a finding of guilt; the judge who is sentencing a juvenile has a great deal more flexibility than a judge sentencing an adult. As discussed in the next section, the definition of delinquent is broader than simply a child who has violated the criminal law. However, the vast majority of children dealt with under the *J.D.A.* are charged with violating the criminal law, and the principles of substantive criminal law are identical to those which apply to adults. There are some special offenses which can only be committed by children, and there are special defenses which are available only to children, and these will be discussed later. In most cases, the definition of the offense and the determination of guilt or innocence, are based on exactly the same principles as apply to adults. These principles are largely to be found in the *Criminal Code*, and other federal statutes such as the *Narcotics Control Act*, and in various pieces of provincial legislation, such as the *Liquor Control Act* and the *Highway Traffic Act*.

In any criminal case, the onus is upon the Crown Attorney, or prosecutor, to prove that the accused is guilty beyond a reasonable doubt and if this does not occur, the accused must be found not guilty. This is a fundamental rule of our criminal justice system, and applies equally to adults and children. There is no obligation upon the accused to prove his innocence or to testify at his trial. The criminal law defines two basic elements to each offense: a physical element, known as the *actus reus* (guilty act), and a mental element, known as the *mens rea* (guilty mind). That is to say that the Crown must prove that the accused actually committed the physical act which he is charged with committing and that he had intended to do this act. For example, if a person is charged with murder, the Crown will have to prove that the accused actually killed the victim, for instance, by pulling the trigger of the gun which was proven to have fired the bullet which killed the victim. This is the *actus reus*. It must also be proven that the accused intended to do the act charged. In this example it must be shown not only that he intended to pull the trigger, but that he intended that the accused die as a result. This is the *mens rea*.

If the accused did not intend this, he may be guilty of some other offense, such as dangerous use of a firearm, but he will not be guilty of murder.

The requirement that the accused have the intention to commit a criminal act is not to be confused with the notion that he must have knowledge of the law; ignorance of the law is no defense. One can intend to do something and not know that it is against the law to do so. For example, a man may come to Canada from a foreign country where the possession of marijuana is not a violation of the law. If he knowingly possesses marijuana in Canada, he is guilty of an offense, even though he may honestly have thought that he was obeying the law. Even if he can convince the judge that had he known that it was illegal he would not have broken the law, his ignorance of the law will not affect his guilt, though it may mitigate his sentence. If, however, a person has marijuana in his possession, but is unaware of its presence, he will not be guilty of the offense of possessing marijuana, for he did not have the necessary intention to commit the offense. Though he committed the *actus reus*, the physical element of the offense, the *mens rea*, the mental element of the offense, is missing. The concepts of *actus reus, mens rea* and ignorance of the law are difficult ones and often trouble law students, lawyers and judges. It is sufficient for present purposes if the reader has only a general understanding of these concepts.[5]

The juvenile charged under the *J.D.A.* has available to him all of the substantive defenses available to an adult, such as self-defense, or like an adult he may rely upon the inability of the Crown Attorney to prove a material element of his case beyond a reasonable doubt: for example, the Crown may be able to prove that a theft occurred, but may not be able to establish beyond a reasonable doubt that this particular child committed the crime.

The relationship of the *J.D.A.* to substantive criminal law can perhaps best be understood by means of an example. A 14-year-old boy is charged with murdering his father. The *J.D.A.* specifies that the trial is to be held in Juvenile Court without a jury and the Act is applied to determine whether the child may be released pending trial. The child enters a not-guilty plea. The onus is upon the Crown to prove its case beyond a reasonable doubt. The substantive law which determines whether an offense occurred and whether there are any available defenses is applied just as for an adult. The laws of evidence, such as those governing confessions and illegally obtained evidence, are those which would apply in adult court, except that where a child testifies, whether in Juvenile Court or in an adult court, special rules of evidence apply. If the child is acquitted (found not guilty) he is released just like an adult. If, however, the child is convicted of the offense, the nature of the proceedings is quite distinct from that in adult court, and the judge will have a very different range of dispositions available and apply quite different principles when deciding which sentence is appropriate.

The structure of the trial for the juvenile is much the same as one in adult court. The Crown Attorney is a lawyer, though often in Juvenile Court he may be represented by a police officer, usually a member of the Youth Bureau, especially if the offense is not serious. The Crown calls its witnesses first with each witness being "examined in-chief," asked questions by the Crown Attorney, and then "cross-examined" by the lawyer for the accused. While questions on examination-in-chief should not be leading, that is should not suggest answers, questions on cross-examination may be quite pointed and suggest answers. After the Crown has called all of its witnesses, there may be witnesses called by the accused, each being first examined in-chief by the lawyer for the defense, and then cross-examined by the Crown. There is, however, no obligation on the accused to have witnesses testify; he may simply rely upon weaknesses in the case for the Crown. After the accused finishes his evidence, the Crown may wish to call "reply" evidence, to counter evidence which has come out. After all of the evidence is heard, each lawyer will make "submissions," suggesting to the judge what evidence is important, and what is the applicable law. The judge will then make a finding of guilty or not guilty. If it is not guilty, the child is free to go; if it is guilty, the trial goes to the disposition stage. If the child pleaded guilty, the case will proceed immediately to the disposition stage, without the hearing of evidence.

Unlike the adjudication or trial stage, which is similar in many ways to that which an adult would face, at the time of disposition, which is analogous to the adult stage of sentencing, the principles applied by the Juvenile Court are very different from those applied in adult court. Here the philosophy of the *J.D.A.* is important. There is not to be an emphasis upon punishment, but, rather, the juvenile is to be treated as a "misdirected and misguided child." It may be that the child can best be helped by keeping him at home, and if there is evidence from a psychiatrist to this effect, the judge may not order the child removed from home, even in a case involving murder. The most severe disposition that can be made by a Juvenile Court is to commit the child to a training school, which cannot last past the child's 18th birthday; under certain circumstances a serious case can be transferred to adult court and dealt with there. The point is not that child offenders are dealt with in a more lenient manner than adults; often times they're not and frequently a child will be sent to training school for a quite trivial offense, if this is felt to be in the child's best interests. The point is that, while in the adjudication stage the proceedings in many ways resemble those facing an adult, if a finding of guilt is made, the proceedings are very different. The three principles governing the sentencing of adults are greatly modified; of the three rationales for punishment, deterrence, retribution and rehabilitation, only the last is important for juveniles. A fourth rationale, that of confining or isolating the individual and preventing the recurrence of the crime while the offender is in custody, may apply equally to adults and children.

Since in juvenile proceedings, as with those in adult court, the vast majority of persons charged plead guilty, and of those who face trial many more are convicted, the difference in sentencing principles is enormously significant.

B. THE NATURE AND CAUSES OF DELINQUENCY

1. Definition

The *J.D.A.*, s. 2(1), provides the following definition:

"juvenile delinquent" means any child who violates any provision of the
Criminal Code or of any federal or provincial statute, or any
by-law or ordinance of any municipality, or who is guilty of sexual
immorality or any similar form of vice, or who is liable by reason
of any other act to be committed to an industrial school or juvenile
reformatory under any federal or provincial statute;

Any child who is proven in a court to have committed any of the acts set out in
this definition, commits an offense known as delinquency. Thus a young child who
shop-lifts a chocolate bar is not convicted of theft, and is not labelled a thief; one
who commits murder is not a murderer. Both are guilty of the offense of "delinquency," and are technically described as "juvenile delinquents."

Although it is true that the vast majority of the children who are brought to
Juvenile Court on charges of delinquency as a result of acts which would result
in criminal charges if they were adults, there are certain acts which are dealt with
more severely if the perpetrator is a child, and even some acts which are offenses
for children, but not for adults. Violations of provincial statutes, such as the *Liquor
Licence Act* or the *Highway Traffic Act*, or of municipal by-laws constitute what
are known as "*quasi*-criminal" offenses for adults. They are less serious offenses,
and there is no criminal record after conviction; a jail sentence will generally only
be imposed if a person fails to pay a fine. For a child, the commission of one of
these *quasi*-criminal offenses can result in a finding of delinquency and a disposition
just as severe as if a criminal offense occurred.

There are certain acts which are not crimes for adults, but may nevertheless give
rise to delinquency charges. They are called "status offenses" as they are only
offenses for persons having a certain status, namely, that of childhood. There are
quite a few children charged each year with status offenses, though they represent
a small fraction of the total number of youths charged. Only a child may be subject
to criminal sanction for "sexual immorality or any similar form of vice." It is true
that there are acts which are crimes for adults and children alike, which many
would consider to be sexually immoral, such as the various sex and obscenity
offenses in the *Criminal Code*. It is, however, only children who can be subject
to judicial sanction on such a vaguely worded charge. The exact judicial interpretation of the words "sexual immorality or any similar . . . vice" will be considered
a little later. Another status offense is truancy, the failure to attend school. In
Ontario, the *Education Act, 1974*, s. 29(7), provides that any child who is required
by law to attend school (generally children between six and 16), and "who refuses
to attend or who is habitually absent from school is guilty of an offence and on

summary conviction is liable to the penalties provided for children adjudged to be juvenile delinquents.'' This provision will be more fully discussed in Chapter 7. What is important now, is to understand that children are subject to penalties for failure to attend school, whereas others, for example, children 16 or older, are not punished for this. Children can be sent to training schools and otherwise subjected to sanctions for failure to attend school. It must not be imagined that the only way to enforce the socially desirable goal of having universal school attendance is to punish children who fail to attend. Some provinces, such as Quebec, rely solely upon sanctions against parents to enforce attendance, apparently without ill effect upon school attendance by children.[6] Status offenses have been enacted by governments concerned with protecting and helping children. One may ask, however, whether it is appropriate to subject children to special judicial sanction to help them, or whether the use of child protection or other non-criminal legislation might be preferable.

The words ''sexual immorality or any similar form of vice,'' which appear in the statutory definition of delinquency, have been subject of a number of interesting, but sometimes conflicting, judicial interpretations.

The proper interpretation of the words ''sexual immorality'' has frequently arisen as an issue when an adult is charged with the offense of ''contribution to a child's being or becoming a juvenile delinquent,'' under s. 33 of the *J.D.A.*; the charge may be the result of an act of sexual intercourse with a female minor. If such an act constitutes ''sexual immorality,'' then the male is guilty. In the Manitoba case of *R. v. Frost*,[7] a young male was charged with ''contributing'' after repeated acts of intercourse with a 17-year-old female; in Manitoba one is a child until the age of 18 for the purposes of the *J.D.A.* After asking the permission of the girl's father, the young man began to ''court her,'' taking her to movies and hotel lounges. The judge described the facts as follows:

> In any event, during an evening when the accused and his girlfriend had indulged in alcoholic libations, the accused persuaded the girl to accompany him to his apartment. The accused's powers of persuasion were considerably assisted by two factors. Firstly, his apartment was in the same building as the apartment of the girl and her parents and, secondly, the girl was somewhat tipsy by an over-indulgence of cocktails with a vodka base. The evening concluded with the young couple sharing the same bed.
>
> .   .   .   .   .
>
> That the experience left an impression upon the girl, there can be no doubt. For the next two months she made a practice of going down a flight of apartment stairs from her residence to the accused's apartment on the average of twice each week to indulge in the same activity with the accused. Although such matters must always enjoy a mutuality of participation, arrangement and consent, the evidence left no doubt in my mind that it was the girl who was the initiator of these trysts.

This pattern of conduct was concluded at some point during the month of November 1976 at the request and action of the accused. The conclusion of the affair caused the girl some upset and anguish. One day her mother found her crying and upon requesting an explanation the girl told all. It was the mother who then brought the entire matter to the attention of the authorities.

.   .   .   .   .

In short, the mother was prepared to seek the assistance of the police and the courts to chaperone the conduct of her daughter insofar as sexual matters were concerned.

The judge acquitted the accused, finding that the couple's conduct did not constitute "sexual immorality." In the *Frost* case, the judge was faced with the case of *R. v. Tomlin,* an earlier decision of a higher court in which a 19-year-old male was convicted of contributing to delinquency after intercourse with a 15-year-old girl. Normally, such a precedent would be binding upon the judge in *Frost;* in *Tomlin* the judge had said:[8]

The term "sexual immorality" connotes sexual behaviour which is not publicly acceptable as being right, good, virtuous or chaste.

.   .   .   .   .

Protection of a child against sexual immorality is one of the objects of the Juvenile Delinquents Act. The protection is afforded notwithstanding the child's will or the will of a stranger or of a parent.

The judge in the *Frost* case noted that the facts of his case were different from *Tomlin* in that the girl there was younger, 15 as opposed to 17, and her parents were aware of the sexual relations and actively attempting to stop them. Further, the girl in *Tomlin* appeared to be more emotionally unstable than the girl in *Frost.* The judge in *Frost* felt that he had to consider whether the sexual activity would tend to disrupt the girl's emotional development. Though the facts of *Frost* were different from those in *Tomlin,* the judge also took a different view of the law:[9]

Public morality cannot be described in such positive terms. Rather it can best be described in negative terms, that is, the absence of principles and righteousness and virtue to such a degree that society cannot tolerate such behaviour that falls below a minimum standard, which standard is set by the community for its own good.
In short, the courts must never confuse sin with crime.
So that one does not fall into the error of confusing private morality with public morality, sin with crime, I would prefer to phrase [the] definition in negative terms. By doing this the definition would then read as follows:

"Sexual immorality connotes sexual behaviour which is not publicly acceptable because it is wrong, bad, vicious or promiscuous."

. . . . .

I cannot conceive that any reasonable person in today's society would equate all sexual intercourse without benefit of clergy as immoral conduct of such reprehensible and vicious nature as to be categorized a vice.

It is not surprising different judges have varying views as to what constitutes "sexual immorality or any similar form of vice." Indeed, it was recently explicitly recognized by a judge that in deciding what it is, one must have "regard to the contemporary mores of the community standards in the city at this time."[10] Such an approach will by definition tend to vary from one location to another and to evolve over time.

The rather vague expression "other similar form of vice" has been used to bring before the Juvenile Court children who have become intoxicated by using solvents, for example, by inhaling glue or nail polish remover. It is clear that the practice commonly known as "glue sniffing" is a serious social problem, with potentially ruinous effects on the health of users, particularly if they are children. It is not clear, however, that the Juvenile Court is the appropriate social agency to deal with the problem. Intoxication by the use of solvents is not a criminal offense for adults. In *R. v. Pandiak*,[11] the Alberta Supreme Court took a quite strict interpretation of the words of the statute, following the generally accepted rule of interpreting criminal laws, that they are to be narrowly construed as they threaten the liberty of an individual. The court found that while there may be a danger to health as a result of inhaling solvents, there was no danger to "morals"; apparently, some emphasis was placed on the word "similar," as indicating that there must be conduct in some way undermining accepted morality. On the other hand, Judge Little in Toronto,[12] was prepared to find that "glue sniffing" constituted a delinquency. He took a quite broad view of the words "similar form of vice" as he was concerned about identifying children in danger and providing them and their parents with suitable guidance. He was evidently following the philosophical bent of the founders of the Juvenile Court, and prepared to have it exercise a *parens patriae* role in society. The concept of *parens patriae* was discussed in Chapters 1 and 3; it involves the courts acting as an agency of the State to protect children. Not all of the Toronto Juvenile Court judges were prepared to follow the lead of Judge Little, and it can be asked whether a criminally based legal response is the appropriate social response.

2. Incidence

The legal definition of delinquency is extremely broad, and virtually every child has committed at least a few acts which fit within the legal definition. A very tiny fraction of the delinquent acts result in official action leading to court proceedings. Studies indicate that only 1% to 3% of all unlawful acts by juveniles result in charges.[13] Many of the criminal acts of children are not detected, or if the acts are discovered, the perpetrators are unknown. Frequently, however, the child is known to have committed an act which could lead to a delinquency charge, but the police or other figures of authority decide not to bring the matter to court. When the police do not feel an offense is very serious, they may simply warn the child, take him home to his parents and discuss the situation with them, or make a referral to a social agency.[14] Such youths are not represented in official delinquency statistics.

It is recognized by the police, and others, that while some children may be helped, or at least not harmed, by the process of going to court, for some youths the experience of going to court may produce a negative behavioural impact. According to the sociological "labeling theory," if a child is brought to court and officially "labeled" delinquent by society, the child and those around him will tend to view him in this way, and he will behave accordingly. This theory will be considered further in the last section of this chapter in the discussion of diversion programs; programs which are designed to prevent a child from going through the court system and being "labeled" delinquent. For present purposes, it is important to realize that juvenile delinquency statistics do not in reality reflect behaviour, or even officially discovered behaviour, but, rather, reflect discovered behaviour which is perceived by the police, judges and others as being best dealt with by a Juvenile Court prosecution.

In 1978, some 44 000 children were brought before the Canadian courts facing charges under the *J.D.A.*[15] Though many of these children were charged with very serious offenses, such as murder, armed robbery, or rape, the majority involved relatively minor offenses, generally entailing only property damage. A relatively small, though still significant, number involved "status offenses." The ratio of male to female offenders was about 5 : 1, with girls having a relatively greater tendency to be involved in status offenses, such as sexual immorality. It has been suggested by some studies[16] that while girls probably do commit fewer delinquent acts, the true ratio of male to female delinquent acts is probably more like 2 : 1 than the officially reported 5 : 1. These same studies suggest that the relative frequency of the occurrence of different types of offenses is roughly the same for males and females; that is about half as many girls commit violent crimes, and about half as many commit status offenses. These studies are generally based on "self-reporting" surveys in which children were asked about the number of delinquent acts which they committed. The official statistics indicated that overall girls are charged in a ratio of about 1 : 5 as compared to males, but for status offenses the ratio is about 1 : 1. It is suggested by researchers that the relatively small number of females charged overall, and the relatively large number charged with status offenses, is due to "sex role stereo-typing." The police and other social agencies do not expect girls to be violent, but they are expected to be sexually promiscuous and there is more concern about the sexual promiscuity of girls. As a result, if a girl commits an assault, this is more likely to be viewed as abnormal behaviour to be dealt with by a psychiatrist or a counsellor, whereas for a boy this is viewed as typical "criminal" behaviour. On the other hand, sexual promiscuity by young females is viewed as a serious social problem, requiring official intervention to protect the child, whereas this type of behaviour by males is viewed as normal, and indeed perhaps even a healthy part of growing up. There is some indication that female behaviour patterns are coming even closer to those of males, and that perceptions of female and male behaviour are also slowly changing, so that the same types of behaviour are coming to be viewed as delinquent, whether committed by a boy or a girl.

3. Causes

All children commit some acts which are delinquent, and so in a certain sense delinquency may be viewed as a universal phenomenon associated with the normal process of growing up. It is, however, important to realize that some children commit a greater number of delinquent acts, some commit acts which are much more serious crimes, and some are more likely to be brought to Juvenile Court for the delinquent acts which they commit.

There is no single theory, or group of theories, which can explain the "causes" of delinquency. A great many theories have been proposed by those involved in such disparate fields as genetics, psychology, psychiatry, sociology, criminology, and philosophy. Though a number of the theories are without any empirical support, many do have at least some "scientific" support. It is true that many observable events are associated with delinquency; many, though by no means all, of the children who are charged under the *J.D.A.* come from single-parent families, have educational and emotional problems, and live in low-income neighbourhoods. It cannot be proven that any of these factors actually *caused* the delinquency, rather than being associated with it in some non-causal way.

One problem with most theories of the causes of delinquency is that they tend to be very poor at predicting which children will be delinquent. For example, many delinquent children come from broken homes, but most children from broken homes are not delinquents, so that merely knowing whether a child comes from a broken home will not assist one in predicting whether the child will become delinquent. This example is very crude, but even quite sophisticated studies which attempted to predict delinquency on the basis of a number of family characteristics were found to greatly overpredict the actual occurrence of delinquency.[17]

There are so many theories of the causes of delinquency, that it is only worthwhile to mention here a few of the leading schools of thought.[18] It is important to remember that the concept of delinquency can be quite vague and difficult to define. Some theories focus upon actual behaviour, while others focus upon children who actually proceed through the courts.

Biological theories focus upon some inherent characteristics to distinguish deviants from others. Low intelligence, facial or body characteristics, glandular or genetic disorders, and pre-natal difficulties have all been advanced as causes of, or at least associated with, delinquency. More recently, attention has been focused upon chromosomal defects.

Psychologists and psychiatrists have suggested that various mental disorders and diseases may cause delinquency. It has been recognized by researchers taking this approach that there are different motivations for different types of children engaging in delinquent behaviour, so that there is no single explanation. The focus of inquiry is upon personality development and learning to explain why certain individuals respond to some situations by engaging in illegal acts; the emphasis is upon individuals rather than groups and sub-cultures.

Sociological theories reject the notion that there are intrinsic characteristics which distinguish the delinquent child. Delinquency is viewed in a social context, and as a result of various social structures. While some sociological theories are concerned with delinquent behaviour, explaining why some persons in society tend to be deviant, for example, juvenile gangs, others focus upon why some type of behaviour comes to be defined as socially unacceptable, and upon why the deviant acts of some are more likely to result in involvement in the judicial system than the deviant acts of other individuals.

Some researchers are coming to realize single-explanation theories of delinquency are inadequate, and that to understand this phenomenon it will be necessary to take a multi-disciplinary approach. The interaction of various biological, psychological, cultural, social and situational influences must be considered. Much work remains to be done in this area. It is important to remember when considering how to prevent delinquent behaviour, which after all is one of the primary objectives of our juvenile justice system, that we are still very unsure of the causes of this behaviour.

4. The Child: Delinquent or in Need of Protection?

The draughtsmen of the original *J.D.A.* did not seem to make a great distinction between children who were delinquent and those who were in need of protection, between those who were to be dealt with by the judicial system because of their own violations of the criminal law and those who were to be dealt with by the system because of circumstances largely beyond their control. There are differences between delinquency and protection legislation, but there are also similarities. Though for many of the children involved in the legal process there are real differences between proceedings under the two types of legislation, for many children the differences may be illusory.

Under the *British North America Act, 1867*, Canada's main constitutional document, the federal government is given jurisdiction over "criminal law," and it is under this heading that the *J.D.A.* was passed. The Supreme Court of Canada has ruled that it is valid criminal legislation, even though its objectives are not simply to deal with crimes that have occurred, but also to prevent future crimes and to alleviate the social conditions which may cause delinquency. In deciding cases under the *J.D.A.*, the Supreme Court has stated that the judge must consider "the community's best interest and the proper administration of justice," but must conciliate this with his views of the child's best interests; obviously, these aims are distinct from, but quite close to, the aims of child protection legislation, enacted under the provincial heading of jurisdiction over "property and civil rights," which has been judicially defined to include "the care and protection of people in distress, including neglected children."[19]

In a trial under the *J.D.A.*, the central issue at the adjudication stage is whether the Crown can prove beyond a reasonable doubt that a child committed a particular act, something quite different from the issue in a child protection hearing where the court must decide whether the child is in need of protection. At the dispositional stage of the delinquency hearing, however, the issues may be quite close, with the focus of attention being how best to help the child. One of the dispositions which can be made after a finding of delinquency is committal to the Children's Aid Society (C.A.S.) or placement in a group or foster home, so frequently children dealt with under different pieces of legislation are found in the same treatment facility.

It is not surprising that there are considerable similarities in the treatment received. A child who has been abused or neglected by his parents is likely to grow up with behavioural problems, problems which inevitably involve the commission of delinquent acts, though not all children who are abused become delinquents, nor have all delinquent children suffered neglect or abuse. There are often differences in the way children are perceived by others, depending upon the piece of legislation used to bring the child to court. The child in need of protection is to be pitied and comforted; the delinquent child is often seen as the "bad" child, needing discipline and correction. The child may not perceive a real distinction. Children generally have a better understanding of concepts like guilt and punishment and are apt to be less confused by delinquency proceedings than protection hearings.

An example of the confusing situation which can arise was the case of *T.S.E. v. C.A.S. of Metropolitan Toronto.*[20] Here, a 13-year-old boy was convicted by Judge Felstiner, sitting as a Juvenile Court judge, under the *J.D.A.*, and ordered to spend three months in a group home. At the end of three months he was brought before the same judge, sitting as a Family Court judge under the *Child Welfare Act*, found to be a child in need of protection, and made a temporary ward of the Society for 10 months with a "strong recommendation" that he be kept in the group home. Though technically the Society could place him elsewhere, the judge's recommendations are invariably followed. It may well have been that it was in the child's best interests to keep him at the group home, but to the boy and his parents it simply seemed that he was being "sentenced" to an additional 10 months for his initial wrongful act; he was not in prison, but he was to be kept from his family against his will.

For many children, there is no doubt as to what is the appropriate legislation to invoke to legally force intervention in their lives. For the young child who is physically, emotionally or socially abused, it is clearly child protection legislation. The older child who has committed a serious criminal offense will clearly be dealt with under the *J.D.A.* For many children, however, particularly older children who are having difficulties in their relationships with their parents, it is often unclear. It may be a matter of chance or a result of social or cultural factors. A young teen-aged girl may be emotionally rejected and turn to prostitution. If the police become involved, the girl may be charged with "sexual immorality" under the *J.D.A.*; if a social worker from the C.A.S. is the first to make contact with the child, she may be dealt with as a child in need of protection.[21] In a study done in Montreal, researchers were concerned with how different ethnic groups responded to behaviour which was delinquent. It was found that French Canadian parents and social agencies were much more likely to respond by having the children charged as delinquents, while the English Canadian children were more likely to be dealt with under child protection legislation.[22]

There are differences between delinquency and child protection proceedings. The issues in a delinquency proceeding, at least at the adjudication stage, generally relate to a specific event. A parent is not legally a "party" to a delinquency proceeding and has no right to participate in the hearing. The range of possible dispositions at a delinquency trial is much greater. For the children involved, the stigma and legal consequences of having been found a delinquent can be quite severe. It is important to remember that though in some cases there can be significant differences for a child if he is dealt with as a delinquent rather than a child in need of protection, it may well be a matter of chance whether he is treated as one or the other.

C. THE CHILD BEFORE THE TRIAL

1. General

If the police believe that any person has violated a law, they have a responsibility to investigate, and if there are reasonable grounds to believe that an offense has been committed, to ensure that the person is brought to trial. If the offense is serious, or it is likely that the person may not appear at trial, the matter may be brought before a judge to determine whether the person should be allowed to be free pending trial, whether certain conditions ought to be imposed upon the release, or whether the person should be confined until the trial. The actual mechanism for commencing a juvenile proceeding will be discussed in the next section. Here our concern will be with the investigation methods the police may use in cases involving juveniles and the situations in which a child may be held pending trial.

At this point, it might be helpful to briefly describe the relationship of the police to the Crown Attorney. There are, in fact, many different police forces in Canada—municipal, provincial, and the Royal Canadian Mounted Police, the national force. For present purposes, however, the role of the different forces does not vary significantly. Each force is created by statute, and has a general responsibility to prevent crime, preserve the peace, and apprehend those persons who violate the law. The officers investigate the complaints of citizens, and in many cases will initiate their own investigations. It is generally the police who decide whether a person will be charged with a particular offense. The Crown Attorney is responsible for the presentation of the case for the Crown in court, both at bail hearings and at trial.

In theory, the Crown Attorney and the police are independent one from the other. The police decide whether to lay an information and commence proceedings, and the Crown Attorney decides whether the charge should be prosecuted to trial; the Crown Attorney may require the police to carry further investigations if he is unsure of whether there is sufficient evidence to prosecute the charges. The relationship cannot be described as one of solicitor to client, nor of supervisor to worker, though there are elements of these relationships. The Crown Attorney must work closely with the police officer. The Crown relies on the officer to bring forward sufficient evidence to "make a charge stick," and the officer relies on the Crown not to "blow the case." The Crown Attorney may act as something of a restraint on individual officers who may be overly zealous in the performance of their duties by informing an officer, or his supervisor, that certain practices are improper, or by refusing to put certain evidence before the court. Theoretically, the concern of the Crown and the police is not to "win" cases and secure convictions but, rather, to see that justice is done. In practice, in individual cases there is usually little emotional investment in securing a conviction, but there clearly is a desire to not lose many cases.[23]

One complicating factor is that in many places the Crown Attorney will delegate his authority to prosecute juveniles to a police "court officer." Busy Crown Attorneys often feel that juvenile charges are not "as important" as adult cases and will exercise only a general supervisory function over the work of a police officer, the court officer, or some other lay person who is responsible for presenting the case of the Crown in Juvenile Court. The Crown Attorney himself may be involved only in the most serious juvenile cases, leaving the less serious ones to a person who is not legally trained.

2. Limitations of Police Investigations

The law imposes a duty on the police to investigate crimes, and though they have broader powers than the ordinary citizen, there are legal restrictions placed upon investigatory powers.

The police may ask any person questions about the occurrence of a suspected criminal act, though an individual is under no obligation to answer these questions. If the individual is not the accused, he may be required to come to court as a witness and testify under oath; failure to do so may constitute contempt of court and lead to imprisonment. But, there is no legal duty placed upon a person, whether or not he is the accused, and whether an adult or a child, to discuss a case with police investigators before trial.

The police may question a suspect before trial, but there is no obligation upon the person to answer questions. The failure of the accused to answer questions put to him by the police cannot be considered in any way to constitute an admission of guilt. It has been held by the courts that failure of an accused to deny an allegation may constitute an admission of guilt if the circumstances are such that a normal person would naturally make a denial. In *R. v. Cramp*,[24] the accused was charged with attempting to procure the miscarriage of a girl whom he had made pregnant. The girl's father later angrily confronted the accused saying, "I have here those things which you gave my daughter to produce an abortion," and the accused said nothing. His silence was held to constitute corroboration of his guilt, as when such an accusation is made by a person who is not a police officer, one would expect some denial or indignation. On the other hand, in *R. v. Eden*, the accused's silence in the presence of an inculpatory statement was not taken as an admission of guilt. In that case three young men were charged with car theft. The accused sat silently in the back seat of a police cruiser, beside a fellow accused who made a statement implicating the accused. The Ontario Court of Appeal stated:[25]

> The right of a trial court to conclude that an accused adopted an inculpatory statement made in his presence rests upon the assumption that the natural reaction of one falsely accused is promptly to deny or assert his innocence. It follows that before such an assumption can be acted upon the circumstances must be such that it would be normal conduct for the person involved by the statement to deny it.

In this case, being questioned by the police and in a highly threatening environment, the exercise by the accused of his right to silence could not be viewed as the basis of an admission of guilt.

The failure of the accused to make a statement to the police has been held to weaken the effect of alibi evidence, as the failure to warn that this evidence may be adduced does not allow the Crown to adequately rebut the evidence; it is not, however, to be used as an inference of guilt.

At trial, the accused, whether an adult or child, is not required to testify. If, however, the Crown has a strong case, the trial judge may draw an adverse inference from the failure of the accused to testify, while recognizing that the obligation is still upon the Crown to prove each element of its case beyond a reasonable doubt.

The issue which most frequently arises in regard to questioning by the police is whether a confession made to them by an accused person is to be admissible as proof of guilt. In our courts, a confession made to the police is only admissible if it is proven by the Crown to have been made "voluntarily." A classical statement of the present Canadian position was made in the English case of *Ibrahim v. The King*:[26]

It has long been established as a positive rule of English Criminal Law,
that no statement by an accused is admissible in evidence against him
unless it is shown by the prosecution to have been a voluntary statement,
in the sense that it has not been obtained from him either by fear or
prejudice or hope of advantage exercised by a person in authority.

The exact meaning of these words, particularly as they relate to children, will be
considered, but a few preliminary points should be understood.

The purpose of this rule excluding involuntary confessions is to ensure that the
judge does not base his decision upon statements which may be untrue. In the
United States, the courts have stated that the primary purpose of having such a rule
is to protect the constitutional rights of the accused; this is not the objective of
Canadian courts. Thus, if there is evidence which raises a reasonable doubt in a
judge's mind as to whether a child was subject to a beating before making a
statement to the police, it will not be admitted into evidence. In Canada it will be
excluded as it is unreliable. In the United States it will not be admitted as admitting
it might encourage the police to carry out beatings in violation of the child's
constitutional rights. The significance of this difference in approach will become
apparent when considering the use of illegally obtained physical evidence.

If there is some doubt as to whether a statement made to a police officer (or,
indeed, as to whether any piece of evidence) should be "admitted into evidence"
(i.e., used as a basis for reaching a final decision), there will be a *voir dire*. A *voir
dire* is a "trial within a trial." At a *voir dire* a judge will listen to evidence about
the circumstances under which the statement was made for the sole purpose of
deciding whether the statement was voluntary. He will then hear arguments from
the lawyers on this point. If he decides the statement is involuntary, the judge must
not consider any part of the statement nor any evidence heard at the *voir dire*. We
rely on our judges to have sufficient clarity of thought to be able to do this. Juvenile
trials occur with a judge alone, but in adult trials, if there is a jury it will be
excluded during a *voir dire* because it is felt that as laymen they would be unduly
influenced by inadmissible evidence which they would, in fact, have heard during
the *voir dire*.

A confession must be voluntary to be admitted; if it is involuntary it is felt to
be unreliable. In Canada, the courts will consider all of the circumstances under
which a statement was made to determine voluntariness and there is no specific set
of criteria to be satisfied. For example, it is usual for the police to warn an accused
person that any statement he makes may later be used in court, but the failure to
do so does not necessarily mean that the statement is involuntary, while the fact
that a warning was given does not necessarily mean that the statement was voluntary.
It is recognized by the courts that children are particularly vulnerable when being
dealt with by figures of authority. They are very suggestible and may tend to adopt
any statement offered as their own. Children have a reduced capacity to understand
what is said to them, and a formal caution by the police indicating that "any
statement made voluntarily, whether inculpatory or exculpatory, may be used in

subsequent proceedings'' will tend to have little significance for a nine-year-old child in a police station for the first time in his life.

The courts have recommended to the police certain steps which should be followed to ensure the admissibility of juvenile statements:[27]

(1) Require that a relative, preferably the same sex as the child to be questioned, accompany the child to the place of interrogation.

(2) Give the child, at the place or room of interrogation, and in the presence of the relative who accompanies him, the choice of deciding whether he wishes his relative to stay in the same room during the questioning or not.

(3) Carry out the questioning as soon as the child and his relative arrive at headquarters, or if this is not possible, detain the child in a place suitable for children.

(4) Ask the child, as soon as the caution is given, whether he understands it and if not, give him an explanation which he understands and which points out to the child the consequences that may flow from making the statement. In particular, it should be pointed out that if he is over 14 years of age and the offense is serious, that there is a chance of the case being transferred to adult court.

These are only recommended guidelines, and in every case the true test is whether the juvenile's state of mind was such that he perceived the statement as voluntary.

In *R. v. Nancy C. and Darlene V.*,[28] two girls, aged 14 and 15, were charged with attempted break, enter and theft. They were apprehended near the scene, evidently suffering from the effects of sniffing glue. The girls were questioned at the police station two to three hours later in the presence of their parents, who were urging the children to make a statement. The police officer questioning the girls did not in any way threaten or intimidate them. Though he read them a caution concerning their right to silence and the possible use of statements made, he did not explain the caution. The officer suggested to the girls that he had fingerprint and footprint evidence to implicate the girls, though apparently he did not. Two social workers who knew the girls were at the station during the questioning. The judge ruled that the statements were inadmissible as he was not satisfied that they were voluntary. Under the circumstances the girls might have viewed the presence of their parents and the social workers as threatening, and the girls' ability to understand the situation may have been clouded as a result of the glue sniffing. The remark by the police officer concerning evidence which did not exist was considered to be an inducement to the girls to make a statement. The judge emphasized the need to consider all the circumstances of the case when determining whether a statement was voluntary.

In Canada, the rules regarding the use of pieces of physical evidence are quite different from those concerning the admissibility of statements. The basic rule is that physical evidence is admissible, regardless of whether it is illegally obtained.[29] Thus, if the police suspect that there are illegal drugs in a house and unlawfully enter the house, the drugs may be used as the basis of a drug charge. The unlawful acts of the police officers may give rise to disciplinary proceedings, or to criminal or civil actions against them, but cannot assist the accused. This is quite different from the situation in the United States where the courts have decided that illegally obtained evidence cannot later be used in trials, as if this was allowed the court would in effect be participating in an illegal activity, or at least condoning it.

The police do have a number of legal ways of obtaining evidence. It is relatively simple for the police to obtain a court order for a search warrant or a writ of assistance allowing the search of dwellings and other places. When a person is arrested, the police have the right to search that person.

It is not clear that the police may require a child to allow himself to be finger-printed. The *Identification of Criminals Act* clearly provides that adults charged with certain offenses may be subject to fingerprinting, and that such force as is necessary may be used to effect this. The courts are divided as to whether the police may use this Act, or any other legal powers, to force a child to submit to fingerprinting. The weight of authority suggests that as the taking of fingerprints constitutes an infringement of individual liberty, there must be clear statutory authority to allow it, and indeed most police forces do not fingerprint juveniles. It is, however, universally agreed in Canada that if the fingerprints of a child are obtained, whether illegally, by trick or by force, they may subsequently be used in a trial,[30] just as any other piece of physical evidence.

3. Rights of the Child Before the Hearing

It is provided in s. 2 of the *Canadian Bill of Rights* that every person charged with a criminal offense has the "right to retain and instruct counsel without delay." Thus, a child who has been arrested has a right to see a lawyer. This right is quite narrow, for there is no obligation placed upon the police to inform the child of this right, nor is there any obligation to provide a lawyer if the child or his parents cannot afford a lawyer. The problem of inability to pay can generally be resolved by Legal Aid, though often with some delay. The lack of knowledge and under-standing of rights is a more severe difficulty. Very often, if a child is informed of his right to see a lawyer, he may waive this right, that is he will formally ac-knowledge the existence of the right to see a lawyer, but voluntarily choose not to exercise this right. The problem is that studies have shown that the vast majority of children who formally waive their rights do so without understanding the nature of these rights.[31] Those who come into contact with children at the early stages of the delinquency hearing should be aware of the child's right to see a lawyer, and do all they can to help make this a meaningful right.

If the police want to charge a child under the *J.D.A.*, it is possible to have a summons given to the child and his parents requiring them to appear in court at a specified time. It is possible that after questioning the child and his parents, the police, perhaps in consultation with the Crown Attorney or social workers who have been involved with the child, will decide that the child should be detained until there can be a hearing. The police may have legitimate grounds for wishing

182 THE CHILD AND THE LAW

to detain the child, though in some cases it seems that pre-trial detention is used to punish a child who has not yet been proven guilty, or to facilitate an investigation into the child or his background. The *J.D.A.* has provisions dealing with situations in which a child may be detained pending a trial.

The amount of time a child may have to wait before trial depends a great deal on the locality in which he is charged, and the speed with which the various parties involved (the Crown Attorney, the police, the child, his parents, the defense lawyer, and the judge) are prepared to deal with the case. There is an initial "return date" set when the proceeding is commenced; commencing the proceeding will be discussed in the next section. On that first return date, the child may enter a plea, or there may be a series of adjournments while the child obtains a lawyer or decides what to do. If the child enters a not-guilty plea, a trial date will be set, invariably several weeks later. After a plea of guilty or a finding of guilt, there may be another adjournment while the judge, probation officers, or various social agencies, consider the appropriate disposition.

The initial return date will generally be one to six weeks after the police decide to lay a charge. The adjournments in a juvenile case before plea will tend to be for one to three weeks, though there may be several adjournments. If a guilty plea is not entered and a trial date is set, this will usually be two weeks to two months after the date on which the not-guilty plea is entered, depending upon how busy the court is. The wait from adjudication to disposition may be another one to three weeks. If the trial is a long one, there may be adjournments in the middle of the trial. Thus, it can be seen that if a child is charged with a juvenile offense and detained until a disposition is made, this may involve a considerable period in custody. It is recognized that this period in detention may be very frustrating for the child, and the judges and various officials involved try to keep the length of adjournments to a minimum if the child is in custody. Further, if the police wish to detain a child before trial, the child must be brought before a Juvenile Court judge, if one is available, within 24 hours and in any event "without unreasonable delay," regardless of the initial return date, for what is commonly referred to as a "bail hearing." The purpose of a bail hearing is to determine the appropriateness of the detention of the child. The decision to detain the child pending trial may be reviewed again at any time before the trial, if circumstances should change.

The *J.D.A.* provides in s. 13 that no child charged under the Act shall be detained with adults pending a hearing. Most urban areas in southern Canada have detention or court homes where children in custody can stay pending a trial. Though some of these facilities are quite rudimentary, a number have quite sophisticated educational, recreational, and assessment programs. There is a real lack of adequate facilities for detaining children in northern Canada and certain rural areas, and the *J.D.A.* has special provisions for detaining children over 14 years of age in adult facilities if there is no juvenile detention home; such detention in adult facilities is permissible only to ensure the attendance of a child in court, and is to occur only upon the order of a judge, or in his absence the sheriff, mayor or chief magistrate. To avoid incarceration in adult facilities, the court may accept the promise of an adult that the child will appear. Also, in some localities judges are prepared to allow the child to stay in his own home provided certain conditions are met, such as supervision by an approved social worker.

A child whom the police wish detained in a juvenile detention facility pending a hearing has the right to bail. The bail hearing is held before a Juvenile Court judge, and the terms under which a child is to be temporarily released are determined at that time; these terms are very similar to those which apply to Canadian adults under the *Bail Reform Act*.[32] Accordingly, a child should be detained pending a hearing only if it is necessary to ensure his attendance, if his detention is necessary in the public interest, or for the protection of the public, having regard to all the circumstances including any substantial likelihood that he will commit a further criminal offense if released. The onus will be upon the Crown Attorney to show that detention pending the hearing is necessary.

In Ontario, the *Provincial Courts Act* governs the operation of facilities used for the detention of juveniles prior to trial. These facilities are known as "observation and detention homes." There are four levels of supervision available: home supervision, open, semi-secure, and secure. Home supervision keeps the child in the community, while the other three levels involve increasingly stringent controls in a residential setting. A judge may simply order that a child be detained, in which case the superintendent of the facility decides what level is appropriate. The judge may also order that the child be kept in a secure setting, which involves constant supervision of the child in a physical environment in which escape would be very difficult. The child has a right to go before a judge for a judicial review of his detention; this may lead to the child's release, or at least being moved out of secure detention into a less controlled atmosphere.

It is also possible for a child to be detained before a hearing for a psychiatric examination. Section 738(5) of the *Criminal Code*, which governs proceedings both for adults and under the *J.D.A.*, allows a judge to send an accused person to a psychiatric facility for a period of up to 30 days if it appears that he is mentally ill. Such an order is to be made after examination by a medical doctor; if one is not available the judge may act on his own. It is also possible for a judge to make an order under provincial mental health legislation for the admission of a child who appears to be suffering from a mental disorder to a psychiatric facility. On occasion the courts have taken a very paternalistic attitude towards the committal of persons for psychiatric examination, noting that such a committal is not a criminal proceeding, but rather done for the "benefit" of the individual involved, and as a result, the child apparently need not even be present in court when the committal hearing is taking place.[33]

D. THE DELINQUENCY HEARING

1. Commencing the Proceedings

All proceedings involving children charged with committing a delinquency must be commenced in Juvenile Court. Each province designates one court to be the

Juvenile Court for the province. In Ontario, the government has decided that the Provincial Court (Family Division) is to be the Juvenile Court, and in most provinces the Family Court is the Juvenile Court. A proceeding is commenced by having a person make a sworn, written statement, known as an information, which is brought to a justice of the peace. If the justice of the peace is satisfied that a reasonable case has been made out, he will issue a summons requiring the accused to appear in court at a certain time and date, or he may issue a warrant for the accused's immediate arrest pending trial. A warrant is only to be issued if the justice believes that it is necessary in the public interest for the accused to be in custody pending trial. The issuance of the summons or warrant is, theoretically, a discretionary matter; practically, as the accused is never present, the justice of the peace will invariably do what the police request.

It should be noted that while police are usually the ones who swear out informations to commence criminal prosecutions, any person who has reasonable and probable grounds to believe that an offense has been committed may swear out an information; in this case, the justice of the peace may exercise his discretion to issue a summons or warrant a little more judiciously. Thus, if a merchant catches a young child shop-lifting, and the police refuse to charge him with commiting a delinquency the store owner may go to a justice of the peace and satisfy the justice that a summons or warrant should be issued. If the Crown Attorney wishes, he may become involved in a charge where a private individual swore the information, or he may allow the individual to carry on with it as a "private prosecution"; such a prosecution is still a criminal prosecution carried on in the name of the State, but by a private individual.

A person may be arrested or detained without an information and warrant, but in this case the information must be sworn after the arrest. If a person is detained after an arrest with or without a warrant he has the right to a bail hearing as outlined above.

The *J.D.A.* provides in s. 10 that not only must the child have notice of the hearing, but his parent or guardian must also be given "due notice" of the hearing. In *Smith v. The Queen*,[34] the father of the child received a short note, which stated in full:

Dear Mr. Smith:—   Re Your son Gerald
    This is to advise you that you must be present with your son for a court hearing on Friday, August 30th, at 10 o'clock in the morning.

A probation officer swore that he orally informed the father of the nature of the charge, an alleged indecent assault on a little girl. The father asked to adjourn the matter on two occasions as his son was out of town, and then failed to appear on the third date. The Supreme Court of Canada held that the written notice was inadequate as it failed to disclose the nature and seriousness of the offense, and therefore the parents were unable to ascertain whether legal assistance was required, or even whether they should be present. The failure to give the statutorily required notice rendered the proceedings a nullity; that is they were without legal effect.

It should be pointed out that a parent who is given notice of the hearing pursuant to s. 10 of the *J.D.A.* has the right to be present at the hearing, though not the right to participate as a party to the proceeding. It is the child who is the accused, and it is the child who has the right to cross-examine and call witnesses and make arguments to the judge, either on his own or more likely through a lawyer, or other agent. The parent's right to participate is usually confined to the dispositional stage of the hearing, if there has been a finding of guilt.

2. Jurisdiction of Juvenile Courts

The Juvenile Court initially has exclusive jurisdiction over all children charged with violating federal or provincial statutes, municipal by-laws, or charged with "sexual immorality or a similar form of vice." As will be discussed below, in certain serious criminal offenses committed by children over the age of 14, the Juvenile Court judge may decide to transfer the case to adult court; otherwise the case must be dealt with in Juvenile Court.

It is an essential element of the Crown's case in every prosecution under the *J.D.A.* that it be proven beyond a reasonable doubt that the accused is a "child," which is defined in Ontario and most other provinces as a boy or girl "actually or apparently" under the age of 16. In Newfoundland it is under 17; in Quebec, Manitoba and British Columbia it is under 18; since October, 1978, in Alberta, it is under 16 for both boys and girls. The relevant time for determining the age of a child is the time when the offense occurred. If the court does not make a finding as to the child's age, it is without jurisdiction to act, and if the Crown fails to prove this fact the charge must be dismissed; frequently, the judge may gently remind the Crown Attorney of the necessity of proving this fact. The age of a child is often proven by calling a parent to testify as to the child's age. As will be discussed in Chapter 8, written documents are generally not admissible in evidence unless the person who originally produced them is available in court to identify them. There are, however, statutory provisions for allowing proof of age by means of a birth certificate in the *Canada Evidence Act*, s. 24. As will also be discussed in Chapter 8, there is a general rule of evidence that a witness may not testify as to matters of which he or she does not have direct personal knowledge, as this is "hearsay" evidence. In *R. v. A.M.P.*, [35] a young adopted boy was charged with break, enter and theft, and the Crown did not have a copy of the birth certificate. The adoptive mother was only able to give "hearsay" evidence about the lad's age, as she was not present at his birth and had no direct personal knowledge of it. The mother had seen the birth certificate and was told the boy's age by the adoption agency. The judge stated that he was prepared to make an exception to the hearsay rule, as the mother's evidence was the best that was available, and it seemed most likely that she was telling the truth; if there was any doubt, the child could take the stand himself to rebut his adoptive mother.

3. The Trial

The *J.D.A.* provides in s. 12 that all trials of children shall take place without publicity and separate from adult criminal trials. In Ontario, juvenile trials are held at the Family Court. In most urban Canadian centres, the Juvenile Court is located in a completely different building from the building where adults are tried for criminal offenses. In smaller centres, however, it may simply be a question of having the hearings at different times in the same location; in such localities it is not uncommon for one person to "wear several different hats" and sit as a judge for both adults and juveniles. In such circumstances, the judge may not, of course, sit for both adults and children at the same time.

Regardless of where the trial is held, there is concern with preventing the child from being commonly known as a delinquent. It is an offense for the media to make any report on a juvenile proceeding which in any way serves to identify the child. Nevertheless, in smaller communities the identities of the children brought before the court are often difficult to keep secret.

As was discussed earlier, the adjudication stage of a juvenile trial, the stage at which a decision is made as to guilt or innocence, is in many ways identical to that found in adult criminal trials. There is, however, often a somewhat more relaxed atmosphere. It is true that for the child and his parents, the experience of going to Juvenile Court is frequently very intimidating. The judge and various officials do realize that they are dealing with children who may have a limited understanding of what is happening, and they generally make an effort to be less brusque than they may be in adult court. The *J.D.A.* specifically provides in s. 17 that proceedings under the Act "may be as informal as the circumstances will permit, consistent with a due regard for the proper administration of justice." This does not mean that a child should not have all of the substantive and procedural rights which an adult has, but simply that the court may proceed in a less formal manner, for example, by calling the child by his first name.

All criminal proceedings begin with the judge or a court official reading the charge to the accused, and asking him how he pleads—guilty or not guilty. If there is a guilty plea, the proceeding moves into the dispositional stage. If there is a not-guilty plea, there will be a trial to determine the question of guilt or innocence. Generally, if an adult is unsure of how to plead, a judge will make a brusque comment and refer him to a lawyer, or simply enter not guilty on his behalf. If a child appears before a Juvenile Court judge and is uncertain of how to plead, the judge will generally be more solicitous. He may explain the charge in the most simple language possible, and perhaps, rather than asking for a plea of guilty or not guilty, words which the child may not understand, the judge may ask the child if he did the act alleged. There are, however, real dangers in taking this process too far. In *Smith v. The Queen*,[36] the following exchange took place between the trial judge and the 14-year-old accused:

> Judge: There's an Information here sonny, that on or about the 7th of
> June, a long time ago, unlawfully and indecently assault Helen

Balaban [*sic*]. What about that, is that correct or not? What did you do?

Gerald: We took her pants down and let her go.

The Supreme Court of Canada held that this was inadequate. The charge should have been explained to him in language he could comprehend, with an explanation of the gravity of the offense. The court further noted:[37]

> . . . he was not asked whether he pleaded guilty or not guilty to the information. On the contrary, the boy was told that there was an information that three months previously he had unlawfully and indecently assaulted Helen Balaban and the questions then put to him were simply an invitation to him to make a statement of what occurred. The boy . . . should not have been permitted by the Judge to make a statement without at least being warned that he was not obliged to say anything.

It must be remembered that the question, "did you do it?" is asking for a factual statement, while the question, "how do you plead?" is asking for a legal position. The boy may well have in fact done the act, but still had a legal defense. It may be that the only evidence the Crown had was the testimony of the young victim, and as we shall see, this is not legally sufficient as the sole basis for a conviction. Clearly, the best way for a judge to resolve the difficulties which can arise when taking a plea, is to advise the child to see a lawyer before coming to court, so that the charge can be explained, and all factual and legal defenses fully explored.

If a not-guilty plea is entered, the trial proceeds as outlined earlier, with the Crown presenting its case, followed by the accused, arguments, and then judgement. A juvenile trial may last anywhere from a few minutes to several weeks. Most juvenile trials last from one to three hours. There are certain features of the juvenile trial which distinguish it from the adult criminal trial, and these will be considered next.

4. Special Defenses: Physical and Mental Incapacity

The onus is on the Crown to prove each and every element of its case beyond a reasonable doubt, and to prove beyond a reasonable doubt that any defense which might be raised is without legal merit. Generally, all of the defenses which are available to an adult are available to a child; defenses such as duress or compulsion by another, self-defense, and defense of property. For example, if a young boy is charged with assault the onus is upon the Crown to prove all of the constituent elements of the offense. One looks to the *Criminal Code*, s. 244, to find the definition of assault:

> 244. A person commits an assault when
>   (*a*) without the consent of another person . . . he applies force
>   intentionally to the person of the other, directly or indirectly;

The Crown will have to prove beyond a reasonable doubt that there was a victim who was in some way struck by another person, and that the person who struck the victim was the accused. It will be necessary to show that the accused acted intentionally. Since intention is a state of mind, it is, in a certain conceptual sense, impossible to actually prove intention, and the courts rely on the things which the accused may have said or done to infer intention. It will be necessary for the Crown to show that the victim did not consent; it is not necessary for the Crown to prove an absence of consent for all criminal offenses, but it is for assault, as otherwise assault charges could arise out of a tackle in a football game, the act of kissing a girl, or thousands of other situations in which a person might find himself in a day. In the case of assault, there may be evidence suggesting that the accused was acting in self-defense. This evidence might be the testimony of the accused, or the victim, or any witnesses. If this evidence arises, the Crown must prove beyond a reasonable doubt that the boy was not acting in self-defense.

Besides the defenses available to an adult, there are special defenses which can only be used by children. These are the defenses of physical and mental incapacity. Section 147 of the *Criminal Code* states that no boy under the age of 14 can be convicted of the offense of rape, sexual intercourse with a female under 16, or incest; that is to say that it is a rule of law that a boy under 14 is deemed to be physically incapable of committing the act of sexual intercourse, though it is a well-known fact that this is not true.

It is recognized in all systems of criminal law that at some stage in their lives, children ought not to be responsible for their acts as they lack the ability to truly understand the significance of their deeds. In the English and Canadian legal systems this concept has been embodied in the defense of *doli incapax* (the incapacity to form the intention to do wrong). This common-law defense is now found in two sections of the *Criminal Code*:

> 12. No person shall be convicted of an offense in respect of an act or omission on his part while he was under the age of seven.
> 13. No person shall be convicted of an offense in respect of an act or omission on his part while he was seven years of age or more, but under the age of fourteen years, unless he was competent to know the nature and consequences of his conduct and to appreciate that it was wrong.

If a child is under the age of seven when he commits the violation of a federal, provincial or municipal law, he has an absolute defense and simply is not charged. If there are serious problems with a child of this age, the child may be dealt with under provincial child protection legislation.

The onus is on the Crown to prove beyond a reasonable doubt that a child between seven and 14 did, in fact, have the mental capacity to commit a criminal offense. The concept of mental capacity must be distinguished from two related concepts; ignorance of the law and insanity. The mere fact that a child did actually know that a certain act was a violation of the criminal law does not constitute a defense to a criminal charge, for the test is whether he had the competence to appreciate wrong. The word "competence" suggests capacity rather than an actual state of knowledge, while the word "appreciate" suggests a degree of understanding rather than the mere ability to have knowledge of wrongness. The defense of insanity is quite different from the defense of mental incapacity for insanity requires proof of a "natural imbecility," or a disease of the mind. Further, the *Criminal Code* creates a unique "reverse onus" situation in regard to insanity, requiring the accused to prove his insanity, whereas there is a presumption that a child under the age of 14 lacks capacity, and the onus is on the Crown to overcome this presumption. It is true, however, that children who are insane invariably lack the mental capacity to commit a criminal offense.

In practice the defense of *doli incapax* is not used very frequently. This is partly because in many cases involving children under 14, it is clear that the child had the sufficient mental capacity to commit the crime. It is also true that many lawyers and judges are somewhat unsure as to the exact nature of this defense and hence are reluctant to apply it. It seems that it could be used more frequently than it is at present.

In some cases it may not be easy for the Crown to actually prove that a child had the required mental capacity. The Crown cannot call the accused child to testify, and must rely on the evidence of other persons. Unless there are witnesses who know the child, or at least have talked to the child, it may be difficult for the Crown to rebut the presumption of incapacity. In *R. v. M.S. and C.S.*,[38] a brother and sister, aged eight and 10 respectively, broke into a cottage with two older children, smashed some windows, and generally made a mess of the cottage. All of the children involved were charged with wilfully causing damage to private property. The older children pleaded guilty and testified against the two younger ones. The judge was satisfied that the acts of the younger children were wilful and deliberate, but he felt that there was not enough evidence to prove that they had the capacity to appreciate that their conduct was wrong. The judge noted that the Crown failed to produce any evidence concerning their intelligence, upbringing, moral training or personalities.

The courts have developed certain rules to assist the Crown in the rebuttal of the presumption of incapacity. The older the child is, the less evidence will be required to rebut the presumption. Parents, teachers, or doctors may be called to testify as to the child's level of moral development and background. His appearance and demeanour in court may be considered. If the child has been interrogated by the police after the occurrence of the crime, any admissions made concerning an appreciation of the nature of the act may be used by the court.

The case of *R. v. B.C.*[39] provides a quite dramatic illustration of the defense of *doli incapax*. A 12-year-old-boy was charged with murdering his stepmother. He admitted shooting her and was ordered by the judge to be sent to a psychiatric facility for observation. The psychiatrists who examined the boy could not positively conclude that he was legally insane. The youth was fascinated by guns and television shows depicting violence; he talked quite openly about his horrific fantasies of war. Though he was of average intelligence and intellectually aware of his act, he did not truly appreciate it and spoke of his stepmother as if she were alive. One doctor testified about the boy in the following way:[40]

> I don't think he would have taken into consideration the full emotional impact that this would have had, not just on himself but on other people, and I think that children tend to be somewhat more impulsive in that age range than adults. They haven't developed the appropriate emotional developments and I think this applies . . .

In this case, the judge felt that the presumption of incapacity was not overcome and he found the lad not guilty. The judge did recommend that the boy should receive immediate and appropriate treatment pursuant to either child protection or mental health legislation, but once he made a finding of not guilty, he had no jurisdiction under the *J.D.A.* to order such treatment. In *R. v. B.C.* there was a clear indication that the boy was not simply immature, but quite possibly insane. If an adult commits a serious criminal offense and there is a finding of not guilty by reason of insanity, the person is committed to a psychiatric facility until it is safe to release that person. If a child successfully raises the defense of insanity, he cannot be dealt with further under criminal legislation, but can only be treated under child protection or mental health legislation.

5. Evidence at a Delinquency Hearing: Testimony of Children

In any trial, the judge can only make a finding of law after he has ascertained the facts. The legal question of guilt or innocence at a delinquency hearing can only be resolved after the judge decides what are the facts of the case. The judge determines the facts by listening to witnesses testify, accepting documentary evidence, and receiving physical evidence, such as photographs or an object used in the commission of a crime, for example, a shot-gun in a murder. There has always been a concern that a judge only make a finding of fact on the basis of evidence which is reliable, and so the laws of evidence have developed to exclude certain evidence which is unreliable, and to subject evidence which is accepted to thorough testing, for example, by means of cross-examination.

The laws of evidence which apply at a delinquency hearing are generally the same as those applicable to other types of proceedings. These rules determine what types of testimony the judge may listen to, and what types of documents and physical objects the judge may accept as evidence. We have already considered one rule of the law of evidence; that concerning the circumstances under which a judge will allow a police officer to relate a statement made by a child. The law of evidence will be considered more fully in Chapter 8. There is one evidentiary matter which arises most frequently in delinquency hearings and seems worth considering now, and that is testimony by children. Often, one or more of the witnesses at such a hearing will be a child. A child may have been the victim of the crime, or more frequently was an observer or accomplice; the child charged with the delinquency may wish to testify.

It is recognized that children, more often than adults, have difficulty in perceiving, remembering and recounting events in a meaningful way, and so special rules of evidence have developed regarding their testimony. One rule of evidence, developed to ensure reliability of testimony, requires witnesses to swear an oath on the Bible to tell the truth. The effectiveness of this procedure depends upon a witness understanding the nature and meaning of an oath.

If a child who is under 14 years of age is to testify under oath, the judge must first inquire as to whether the child understands the nature of the oath; that is to say that the child understands the moral obligation of telling the truth. When a child is over 14, the judge may hold an inquiry if he feels it appropriate. In *R. v. Bannerman*, a 13-year-old boy was called upon by the Crown to testify against a man accused of sexually assaulting the boy and his sister. The questioning of the boy by the Crown Attorney, the judge, and the lawyer for the accused went as follows:[41]

Crown: Do you know what it is to swear to tell the truth on the Bible?
Boy: No.

.   .   .   .   .

Crown: If I asked you a question and asked you to tell the truth about what happened what would you tell me, the right thing that happened or the wrong thing?
Boy: The right thing.
Crown: If you put your hand on the Bible and His Honour asked you if you would swear to tell the truth do you know what is meant?
Boy: Yes.
Crown: All right, put your hand on the Bible. What would this mean?
Boy: To tell the whole truth.

.   .   .   .   .

Crown: Does Your Honour wish to examine further of this witness as to whether he is capable of understanding an oath?
Judge: Did you ever go to church or Sunday School?
Boy: I go to catechism.
Judge: Do they tell you there you must tell the truth?
Boy: Yes.
Judge: And what do they say if you don't tell the truth?
Boy: I don't know.
Judge: That it is bad?
Boy: Yes.

Judge: Do you believe that it is?
Boy: Yes.

.   .   .   .   .

Judge: I look at the boy, he is a very bright looking boy, an intelligent
       boy. He goes to catechism and knows what the truth is and knows
       on all occasions he should tell the truth and particularly when he
       swears he shall tell the truth, is that correct?
Boy: Yes.
Judge: And you know it is wrong not to tell the truth, don't you?
Boy: Yes.
Lawyer for the accused: May I ask some questions?
Judge: Yes.
Lawyer: You are fourteen years of age?
Boy: Thirteen.
Lawyer: And you are in grade 4?
Boy: Yes.

.   .   .   .   .

Lawyer: Now what would happen to you if you didn't tell the truth, do
        you know?
Boy: No.

The boy was allowed to give testimony under oath, and in large part due to this
testimony a conviction was obtained. The Manitoba Court of Appeal upheld the
decision of the trial judge, allowing the boy to testify under oath, stating that all
of the circumstances of the boy's competence to be sworn were to be considered.
One of the judges of the Court of Appeal remarked:[42]

> I doubt whether the greatest of present day theologians or moralists would
> have answered the question put to this 13 year old boy with any degree
> of certainty or unanimity. King Solomon himself found it necessary to
> pray for knowledge of good and evil. It is therefore understandable that a
> 13 year old boy, in the midst of what was to him a strange and embarrassing
> environment, found it difficult to give a positive answer to the abstract
> question put to him by counsel for the accused.

It should be noted that even if a child is found competent to be sworn, and testify
under oath, the courts are reluctant to put as much reliance on the testimony of a
child as that of an adult. It is felt that a child's capacity to observe, recall and
answer questions about an event are poorer than those of an adult, and that even
under oath the child's[43] sense of moral responsibility may be more limited than an
adult's.
   If a child is not able to understand the nature of the oath, the child may still
testify. The *J.D.A.* provides in s. 19(1) that such a child may testify without an

oath "if in the opinion of the judge the child is possessed of sufficient intelligence to justify the reception of the evidence and understands the duty of speaking the truth." The Act goes on to provide that no person shall be convicted upon the unsworn testimony of a child unless that evidence is "corroborated in some material respect." An exact appreciation of the legal concept of "corroboration" is quite complex and beyond the scope of this book; suffice to say that evidence which can corroborate the unsworn testimony of a child must be independent evidence that confirms that the accused committed the crime with which he is charged. Thus, in a case where a 15-year-old boy is charged with sexually assaulting a 10-year-old girl, if the girl testifies about the incident without being sworn as a witness, her evidence must be corroborated or the boy cannot be convicted. Her evidence could be corroborated by finding at her house his underpants, and traces of pubic hair which could have been his.[44]

It is not infrequent for two or more juveniles to be accomplices in a crime. It is a rule of law that where a person is charged with a crime, the judge should be reluctant to convict that person solely on the basis of the testimony of an accomplice unless that testimony is corroborated. The reason for this rule is that an accomplice may be tempted to implicate the accused to improve his own position. For example, if two girls, Betty and Sue, are charged with shop-lifting, Betty may admit her guilt, but say that Sue was the instigator of the episode. It can be argued that Betty made her statement to improve her own position, and so the judge would usually expect some corroboration of Betty's testimony before convicting Sue. An example of corroboration would be the testimony of a sales clerk who saw both girls run from the scene of the crime together, as Betty's flight would indicate a guilty conscience.

6. Disposition

It is the disposition stage of the delinquency hearing which most clearly marks this type of proceeding as different from that which occurs when an adult faces a criminal charge. If there is a plea of guilty or a finding of guilt, the judge in Juvenile Court has a much broader range of possible dispositions. His main concern is generally not to punish the young offender, but rather to help ensure that the child does not commit further crimes. Unlike the judge in adult court, his primary focus is upon the offender and not the offense, and the ultimate disposition varies more with the nature of the child and his problems than with the nature of the crime.

Section 20(1) of the *J.D.A.* sets out the following possible dispositions, in roughly increasing order of severity:
(1) suspension of final disposition or adjournment without disposition;
(2) fine of up to $25;
(3) probation, including supervision of a probation officer, or other terms such as restitution;
(4) committal to foster home, group home, or care of a suitable person;

(5) committal to the care of the C.A.S.;

(6) committal to training school.

Each of these dispositions will be discussed in turn, and then consideration will be given to the question of how the judge decides which is appropriate in a particular case.

A. No Immediate Sanction

Many, if not most, of the children who appear in Juvenile Court, appear only once. They are not young criminals, but rather are youths who have violated the law. Perhaps they have committed a couple of infractions and have been warned, and now a person in authority decides that it is time to take some firm action to impress upon the child the increasing seriousness of the situation. It is hoped that the child will be affected by the situation, and perhaps be a little bit frightened by the experience of attending court. The relatively formal nature of the setting, and the large number of strange adults, clearly people in authority, people who even intimidate the child's parents, will have an impact on most children. For a child who appears for the first time in Juvenile Court, has not committed a serious offense, and appears to have no unusual problems, it is often felt that an official warning from the judge is sufficient. Some judges will make quite a production of the process, raising their voices, gesturing forcefully, and stressing the potential moral and legal implications of a continuation of the type of behaviour which brought the child to court. Other judges take a somewhat more relaxed approach, but it is always hoped that the effect will be the same.

There are a number of legal devices for giving an "official warning." The judge may adjourn the proceedings, either before or after making a finding of delinquency. The adjournment may be to a definite date, or for an indefinite period which lawyers describe with a Latin expression, to adjourn *sine die* (without a date). Typically, the judge may not even make a finding of delinquency, but simply warn the child and adjourn the matter indefinitely; in this way, there is no record of a juvenile conviction. Theoretically, if the child causes further trouble, the matter may be reopened, but it rarely is. If there is an adjournment to a definite date, the judge will expect a progress report of some kind to be presented at that time. The judge may make a finding of delinquency, but suspend making any decision as to disposition. The effect of this is that the child has a record of a Juvenile Court conviction, but no sanction beyond the warning has been imposed. Again, theoretically, it is possible that the child may be brought back to Juvenile Court for the imposition of a sanction at some later date, but this would be very unusual.

Some Juvenile Court judges are prepared to adopt the concept of absolute and conditional discharges from provisions of the *Criminal Code* dealing with adult offenders, even though there is no specific provision for this in the *J.D.A.*[45] An absolute discharge takes effect immediately, while a conditional discharge takes effect upon the satisfaction of certain conditions, such as restitution, or the offender's avoidance of any future appearances in Juvenile Court for a specified period of time. When a discharge is made, there is no record of a conviction, which may be significant for immigration or employment purposes.

B. Fine

A fine of up to $25 may be imposed upon the child. Since the maximum amount is small, and parents have a tendency to end up paying the fine in any event, this disposition is only rarely made. As we shall see, s. 22 of the *J.D.A.* allows for the imposition of quite substantial financial penalties upon parents found to be responsible by reason of their failure to exercise due care for their child's delinquency.

C. Probation

A judge may feel that it is most appropriate for the child to remain at his home in the community, but that certain conditions should be placed upon his behaviour for a period of time or certain obligations should be corrected. This is generally known as placing a child on probation. One stipulation of a probation order can be that the juvenile report to a probation officer, though it is not a necessary condition of a probation order that there be supervision by a probation officer. Juvenile probation officers are generally provincial employees, or may in some cases be volunteers. A probation officer should provide a youth with counselling and advice, as well as practical assistance, and general supervision. The officer will report to the court. Other possible terms of probation orders could include keeping a curfew, attending school, or consulting a psychiatrist. An increasingly popular term of probation orders is that the juvenile should make restitution to his victim; this might involve the payment of money to the victim, or providing services for the victim. If restitution is impractical or there is no individual victim, the judge may order that the child carry out a certain number of hours of community service work; this could involve working at a senior citizen's home, in a hospital, or doing some work for the local municipal government.

If the child fails to carry out the terms of the probation order, he may be required to appear before the judge again for further disposition.

D. Placement Out of the Home

After making a finding of delinquency, a judge may feel that a juvenile has quite serious emotional or behavioural problems which can only be dealt with by removing the child from the home, either for a definite period or for some indeterminate period. Placement with the C.A.S. or in a training school will be considered later; for the moment we will concern ourselves with various foster homes and group homes. These homes are generally used if it is felt that the child's home situation is not satisfactory and is unlikely to improve significantly, even if there is supervision by a probation officer, or other suitable social worker. It is recognized by Juvenile Court judges that though the experience of being separated from family may be beneficial and necessary, it can be potentially traumatic for many children.

A placement in a foster home involves the child's living with another family. This family is usually recruited by probation officers and workers from another agency, and receives some minimal financial compensation. Generally, foster parents are ordinary citizens who have a special interest in children, but no extensive professional training. Group homes (or treatment homes as they are sometimes called) usually have several children on placement and are operated by a professional staff. Though relatively small, they generally exist for the sole purpose of having children on placement; foster homes are the existing homes of natural families. Many group homes are operated by various non-profit corporations and agencies. Although a child cannot be technically committed to the care of a corporation which operates a group home, this problem is solved by having the child committed to the care of the director of the home which the corporation operates. The director is an employee of the corporation, and the committal is on the condition that the child stays in the home. A probation officer is usually assigned to supervise each child in a foster or group home, and reports back to the judge. The case may be brought back to court if the placement is, for any reason, unsatisfactory; the child or probation officer may request such a review.

It is also possible for the judge to place the child with "any . . . suitable person" after making a finding of delinquency. It may become apparent at the disposition stage of a hearing that the child would be better off with a neighbour or relative than in his own home. In R. v. F.G.,[46] a 15-year-old boy was in court as a result of a number of incidents. His parents were separated and his mother had obtained a custody order in the Supreme Court of Ontario. The boy had been in court on delinquency charges and he had been placed in a group home. After hearing testimony from a number of expert witnesses, the judge placed the boy in the care and custody of his father. The judge felt constrained only by a consideration of "the child's own good and the best interests of the community." He did not feel bound by the Supreme Court order, even though it was the decision of a higher court, as the issue he was considering was not really the same as that dealt with by the higher court, namely, custody, but rather what was the best way to deal with this particular delinquent child, a matter within his sole jurisdiction as a Juvenile Court judge.

E. Placement with the Children's Aid Society

When making a committal to a foster home or a group home, a judge must specify exactly which home the child is being sent to. It is also possible for the judge to simply commit the child to the care of the local C.A.S. The C.A.S. operates its own group and foster homes, as well as other assessment and treatment facilities. Once committed to the C.A.S., the Society will decide what is best for the child without having to refer the matter back to the Juvenile Court judge. In Ontario, and most other provinces, there are specific statutory provisions that if a child is committed to the C.A.S., this is deemed to be a wardship for the duration of the committal, or if an indefinite committal, then it is deemed to be a 12-month wardship.

F. Training School

The most serious disposition which can be made by a Juvenile Court judge is committal to a training school (other than transferring the matter to adult court and having an adult trial and disposition, a topic which will be discussed later). Training schools are also known as industrial schools, reform schools, and borstals. In a certain sense a training school is a jail for children. The philosophy of the staff and the nature of the facilities and inmate population are very different from those found in adult penal institutions, but children are forced to go there if they have violated the criminal law, will be restrained if they try to leave, and are subject to quite structured programs while there.

Training schools are controversial institutions and have been subjected to much criticism. It has been argued that no child can be truly helped in such a coercive environment. Clearly, it is true that at one time many training schools were little more than schools for crime for the majority of children attending, where often the children taught one another "the tricks of the trade." Facilities were inadequate, overcrowded and understaffed. It must be recognized that the nature of training schools varies considerably from one part of the country to another. Still, it seems fair to say that growing public and professional concern has led to considerable improvement in most training schools. There has also been a significant decline across Canada in the use of training schools during the past decade.

In British Columbia, from 1969 to 1977, the provincial legislature effectively took from Juvenile Court judges the authority to send children to training schools. The physical facilities were not closed, but their use was curtailed and they were operated under the auspices of the Superintendent of Child Welfare, who decided which children should be sent there. At present, the use of training schools in British Columbia is still restricted, and subject to considerable controversy.[47]

It is clearly beyond the scope of this book to examine the effectiveness of different institutional arrangements of training schools, or of training schools in general. Suffice to say that, as with adult prisons, there tends to be a high recidivism rate, but at least some of the children who enter are clearly helped by the stable environment and are less likely to commit crimes upon their release. Further, many training schools have educational and recreational facilities superior to those available to the children in the community. Finally, as long as a child is in a training school, society can at least be assured that he will commit no additional criminal acts.

In Ontario, as in most other provinces, once committed to training school the child is dealt with under provincial legislation. The committal is generally an indefinite one, in the sense that a child is not "sentenced" for a definite period, but rather committed to training school, and stays there until the training school authorities, as governed by provincial legislation, decide that the child is ready to

leave. The legislative scheme governing training schools is similar in most provinces, and Ontario's scheme as set out in the *Training Schools Act* will be considered
here. Upon being committed to a training school, a juvenile becomes a Crown
ward, though not the same type of Crown ward under the supervision of the
C.A.S., but, rather, a Crown ward under the supervision of a training school.
During the period of wardship, the parents' rights and duties are suspended and
the training school authorities are responsible for the child.

At some point these authorities will decide that the child may be moved back
into the community and so he might move to a foster or group home, and then
perhaps back to his own family. During this entire period, he is still a Crown ward,
and once in the community he will be supervised by a probation or "after-care"
officer. If there are difficulties in the process of readjusting to the community, the
child may be taken back to the training school without a new court hearing. It is
only upon termination of the Crown wardship that the training school authorities
lose their power to act; such a termination will occur at the request of these
authorities, or automatically when the child reaches the age of 18. It should be
noted that, in Ontario, no child under 12 can be sent to a training school, while
other provinces have limitations on juvenile charges for children under 12. The
J.D.A. provides in s. 25 that a child under 12 shall only be sent to a training school
if there has been an attempt at another placement outside the home.

Most training schools are in rural settings and some distance removed from the
places where the children live. Families are generally encouraged to visit, and some
efforts are usually made to send children who appear to be adjusting to the training
school home for visits.

G. Deciding the Disposition

After a judge makes a finding that a child is guilty of an offense which constitutes
a delinquency, and before making a determination as to what is the appropriate
disposition, the judge will usually seek some sort of expert advice, at least if the
case involves the possibility of one of the more serious dispositions which might
take the child out of the home. Before the judge decides which disposition to make,
the case may be adjourned for several weeks to allow all concerned to prepare for
the "disposition hearing." The judge may seek out independent assessments. This
may be a "social history" prepared by a probation officer explaining the child's
background and suggesting a disposition, or it may be a more sophisticated report
from a psychologist or psychiatrist. If there have been a number of social workers
and other professionals involved with a child before he came to court, there may
be a "case conference" which will result in a report based upon the views of a
number of people. If it is felt to be necessary to assist in the assessment of the best
disposition for the child, the child may be held in a detention facility or location,
pending disposition, though as with detention before trial, the child is not to be
confined with adults.

At the disposition hearing, the Crown and the lawyer for the child will each have
an opportunity to call witnesses, produce reports and make arguments to assist the

judge. The normal rules of evidence do not apply at a disposition hearing, and the proceeding is generally considered to be less adversarial in nature than the adjudicatory stage. The sections of the *J.D.A.* which set the philosophical tone of the Act are generally thought most applicable at this stage; sections such as s. 38 which provide that the child shall be treated "not as a criminal, but as a misdirected and misguided child, and [in need of] aid, encouragement, help and assistance." In the interests of fairness, however, each party usually has prior access to any report which will be filed, and can, if desired, request that the author be present in court to explain its contents and answer questions.

The judge will consider many factors when deciding what is the appropriate disposition for a child. The record of previous convictions and the nature of the offense are important, but less so than for adults. The judge is generally concerned with trying to provide help for the child, though in some cases deterrence to the child and other juveniles may be a factor. Considerable weight is usually given to the reports of the various professional persons who may have been involved with the child (probation officers, social workers, doctors and psychiatrists). Ultimately, the judge will focus upon all of the circumstances, the child's age and personality, and the nature of the facilities available. The child is likely to be taken out of the home only if efforts to help the child while at home have failed. And training school is used only as a last resort.

H. Financial Responsibility

If a child is found to be delinquent, there may be financial consequences both for society as a whole, and for the child's parents. It is always true that someone must bear the cost of crime, but invariably the cost of rehabilitating the young offender may be even greater than the cost of the original crime.

The *J.D.A.* provides in s. 20(2) that when a child is placed outside of his home, the parents of the child, and the municipality where the child resides, may be required to contribute to the "support" of the child. Practically, this issue will generally only arise if the child is placed in a foster home or a group home, as other facilities such as training schools and the C.A.S. receive funding from other sources and do not require court-ordered assistance. The cost of foster care is generally under $10 per day, but the cost of keeping a child in a group home, with its relatively large staff and sophisticated program, can easily amount to $40 to $50 per day or more. The parents of the child will be required to contribute according to the level of their income. Invariably, the municipalities end up bearing the largest load. This has become quite a sensitive political issue, with municipalities bearing the cost for programs they had no part in designing, and as a result of the decisions of judges over whom they have absolutely no control. This has also resulted in a number of cases where municipalities have challenged the validity of various dispositions.[48] It is perhaps regrettable that some of the most fiercely contested cases involving dispositions of juveniles revolve around the issue of how much each level of government is to pay to help the child.

If a judge is satisfied that the parent of a juvenile delinquent "has conduced to the commission of the offense by neglecting to exercise due care of the child," s. 22 of the *J.D.A.* allows the judge to order the imposition of a fine on the parent, or order the parent to pay damages or restitution to a victim. The parents must be given adequate notice of the possibility of such an order being made to allow them to prepare for and attend this portion of the hearing. It is not enough for an offense to have occurred, it must be shown that they have, in some way, contributed to the occurrence of the offense. One interesting case where the parents were fined was *R. v. B.*[49] The parents were Americans and had sent their 17-year-old son to study at McGill University in Montreal; in Quebec, the age of delinquency is up to 18. The boy was involved in a student demonstration at Sir George Williams University, in which several million dollars' damage was done to computer facilities, and the boy was convicted of committing a delinquency by violating s. 372(1) of the *Criminal Code* by wilfully obstructing the lawful use and enjoyment of facilities at the university. The parents were fined as the judge felt that by sending their young son to a foreign country to study and live without any real supervision, they failed to exercise the care the boy required. Section 22 is rarely invoked. Its purpose is to give parents an incentive to properly supervise their children. It is, however, recognized that in many situations punishing parents for the acts of their children may tend to aggravate an already unhappy home situation.

7. Juvenile Records

It is a widely accepted piece of Canadian folklore that the record of a juvenile delinquency conviction has no legal significance when a child becomes an adult. This, however, is not the law in Canada.

Many people feel that the mistakes a person committed as a child, mistakes which resulted in delinquency convictions, should not be held against that person when he becomes a mature adult. Historically, probation officers have told juveniles with records that upon reaching adulthood they could honestly state on employment and other application forms that they had not been "convicted" of a criminal offense. Police departments have traditionally kept a record of juvenile offenders, but once a child becomes an adult these have been destroyed. No record of juvenile convictions has been kept on the centralized computer record known as the Canadian Police Information Centre. All of this may change as a result of a recent decision of the Supreme Court of Canada.

In *Morris v. The Queen*,[50] a 19-year-old young man was charged with breaking into a building with the intent to commit an offense therein. He admitted being in the building, but said that he entered not for an unlawful purpose, but simply to seek shelter from the rain; he thus admitted trespassing, but denied committing the relatively serious offense with which he was charged. His entire case depended upon whether the jury believed his story, and so his credibility was very important. When he testified, the first question which his lawyer asked him was whether he had ever been convicted of a criminal offense. He answered in the negative. On cross-examination, the Crown Attorney questioned him about a series of convictions in Juvenile Court, which he admitted occurred. In addressing the jury before they retired to make a decision, the trial judge said:[51]

> Now, just before terminating, I'd like to say one word about the record, which was brought out. First of all, it seems quite clear to me that in his evidence in chief, the accused lied. When he started out, the very first thing he said was that he had never been convicted. . . . You can draw what conclusions you like from that. You may choose to think that he was frightened, didn't want to bring out before you the fact that he'd been in trouble with the police before, as a juvenile. You may choose to think that he felt that his record as a juvenile was not important or wasn't covered by what was asked of him. You may also choose to think that even if he deliberately lied to you on this matter, that what he told you in the rest of his testimony is the truth. . . . It would be equally within your realm, in your power, to come to the conclusion that having lied to you on this matter, which you may think is pretty important, that the rest of his story is pretty doubtful. That's your decision to make. The only thing that I would ask you to do, and I'm sure that your common sense will tell you this, I would ask you to be very careful not to convict the accused simply because he has been convicted before. . . . So you can take that record of his into account when your's [sic] assessing his credibility, and you may feel it's of great importance, but I would not want you to convict a man simply because he has been previously convicted.

The Supreme Court of Canada held that the comments of the trial judge were quite proper, and that for the purposes of bringing credibility at a trial into issue, the effect of a juvenile record was the same as an adult record.

It would seem that the way is now clear for courts to use juvenile records for other purposes, such as determining an appropriate sentence for an adult offender or deciding whether an adult ought to be released on bail pending trial. Since Juvenile Court proceedings are not now open to the public, and as no central records are kept of juvenile convictions, it does not seem likely that immediate use will be made of such records, but the door has clearly been opened.

8. Transfer to Adult Court

The most severe step which can be taken by a Juvenile Court is for the judge to decide that the case is so serious that it should not be dealt with in Juvenile Court, but rather should be dealt with in the ordinary adult courts. In these courts, there are some procedural safeguards which are not available in Juvenile Court, such as the right to a preliminary inquiry to determine whether there is sufficient evidence to require a trial, and the right to a public trial, often with a jury. In adult court, however, the adult rules regarding sentencing are to be followed. This invariably means that the child will receive a much longer custodial sentence in an adult facility. Thus, though it is true that when considering whether to transfer a child to adult court, reference is always made to the interests of the child, all too often the main reason for the transfer appears to be to ensure that the child receives an "adult punishment."

Section 9 of the *J.D.A.* deals with the question of the transfer of juvenile cases to adult court. This section allows a Juvenile Court judge to order that a child of the age of 14 or over who has committed an indictable offense (one of the more serious offenses), be proceeded against in the adult courts, if the judge feels that "the good of the child and the interest of the community demand it."

It is recognized that a transfer to adult court is an "exceptional procedure," and is not used very often. It is not enough that the circumstances merely indicate that transfer would be desirable, they must be such that this course is "demanded," both for the good of the child, and the good of the community. Judges will consider many factors at such hearings, including the child's age, character, academic record, psychological condition and record of previous juvenile offenses, and the seriousness of the offense. When considering the interest of the child, particular attention will be given to the nature of the facilities available for children being sentenced from Juvenile Court as opposed to those available upon sentencing from adult court, and whether this particular child is amenable to rehabilitation at the juvenile facilities. The court must consider whether the long-term interests of the child would be served by a transfer to adult court. Until relatively recently, it was felt that in serious cases a juvenile's rights might be better protected in adult court. This was probably a much more important factor at a time when the practice was to appoint laymen who had an interest in children, but no legal training, as Juvenile Court judges; now virtually all Juvenile Court judges have had formal legal training, and have been practising lawyers before being appointed judges, and so it is generally felt that the child's rights can be adequately protected without a transfer to adult court.

The concept of promoting the "interest of the community" is usually considered in terms of the additional protection society will receive from the longer custodial sentence which an adult court will give, though consideration is also given to the desire to have an open and publicly reported trial in adult court. If a juvenile and an adult are accused of having jointly committed a criminal act, such as robbing a bank, one factor a judge may consider is that it is desirable to have them tried together, which necessitates having the juvenile transferred to adult court. Such a procedure saves the community the inconvenience and expense of separate trials.

One of the most famous instances of a transfer to adult court was the *Steven Truscott* case.[52] Steven, a 14-year-old boy at the time, was charged with the rape and murder of a 12-year-old friend. The case received a great deal of publicity before the boy was even brought to Juvenile Court. At the transfer hearing, there was little evidence presented about the benefit which the boy would receive from being tried in adult court, but the order was made, and when the transfer decision was appealed, the appellate judge remarked:

> Counsel for the accused has strongly argued that it is not for the good of the child that he should be tried in the High Court with the attendant publicity and strain of a public trial. . . . In any case notwithstanding the publicity and strain of a trial it is my opinion that it would be for the good of the child to have his position in respect of such a serious charge established by a jury which would remove any possible criticism of having such a serious matter determined [in Juvenile Court].
>
> I think it is also in the interests of the community that the public be assured that in a matter of this kind where public sentiment may have been aroused, the trial and disposition of the matter shall be in the ordinary course and free from any criticism.

Steven was convicted by a jury on the basis of circumstantial evidence; his trial remains a controversy to this day. His death sentence was commuted to life imprisonment, and he was eventually released on parole. It is difficult to this day, however, to conceive of the benefit he received from a trial in an adult court.

The transfer hearing is something of a legal anomaly and a special set of rules has evolved to govern the proceeding. The application for a transfer may be made by the Crown Attorney, or by the judge, or even, theoretically, by the accused juvenile. If the judge considers that a transfer may be appropriate, he should be very careful not to take a biased view of the hearing.[53] There must be an opportunity for a full and fair hearing with a right to call witnesses; like a disposition hearing, it may be possible to file reports instead of having witnesses testify, but the authors of the reports should be available for cross-examination. A transfer hearing can occur at any stage of a juvenile prosecution. It can be heard before or after adjudication. It can also be heard after disposition. Section 20(3) of the *J.D.A.* allows a juvenile delinquent who has already been given a particular disposition to be brought back before the Juvenile Court for further disposition, including a transfer to adult court, at any time before reaching the age of 21; this provision does not generally apply once the child has been sent to a training school or committed to the C.A.S.[54] Section 20(3) may be used if a particular disposition has been tried without success. As well, the threat of recalling a juvenile and transferring him to adult court can be used to enforce a strict probation upon him. Such probation can continue until a juvenile reaches the age of 21.

9. Appeals

After an adult has faced a criminal prosecution, there is a broad right of appeal. The right of appeal does not go so far as to grant a right for a full rehearing, with witnesses being called to testify again, but it does provide for an argument before the Appellate Court concerning any point of procedure or law which appears, from a reading of the transcript of the trial, to have been incorrectly applied. The fact that an adult may have an appeal heard does not, of course, mean that the appeal will be successful. The right of appeal after a juvenile hearing is considerably narrower than that provided for an adult. As with an adult, the juvenile appeal does not involve a new hearing with witnesses testifying again, but rather involves a consideration of the transcript only. An appellate judge may order a new trial if this is appropriate. A juvenile appeal is governed by s. 37 of the *J.D.A.* and requires special "leave" or permission, which is to be given only if "in the particular circumstances of the case it is essential in the public interest or for the due administration of justice that such leave be granted." The word "essential" suggests that quite a high standard must be satisfied before an appeal is allowed. An application for leave to appeal must be made to a superior court judge very quickly, and in any event within 30 days.

The rationale for having such strict rules governing appeals is to restrict the number of appeals, and expedite the hearing of those appeals which are heard. It is felt that it is undesirable for any proceedings involving children to be unduly protracted, and that the dispositions which may be ordered by the Juvenile Court should be implemented without delay. The restrictive rules can, however, cause real injustice for some of the children dealt with in the Juvenile Courts.

In *R. v. W. & W.*,[55] a boy was charged with violating the *J.D.A.* by committing the offense of breaking and entering. The boy appeared without counsel, and without his parents being present. After the charge was first read out, the Juvenile Court judge decided to transfer the case to adult court. This judge was also the local adult criminal court judge, a situation not too uncommon in smaller Canadian centres. He reconvened the court a few minutes later as an adult court, asked the lad to enter a plea, accepted a guilty plea from the boy, and sentenced him to 12 months in an adult facility. The boy appealed the decision to transfer him into adult court. The appellate judge described this as "the most serious miscarriage of justice I have ever seen while at the bar and on the bench of this Province." He stated that he had "no doubt whatsoever that the appeal . . . should succeed," but that because it had not been commenced within the statutory 30-day time-limit, it had to be dismissed. The failure to launch the appeal earlier was a result of the fact that the boy had been incarcerated and unable to obtain legal aid and the services of a lawyer until after the 30 days had expired. The *Criminal Code* specifically provides in s. 607 that any time-limits which apply to adults in connection with an appeal may be extended by the court, and in similar circumstances, the time-limit for an adult would doubtless have been extended.

Circumstances in which s. 37 of the *J.D.A.* has been found to apply and which have been such that it has been deemed to be essential to the "public interest or for the due administration of justice," include cases where the judge limited the accused's right of cross-examination, or allowed the Crown's witness to make seriously prejudicial statements which the laws of evidence excluded. It is, however, not enough for an appellate judge simply to believe that he would have reached a different conclusion about the matters at issue; he must consider the whole course of the juvenile trial and determine whether its cumulative effect makes it essential for the due administration of justice that the appeal be heard.

It should be noted that in some circumstances there may be ways of avoiding the strict appeal limitations contained in the *J.D.A.*, for example, by arguing the

Juvenile Court judge really exceeded his jurisdiction and was not acting under the Act at all, or by arguing that the judge was not really acting under the *J.D.A.*, but under some other piece of legislation, such as the *Training Schools Act*, for which the strict time limitations do not apply. A lawyer should always be consulted if there is a possibility of an appeal.

10. The Role of Counsel in Juvenile Court

As discussed earlier, the *Canadian Bill of Rights* guarantees that a child charged with committing a delinquency has the right to have a lawyer represent him in Juvenile Court. This guarantee does not go so far as to ensure each child who comes to court adequate legal representation. Indeed, historically, very few children who appeared in Juvenile Court had lawyers. Most children were from low-income families which could not afford the cost of legal representation, and the government did not see fit to provide these services. Besides, many social workers, probation officers and judges involved in the juvenile justice system felt that it was unnecessary for lawyers to be present. In recent years, there have been great changes in the area of legal representation for juveniles. Government-funded legal aid schemes have ensured that most children appearing in Juvenile Court, at least on serious charges, have access to some legal advice, and most of the social workers, judges and other persons involved, have come to accept that lawyers do have an important role to play in Juvenile Court.[56] There continues to be, however, great uncertainty as to what is the appropriate role for lawyers in this setting; this uncertainty is shared by lawyers, and by all those concerned with the juvenile justice system.

The role of the lawyer representing an adult accused of committing a criminal offense is fairly clearly defined. Subject to certain ethical considerations, the major decisions about a case are ultimately made by the client, and the lawyer will never take a course of action contrary to the client's express instructions, out of a desire to promote the lawyer's view of the client's interests. A lawyer may well indicate to a client that as long as he is retained, he will make the tactical decisions, but the ultimate control over the case rests with the client. Ethical considerations prevent a lawyer from knowingly misleading a court, for example, by putting forward testimony known by the lawyer to be perjured. But these considerations do not prevent a lawyer, who knows his client to be guilty, from relying upon any technical, procedural or evidentiary defense, and they do not prevent him from seeking the lightest possible sentence regardless of the lawyer's personal belief that the client might benefit from a stiffer sentence.

There are some who argue that the lawyer's role in Juvenile Court is the same as in adult court. According to this view, any form of intervention in the child's life represents an infringement of the client's liberty, and must be as vigorously resisted as the client directs; the lawyer is the only person in court who can truly "represent" the child, and there are others, such as parents, probation officers, and the judge, who can promote the child's best interests.

Others feel that lawyers should take a very different position when representing a juvenile. They are concerned that an unduly adversarial stance does not fit with the purpose of the court, and will not ultimately help the child. A Manitoba Juvenile Court judge commented:[57]

> As I have said, a lawyer is the representative of his client, but the servant of the law. A lawyer who represents a juvenile may find that he best represents his client and best serves the law if he ensures that his client gets the help and guidance and proper supervision that he may obviously need. For a lawyer to offer a technical defense which leads to a finding of not delinquent may be in the very worst interest of his client. To beat the rap is an invitation to a juvenile to try it again. If he follows this course he may become beyond all help and guidance and proper supervision. He may become confirmed in the habit of law-breaking.
> The juvenile court is a special kind of court and needs a special kind of lawyer.

According to this view, a lawyer representing a child must weigh his own views of the child's best interests against any wishes expressed by the child.

Lawyers in Juvenile Court often face considerable pressure to take a particular approach to a problem. Though the child is the client, the parents may often try to directly influence the manner in which the case is conducted, or pressure their child into taking a certain position; difficulties may be exacerbated if the parents are paying the lawyer's bill. Also, the social workers, probation officers, and judges may have a certain view as to the appropriate role for a lawyer, and this may subtly, or not so subtly, affect the lawyer's actions. The continuous protestations of these various persons that they are all concerned only with the child's best interests may curb the lawyer's adversarial instincts. Further, there are studies which indicate that if counsel insists upon playing a role in juvenile proceedings which is different from that expected by the judge, particularly if it constitutes conduct which the judge views as unduly adversarial, then his clients will tend to receive more severe dispositions than if the lawyer adopts the expected role.[58]

Another problem lawyers representing children face is that of receiving suitable instructions. An adult is presumed to have the capacity to instruct his counsel; it is not always clear that children have this capacity, even in regard to the most basic issues of a case, such as whether to enter a plea of guilty or not guilty. The child's capacity to instruct a lawyer depends upon his ability to communicate effectively with his lawyer, and upon his ability to make a competent decision. If the child does not have the capacity to instruct his counsel, then there is a greater onus placed upon the lawyer to develop a position on his own.[59]

Each lawyer will have his own views as to what is his appropriate role in Juvenile Court, and each will usually be prepared to modify his stance according to the circumstances. One factor already mentioned is whether the child is in fact expressing his wishes, and whether the lawyer believes that the child is competent to adequately make a decision. Many lawyers tend to feel that their role should be different at each stage of the proceedings. At the adjudication stage, when the question of guilt or innocence is being resolved, a strict adversarial stance may be called for with full reliance upon all technical defenses. If a finding of delinquency is made, however, the lawyer may be prepared to take a less adversarial role and relax the technical legal rules; at this stage he may also feel less obliged to simply follow the instructions of his young client and may be prepared to express his own views. According to this position, no child should be found delinquent simply to help the child, as there is other legislation which can be used to provide help, but if a child is found delinquent, all efforts should be made to promote the child's best interests regardless of the child's express wishes.

Although there are many views about this, there is no agreement; there is agreement about many of the functions of counsel in Juvenile Court. He should ensure that the parents and child understand what happens in court, and that their views are at least expressed to the court. He can ensure that all relevant facts and law are brought to the judge's attention, and that statutory procedures are followed. He can ensure that the basic elements of procedural fairness are met, and that the opinions of various witnesses are properly tested through cross-examination, and that the judge is not swayed by unreasoned views. Within this framework of agreement, there is still a broad scope for disagreement.

In view of the confusion among adults, it is perhaps not surprising to learn that children who attend Juvenile Court often do not have even the most basic understanding of the role of the lawyer in the proceedings. Often the child who goes to court believes that it is the lawyer and not the judge who brought about the punishment. Not only is there a lack of understanding, but many children who go to court express feelings of distrust and dissatisfaction towards the lawyers who represent them.[60] Such feelings are, of course, exacerbated if the lawyer feels he must put forward his own views, rather than those of the child. Some of the feelings may be a result of a lack of understanding on the part of the children, but some blame must be laid at the feet of lawyers, some of whom are prepared to treat juvenile matters as affairs of relatively slight importance. Clearly, lawyers will have to develop greater expertise and knowledge to perform effectively in Juvenile Court, a setting in which lawyers are increasingly being found.

E. NEW DIRECTIONS IN JUVENILE JUSTICE

1. General

It is hardly surprising that a piece of legislation based on a philosophy prevalent in the late 19th century should come under increasing scrutiny and attack as we enter the last decades of the 20th century. The *J.D.A.* is based on the philosophy of "child saving," a belief that children who violate the law should be saved from a life of crime. As a result of this philosophy, special courts, treatment personnel, and facilities have come into existence. In view of the absense of conspicuous success of the present juvenile justice system, the sustained criticism which the present system has provoked is to be expected. Consideration will be given here to three related developments which may indicate the course of new approaches to juvenile crime. The first is the articulation of a philosophy of "non-intervention" to replace the old child-saving philosophy; this philosophy postulates that intervention in a child's life will frequently not be helpful, and may even be counterproductive. Out of this philosophy arose diversion programs, which will also be considered here; children in these programs are diverted away from the traditional juvenile justice system with all the problems it is believed to create for children perceived as "delinquent." The final development which will be considered here is the proposed *Young Offenders Act,* which largely reflects a non-interventionalist philosophy, and may replace the *J.D.A.* The topics which will be considered here are by no means exhaustive of the topics which could be discussed, but rather are representative of some of the most significant developments.

2. Non-Intervention

Many of those who accepted the validity of the labeling theory as an explanation of delinquency came to adopt a non-interventionalist philosophy as a basis for policy reform. The labeling theory was discussed earlier in this chapter. This theory does not focus upon the delinquent child and his acts. Rather, the focus of concern is the societal reaction to the delinquent child. Proponents of this theory argue that certain youths, youths who do not differ much from other children, are designated "delinquent" by the juvenile justice system. The result of such a process of designation, or "labeling," is that these youths come to perceive themselves as delinquent and act accordingly. Further, society perceives them as delinquent, creating patterns of reaction and expectation. In 1971, Edwin Schur wrote a theoretical sociological work, dealing with labeling deviant behaviour.[61] Two years later, to outline appropriate policies for dealing with delinquency, Schur describes the policy of non-intervention as follows:[62]

> . . . delinquents are seen not as having special personal characteristics, nor even as being subject to socio-economic constraints, but rather as *suffering from contingencies.* Youthful "misconduct," it is argued, is extremely common; delinquents are those youths who, for a variety of reasons, drift into disapproved forms of behavior and are caught and "processed." A great deal of the labeling of delinquents is socially unnecessary and counterproductive. Policies should be adopted, therefore, that accept a greater diversity in youth behavior; special delinquency laws should be exceedingly narrow in scope or else abolished completely, along with preventive efforts that single out specific individuals and programs that employ "compulsory treatment." For those serious offenses that cannot simply be defined away through a greater tolerance of diversity, this reaction pattern may paradoxically increase "criminalization"—uniformly applied punishment not disguised as treatment; increased formalization

of whatever juvenile court procedures remain, in order to limit sanctioning to cases where actual antisocial acts have been committed and to provide . . . safeguards for those proceeded against.

The non-interventionalist approach stresses that society should not intervene in the lives of children under the guise of trying to "help" them. One can only hope that sending a young juvenile offender to a training school will help him to resolve some of his emotional and behavioural problems. Realistically, it must be recognized that many children who go to training schools will be more influenced by the other "inmates" than by the custodial staff, and leave the institution more thoroughly committed to a deviant life-style than upon their entry into the institution. According to this view, treatment must be voluntary to be effective. Anything other than voluntary treatment should be recognized as a form of punishment, and should be the consequence of serious criminal acts. The nature and duration of the punishment should be related more to the offense than the offender. It follows that non-interventionalists are clearly opposed to the continued existence of status offenses, offenses which can be committed only by children, as it is felt that this type of offense is used as a justification for unnecessary intervention.

3. Diversion

Diversion refers to a process whereby young offenders are not dealt with through official action by the juvenile justice system, but rather are "diverted" and dealt with in some other manner.[63] The term "diversion" has actually taken on a number of slightly different but related meanings. Some diversion programs are mainly concerned with diverting juveniles *from* the Juvenile Courts, while others are concerned with diverting them *to* some other less formal system for dealing with problematic behaviour. Other diversion programs are highly structured and formalized, while many types of diversion have been carried on informally since the inception of the juvenile justice system.

Diversion is generally based on a belief that too many children are being unnecessarily processed by the juvenile justice system, and that for many of them, particularly first offenders, the harm done by contact with the system may outweigh any possible benefits. It is hoped that the process of diversion will avoid the consequences of "labeling," and that "diverted" youth will not be viewed by themselves and others as "delinquent." Most diversion programs are designed to be more humane, and at the same time less expensive to operate than the more formal system. Many programs actively involve members of the community and the youngster in working out a consensual arrangement to deal with the undesirable juvenile conduct.

The oldest and most informal type of diversion has long been carried out by the police and members of the public, though it has not always been called by this name. If a child is not perceived as "bad," that is, he has not had previous contact with the police and the juvenile justice system, there has always been a tendency to "give the kid a break," and after he has been caught breaking the law, he is given a warning and perhaps taken to his home for parental discipline. This type of diversion has been a result of action by police, but also by ordinary citizens, such as merchants who apprehend young shop-lifters.

In recent years a number of formal diversion programs have been developed to deal with youngsters after they have been officially apprehended and before the child is brought to court. The child will be asked if he wishes to participate in the diversion program rather than going to Juvenile Court, and if the police and Crown Attorney consent, the child enters the diversion program. Once in the program an appropriate plan will be devised to deal with the child. This may involve restitution to the victim, or some kind of community service work. It might also involve attending some type of counselling session or rules regarding behaviour, such as a curfew. Participation in diversion programs is generally voluntary, but a failure to do so will usually bring the child back into the juvenile justice system.

This formal type of pre-court diversion program is by no means free from problems. One difficulty is that it is usually a condition of participation that a child accept responsibility for the situation he is in and admit guilt. There may be considerable pressure for some youngsters who are innocent to forego their right to a trial for the sake of getting into a diversion project. It is a generally accepted principle of sentencing, for both adults and children, that a more severe penalty should not be imposed because a person pleaded not guilty and chose to have a trial, as otherwise accused people would have an incentive to plead guilty. But with diversion programs, this is exactly what happens, for if the child wishes to have a trial he must go to court and give up the possibility of participating in a diversion program, with its low level of stigma and generally less severe dispositions. Another problem is that many cases which might have been informally diverted before, cases where the child would simply have been given a warning, will now be processed through a diversion program, leading more children, rather than fewer, through at least an informal kind of juvenile justice system. Related to this may be a temptation for the police to lay charges they know could not be proven in Juvenile Court, but which they believe a child might be willing to accept responsibility for if the only consequence is participation in a diversion program.

Various programs have also been developed to involve members of the community in diversion. In Scotland, a quite elaborate system of Children's Panels has existed since 1971. A child who admits that he is guilty of a criminal offense, or who has been convicted of an offense in a court, is brought before a special board of laymen for disposition. There, the child, his parents, a social worker, and volunteer representatives of the community, internally discuss the child's problems, and formulate a plan to deal with them.[64] Experimental projects are also being tried in North America. In Duluth, Minnesota, some convicted first-time juvenile offenders have a choice of being sentenced by an ordinary judge or by a "jury" of eight fellow teenagers. Though offenders might expect more lenient treatment from their peers, this is often not the case. The experience can prove educational for all concerned.[65]

A difficulty with all diversion programs is that as they become more structured and formalized, they may be moving further away from their initial objective of avoiding labeling. It may well be that most children are not sufficiently sophisticated to perceive any differences between the "informal" diversion program and the more formal justice system. And indeed, there may not be much difference. The sanctions imposed by a diversion project, though in a sense voluntary, may be every bit as real. The social perceptions attached to participation in a diversion program may come to be similar to those concerning the Juvenile Court. It must be remembered that the juvenile justice system was initially established to "divert" child offenders from the more formal adult system, and that the term "delinquent" was used in the hope of promoting a less critical attitude towards young offenders than the adult term "criminal."

4. The Young Offenders Act

The federal government has been aware of many of the deficiencies in the *J.D.A.* for many years, and a number of quite radical proposals have been made to alter the laws dealing with children who violate the criminal law. It is recognized that this is a matter on which there must be at least a certain degree of agreement and co-operation between the federal and provincial governments. While the federal government is responsible for substantive criminal law, the provincial governments are responsible for providing facilities and much of the complementary legislation, such as laws concerning mental health and child protection; as a result co-ordination between the two levels of government is essential.

For approximately 15 years, the two levels of government have discussed the problem, but to date it has not been possible to reach agreement, and we are still left with the old *J.D.A.*, a piece of legislation which is well recognized as having many deficiencies. In 1965, the Department of Justice Committee on Juvenile Delinquency proposed a *Children and Young Persons Act*. This was followed in 1971 by a proposal for a *Young Offenders Act*; in 1975 by a Bill to be entitled *Young Persons in Conflict with the Law Act*; in the late 1970s, by yet another proposed *Young Offenders Act*, different in content from the 1971 version.[66]

In view of the relative fluidity of the situation, a detailed examination of these proposals seems pointless. There are, however, certain common themes found in all of them, and these should be briefly considered. The "child saving" philosophy of the *J.D.A.* has been replaced by a philosophy which is basically non-interventionist in nature. This philosophy is well summarized in the preamble to the latest draft of the *Young Offenders Act*:

> Young persons who commit offences should bear responsibility for their
> contraventions and while young persons should not in all instances be
> held accountable in the same manner and suffer the same consequences for
> their behaviour as adults, society must nonetheless be afforded the
> necessary protection from such illegal behaviour.

In affording society protection from illegal behaviour, it is to be recognized that young persons require supervision, discipline and control, but also, because of their state of dependency and level of development and maturity, young persons have special needs and require guidance and assistance.

. . . . .

In determining the responsibility of young persons under this Act, it is to be recognized that young persons have rights and freedoms including those stated in the Canadian Bill of Rights; and in particular a right to be heard in the course of, and to participate in, the processes that lead to decisions that affect them as well as special guarantees of these rights.

In the application of this Act, the rights and freedoms of young persons include a right to the least interference with freedom, having regard to the protection of society, the needs of young persons, and the interests of their families.

. . . . .

It is recognized that parents have responsibility for the care and supervision of their children, therefore, young persons should be removed from parental supervision either partly or entirely only when all other measures that provide for continuing parental supervision are inappropriate.

In keeping with the non-interventionalist philosophy, the proposed legislation will only deal with children who violate federal statutes and the *Criminal Code*. Status offenses will be eliminated, and it will be up to the provinces to decide how they want to deal with children who commit offenses against provincial law; offenses which are generally less serious. In recognition of the fact that the criminal law is a relatively blunt social instrument and not perhaps suitable for dealing with young children, the minimum age of criminal responsibility will be raised from seven to 12, and children under 12 who commit criminal acts will be dealt with under provincial child protection law. The proposed legislation has provisions dealing with many of the problems with the existing legislation. These provisions provide for reforms in many areas, including diversion, detention prior to court disposition, legal representation for children, admissibility of children's confessions, medical and psychological examinations, pre-disposition reports, the range of possible dispositions, reviews of disposition, records of convictions, and appeals.

FOOTNOTES

1. For a fuller description of the "child saving" movement, see Anthony Platt, *The Child Savers: The Invention of Delinquency* (Chicago, 1969)
2. See Jeffrey S. Leon, "The Development of Canadian Juvenile Justice: A Background for Reform," 15 Osgoode Hall L.J. 71 (1977) at p. 76

3. *Annual Report of the Department of Neglected and Dependant Children* (1906), at p. 15; and see Leon, *supra*, at p. 86
4. *Attorney-General of British Columbia v. Smith*, [1967] S.C.R. 702 at p. 710
5. For a fuller description of these concepts, the reader who has not had legal training is referred to Kenneth L. Clarke *et al.*, *Criminal Law and the Canadian Criminal Code* (McGraw-Hill Ryerson, 1977: Toronto), especially Chapter 3
6. See unpublished paper by Andrea Margles and Neil Boyd, "The Repeal of Section 29(5) of the Education Act" (1975), available from Osgoode Hall Law School
7. (1977), 40 C.R.N.S. 119 at pp. 120-21
8. [1977] 2 W.W.R. 277 at pp. 279-80
9. *R. v. Frost* (1977), 40 C.R.N.S. 119 at pp. 126-27
10. *Re Lewis* (1977), 1 R.F.L. (2d) 337 at p. 341
11. (1967), 61 W.W.R. 207
12. See Graham Parker, "Glue Sniffing," 11 Crim. L.Q. 175 (1968); *R. v. Mack* (1973), 11 C.C.C. (2d) 386
13. See Sherri Barnhorst, "Female Delinquency and the Role of Women," 1 Can. J. Fam. L. 254 (1978) at p. 256
14. John Gandy, "The Exercise of Discretion by the Police," 8 Osgoode Hall L.J. 329 (1970)
15. Statistics Canada, Justice Statistics Division, "Juvenile Delinquents" (1978), at p. 53, reported 44 868 children brought before the courts on delinquency charges but no reports were received from Prince Edward Island, British Columbia, or the Northwest Territories
16. See Barbara Landu, "The Adolescent Female Offender," 17 Can. J. Crim. & Corr. 146 (1975); and Sherri Barnhorst, "Female Delinquency and the Role of Women," 1 Can. J. Fam. L. 254 (1978)
17. See Edwin Lemert, *Instead of Court: Diversion in Juvenile Justice* (Washington, 1971), especially at pp. 73-74
18. There is a tremendous amount of literature on the causes of delinquency. For a general discussion see Martin Haskell *et al.*, *Juvenile Delinquency* (Chicago, 1970), Part 3, "The Causal Context of Crime and Delinquency"; and Marvin Wolfgang *et al.*, *The Sociology of Crime and Delinquency* (New York, 1970), Section III, "The Concept of Cause."
19. *Attorney-General of British Columbia v. Smith*, [1967] S.C.R. 702
20. (1977), 4 R.F.L. (2d) 45. See also *C.A.S. of Winnipeg v. R.* (1979), 11 R.F.L. (2d) 198
21. Cliff Nelson and Ray Steel, "The Vagrancy Dilemma: An Empirical Study," 7 Osgoode Hall L.J. 177 (1964)
22. See Commission on Educational and Learning Disorders in Children, *One Million Children* (Toronto, 1970), at p. 224
23. For a fuller discussion of the relationship of the police and the Crown Attorney, see Brian A. Grosman, *The Prosecutor: An Inquiry into the Exercise of Discretion* (Toronto, 1969)

24. (1880), 14 Cox C.C. 390 at p. 391
25. [1970] 3 C.C.C. 280 at p. 283
26. [1914] A.C. 599 at p. 609
27. See *Re A*, [1975] 5 W.W.R. 425
28. (1978), unreported decision of Judge A.P. Nasmith (Ont. Prov. Ct. (Fam. Div.))
29. *R. v. Wray* (1970), 11 D.L.R. (3d) 673
30. In *R. v. A.N.* (1978), 83 D.L.R. (3d) 370, it was suggested that it was illegal for the police to take fingerprints from a child. The opposite view was taken in *R. v. D.G.* (1978), 5 R.F.L. (2d) 378. In both cases, however, it was agreed that once taken, whether legally or not, the fingerprints were admissible.
31. See A.B. Ferguson and A.C. Douglas, "A Study of Juvenile Waiver," 7 San Diego Law Rev. 39 (1970)
32. See the *Criminal Code*, ss. 457 and 457.1, and the *J.D.A.*, s. 15
33. *Ex parte Branco*, [1971] 3 O.R. 575
34. *Smith v. The Queen*, [1959] S.C.R. 638 at p. 640
35. 2 Fam. L. Rev. 58 (1977)
36. [1959] S.C.R. 638 at p. 641
37. *Supra*, at p. 649
38. (1979), 2 Fam. L. Rev. 66
39. (1977), 39 C.C.C. (2d) 469
40. *Supra*, at p. 474
41. (1966), 48 C.R. 110 at pp. 130-32
42. *Supra*, at p. 120
43. *R. v. Kendall*, [1962] S.C.R. 469
44. See *R. v. Boucher*, [1963] 2 C.C.C. 241
45. See *Kroh v. The Queen* (1976), 24 Chitty's L.J. 345; and *R. v. K* (1978), 1 Can. J. Fam. L. 297
46. (1977), 34 C.C.C. (2d) 333
47. See John A. MacDonald, "Juvenile Training Schools and Juvenile Justice Police in British Columbia," 20 Can. J. Crim. 418 (1978). In 1977, the government of British Columbia enacted the *Corrections Amendment Act* providing that under some circumstances judges could order juveniles to "youth containment centres," in effect training schools, but the courts have questioned whether such legislation is within the constitutional jurisdiction of the province. See *R. v. P.D.P.* (1979), 94 D.L.R. (3d) 564.
48. See *Attorney-General of Ontario and Viking Houses v. Regional Municipality of Peel* (1979), 49 C.C.C. (2d) 103; and *Re County of Grey* (1976), 13 O.R. (2d) 352
49. (1969), 7 D.L.R. (3d) 91
50. (1978), 43 C.C.C. (2d) 129
51. *Supra*, at p. 134
52. *Re S.M.T.* (1959), 31 C.R. 76 at p. 78. See also Isabel Lebourdais, *The Trial of Steven Truscott* (Toronto, 1966); Steven Truscott, *The Steven Truscott Story*

(Richmond Hill, 1971); and *Reference re Regina v. Truscott*, [1967] 2 C.C.C. 285
53. See *R. v. G* (1978), 6 C.R. (3d) 241
54. See *R. v. Mero* (1977), 30 C.C.C. (2d) 497
55. [1970] 5 C.C.C. 298
56. See Patricia G. Erickson, "The Defense Lawyer's Role in Juvenile Court," 24 U.T.L.J. 126 (1974)
57. Roy St. George Stubbs, "The Role of the Lawyer in Juvenile Court," 6 Man. L.J. 65 (1974) at pp. 70-71
58. See W. Stapleton *et al.*, *In Defense of Youth* (New York, 1972)
59. See Jeffrey S. Leon, "Recent Developments in Legal Representation of Children: A Growing Concern With the Concept of Capacity," 1 Can. J. Fam. L. 375 (1978)
60. See Stephen G. Walker, "The Lawyer – Child Relationship," 9 Duquesne Law Rev. 627 (1971) at p. 641
61. Edwin Schur, *Labeling Deviant Behavior: Its Sociological Implications* (New York, 1971)
62. Edwin Schur, *Radical Nonintervention: Rethinking the Delinquency Problem* (Englewood Cliffs, 1973: New Jersey)
63. For a fuller discussion of diversion, see Reker *et al.*, "Juvenile Diversion: Conceptual Issues and Program Effectiveness," 22 Can. J. Crim. 36 (1980)
64. See Fox, "Juvenile Justice Reform: Innovations in Scotland," 12 Amer. Crim. Law Rev. 61 (1974)
65. Sheppard, "Teenage Jury Tough on Young Offenders," *The Kingston Whig Standard*, April 7, 1980, at p. 1
66. On March 21, 1977, the Solicitor-General of Canada released "Highlights of the Proposed New Legislation for Young Offenders," 37 C.R.N.S. 113. Subsequent drafts have been tabled in the House of Commons, but have yet to be enacted; the general thrust of these proposals is similar though the details have continually changed.

Chapter 7

The Child in Society

A. INTRODUCTION

> In order to prevent, as far as is possible, the evils which would arise from the imbecilities and inexperience to which every man is subject who enters the world, the legislature has imposed upon him, for a given period, those disabilities, and endued him with those privileges, which, with their modifications, are implied in a legal acceptation of the term infant; and every person is, in our law, considered as an infant until he has completed the age of twenty-one years. [P. Bingham, *The Law of Infancy and Coverture*, London, 1812]

The above statement of English law accurately summarizes — except for age — the law's attitude toward the legal position of children in Canada since the earliest days of Confederation.

In the eyes of the law an infant (or a child) is a "natural" but not a "legal" person. He is possessed of a limited legal capacity. The word "capacity" as it is used here refers to a child's status or standing within certain legal contexts, for instance, the right to enter into contracts, to own property, and even to marry. To consider it in another light, one might say that it is a question of a child's qualifications. A person qualified in a certain area of expertise is granted certain rights and privileges, and assumes corresponding duties and obligations. In most civil matters, a child is not qualified, that is, he lacks the capacity to act on his own behalf. In legal terms, a child is described as not being *sui juris*, rather he is described as possessing only a limited legal personality. He becomes qualified (in almost all of the provinces) when he attains the age of 18. On this birthdate, he becomes *sui juris* and possesses a legal personality independent of any other person. In other words, for better or for worse, he leaves childhood behind and enters the world of the adult.[1]

Age 18 is known as the age of majority and most provinces have an Age of Majority and Accountability Act which confers "official" adult status on a child upon reaching this age. The effect of "Age of Majority" statutes is to vest in a person the capacity to enter into legal relationships without requiring another party to act on his behalf.

As a result of his legal incapacity, a child is subject to certain legal handicaps and restrictions which do not apply to adults. These restrictions prohibit a child from engaging in activities which may be injurious to his health, morals or general well-being. Such laws have been enacted for the protection of the child. It is assumed, of course, that the child lacks the emotional development and maturity to decide such matters for himself. The wisdom of such a protective and "parental" attitude, while remaining intact within the laws of the land, is subject to frequent attacks by social scientists, and by children themselves. In *Escape from Childhood*, referred to in Chapter 1, the author advocates that the distinction between childhood and adulthood should be abolished as far as legal capacity goes. The author makes the following observation:[2]

> What would it mean to give a young person full legal and financial responsibility? Just what it now means for adults. It would mean that he was accountable to his fellow citizens and the law for what he does. It would mean that he could sue others and be sued by them. It would mean that he could own, buy and sell property, make contracts, establish credit, borrow money and do all the other things an adult may now legally do.

This rather novel view does not appear to have won much sympathy, either from the general public (in particular parents), or from the country's lawmakers. One suspects this radical approach is destined to attract only the attention of philosophers, children's activists, and students engaged in the study of children and the law.

B. THE CHILD ON HIS OWN

As a general rule, a child may legally leave home and withdraw from parental control at the age of 16. A child leaving "the nest" is often a traumatic time for parents, particularly if the child's life-style and means of livelihood do not fulfil parental expectations. In extreme circumstances, for instance, a 16-year-old girl moving in with a 30-year-old man, or a teen-aged child joining a controversial religious cult, parents often contact the police for help. For better or worse, the police and the child welfare authorities can do nothing. Their hands are tied, as are the hands of the parents. Although age 18 may be the "magic" age of adulthood, age 16 really sets the stage for entering the world of the adult. At 16, a child may withdraw from school, leave home, get a job, and set up house for himself. However, his ambitions to establish full independence at this age are hampered by certain legal restrictions. For instance, he cannot own a family residence without the supervision of the court, and in most provinces cannot marry without parental consent. Nor can he be served alcohol, or even attend certain movies. As well, he will find it next to impossible to borrow money or obtain a credit card (or establish other lines of credit) and of course he will not be able to vote. He is a "child–adult," a person treated sometimes as an adult, sometimes as a child, the deciding factor being the particular legal context.[3]

In Ontario, parents are obligated to provide support (according to s. 16 of the *Family Law Reform Act, 1978*) as follows:

16(1) Every parent has an obligation to the extent the parent is capable
of doing so, to provide support, in accordance with the need for his or
her child who is unmarried and is under the age of eighteen years . . .
(2) The obligation . . . does not extend to a child who, being of the age
of sixteen years or over, has withdrawn from parental control.

Further, the *Criminal Code* of Canada stipulates that it is an offence not to provide the necessaries of life for a child under the age of 16 years. Thus, a child who voluntarily departs the family home upon turning 16 cannot turn around and demand support from his parents. He must earn his own livelihood. Upon attaining the age of 18, a parent is under no legal obligation to support his child (unless the child's parents are divorced in which case the obligation may extend beyond the child's 18th birthday (see Chapter 3)) and may even "turn him out" of the family home.

A recent Ontario case[4] highlighted the situation where a child who left home at age 16, subsequently sued his parents for support. Ontario's *Family Law Reform Act, 1978* allows a child to "sue" his parent. The boy, named Scott, left home because of his stepfather's chronic alcoholism. At the trial, Scott's mother made the following observation:[5] "The home life has been one hell. It has caused psychological damage not only to Scott, but also to my infant son." Scott moved in with another couple who charged him for room and board. He was an excellent student and a young man of exemplary character. In deciding whether Scott could actually sue his own parents for support the court expressed its wisdom as follows:[6]

In the view of this Court the concept of the withdrawal from parental control
at age 16 means a "voluntary" withdrawal. The free choice, indeed, of
the child to cut the family bonds and strike out on a life of his own.
On taking this personal freedom the child assumes the responsibility of
maintaining or supporting himself. It is his choice, freely made, to cut
himself away from the family unit. Once this choice is freely made and
the responsibility accepted by the child, the family unit has, in effect,
been severed and the responsibility of the parents to support the child thus
ceases.
If the child is driven from parental control by the emotional or physical
abuse in the home brought on due to the circumstances in the home,
then surely he cannot be compelled to remain there. These cases may be
analogized to a term of "constructive" withdrawal from parental control.
The choice of leaving was not voluntary but of necessity to ensure the
physical and mental well-being of the child.
There will be cases where the parent or parents due to the inability of
the child and the parents to get along will, in the best interests of the
family unit and perhaps with the consent of the child cause a child to set
up residence elsewhere on attaining the age of 16. This is not a withdrawal
as envisaged by the Act.

The court held that Scott had, in effect, been forced to leave home and was, therefore, entitled to support. However, it should be noted, as the above case illustrates, if a child *voluntarily* withdraws, he cannot collect support.

C. CIVIL STATUS

1. General Restrictions

In most provinces, a child may not marry until he or she reaches the age of 16, and contrary to popular belief, pregnancy does not create an exception to this rule of law. A person 16 years of age or over, but not yet 18 may be married if he or she has the written consent of both parents. If this consent is not available, or is unreasonably or arbitrarily withheld, the person in respect of whose marriage the consent is required may apply for a court order dispensing with the consent. A person over the age of 18 does not require a consent to marry.

A will made by a person under 18 years of age is not valid unless special circumstances exist. The *Succession Law Reform Act, 1978* of Ontario states that a will made by a person under 18 will only be valid if: (1) at the time of the making of the will, the person is, or has been, married; or (2) is contemplating marriage and the will states that it is made in contemplation of marriage to a named person. Such a will is not valid unless the marriage to that named person actually takes place. Certain types of employment allow a person under the age of 18 to make a will whether or not the above-described circumstances exist. For instance, a member of the Canadian Armed Forces, or a member of the merchant marine, may make a will while at sea.

There are a number of other restrictions on certain activities which apply only to children. Perhaps the most visible restriction involves the consumption of alcohol. A number of years ago the drinking age was lowered in most provinces from 21 to 18, then in 1979 many of these same provinces raised it to 19, primarily because of alarming statistics about teenage drinking and motor vehicle accidents. It is interesting to note that an owner of a tavern or pub may be found liable if he permits children to enter licensed premises, notwithstanding his lack of personal knowledge, or his employees' carelessness in failing to exclude the children. This is yet another indication of society's concern about under-age drinking, and the onus is placed on those in the business of selling alcohol to exercise caution to whom they serve.

With respect to driving, a person must be at least 16 years of age before he or she can obtain a driver's licence. This age limitation applies also to motor cycles and to snowmobiles. With respect to tobacco, it is perhaps a little-known fact that it is against the law in many provinces for a person to sell to someone under 18 years of age, cigarettes, cigars, or tobacco in any form. This is an example of law directed at protecting children from a particular vice but one which is rarely en-forced, and is perhaps out of tune with the times. In any event, it is generally not against the law for children to smoke tobacco and, unfortunately, many young people develop a nicotine habit at an early age.

Everyone is probably aware of the "X" rated movie. Children certainly are—they're not allowed to see them! Actually, an "X" rating is not a legal definition in most provinces. A movie to which such a rating might apply is now generally referred to as a "restricted entertainment," and in most instances a movie so rated is off limits to those persons under 18. Regardless of the rating, most provincial Theatre Acts also prohibit a child under the age of 12 from going to a movie during school hours, or in the evening, unless he is accompanied by an adult.

Another important area where the law places a restriction on a person under the age of 18 involves the question of voting. The *Canada Election Act* provides that a person must be 18 years old before he can vote. Youthful politicians take note: to become a member of the legislative assembly of Ontario (and most other provinces), or to be eligible to run as a candidate of the Federal Parliament, you must be at least 18.

It has often been said that "there is nothing in a name." Yet a change of name is a relatively frequent occurrence in today's "mobile" society. Most provinces have an Act entitled, appropriately enough, the Change of Name Act. These Acts outline procedures whereby a person may change his name. A person under the age of 18 cannot legally change his name. On the other hand, if a parent is attempting to change his or her own name, and in the course of such an application is attempting to change the name of the child, the child's consent is mandatory before approval may be given, if the child is 14 years of age or over. Situations in which a change of name arises often occur upon matrimonial separation. For instance, a mother divorces her husband, remarries and wishes the children to assume the surname of the children's stepfather. Generally speaking, both the natural parents of the child must consent to such a name change; as indicated, if the child is 14 or older so must he (or she). Incidentally, a change of name does not necessarily have to be effected through the mechanism provided by a Change of Name Act. A person, and apparently this would include a child, who has left home may "create" a name change by usage and reputation.

2. The Child as Plaintiff or Defendant

With respect to suing and being sued, a child is not a legal person because he is incapable of instituting a lawsuit without the assistance of some other person. This other person is described as the "next friend" of the child, and usually is a parent or legal guardian. The next friend is responsible for court costs and other legal expenses, and is a person through whom the court may compel obedience to its directions. It should be noted that a next friend does not have an interest in the child's claim, or in any monetary sum which may be awarded. If the infant is successful in a suit (for instance, because he suffered injuries in a car accident caused by another person's negligence), and is awarded a sum of money, then that money must be paid into court, and as a general rule, it will remain in court until such time as the child reaches the age of 18. A parent or legal guardian may, however, make an application to the court to have sums paid out in order to support the child, for instance, to pay for educational expenses, clothing, room and board.

On the other hand, if a child is sued he is sued as a normal adult defendant. He may be sued due to his own negligence, or because he breached a contract for which he is responsible, or because of any other legal obligation for which he is liable. (Contracts to which a child is party are discussed later in this chapter.) Should this occur, an individual described as a *guardian ad litem,* once again usually a parent, will be appointed by the court to defend the child's interests. The one exception to this rule is when a child is sued with respect to his interest in an estate. In such circumstances the child is automatically represented by the Official Guardian.

D. PROPERTY

A child can own real estate (and other property). However, he is unable to buy, sell, or otherwise "trade" in his investments without the involvement of an adult, usually a parent or guardian, and without the intervention of certain statutory requirements. For instance, in Ontario, a child (more accurately, the person acting on his behalf) cannot sell land unless a court is satisfied that the sale is necessary or proper for the maintenance, education, or advancement of the child. In other words, the sale must be for the benefit of the child; not incidentally, for the benefit of his parents, a distinction which is sometimes blurred by those acting supposedly in the child's best interests.

Re Hibbard,[7] an American decision, is an example of a case in which a conflict arose between a parent and a child over the sale of land owned by the child. The child's father was in poor health and it was recommended that he move to California. An application was brought for leave to sell a portion of the child's property to provide funds for the father's move. In finding any such sale to be "contrary to the law of the land and thus void," the court stated:[8]

Now, the power to sell is only for maintenance or education of the infant, or on account of the deterioration of the property; where in these instances it appears to be for the interest of the infant owner to dispose of the land, it may be done. The present application is to raise money out of the land to enable the father of the infant to go to California for the benefit of his health. It is suggested that this expenditure may save the parent's life; but, however persuasive may be the domestic and humane reasons involved, these cannot bestow jurisdiction upon the court.

In the circumstances the court refused to sanction the sale of the child's land.

A child may inherit property through a person's will, or if the person dies intestate (without a will) according to provincial succession laws. Generally, the Official Guardian of the particular province becomes involved and monitors the child's property interests, or as noted in Chapter 3, a "guardian" may be appointed to look after the property. Further, sums of money payable to a child regardless of their origin (from a will or damages awarded to the child as a result of another person's negligence) are generally paid into court. The funds earn interest and are not paid out to the child until he attains the age of majority. However, a parent or guardian may apply to the court (usually the Supreme Court of the province) to have part of the funds paid out in payment of such necessities as room and board, unusual medical expenses, and educational expenses. For instance, a child who wins a provincial lottery prize could not claim the money in the sense of directing that it be placed into his bank account. The money would go into court and the child would not be free to dispose of it until he legally qualified as an adult.

One may question this procedure or the general procedure of restricting a child from controlling the destiny of his own property. However, there is an underlying concern that a person under the age of 18 may lack the maturity required to deal intelligently with his assets. He may squander an inheritance or lottery winnings, or be subject to manipulation by dishonest and unscrupulous persons who may use the child and his wealth to advance their own financial positions. For these reasons the child's property is sheltered during the years of his childhood. Incidentally, it is also for this reason that many parents, in their wills, stipulate that their children's inheritance is to be kept invested in a trust fund until a child attains the age chosen by his parents, usually age 21, although frequently age 25 is the more popular age at which time the child is entitled to take possession of his inheritance. A child in these circumstances cannot "attack" his parent's will in order to secure the release of the money in the trust fund until he achieves the stipulated age, unless he is in extreme financial difficulty. It should be noted that as a general rule, a parent can exclude his offspring from sharing in his estate by not mentioning the child in his will. However, a child who is excluded from his parent's will and was financially dependent on his parent prior to the parent's demise, may seek a court order varying the terms of the will to gain financial support. On the other hand, if a parent dies without a will, then under various provincial succession laws, a child is entitled to share in his parent's intestate property.

There is yet another issue dealing with children's property and that is the question of a gift to a child. A gift to a child is irrevocable. In other words, a person cannot give something to a child and then upon a change of heart retrieve the gift. This general rule applies even if the person giving is the child's parent. Thus, a parent may give his child property and later be prevented in law from "re-capturing" the property. If a gift is made by the child, the child may, upon attaining the age of majority, repudiate the gift. In other words, the gift stands until the child becomes an adult, unless prior to achieving such status the child changes his mind.

E. CONTRACTS

1. Definition

A contract is briefly defined as an agreement entered into by two or more persons. The agreement is supported by a "consideration." The term "consideration" is a rather obscure legal concept, however, it may be generally translated as meaning "something," or some promise exchanged by the parties.

The above is only a summary definition. The law of contract is very complex. It should be emphasized that agreements must conform to certain other rigorous requirements before they will be legally accepted as contracts. The simple mechanics of a contract are that one person offers to perform a certain act, and a second person undertakes to accept the promise. It is more than a mere offer to do something (or to refrain from doing something), or a mere statement of intention. In other words, a *legal* rather than a *moral* obligation is created.

2. Children's Contracts

All parties to a contract must have the legal capacity to enter into a contract. An infant is handicapped in contract law because he is deemed not to have the capacity and, therefore, the law of contracts relating to children is made up of a special set of rules. Children's contracts are generally classified as: (1) void; (2) voidable; or (3) binding.

As noted above, under most contracts each party receives benefits and assumes burdens. Therefore, in nearly all contracts to which a child is a party, the child will assume obligations of some kind. If these obligations are so onerous that they outweigh the general benefit which the contract confers on the child then the contract is void. A void contract cannot be enforced. In other words, it cannot be sued upon or, to put the matter more simply, it is as if the contract does not exist.

The second class of contract is one which is described as voidable. Voidable contracts fall into two groups: (1) contracts which are valid and binding until repudiated, and (2) contracts that are not binding until ratified.

The "voidability" rules permit a child to contract with an adult. They offer him protection in the sense that there is no permanent liability until the child becomes an adult whereupon he is deemed to have the maturity and understanding required to measure the consequence of entering into a contractual relationship. It is important to understand that although the term "voidable" appears to have two different meanings, it is used in both categories to refer to the right of the child to choose not to be bound by the contract he has entered into. In the first instance, he may choose to repudiate, that is to reject the contract; in the other he may choose not to ratify, that is, to confirm the contract. Only the child may void it. The adult party to the contract is fully bound under the terms of the contract.[9]

An example of a contract which is void is to be found in *Phillips v. Greater Ottawa Development Co.*[10] In this case, a child entered into a contract to buy some land. The contract provided that if the child defaulted on his payments then he would have to forfeit the property. The court held the contract was void because it was clearly detrimental, or unfair, to the child. In other words, the contract was held to be invalid from the outset.

An example of a contract which is voidable but valid and binding until repudiated would involve the situation of a child signing a lease, a lease being a special type of contract. The child is liable for the rent as it becomes due. However, the child can repudiate the contract at any time, that is reject it, and if he does so then the contract is treated as having come to an end.

An example of a voidable contract that is not binding until ratified would involve an infant being extended a line of credit. Many department stores cater to the teenage market and as a result extend credit to them. If a child fails to pay, then the person giving the credit (usually a department store) cannot take the child to court to force payment. However, as soon as the child reaches the age of majority, he can confirm (ratify) the contract. Using the example described above, the child would confirm the amount of his credit debt. The important thing to note is that the contract is unenforceable by the adult party. You may be wondering why anyone would extend credit to a child. The simple truth is that most individuals and department stores do not extend credit; if they do usually they insist upon a parental "guarantee" that if the child fails to pay, his parents will cover the debt.

There is a type of contract which *is* enforceable against a child and that is a contract for necessaries. If the child contracts for necessaries (which would include food, clothing and rent), he will be liable under the contract and may be sued thereon. In Ontario, the *Sale of Goods Act* provides a statutory basis for enforcing contracts for necessaries against children.

> 3. When necessaries are sold and delivered to a minor . . . he shall pay a reasonable price therefor.

There is a second exception to the void and voidability rules and that is a contract for service or employment which is beneficial to the child. Such a contract will be seen as binding upon the child. A contract of service is defined as an agreement between an employer and an employee.

In a recent Ontario Court of Appeal decision,[11] the issue surrounded a contract entered into by a child, John Tonelli. Briefly, when Tonelli was 17 years old, he signed a contract to play with the Toronto Marlboros Junior "A" hockey team. Tonelli was obligated to play hockey for the Marlboros for a period of three years, or at the team's option, four years, and further, to pay to the Marlboros 20% of his earnings during his first three years as a professional hockey player. When Tonelli turned 18, he repudiated the contract and entered into an agreement with the Houston Aeros of the now-defunct World Hockey Association. The Houston club contracted to pay Tonelli $90 000 for his first year, $110 000 in his second year, and $120 000 in his final year. At the heart of the court action was the question of whether or not the contract made between Tonelli and the Toronto Marlboro Hockey Club (when he was 17 years of age) was enforceable against him. The trial judge concluded that considering Tonelli's exceptional ability and the owner's terms of the contract—a minimal salary of $15 to $20; the requirement to pay 20% of his earnings for the first three years of his professional career; and that he only play hockey for the Toronto Marlboros—the contract was not beneficial to Tonelli and, therefore, could not be enforced against him.

F. CHILDREN AND EMPLOYMENT

The *Tonelli* case brings up the question of children and employment. Chapter 1 described the brutal working conditions of children during the years of the Industrial Revolution. Until various child labour laws were enacted, there was no governmental regulation of child employment during this period. Today, in all of the provinces and territories, children are restricted in terms of their employment.

Generally, a child under the age of 16 must attend school and, therefore, unless special circumstances exist (see p. 234), working during school hours is forbidden. Of course, nothing prevents a child from working after school or on week-ends. There are, however, statutes which limit the environment in which a child may work, and which specify minimum age requirements, even in part-time employment situations. For instance, a child under age 16 cannot work on a construction project in the province of Ontario, or in most other provinces. If a contractor knowingly hires an under-age person, he may be liable to a $10 000 fine, or even a term in jail. As well, similar restrictions are placed on children working in factories and in mines.

G. TORT LAW

1. Definition

Tort law is perhaps most commonly understood as the law of negligence. Putting it simply then, a tort is an act of negligence. What is a negligent act? Generally, we are all required to conform to a certain standard of care in our day-to-day activities. Our actions in this sense are often compared to those of a fictitious person known as the "reasonable man." The reasonable man (perhaps the law will soon refer to such an individual as the reasonable "person" in order to avoid being labeled sexist) is someone who exercises reasonable judgement and care in his day-to-day interactions with his fellow man. If our behaviour, measured against that of the reasonable man, falls below his standard of care, then we may be negligent in the eyes of the law.

A more particular way of viewing negligence is to ask whether a person is able to understand the nature and likely consequences of his actions. If we can say that he understood the likely consequences, then he may be liable if the consequences involved injury to another party. This is the approach adopted by the law when judging the alleged negligent actions of children. There is no fictitious person known as the "reasonable child" because of the uneven emotional development and maturation of children.

2. The Negligent Child

A child can be liable for a negligent act and can be sued in court (just like an adult). The standard of care that applies to children is not the same as that defined for adults. If a child is capable of understanding the nature of his acts and foreseeing the consequences, then the child commits a tort if his acts cause injury. Unlike in the criminal law (see Chapter 6), the common law does not provide automatic immunity for a child under the age of seven. The question is this: Given the individual child's particular emotional and mental development, can he be said to be blameworthy for the injuries caused? In a British Columbia case, *Walmsley v. Humenick*,[12] a five-year-old boy who shot a playmate in the eye with an arrow while playing cowboys and indians was held not liable for the act because he had not reached that stage of mental development where it could be said that he should be held legally responsible for his acts. On the other hand, in a Tasmanian case,[13] a five year old who intentionally slashed another with a razor was held liable. Although he did not appreciate the seriousness of his action, he nevertheless intended to harm his victim and recognized the fact that he was doing so. In yet another case,[14] a three-year-old child dragged a baby from his carriage. The three year old was found not liable because of the lack of emotional maturity required to understand the nature and consequence of his act.

Briefly, summarizing the case-law, it is apparent that each child will be treated individually in determining his particular state of emotional development.

3. The Negligent Parent

A parent may be joined in an action against a child for the child's negligence.

If a father or mother has knowledge that a child is engaging in behaviour which may cause harm to another person, and the parents refrain from taking any steps to curb that behaviour, the parents may also be negligent. A recent New Brunswick case[15] deals with the issue of parental negligence in this context. In this case, the infant plaintiff was a four-year-old girl and the action was "brought" by her father who was her "next friend." As a result of a rock thrown by the defendant child (who was an 11-year-old boy named Dennis, defended by a *guardian ad litem* appointed by the court), she lost an eye.

An analysis of the facts indicate that the throwing of the rock, resulting in the little girl's loss of her eye, was not an isolated episode. In fact, the problem had existed for some time. The father of the little girl related that on a previous occasion, his daughter had been cut on the forehead by a thrown rock and that he himself had been hit on numerous occasions. The judge stated:[16]

> The cumulative effect of the evidence satisfies me that the Dupuis children, especially Dennis, the defendant, have developed a propensity for throwing rocks around in a reckless manner with complete disregard to the safety of other people. Dennis is reported by his father to be a normal child and was eleven years of age when this incident occurred. At that stage, a child who is told by his parents and who is normal is certainly capable of understanding the nature of his acts and to reasonably foresee the natural consequences.

The judge went on to state: "there is no evidence of malice in this particular case but there is evidence of want of due care by Dennis." Having thus settled the question of Dennis' negligence, the court went on to consider the issue of parental liability. Upon reviewing the evidence, the court was satisfied that the father was well advised of the fact that his children were throwing rocks. In fact, it appears that the father actually showed an indifference to the problem and took no steps to discipline the children (in particular, Dennis), or to exercise proper control and supervision. In the circumstances, the parents were also found to have been negligent.

The *Walmsley v. Humenick* case, mentioned previously, illustrates a situation in which parental supervision was found to be adequate. The parents' child injured a playmate by shooting an arrow into his eye. The child himself was not found negligent because, given his age, his standard of care was not unreasonable. With respect to parental negligence, the court was advised that the parents had directed their son not to play with the bow and arrows and had instructed him on the "weapon's" dangerous character. Further, at the time of the incident the parents were unaware their son had removed the equipment from the house. In the circumstances the court found the parents had exercised reasonable care in supervising their son. This case should cause parents to breathe a collective sigh of relief as it suggests that parents are not expected to maintain a constant vigil over the activities of an energetic young child. Query: What if the parents, having instructed their son not to play with the bow and arrows, took no steps to actually store the equipment in a safe place? Another case, *Moran v. Burroughs*,[17] indicates the parents would be negligent. In this case a 12-year-old boy shot his friend with a rifle. The father was aware of his son's possession of the weapon yet took no steps to remove it from him.

The *Michaud*, *Walmsley* and *Moran* cases demonstrate the principle that parents are required to exercise reasonable control and supervision over the activities of their young children. On the other hand, it should be stated that the degree of that control and supervision and the standard of care required bears some relationship to what is practicable in the light of all the circumstances of each case.

The common-law rule is that the father is not liable in damages for the torts of his child. In other words, he cannot be made to pay compensation. One exception, however, is that the father is liable for the conduct of his young child if he knows of the child's frequent wrongdoing in a particular direction and, by his attitude or his inaction, indicates his unwillingness to halt this misconduct should it be repeated. As a result, in the *Michaud* case, the father was ordered to pay damages ($15 000 for the loss of the eye).

There is also a concept in tort law described as contributory negligence. Simply stated, this principle dictates that if a person contributes by his own carelessness to an accident, for instance, a child running in front of a speeding car, then the amount received by that person will be diminished in relation to how much he contributed to the cause of the accident. In the example of the child running in front of a speeding car, it may be that 50% of the blame will be attributed to the driver of the car, with the remaining 50% being attributed to the child. As a result, the motorist may be required to pay only half of any awarded damages to the child.

H. EDUCATION

1. General

Education is a provincial responsibility under the *British North America Act, 1867,* and therefore each provincial legislature has the task of administering and organizing the educational system in that particular province or territory. Most provinces have an Act similar to the *Education Act, 1974* of Ontario.

Education is generally provided for the benefit of three different parties: the child, the parent and the State. The State's benefit was emphasized in an old Ontario case, *Ottawa Separate School Trustees v. City of Ottawa*:[18]

> The creation of the office of Minister of Education, and the enactment of all the elaborate legislative provisions of this province, respecting education . . . were not for the mere benefit of parent or child; the paramount purpose, the dominant intention, was the public interest of the province, the making of true and efficient subjects of all its children . . . loyal and efficient subjects and citizens, the best assets of every state.

There are a number of administrative issues addressed by provincial laws dealing with education. These matters include the question of residency, in order to determine the particular school which the child is eligible to attend, matters of curricula, the question of religious instruction, attendance, and the newly emerging question of student rights. These issues will be discussed individually.

2. The Right to Attend School

A person has the right to attend a school without payment of tuition in the school district in which he is qualified to be a "resident." The child qualifies as a resident where his parent or legal guardian is registered on the tax rolls of the geographical region in which the school is located. The more simple criteria is that the child simply resides in the school district in which his parents or guardian resides.

If a child is in the care of a person other than his parent or guardian, special rules apply. For instance, if the child is a ward of the Children's Aid Society, then he will attend the elementary or secondary school in the district in which he is living, regardless of the location of his parents or guardian.

The obligation to attend school commences at the age of six and continues until that person reaches the age of 16 years. After age 16, attendance is voluntary and in most provinces may continue until age 21.

3. The School Board

The administration of the *Education Act, 1974* and the organization of education within a particular geographical region (often described as a district) is usually the responsibility of a board of education. As a general rule, these boards are comprised of elected officials whose responsibility it is to ensure that the guidelines and provisions of any government authorities and legislative Acts are carried out. Some of the responsibilities of the board of education include the responsibility to provide "adequate accommodations" during a school year for people having the "right" to attend school within its jurisdiction. Accommodation in this context means school facilities. With declining enrolments, resulting from a dramatic decrease in the birth rate, communities are often embroiled in controversy over the closing of various schools. However, the board of education has the authority to determine the particular school needs for its district and may direct the closing of an under-populated school.

In an Ontario case,[19] an application was brought by a group of parents who wanted to have the Ottawa Board of Education cancel a plan which would have created a French-language high school in an existing English-language high school (thereby depriving students from access to that particular English-language school). The parents' application was dismissed. On appeal the Ontario Court of Appeal stated:[20]

> The Board is not under any obligation to maintain, in a sense of "to perpetuate" any particular school it establishes. "Maintain" in the Ontario Acts is not a direction to keep forever. It encompasses only authority and obligation to expend the money upon the school and keep it in operation so long as the Board feels it is desirable to do so for the provision of the educational needs of the people for whom it is responsible. "Maintain" . . . means the duty from year to year to keep up the operation of the school so long as the Board is of the opinion that such school should be operated as an appropriate means of discharging its duty to provide accommodation for its pupils.

This case underlines the power vested in school boards to direct the use of school facilities within their districts.

Every board of education, as noted above, must provide instruction to pupils who qualify and thereby have the right to attend a school within its area of jurisdiction.

However, should a child be unable, by reason of mental or physical handicap, to benefit from "normal" instruction, then that child may be excluded from a particular school. On the other hand, government authorities have the power to establish special education programs for those children who are unable to profit by regular teaching methods. Therefore, most school boards have established special education programs to assist handicapped children in attaining their full potential.

A board of education has a responsibility to its students to ensure reasonable care is taken to protect the students during various school activities. In a case decided in Ontario,[21] a 16-year-old high school student suffered a fractured dislocation of his elbow during a "take-down" in a gym class. The boy struck the hardwood floor of the gymnasium at a place where the wrestling mats had become separated immediately prior to the fall. The only precaution taken against separation was a standing instruction to non-participating students to sit around the perimeter of the mats with their feet pressed against the edges of the outside mats. The injured student sued not the teacher involved, but rather the school board. The lawsuit was based on negligence in the system adopted by the defendant school board in the provision of safety equipment in the operation of the wrestling class in one of its high schools. The following excerpt summarizes the judicial position:[22]

If the Board of Education undertakes to include the art or sport of wrestling in the compulsory education programme, as it did in the present instance and as, no doubt, many Boards throughout the Province do, there is a burden placed upon it to take the best safety precautions reasonably possible. With physical education for boys in several grades concentrated exclusively on wrestling during certain periods of the year, as was the evidence in the present case, and with three gymnasia available, to require that one gymnasium be provided with a mat large enough to fill the floor space and to be left permanently in place, or, at least, with two or three large mats which together would fill the space, is not, in my view, an unreasonable requirement. Such a practice would meet the safety standards which, in the opinion of the experienced witnesses other than those employed at the Royal York Collegiate, which opinion I accept, are the minimum required for competitive wrestling.

As a consequence, the school board was found liable and was ordered to pay damages to the injured student.

4. Curricula

The question of curricula is often a controversial issue, particularly in recent years. Secondary school curricula have been attacked for the lack of attention to those basics often referred to as the "three R's" (reading, writing and arithmetic). The question of curriculum is not exclusively within the control of any particular school board. Rather, the Ministry of Education issues curriculum guidelines and requires that courses of study be developed conforming to these guidelines. Procedures are also established for the approval of courses of study that are not developed within specific curriculum guidelines. In other words, there is a system of approval by which school boards are required to follow governmental guidelines but which allow for a school board to have a say in curriculum content. Similarly, the selection and approval of books is subject to government guidelines and approval.

Recently, a great furor has erupted in Ontario with respect to whether the Lord's Prayer should be recited at the commencement of each school day. The role which religious instruction is to play in a school is usually defined by a particular government statute. In Ontario, the Regulations of the *Education Act, 1974* provide that a religious exercise is to be held daily in each class-room. In other words, religious instruction is to form part of the curricula of every school in Ontario. However, if a parent sends written notice to the teacher that he does not, for religious reasons, wish his child to participate in the exercises, the student is to be excused therefrom.

Unlike the question of religious instruction, students may not be exempted from what are described as "patriotic exercises." The Ontario *Education Act, 1974*, s. 229(1), requires that a teacher:

(c) . . . inculcate by precept an example respecting religion and the principles of Judaeo-Christian morality and the highest regard for truth, justice, loyalty, love of country, humanity, benevolence, sorority, industry, frugality, purity, temperance, all other virtues.

Another particular area of education which is subject to considerable controversy by the public involves the question of French-language instruction. There is no question that a board of education may require a student to take a course of instruction in the French language. Usually, such courses are compulsory in the elementary school years but are made optional at the secondary school level. A larger issue is the question of creation of French-language schools. The board of education is empowered to establish elementary and secondary schools in order to provide for an education in the French language. Indeed, if there are a sufficient number of French-speaking people living within the school board's jurisdiction, and within the particular school district, who elect to have their children taught in French, the school board must provide classes conducted in the French language.

School boards defined by religious affiliation are really creatures of statute. The *British North America Act, 1867* provides in s. 93 that each province has exclusive jurisdiction to make laws in relation to education. However, no provincial law "shall prejudicially offset any Right or Privilege with respect to the Denominational Schools which any class of persons have by Law in the Province at the Union." In other words, denominational schools (those with religious affiliations) in existence at the time of Confederation, cannot be prejudicially affected by provincial laws today. Thus, Roman Catholic and Protestant school boards continue to exist today although there are many who think the distinction is anachronistic. In any event, governmental guidelines have equal application to both "species" of school boards.

With respect to private schools, the Ministry of Education enjoys much the same control as it does over public schools. As a result, the government has the right to inspect such a school and has curricula and quality control over the question of instruction.

5. The Obligation to Attend School (Truancy)

The issue of school attendance has also been dealt with by legislation. Many parents have been confronted by a child asking, "Must I attend school?" The answer in all but the most unusual circumstances is an unqualified "yes." This leads to consideration of the issue of truancy. Section 29(5) of the *Education Act, 1974* of Ontario creates the offense of truancy, while s-s. (1) deals with a parent's duty and responsibility to ensure his child's attendance at school:

> 29(5) The child who is required by law to attend and who refuses to attend or is habitually absent from school is guilty of an offence and on summary conviction is liable to the penalties provided for the children adjudged to be juvenile delinquents under The Juvenile Delinquents Act (Canada) . . .
>
> . . . . .
>
> (1) A parent or guardian of a child of compulsory school age who neglects or refuses to cause a child to attend school is, unless the child is legally excused from attendance, guilty of an offence and on summary conviction is liable to a fine of not more than $100.00.

Truancy is often described as a status offense, and is discussed more fully in Chapter 6.

There is an important exception to the truancy rules however. If a child is not attending school because he is receiving satisfactory instruction at home (or elsewhere), then he (and his parents) will not be contravening the truancy rules. In a recent Family Court decision,[23] the mother of a 10-year-old boy (Marc) removed him from school because she believed he was not getting proper religious and moral instruction. She was charged under s. 29(1) of the *Education Act*. The boy was attending school in Sarnia, Ontario, at the time he was removed. Upon his removal, the mother enrolled him in correspondence courses offered by the Christian Liberty Academy, an educational institution based in the state of Illinois. A truancy officer reported the child's absence and the matter was then brought before the court.

With the assistance of materials from the "academy," the mother had set up a program of instruction which included the study of language arts, spelling, social studies, history, mathematics, and physical education. The Board of Education was, however, concerned about the adequacy of Marc's education in several areas:[24]

(1) That Marc is deprived of the stimulation of other students in a classroom.
(2) That the "teaching strategies" of his mother may be inadequate and detrimental.
(3) That the social studies programme lacked appropriate Canadian content.
(4) That the "maturity level" of the work "may be ill-chosen."
(5) That Marc may face "almost insurmountable obstacles" in returning to the regular stream should the alternative prove unsuitable or should he later wish provincial certificates.

On the other hand, investigators from the Ministry of Education reported that the boy was getting an adequate education at home, although they added that "it is difficult to determine what effect the home learning has been in relation to the school's instruction."

This case illustrates the tension between the State and the parent in the area of who has the right and responsibility to educate a child. The judge, in considering the dilemma, made these comments:[25]

I have no doubt that the legislature of Ontario, in enacting the Education Act, intended a purpose with which the majority of the population agrees, and that is to maintain at least a minimum degree or standard of education for its citizens; and to that end the state is accorded the right to interfere with the rights of parents to educate their children as they wish.

Obviously, there will always be persons who for religious, cultural or other sectarian purposes reject all or part of the public educational system, and pressing against them will be the intent of the state to protect their children from what may be the ignorance, excess, or folly of their parents which may, in turn, deprive their children of the right to full and free development and may result in them becoming a burden and a charge upon society as a whole.

It is very important that there be a fine balance between these contending rights and interests.

The judge then went on to quote an American case:[26]

The child is not the mere creature of the state; those who nurture him and direct his destiny have the right, coupled with the high duty, to recognize and prepare him for additional obligations.

In the end, the judge concluded that Marc's mother was providing him with adequate instruction. In other words, the boy was receiving "satisfactory instruction at home or elsewhere," and therefore, the *Education Act, 1974* had not been contravened.

The trend towards home instruction is apparently gaining momentum across Canada. A group of parents in Ontario, dissatisfied with school curricula, have formed an organization known as the Canadian Alliance of Home Schoolers. The aim of the group is to make home schooling an available legal alternative to what they describe as "packaged" school curricula. In Manitoba, provincial educational laws make it difficult for home schooling to occur. As a result, a group of parents (the Manitoba Association for Schooling at Home) are attempting to have that province's laws relaxed to allow home study programs.

6. Leaving School

The law requires a child to attend school until he reaches the age of 16 years. However, most government legislation provides for situations whereby a child who has reached the age of 14 years may be excused from attendance in school, or be required to attend on a part-time basis only. The Ontario *Education Act, 1974*, s. 3(1), provides that the parent of a child who is of compulsory school age and is past his 14th birthday may apply "to the principal of the school the child attends or has a right to attend to have the child excused from attendance . . . the parent should state in the application why he considers the child be so excused." Such an application must be in writing and should contain information regarding the provision of an alternative program of instruction, although in fact such information is not mandatory. The application is reviewed by an "Early School Leaving Committee." Such a committee is made up of a supervisory officer employed by the school board, and at least two other persons. The committee conducts a hearing to consider any applications placed before its members. Teachers, school guidance counsellors, or any other persons (parents, employers, etc.) involved who may be able to assist in reaching a decision are invited to participate. The committee must also interview the child and his parents. Generally, the committee can require the child to attend school until he reaches the age of 16, attend school on a part-time basis, or be excused from attendance at school altogether, provided the child is enrolled in an alternative education program approved by the committee. It has not been determined whether a student, independent of parental approval, should be able to make application before an "Early School Leaving Committee."

7. Student Discipline

The question of discipline and the teacher–student relationship are inextricably entwined. The *Criminal Code* of Canada is explicit in sanctioning discipline as a means of maintaining control of an "errant" or disobedient child. Section 43 of the *Criminal Code* which follows, includes parent–child discipline as well as that of teacher–student.

> 43. Every school teacher, parent or person standing in the place of a parent is justified in using force by way of correction toward a pupil or child, as the case may be, who is under his care, if the force does not exceed what is reasonable under the circumstances.

Generally, this provision gives a teacher (or a parent) immunity from criminal prosecution for disciplinary action which otherwise might be treated as criminal conduct. The key phrase is "the force may not exceed what is reasonable under the circumstances." Should the force exceed what is reasonable, then the teacher may be subject to an action in which an assault is alleged by the student. Whether the corrective action taken is excessive or unreasonable is a question of fact depending upon the circumstances of each case. Incidentally, it should be added that because the teacher's authority is seen as essential for maintaining order in the class-room setting, he can exercise the necessary discipline even over the objections of a parent.[27]

Certainly, it would appear that s. 43 authorizes the teacher to use that "old-fashioned" means of discipline—the strap. With respect to discipline, the Ontario *Education Act, 1974* provides:

> 299(1) It is the duty of the teacher . . . to maintain, under the direction of the principal, proper order and discipline in his classroom and while on duty in the school and on the school ground.

Section 37(1)(*b*) provides that a pupil shall "submit to such discipline as would be exercised by a kind, firm and judicious parent."

The case of *Campeau v. The King* is illustrative of where the line is drawn between what is reasonable punishment and what is not. The judgement in that case states:[28]

> That punishment may naturally cause pain hardly needs to be stated; otherwise, its full purpose would be lost. If in the course of the punishment pupils should suffer bruises or contusions, it does not necessarily follow that the punishment is unreasonable. However, if the teacher is careless in the manner of punishment, he may by that fact alone be held responsible. There will be no disagreement that if a teacher strikes a pupil on the head by way of discipline, the act is completely unjustified; the reason of course being that there is danger of doing permanent harm by striking a delicate part of the body such as the head. For the same reason, to hit a child on the spine with a hard object such as a ruler, would in my opinion, be unjustified no matter what his offence. Also (as in the present case) though to a lesser degree, to discipline a nine year old child and one of six years by banging their knuckles on the corner of the desk is dangerous and may be unjustified. The covering over the bones on the back of the hands is very thin and the risk of permanent injury is correspondingly great . . . There are a number of parts of the body where the bones are well protected by thick flesh and it is to those parts that the force should be applied.

The suspension and expulsion of students is within the authority of the principal of the school, although school boards are usually required to review such a decision. Most often pupils are expelled or suspended from school for chronic truancy and/or persistent opposition to authority, authority being represented in the form of a teacher or other school official. Other behaviour which may lead to suspension or expulsion includes smoking marijuana within the school, or even defacing school property. The *Education Act, 1974* of Ontario also provides that suspension or expulsion may be appropriate where the offending student is guilty of conduct offensive to the moral tone of the school, or to the physical or mental well-being of other students. Expulsion can usually be exercised only after a decision of the school board acting upon the request of the principal. This is an extreme measure and only a student displaying the most maladaptive behaviour (persistent truancy and uncontrollable opposition to the school environment) would warrant such action.

The sort of behaviour which may result in suspension may appear, at least on the surface, to be rather trivial. In the Saskatchewan case of *Ward v. Blaine Lake School Board*,[29] an 11-year-old pupil in grade 6 was temporarily suspended until he obeyed a resolution of the school board which defined the maximum length of hair for male students. At first glance the decision in this case may come as somewhat of a surprise. After all, one would hardly think a student's hair-style would be sufficient grounds for keeping him out of school. However, a student's hair-style and/or manner of dress may be the subject of school board policy, or provincial regulations. If the flaunting of such a policy or regulation can be construed as "persistent opposition to authority," or at the risk of stretching the issue, "conduct injurious to the moral conduct of the school," then a suspension may be authorized. Incidentally, the defense of the 11-year-old boy in the *Ward* case was based on the concept of freedom of expression. The defense, unfortunately, fell on unreceptive ears and the boy was forced to pay a visit to his barber.

The issue of student rights enjoyed a certain notoriety in the United States during the Vietnam War. Both university students (most of whom were adults in the eyes of the law) and high school students (children in the eyes of the law) protested the war. Students in several high schools in Des Moines, Iowa, sought the right to wear mourning-bands (black armbands) as part of a protest against the war. In *Tinker v. Des Moines Independent Community School District*,[30] the United States Supreme Court firmly struck down the schools' refusal to allow them, saying that neither "students nor teachers shed their constitutional rights to freedom of speech or expression at the schoolhouse gate." American courts have spread this protection to student newspapers, pamphlets and petitions.

Yet there is still a reluctance on the part of many schools to obey the spirit of the law. Certainly the student in the *Ward* case could argue that point. Apparently any student behaviour which can be construed as a disregard for authority is subject to censure. One might well question whether a student's hair-length, or the wearing of a mourning-band amounts to such a flagrant disrespect for authority that it warrants suspension or any type of intervention by school officials. The need for discipline in the school setting is obvious, yet it would appear that student rights (in the form of students being allowed to express themselves — a natural and healthy part of growth) will be subordinated to the maintenance of good order.

FOOTNOTES

1. See paper by Alberta Institute of Law Research and Reform, "Status of Children" (Edmonton: University of Alberta, 1976)
2. *Escape from Childhood* (New York: E.P. Dutton, 1974), at p. 236
3. See F.R. Marks, "Detours on the Road to Maturity: A View of the Legal Conception of Growing Up and Letting Go," "Children and the Law," 39 Law and Contemporary Problems 78 (1975)
4. *Re Haskell and Letourneau* (1980), 25 O.R. (2d) 139
5. *Supra*, at p. 142
6. *Supra*, at p. 151
7. *Re Hibbard* (1891), 14 P.R. 177
8. *Supra*, at p. 179
9. See "The Present Law of Infants' Contracts," 53 Can. Bar Rev. 1 (1975)
10. (1960), 33 D.L.R. (2d) 259
11. *Toronto Marlboros Major Junior "A" Hockey Club v. Tonelli* (1979), 23 O.R. (2d) 193
12. [1954] 2 D.L.R. 232
13. See Fleming, *The Law of Torts*, 3rd ed. (1965), at p. 25
14. *Tillander v. Gosselin* (1966), 60 D.L.R. (2d) 18
15. *Michaud v. Dupuis* (1978), 20 N.B.R. (2d) 305
16. *Supra*, at p. 308
17. (1912), 27 O.L.R. 539
18. (1915), 24 D.L.R. 497 at pp. 499-500
19. *Crawford v. Ottawa Board of Education* (1971), 17 D.L.R. (3d) 271
20. *Supra*, at p. 281
21. *Piszel v. Board of Education for Etobicoke* (1977), 16 O.R. (2d) 22
22. *Supra*, at p. 23
23. *Lambton County Board of Education v. Beauchamp* (1979), 10 R.F.L. (2d) 354
24. *Supra*, at pp. 359-60
25. *Supra*, at p. 361
26. *Pierce v. Society of the Sisters of the Holy Name of Jesus and Mary* (1925), 268 U.S. 510 at pp. 534-35
27. *Murdock v. Richards*, [1951] 1 D.L.R. 766 at p. 769
28. (1951), 103 C.C.C. 355 at pp. 360-61
29. [1971] 7 W.W.R. 161
30. (1969), 89 S. Ct. 733

Chapter 8

The Laws of Evidence and the Trial Process

A. INTRODUCTION

In every trial, there are two basic types of issues: issues of fact and issues of law. Issues of fact involve the resolution of questions concerning what actually occurred in a particular situation, or in some cases, such as custody cases, may involve a decision at to what might happen in the future. Issues of law involve the resolution of legal questions, and the determination of the legal consequences which are to follow from certain facts which have been proven. Evidence may broadly be defined as something which tends to prove or disprove the existence of facts which are in dispute. The laws of evidence are those rules which determine which evidence is to be received to allow a finding of fact to be made. Lawyers will generally say that the rules of evidence determine which evidence is "admissible."

An example may clarify these concepts, At a hearing concerning the custody of a little girl, the father may allege that the mother is a lesbian. This is a question of fact which can be determined. Evidence, usually in the form of testimony from various witnesses, may be heard to determine whether the alleged fact is true. The laws of evidence determine what evidence may be heard. The laws of evidence provide that the father may not testify that another woman told him that she had homosexual relations with the mother, as this violates the "hearsay" rule, a rule which will be discussed later in this chapter. Once a determination of fact is made, for example, that the mother is a lesbian, the legal issue must be faced. This is resolved after the judge hears arguments from the lawyers about the law. At one time, the law provided that a homosexual parent would automatically lose custody to a heterosexual parent, but now the law provides that the sexual preference of a parent is only one factor to be taken into account in determining custody. It should be noted that in most cases involving children, the distinction between questions of fact and law is often very fine. In our example, the matter might call for a psychiatrist to testify that as a matter of fact this girl will not be harmed by residing with a lesbian mother.

In most types of court cases, the main factual issues concern past events. The entire focus of the proceedings is retrospective. Did the accused shoot the deceased? Was the motor vehicle accident the defendant's fault? Most cases involving children, however, are concerned about the future. The focus is prospective. With which parent will the child be happiest? Will physical abuse be likely to recur if the child is returned to his home? Thus, in cases involving children, the factual issues, those questions which can be resolved by the presentation of evidence, are quite broad and not narrowly focused on certain, specific, past events. The type of testimony which will be heard may deal with broad issues, and tend to be somewhat speculative. Perhaps in the custody example just considered, experts will testify not simply as to what is the situation with this particular girl, but also explain what generally happens to children raised by homosexual parents. Such general testimony may assist the judge in deciding what is likely to happen with this child in the future if she resides with a lesbian mother.

Generally, the same rules of evidence as apply to other types of proceedings will govern the admissibility of evidence in cases involving children, and it must be recognized that some of these rules may not be particularly well suited to dealing with the issues which may arise. The laws of evidence can only be understood in the context of an adversarial system. The laws of evidence do not exist solely to promote a search for the truth, but also serve the function of promoting a fair contest between the litigants. As we shall see, these two goals are not antithetical in all situations, but often they are, and often if they conflict the object of promoting a fair contest seems to take precedence.

The laws of evidence must also be understood as having evolved in a certain historical and institutional context, a context which may not be applicable today, particularly in cases involving children. Many of the very strict exclusionary rules, rules restricting the admissibility of evidence, developed in the 18th and 19th centuries, a time when the death penalty was invoked for a theft conviction, and when the accused was not permitted to give testimony on his own behalf. As a result, it was hardly surprising that rules developed to promote a fair hearing. Other rules developed in the context of jury trials. It was felt that juries might be unduly swayed by certain types of evidence, and had to be "protected" from making erroneous findings of fact. It was felt that juries could not adequately "weigh" the evidence, and that it was best to simply totally exclude certain types of questionable evidence from their consideration. In cases tried by a fully trained professional judge, and almost all trials involving children are heard without a jury, such rules may not make much sense, but continue to apply. The common-law rules of evidence are gradually being altered by legislation, but the process is slow. Though many of the laws of evidence are eminently reasonable, it must be recognized that in the context of our present legal system some are not.

The purpose of this chapter is not to fully survey the laws of evidence.[1] Rather, it is to familiarize those who may be dealing with cases which may end up in court with some of the basic rules of evidence which they are most likely to encounter. This can be of assistance for actually testifying in court by alerting the reader to the nature of evidence which may be heard, and perhaps more importantly, can assist the reader in the handling of a case, and the accumulation of evidence in a case, which may only potentially go to court. When actually preparing a case which is about to go to court, it is always best to have adequate legal advice and discuss all potential evidentiary problems with a lawyer.

It is doubtless clear to anyone who has frequently attended court that the laws of evidence are extremely complex and subject to many rules and exceptions to rules, and exceptions to exceptions. It is important, however, for those who handle cases before they go to court to be aware of the basic rules of evidence. For example, a worker with the Children's Aid Society (C.A.S.) may be handling a case involving suspected physical abuse of a child. The worker may not initially plan to go to court, but rather hopes that a voluntary plan can be effected. After a period of months, the worker may decide that the situation is in fact deteriorating and feel that there is sufficient "evidence" to get a wardship order. Often this "evidence" will be the type of information upon which a reasonable person would base his actions, and it may be enough to persuade the agency to act. If, however, it is not "evidence" which is admissible in a court of law no wardship order will be made. So it is important for the worker to be continually considering whether there is an accumulation of "evidence" which will persuade a court.

Before considering the actual rules of evidence, the context in which these rules are applied should be understood. A witness may be asked a question which will obviously produce a response which is not admissible, or the witness may begin to give inadmissible testimony spontaneously. At this point, one of the counsel, usually the one who was not questioning the witness, will interrupt and "object" to the admission of the evidence. There may be an argument between the lawyers as to the admissibility of the evidence, and the judge will order the witness not to go on with the inadmissible testimony and will ignore any inadmissible testimony already given. The judge may act on his own to interrupt a witness who is giving inadmissible testimony, but usually he will rely on the parties to do this, particularly if they are represented by lawyers. It must be recognized that the judge sits between the litigants and if they do not wish to enforce their rights to have evidence excluded, it is not his role to do so. The parties may choose to not enforce their rights, either by not objecting, or by expressly waiving their rights. This happens particularly frequently in cases involving children. It may be that the parties do not feel that the inadmissible evidence is particularly damaging, or they may wish to expedite the hearing or perhaps even feel that given the type of hearing the judge should hear as much evidence as possible. If the parties take this view, the judge will invariably be prepared to base his decision, at least in part, on technically inadmissible testimony. Thus, witnesses should be prepared to give testimony which may be inadmissible. But parties must always be prepared to prove their cases by relying on legally admissible evidence; it is usually in the most difficult and closely contested cases that parties rely on their strict evidentiary rights, for it is here that the rights are most significant.

B. THE NATURE OF EVIDENCE

1. Testimony and Real Evidence

There are many different ways of classifying types of evidence into various categories. For present purposes, it will suffice to consider two broad classifications;

the first is the distinction between testimony and real evidence, and the second is the distinction between direct and circumstantial evidence. The classifications are offered to explain certain concepts, and it must be recognized that other authors may use different classifications for other purposes.

Testimony can be defined as the statements of witnesses given upon the witness-stand. Real evidence is defined as any material object presented to a court, but may be more broadly defined to include the appearance and demeanour of witnesses.

Testimony is all that which is said by the witnesses in a trial. Testimony is generally given under oath and is sworn on the Bible to be true, though as discussed in Chapter 6, the testimony of a child may be accepted by a court even if the child does not understand the oath. There are also provisions for accepting testimony from persons who object to taking an oath for religious reasons, or do not feel that the taking of an oath would be binding on their conscience.[2] A witness who does not take an oath usually simply makes an affirmation, solemnly affirming to tell the truth. It is also possible for a witness to have a more exotic ceremony if this is appropriate to indicate the solemnity of the occasion. For example, a Chinese witness may testify after giving the "chicken oath" which involves the slaughtering of a live chicken.[3] The criminal offense of perjury is committed by a witness who knowingly gives false testimony, regardless of the form of oath or affirmation.[4] A record is kept of the testimony at a trial by a shorthand stenographer, or with some other recording device, which if required can be typed into a "transcript."

Real evidence can be considered to be all things which are admitted and filed as "exhibits." They are generally things which are identified by a witness who is present in court, and kept by the court as part of the record of the proceedings. Though most exhibits must be identified by a witness who can testify under oath as to their relation to the proceedings, some exhibits, especially documents, can be said to speak for themselves and do not require an identifying witness. Real evidence includes material objects, such as a weapon used in an assault. Photographs can be extremely useful pieces of real evidence, especially in child abuse cases. It is not necessary to have the person who actually took the picture testify, though this may be helpful; it is sufficient to have a witness who will testify from personal knowledge that the picture accurately represents the scene in question. Real evidence is usually considered to include movies, tape-recordings and fingerprints. Documents are generally filed as exhibits and are considered to be real evidence, though a witness may identify a document as his own and read it aloud on the witness-stand, making it part of his testimony. Affidavits are documents which contain statements made under oath. Documentary evidence will be discussed more fully in the section of this chapter dealing with hearsay. It should be noted, for the present, that if the author of a document is not present to identify the document as having been made by him, it may not be admissible.

Some legal authorities[5] include the appearance and demeanour of witnesses as real evidence. Clearly, when assessing whether a witness is telling the truth, if it is observed that he gives his testimony in a forthright way and is unperturbed by cross-examination, this will buttress his credibility. This can be considered to be real evidence.

2. Direct and Circumstantial Evidence

Direct evidence is when a witness testifies about a matter which is at issue, and positively makes a statement about the matter. Circumstantial evidence is when evidence is presented which, when considered with other evidence, supports a logical inference about a matter which is at issue. For example, in a child protection case it may be admitted that the child has been bruised, but the parents will say that it was the result of an accidental fall, while the C.A.S. will argue that it was the result of abuse. If a neighbour testifies that he saw the father hit the child, or if a social worker testifies that the father admitted striking the child, this will constitute direct evidence. This type of evidence is frequently not available in a child abuse case. More frequently, circumstantial evidence is required. The testimony of a doctor might be that from the size, shape and location of the bruise, it would not seem likely that it could have been the result of a fall; two social workers might report that the parents each gave a very different story about how the "accident" occurred. Both of these pieces of evidence would be circumstantial evidence. They tend to show that the parents were lying in their explanation and so are hiding something, but do not directly prove that the child was physically abused by his parents.[6]

It is invariably preferable to have direct evidence rather than circumstantial evidence. If a case is based upon circumstantial evidence, it is not only necessary to prove to the satisfaction of the judge that the circumstances in fact existed, it is also necessary to convince him in argument of the logical soundness of drawing the desired conclusion. It is not sufficient for the proven circumstances to merely be consistent with the desired conclusion; the circumstances must be such that the desired conclusion can clearly be inferred. This is particularly important in criminal cases, such as under the *Juvenile Delinquents Act*, where guilt must be proven beyond a reasonable doubt. The old English rule from *Hodge's Case*[7] provides that if the case against an accused is based on circumstantial evidence, the jury is to convict if satisfied,

> . . . not only that those circumstances were consistent with his having committed the act, but they must also be satisfied that the facts were such as to be inconsistent with any other rational conclusion than that the prisoner was the guilty person.

The principle embodied in this rule is an accepted part of Canadian criminal law.[8]

In civil cases, such as custody or child protection hearings, facts need not be proven true "beyond a reasonable doubt." It is only necessary to prove facts on "the balance of probabilities," to prove that the existence of a fact is more likely than its non-existence. In such cases, the conclusion to be drawn from circumstantial evidence must be more than mere conjecture, it must be at least a "reasonable deduction."[9] When considering whether the conclusion is one which ought to be drawn, the court will consider all of the relevant circumstances, in a sense considering whether all of the pieces of the puzzle fit together to make a clear picture.

In many cases involving children, there may be a real difficulty in securing direct evidence about particular matters, and it is important to remember that, effectively used, circumstantial evidence can secure the same purpose.

3. Civil and Criminal Proceedings

It might be helpful at this stage to explain the difference between the civil standard of proof, "on the balance of probabilities," and the criminal standard of proof, "beyond a reasonable doubt." The exact distinction is the subject of much theoretical discussion, though in practice it may be hard to make. In a criminal case, where the liberty of an individual may be at stake, a court will not make a finding unless there is very strong evidence, unless a matter is proven "beyond a reasonable doubt." In a civil case, which is not viewed as a contest between an individual and the State, a court may act on the basis of slightly less convincing evidence. An example may be considered in which a parent is alleged to have abused a child. This may give rise to a criminal prosecution, in which the parent is charged with assault. It may also give rise to a civil proceeding to determine whether the child is in need of protection. Though the issues in these proceedings will often be somewhat different, we can, for the moment, assume that they are the same. If exactly the same evidence is presented on the issue of whether the parent assaulted the child, it is theoretically possible for the judge in the civil proceeding to conclude that the parent did assault the child, but for the judge in the criminal proceeding to feel that there is not enough evidence to satisfy the criminal standard of proof beyond a reasonable doubt.

In addition to the differences in the standards of proof in civil and criminal proceedings, there are some situations in which the actual rules of evidence differ. Generally, the criminal rules of evidence are stricter, and evidence which is sometimes admissible in a civil proceeding may sometimes be excluded in a criminal prosecution. One such difference is the rule regarding "admissions"; this is considered a little later in this chapter.

C. EXCLUSIONARY RULES

1. General

As a general rule, all evidence which is logically relevant will be admitted unless there is a specific exclusionary rule which provides that the evidence is not to be admitted. There are many legal rules excluding evidence which is logically relevant to an issue, and some of these will be considered a little later; these include the rules concerning hearsay and opinion evidence, and evidence of character or previous conduct. Subject to these rules, any evidence which is relevant is admissible. It is important to understand the concept of relevance before considering specific exclusionary rules, as the search for relevant evidence will naturally shape much of the preparation for court.

The classical legal definition of the term "relevant" means that:[10]

> . . . any two facts to which it is applied are so related to each other that according to the common course of events one either taken by itself or in connection with other facts proves, or renders probable the past, present, or future existence or non-existence of the other.

The legal concept of relevance is based on logic and ordinary common sense. In a contested custody case between two separated parents, it would probably be very relevant to know that prior to the separation the mother had a relationship with another man and that she was very open about this with her young children. It would be relevant because it would demonstrate great insensitivity towards the feelings of her children, and that she was quite prepared to disrupt the home environment and therefore should not have custody.[11] On the other hand, the fact that the mother may have had extra-marital sexual relationships would not seem relevant to the issue of custody.

Not all evidence which is relevant is legally admissible. If a man is charged with rape, the fact that he was convicted of the same offense on three previous occasions would seem relevant, just as a person betting at the race-track doubtless finds the records of horses in previous races to be relevant. Generally, however, evidence of conduct on previous occasions is not legally admissible, even though logically relevant; the rule excluding evidence of previous misconduct will be discussed later in this chapter.

2. The Hearsay Rule

A. The Rule Defined

One of the most frequently encountered, but nevertheless confusing, exclusionary rules, is the rule that "hearsay" evidence is inadmissible. The rule may be succinctly stated as follows: "A statement other than made by a person while giving oral evidence in the proceedings is inadmissible as evidence of any fact stated."[12] The basic idea behind the rule is that a witness cannot relate the statement of another person who is absent for the purpose of convincing the court that the statement is true. The rationale behind the rule is that the person who made the statement is not under oath and not subject to cross-examination, and that the statements thus cannot be adequately "tested."

An example of hearsay evidence might arise in a child protection case in which the C.A.S. alleged physical abuse. If a worker for the Society testifies that a neighbour told the worker that he saw the parents strike the child, this would be a hearsay statement. The witness, the worker, is offering the statement of another, the statement of the neighbour, to attempt to prove the truth of the statement (that the parents struck the child). The problem with the hearsay statement is that it can be very unfair to the parents, who have no way of testing the accuracy of the statement. Unless the neighbour is testifying, how can the accuracy of the neighbour's eyesight be tested? The neighbour might be blind. How can the honesty of the neighbour be tested? There might be a long-standing grudge with the parents. How can other details be elicited? The neighbour might have forgotten to tell the worker that the child was struck as part of being disciplined for running into the street.

One important point to understand is that the testimony of a witness will not be hearsay merely because the witness repeats the statement of another person. It must be repeated to prove the truth of the statements. If the only issue is whether the statement was made and not whether the statement was true, the testimony is not hearsay. In the case of *Subramanium v. Public Prosecutor*,[13] the accused was charged with unlawfully being in possession of firearms. He argued that he was acting under duress as terrorists threatened to kill him if he did not assist them. It was held that he could testify as to threatening statements made to him by the terrorists, as this was not hearsay. The issue was not whether what the terrorists said was true, and not whether they in fact intended to kill him. Rather, the issue was whether the statements were made, for if the threats were made, this gave a basis to the defense of duress. The accuracy of the matter at issue, whether the statements were made, could adequately be tested by cross-examination of the accused. The only thing that mattered was whether the witness, who was on the stand and testifying under oath, was telling the truth, and whether he could properly hear and comprehend the statements made by the persons who were not present.

The case of *Re Harris*[14] demonstrates the importance of understanding that the definition of hearsay only serves to exclude the statements of persons who are not witnesses if they are tendered to prove the truth of those statements. *Re Harris* was a wardship hearing and the social worker for the C.A.S. wanted to testify about statements made by the children to the worker. The lawyer for the parents argued that the statements were hearsay and not admissible. The judge ruled that the statements were admissible, saying:[15]

> In this case I am satisfied that the statements are admissible not as to the truth of the facts in the statements but because of the inferences that might reasonably be drawn from the fact that such statements were made. For example, if a child, and that's not this case, but if a child woke up in the night screaming irrelevancies that might tend to indicate that something was wrong in the child's life. If a child told the teacher that his father had tried to murder him that morning, the fact that the child chose to make such a statement might lead to an inference, not necessarily that there had been attempted murder, but that there was something wrong with the child's environment; that is, it could be indirectly relevant to the issue of protection, quite apart from whether or not the statement was true. I rule therefore that questions relating to statements made by the children to the social worker are proper and that answers to those questions are admissible, but solely for that purpose.

If a witness is to give testimony which is within the definition of hearsay, it is generally not admissible. This considerably reduces the scope of evidence which witnesses can give. There are a number of exceptions to the hearsay rule, and if what a witness says is hearsay, but it fits within one of the exceptions, then it will be admissible. Most of the exceptions reflect situations in which it may well be essential to accept the hearsay evidence as it would be very difficult or impossible to obtain the evidence otherwise, or situations in which the nature of hearsay evidence is such that the circumstances indicate that the evidence seems to be trustworthy.

B. Documentary Evidence

(i) General

It must be remembered that not only oral statements, but also written documents constitute hearsay. In a child protection case, a social worker cannot testify that a neighbour stated that he saw the mother strike the child as this is hearsay evidence. Equally, it is hearsay for the worker to produce a letter written by the neighbour stating that he saw the mother strike the child; there are exactly the same difficulties in attempting to ascertain the accuracy of the neighbour's observations and his honesty as was discussed above.

It is, of course, possible for a witness to identify a written document as his own, adopt its contents, and file this as an exhibit with the court. For example, a psychologist may be called to testify in a child custody case. The psychologist may have prepared a written report. He may simply be called to the witness-stand, identify the report as his own, and be available for questions. Similarly, a witness may identify a letter as one which he wrote and file this as an exhibit.

If it is inconvenient or impossible for a witness to attend at court, it may be possible to make use of an "affidavit." An affidavit is a written and signed statement. The person making the statement must swear or affirm before an appropriate person, called a "commissioner of oaths," that its contents are true, and commits the offense of perjury if the affidavit contains a statement known to be false.[16] Though affidavits cannot be used in criminal proceedings, the judge has the discretion to admit affidavit evidence[17] in most other types of proceedings. If the affidavit contains statements which are hotly contested, the judge may refuse to admit the affidavit, or give it little consideration. It is possible to have the person who made the affidavit examined on its contents under oath, even if the person lives in another city or province, and if this is done, the judge is more likely to allow the affidavit, and a transcript of the examination, to be admitted.

(ii) Business Records and Official Documents

Accurate written records play an important role in the efficient operation of most businesses and non-commercial establishments, such as hospitals. It is recognized that it may be difficult or impossible to locate the author of such records. Further, it is accepted that as long as the primary purpose of the making of the records is the efficient operation of the enterprise, whether or not it is a commercial establishment, that it is most likely that the records are accurate; it is, of course, recognized that if records are kept solely or largely for the purpose of preparing to go to court, that they may tend to be biased. As a result, a number of common-law and statutory rules have developed concerning the admission of "business records."

In Ontario, the relevant statutory provision is s. 36 of the Ontario *Evidence Act*; the federal government and the other provincial governments have enacted similar legislation. The term "business" is broadly defined to include "every kind of business, profession, occupation, calling, operation or activity, whether carried on for profit or otherwise." The legislation allows for the admission of any writing or record of any transaction, occurrence or event provided that it occurs in the "ordinary and usual course" of the operation, and that it is in the "ordinary and usual course" of the procedure of the operation of the establishment that the writing or record was made. If a business record is being produced, it is not necessary to have the person who originally made the record present in court; it is, however, necessary to have some person present to testify and explain from personal knowledge how the records are made, and satisfy the judge that they are indeed made and kept in the "usual and ordinary" course of the operation. For example, if hospital records are to be produced, it is customary to have the hospital librarian present in court to testify about these matters.

One very important procedural point is that before use is to be made of a "business record," it is generally necessary to give the other parties adequate notice of the fact that use is to be made of such record. Section 36(3) of the Ontario *Evidence Act* provides that at least seven days' notice must be given of the intention to make use of the statutory provisions, and further that any other party may require production of the documents prior to the hearing. This is to allow time to prepare any possible challenges to the accuracy of the records, as the person who made the record will probably not be present to answer questions. The statutory provisions allowing the use of business records can be used in many situations in cases involving children, for example, hospital records or school records. In a Nova Scotia case,[18] the court decided to admit the record kept by a C.A.S. The judge decided that it was a "business record," though he noted some of the information in it might be unreliable, and all of the circumstances must be considered before deciding how much reliance to place on such a record. This case might not be followed elsewhere, however, and C.A.S. workers should be present in court to testify.

As it is accepted that government officials will perform their tasks properly and that the records and documents of such officials will be accurate, various common-law and statutory provisions have allowed for the admission of public documents. Thus it is possible to have court orders and judgements, birth certificates, and other records admitted without their authors being present, and indeed generally without any means of identifying them other than an official seal or certificate.

Before planning on making use of any of the statutory provisions governing the admission of documents, it is wise to ensure that the specific terms of the legislation are complied with.

(iii) Medical Reports

Being a witness in court is often a very time-consuming process, with witnesses having to wait hours, or even days in court-house corridors. This is a problem for any witness, but governments have tended to be particularly sensitive to the difficulties this can cause to doctors. Doctors are frequently required to give evidence in court cases, especially ones involving personal injuries, such as those arising out of motor vehicle accidents. Their testimony is often very important, but they tend to be reliable professionals who are making statements of medical fact which are not often controversial. For example, in an action claiming damages after a car accident, it may be crucial to establish that a person has suffered permanent paralysis from the waist down, but this may be a fact upon which any doctor would agree. It is recognized that doctors are very busy professionals, whose time is in great social demand. Thus most of the provinces have enacted legislation allowing a doctor to file a written report instead of being called as a witness to testify.

Such a "medical report" may simply be a letter, or it may be a more formal document. The provisions of s. 52 of the Ontario *Evidence Act* are to be found in the legislation of most of the other provinces. Any medical report prepared by a medical practitioner qualified to practice in any part of Canada may be admitted without the doctor being present. The other parties must have at least seven days' notice of the fact that a report will be filed, and may inspect the report prior to the trial. Further, the other parties have the right to have the doctor attend if they wish to be able to cross-examine him in person.

The judge has a discretion as to whether to allow a party to make use of these legislative provisions. He may choose not to admit a medical report if it goes beyond giving a diagnosis, the prognosis, and a statement of the treatment given. For example, it has been suggested that a report containing a statement by a patient to his doctor as to how an accident occurred, a statement which would be hearsay and inadmissible if the doctor were present and testifying in person, should not be admitted.[19] In *Re Brady Infants*,[20] a child protection hearing, the C.A.S. tried to make use of the reports of a psychiatrist. The reports indicated that the children in question suffered from serious psychiatric disorders and recommended their removal from their mother's care. It was held that judicial discretion should be exercised to exclude the reports as they contained assessments of the home life of the children totally based upon information the psychiatrist received from a social worker; the court held that as the psychiatrist had never met mother the reports were not acceptable. If the psychiatrist had been present in person, at least some of his testimony would have been admitted; as it was the court held that the reports should be entirely excluded.

A party wishing to have medical testimony brought before the court will, in general, initially have the choice of whether to call a doctor to give testimony, or simply rely on his report. The opposing party may require the presence of the doctor for cross-examination. A party unnecessarily requiring the attendance of a medical practitioner for testimony may be penalized by being required to pay the cost of his attending. If a party does not wish to simply rely on a medical report, but wants to have the doctor present to testify, it is still generally necessary to provide the other party with a copy of the report on which his testimony will be based to give the other party time to prepare. Judges may be prepared to allow testimony without such a warning, especially where children's futures are at stake, but it is best not to test their patience.[21]

In Alberta and the Maritime provinces, there is no provision similar to that in s. 52 of the Ontario *Evidence Act*, and it is necessary to have the doctor present, unless, of course, the opposing party agrees to waive the right to object to the admission of hearsay evidence. Also, in proceedings governed by the federal government's *Canada Evidence Act*, such as trials under the *Juvenile Delinquents Act*, doctors must generally be present, though at some times, such as the disposition stage of a deliquency hearing, the normal evidentiary rules may be relaxed and it may not be necessary to have the doctor or psychiatrist present.

C. Admissions

If a witness relates a statement made outside of court by a person who is a party to the proceedings in question, this is known as testimony concerning an "admission." Though such testimony constitutes hearsay evidence, it will generally be admitted into evidence under the "admissions exception" to the hearsay rule. Thus, in a child protection case, a social worker may testify that on a visit to the home the mother told him that she often lost control of her temper and struck her children when they misbehaved.

The rationale for this exception to the hearsay rule is that the usual dangers of allowing hearsay evidence are not present, since the person who made the statements is in court and can take the stand to deny having made them, or put them into context. Both the nature of the adversary system and the goal of seeking the truth indicate that such statements should be admissible. A person who is a party can hardly argue that a witness should not be allowed to relate statements the party himself made because of the difficulty in evaluating his own honesty or perception; the party can simply take the stand himself to explain the situation. Thus, in the example of the child protection case, the mother may take the stand and deny ever having made such a statement, in which case the judge must decide whom to believe. Alternatively, the mother may admit having made the statement, but say that when she loses her temper and strikes her children, these are very mild incidents and the blows are weak and controlled.

When a statement which is an admission is entered into evidence, the whole of the statement must be heard and considered by the court. The judge must hear the total context of a statement, and be permitted to draw both favourable and adverse inferences. In a child protection proceeding, the C.A.S. may allege that the parents repeatedly assaulted the child and have evidence of repeated bruising. The mother may have admitted to a social worker that she did strike the child causing a bruise on one occasion, but state that this was the only occasion on which she hit the child. If the social worker testifies about this conversation, she must relate the whole conversation. It should be noted that generally the previous statements made by a party to an action which are consistent with the position or testimony at trial are not admissible. Such statements are felt to be self-serving. It is too easy to fabricate such statements for the purpose of the trial. A person is seen as having very little motive for making a previous statement which is unfavourable to his position, but ample motive for making a previous statement consistent with his position at trial. Thus, in the example of the child protection case, the grandmother of the child could not be called to testify that the mother told her that she never struck the child, as this would be viewed as self-serving evidence. It is only as a part of an unfavourable previous "admission" that such favourable remarks may be admitted.

There are special rules of law regarding admissions in criminal cases. Such a statement is known as a "confession," and is only admissible if the prosecution can prove beyond a reasonable doubt that the statement was "voluntary . . . in the sense that it has not been obtained . . . either by fear of prejudice or hope of advantage exercised or held out by a person in authority."[22] The "confessions" rule is very important in police investigations. Its purpose is to ensure that only statements which are likely to be true are accepted as evidence; it is recognized that, faced with some sort of threat or inducement, many people accused of criminal acts will make false statements for the sake of an advantage which might prove quite temporary. This rule is particularly significant in cases involving juveniles charged with criminal offenses, as they are especially susceptible to threats and promises, as was more fully discussed in Chapter 6.

D. Other Exceptions

There are a number of other exceptions to the hearsay rule which, though frequently both interesting and complex, are relatively rarely raised in cases involving children. The legislatures and the courts[23] are taking an increasingly narrow view of the hearsay rule and recognizing that it should not be applied in its more rigid forms.

Needless to say, though these other exceptions may be applied less frequently than the ones previously discussed they can be absolutely crucial to any particular case and it is always wise to seek legal advise if the situation requires.

3. The Opinion Rule

A. The Rule Defined

It is a general rule of the law of evidence that witnesses are to give testimony about events which they have observed, while it is the role of the judge to draw inferences and make conclusions on the basis of these facts. Put another way, the witness is to testify as to facts, and not opinions. There is an important exception to the opinion rule; if the witness is an "expert witness" who has special skill or training he can express an opinion to the court about a matter within his area of expertise.

The reason that ordinary witnesses are prevented from giving opinion evidence is that ultimately their opinions are not relevant; only the judge's opinions are of significance. Allowing a witness to express an opinion will only lengthen the trial, and potentially cloud the issues. For example, in a trial over the disputed custody of a child, a neighbour who knows the family may be called to testify. Testimony concerning the neighbour's views as to whether the mother or father should get custody of the child is opinion evidence and inadmissible. It is irrelevant what the neighbour's views are; it is the judge who must decide which parent is better suited to have the child.

The rule against the giving of opinion evidence can never be very strictly applied. One basic difficulty is that though the concepts of fact and opinion can theoretically be distinguished, when a witness is giving testimony the distinction may be impossible to make, and there may be little useful purpose in attempting to exclude opinion evidence in any event. A witness can never truly state a fact, but must always be giving his impression of events. An author in the field of evidence has written:[24]

> The words of a witness cannot "give" or recreate the "facts", that is, the objective situations or happenings about which the witness is testifying. Drawings, maps, photographs, even motion pictures, would only be a remote and inaccurate portrayal of those "facts" and how much more distant approximations of reality are the word pictures of oral or written testimony. There is no conceivable statement however specific, detailed and "factual", that is not in some measure the product of inference and reflection as well as observation and memory. The difference between the statement, "He was driving on the lefthand side of the road" which would be classed as "fact" under the rule, and "He was driving carelessly", which would be called "opinion" is merely a difference between a more concrete and specific form of descriptive statement and a less specific and concrete form. The difference then between a so-called "fact", then, and "opinion" is not a difference between opposites or contrary absolutes, but a mere difference in degree with no recognizable line to mark the boundary.

Thus in the example of the custody case, it is opinion evidence for the neighbour to state that the mother should get custody. It may be more acceptable to specify that the mother loves the child, though clearly this is not simply a statement of fact, but involves the formation of opinions. The neighbour might state that the mother displays warmth towards the child, but this, too, may involve an opinion. Even a more specific statement such as one that the mother affectionately hugs the child may be an opinion; did the witness incorrectly conclude that the hugs were affectionate when they were in fact aggressive?

It is commonly accepted that the opinion rule cannot be strictly applied. Witnesses of ordinary intelligence may give opinion evidence about matters of which they have personal knowledge, such as the identity or age of individuals, the physical or mental condition of a person, or whether a person was intoxicated.

Perhaps the greatest effect of the opinion rule is that it creates a certain area of testimony which is the exclusive preserve of the ''expert'' witness. The exact extent of this area will depend upon the type of case and the matters which are at issue, but in virtually every case there will be a sphere restricted to ''experts.'' Thus, in a case involving child abuse, a social worker may generally testify as to the location, size and colouration of bruising, but only a doctor who is a qualified ''expert'' may express an ''opinion'' as to the probable cause of such bruising. The greatest difficulties often arise when social workers, or other persons lacking extensive psychological or psychiatric qualifications, attempt to give testimony about behaviour patterns, or interpersonal relationships. If the statement of a witness is objected to on the grounds that it violates the opinion rule and the witness is not an expert, it is often possible to have at least part of the basis of the opinion entered into evidence by asking a more specific question. For example, generally only a psychologist can give testimony about a person's score on intelligence tests and clinically describe a person as having ''sub-normal intelligence.'' It would usually, however, be quite possible for any witness to state that a person had a limited vocabulary, appeared to have difficulty comprehending instructions, or otherwise describe the characteristics which would lead a lay witness to believe a person was retarded.

The area which will be left to expert witnesses will vary from one case to another, often depending as much upon the attitude of the judge as upon the nature of the issues, but in virtually every case there will be questions which can only be directly answered by ''experts.''

B. Expert Witnesses

An expert witness is one who is qualified, by experience or study, to give a valid opinion about a matter within his area of expertise to the court. The expert can perform two basic functions. He can provide basic information to the court to assist the judge in understanding scientific or technical issues, and he is permitted to draw an inference and make conclusions in a way that an ordinary witness cannot. For example, a psychologist might be called as a witness to explain basic concepts in developmental psychology to the judge, by way of providing information to the court. Though it is true that most judges are men and women of considerable general knowledge and experience, too much reliance should not be placed upon this, especially if the issues are at all complex or controversial. Generally the expert's more important function is to relate the background information to the questions at hand and express some opinions about the matters at issue. Thus, in a child protection case, where the child's emotional development may be lagging, after explaining basic concepts in developmental psychology, an expert witness might state that it is his opinion, as a psychologist, that the emotional development of the child in question is lagging, and that this is due to a lack of stimulation in the home environment.

Simply because an expert is called to testify, it does not mean that the court is obliged to accept his opinions. It is not uncommon for opposing parties to each call their own experts, who may express quite different opinions. It is then for the judge to determine whom to believe. Indeed, even if only one expert is called, the judge may still reject some, or all of this testimony. It is important to remember that while an expert can express an opinion upon the very question which the judge is to decide, it is ultimately the decision of the judge. The judge must assess all of the evidence, and not simply listen to the expert. Often experts have a particular institutional or intellectual bias which affects their views, and though the judge will invariably respect the opinion of an expert witness, he will be loath simply to accept it as deciding an issue.

There are basically two types of opinions which an expert can express. The first is based upon his own involvement with the particular case before the court, while the second is simply giving an opinion as an expert on the basis of the facts which he is told about in court, without having had personal involvement with the case.

When an expert is called to testify, he will be asked his opinions about a case, and also how he came to hold those opinions. It may be that he has had personal involvement with a case, and that he can fully relate the basis of his opinion to the court, making the basis of that opinion evidence in itself. In a child abuse case, a doctor can testify about the nature of injuries which he himself observed, and then, as expert, express some opinions as to the cause of the injuries; then the court will receive in evidence both the existence of the injuries and the doctor's opinion about the case, ultimately accepting as true as much of this evidence as the judge sees fit.

It is also possible that an expert will have had personal involvement with a case and be asked to relate something which may not, in itself, be admissible in evidence. In this situation the opinion may be heard, and the basis of the opinion will be heard by the court, but the judge will only accept the testimony which he hears about the basis for the opinion to assist him in evaluating the worth of the evidence, and not as proof of the facts which form the basis of the opinion. For example, a psychiatrist who has examined a child charged with committing a criminal offense may be called to testify at the child's trial on the issue of whether the juvenile was sane and had the necessary mental capacity to be convicted of a criminal offense. The psychiatrist will base his opinion on direct observation, but mainly will rely upon what he has heard from the accused and from other sources. If the psychiatrist were an ordinary witness, he might not be able to relate the statements of the accused (as these would be viewed as self-serving), nor could he relate the reports from various sources, such as psychologists' reports, school records and investigations by social workers (as all would constitute hearsay). The Supreme Court of Canada has commented:[25]

> The evidence . . . indicates that to form an opinion according to recognized normal psychiatric procedures, the psychiatrist must consider all possible sources of information, including second-hand source information, the reliability, accuracy and significance of which are within the recognized scope of his professional activities, skill and training to evaluate. Hence,

while ultimately his conclusion may rest, in part, on second-hand source material, it is nonetheless an opinion formed according to recognized normal psychiatric procedures . . . The value of a psychiatrist's opinion may be affected to the extent to which it may rest on second-hand source material; but that goes to the weight and not the receivability in evidence of the opinion. . . .

There is still some uncertainty as to the exact extent to which the courts are prepared to rely on the testimony of experts who have relied on "second-hand" sources.[26] It seems reasonably clear, however, that judges are prepared to hear from doctors, psychologists, psychiatrists and other experts who must, from the nature of their professions, rely upon others to assist them in forming professional opinions and that judges generally give considerable weight to expert testimony.

It is also possible to have an expert who has had no involvement with a case prior to coming to court testify. Such an expert will be asked "hypothetical questions." That is, the expert will be asked to express an opinion on the matter at issue, after being given a certain set of assumed facts. It will then be up to the parties to attempt to prove that these assumed facts existed. If the judge is satisfied that the assumed facts are proven to have existed, he can then consider the expert's opinion. When use is being made of hypothetical questions, it is common to ask the witness a number of different questions, varying the assumed facts.

It is necessary for a witness to possess special knowledge to be able to give "expert" testimony. This knowledge may be acquired through formal education, but it is important to realize that practical experience is sufficient. The law was well stated in the old case of Rice v. Sockett:[27]

The derivation of the term "expert" implies that he is one who by experience has acquired special or peculiar knowledge of the subject of which he undertakes to testify, and it does not matter whether such knowledge has been acquired by study of scientific works or by practical observation. Hence, one who is an older hunter, and has thus had much experience in the use of firearms, may be as well qualified to testify as to the appearance which a gun recently fired would present as a highly educated and skilled blacksmith.

If a witness is to give expert testimony, the first questions asked will concern the witness's qualifications and it is often helpful if the witness has a copy of his curriculum vitae available for the court.

There may be a challenge to the qualifications of the witness to give an expert opinion testimony. In this case, there may be quite extensive questioning of the witness by all parties. This questioning will solely concern the witness's qualifications to give expert testimony. It may be followed by argument, and the judge must then decide whether the witness is qualified to be an expert witness. In cases involving children, the issue of who is qualified to express an opinion about human behaviour and development can be extremely controversial.

The exact areas of expertise of various types of professionals and para-professionals are far from clear. In each case it is for the judge to decide who is an expert on various topics. In *C.A.S. v Paquette*,[28] a play therapist was called to testify about her treatment of a young child. There was a challenge to the qualifications of a play therapist to interpret the play of a child and relate it to the child's personality and home life. The judge was only able to decide about the witness's area of expertise after a psychologist was called to testify about the nature of play therapy.

There is considerable controversy about the qualifications of social workers to give expert opinion testimony about subjects relating to child development and behaviour. When dealing with these questions, judges have tended to rely on the testimony of formally qualified professionals, such as psychologists and psychiatrists. Some observers have described the mystique which attaches to these professionals as creating a "witch-doctor cult," with undue emphasis being placed on their opinions. Today, many social workers have extensive formal training and considerable experience. Dr. John Bowlby, the noted English child psychiatrist, suggested that social workers should raise their professional esteem and "stand up to the doctors and judges." Dr. Bowlby has argued that the professional status of social workers must be raised, remarking that, "In many cases, I would trust a social worker far more than a psychiatrist."[29] If the testimony of a social worker is challenged as constituting an opinion which can only be given by an "expert," it may be possible to qualify the witness as an expert, based on experience and training, and not on formal qualifications. As discussed earlier, another way of dealing with such a challenge is for the witness to relate the basis for formulating this opinion and allow the judge to form his own opinion.

If a person is qualified as an expert witness, he may make use of various texts, articles, or tables to assist in his testimony. The extent to which ordinary witnesses can make use of documents or notes will be discussed a little later; suffice to say that it is much more restricted than the opportunity offered an expert. The expert is able to refer to the works of other experts in the field on the theory that he is in effect adopting their ideas as his own. It is not possible for a lawyer, or a person who is not an expert, to simply start reading from a textbook to make a point, as this is clearly hearsay evidence. It is only when there is an expert present in court who adopts the ideas as his own, and is prepared to be cross-examined on the material in the text, that this is admissible.

The opinion of an expert witness may frequently be challenged[30] on cross-examination by confronting the expert with authoritative works in his field, espousing an opposing point of view, to cast doubt upon the correctness of his opinion. This can only be done if the expert witness himself acknowledges the work as authoritative. This places the expert witness in a position where he must explain any discrepancies in the views expressed in the text and his own. If the witness does not accept the work as authoritative, cross-examination on the basis of that work will not be allowed, as if it occurred, the judge could be forced to weigh the opinion of a sworn witness against that of a person not present to answer questions, surely a most unfair situation.

Another technique[31] used to cross-examine expert witnesses is to put questions to the expert which place a different interpretation on the facts upon which the expert is relying, and if possible show that the different interpretation is reasonable. An alternative technique is to show that the expert formed his opinion without taking into account facts which have either been established, or which the examiner hopes to establish. This latter technique may often be employed through the use of hypothetical questions, with the examiner making different factual assumptions, and asking the expert for an opinion.

One final note about expert witnesses is that in most jurisdictions there are statutory limitations on the number of expert witnesses which each party in a case can call to testify. Section 12 of the Ontario *Evidence Act* limits the number to three, though permission of the judge can be obtained to allow a party to have more experts testify.

4. Evidence of Character and Previous Conduct

It is a general rule that evidence of bad character or previous misconduct is not admissible to prove that a person is likely to have committed a particular act. It is true that, in ordinary life, one person's judgement of how another will behave in a particular situation will be greatly influenced by the way in which the latter person has acted in the past when confronted with the same situation. Similarly, when attempting to assess how a person will behave, one would generally be very interested in knowing what his reputation is and how his friends and neighbours think he might react. This type of evidence, however, is generally not admitted as it is considered extremely prejudicial to having a fair trial.

If the issue in a trial is fault in a motor vehicle accident, evidence that one of the drivers was previously found responsible for other accidents, and had a reputation among his friends for being a careless and speedy driver, is not admissible. The issue must be resolved by evidence relating directly to the conduct of the driver at the time of the accident in question.

In *R. v. Drysdale*, the accused was charged with murdering Angela Hawkins, the three-year-old daughter of his common-law wife. At the trial, witnesses gave testimony that on previous occasions the accused had abused the deceased child and her siblings. The Manitoba Court of Appeal ordered a new trial due to the improper admission of this evidence, remarking:[32]

> . . . that the previous acts of mistreatment of the child could not be used as evidence that the accused was a person of bad character of a propensity to commit the crime with which he was charged.

> . . . . .

> Concerning the evidence of prior acts relating to others than Angela, I am decidedly of the view that these were irrelevant and inadmissible. Their introduction in evidence was highly prejudicial to the accused.

Though one could argue that, logically, such evidence is not "irrelevant," as a matter of law it is clearly inadmissible.

There are a number of exceptions to the rule excluding evidence regarding character and previous conduct. Consideration will be given here to one very important exception for trials concerning children.

In cases where the issue arises of whether a person is well suited to care for a child, evidence concerning the past ability of that person to care for the child in question, or any other child, and evidence concerning that person's character or reputation will be admissible. The issue of whether a person is well suited to care for a child may arise in child protection cases, and also in cases where separated parents are disputing custody, or even access.

The issue in such a case is very different from that normally faced by a court. In most trials, the issue is whether a particular person did a particular act at a particular time. In this situation, the fact that that particular person committed the same act a previous time is generally not admissible as evidence. In a trial where the issue is whether a person is well suited to care for a child, the real question is whether, at that particular point in time, the person can care for the child. The only real way to deal with this question is to hear evidence of how that person has cared for children in the past.

In *C.A.S. of Winnipeg v. Forth*,[33] the Society was seeking permanent wardship of a physically abused child, and sought to introduce evidence about how the parents treated two older siblings of the child in question. The lawyer for the parents argued that this was irrelevant and evidence of "past conduct" which was inadmissible. The judge allowed the evidence to be heard, stating that it was evidence of "past-parenting" practice. If the parents had been charged with the criminal offense of assaulting their child in the *Forth* case, as they could have been but were not, such evidence would not have been admissible at the criminal trial following the principle set out in *R. v. Drysdale*. In the *Forth* case, the judge remarked:[34]

> In deciding whether a child's environment is injurious to himself, whether the parents are competent, whether a child's physical or mental health is endangered, surely evidence of past experience is invaluable to the court in assessing the present situation. But for the admissibility of this type of evidence children still in the custody of chronic child abusers may be beyond the protection of the court. . . .
>
> On the other hand, whereas it is my opinion that prior conduct is admissible because it is relevant, care must be taken when weighing "old" evidence. No court has yet been bold enough to invite birth-date apprehension on the basis of prior abuse to other children. An apprehending authority often has a difficult decision to make in abuse cases, wondering whether there is yet sufficient evidence upon which to secure an order.

Unfortunately, it has become clear that in some extreme cases "birth-date apprehension" may be necessary. In the case of *Vicky Ellis*,[35] an Ontario child protection case, testimony concerning the ill-treatment of older siblings of the child Vicky was not admitted into evidence. The child was returned to her parents and died shortly thereafter. Largely as a result of this case, the law of Ontario has been changed, and the *Child Welfare Act, 1978*, s. 28(4), now provides that in a child protection hearing, before a decision is made to return or place a child with an adult, the court may consider the past conduct of that adult towards any child that was in his care at any time, and that the judge may suspend the ordinary rules of evidence when attempting to determine the nature of such conduct. Children's Aid Societies are now prepared, in very serious cases, to apprehend the children of some parents at birth.

D. TESTIFYING IN COURT

1. The Obligation to Testify

The legal system can only operate effectively if all those persons who have knowledge of a case are available to testify in court, and rules have been developed to ensure the co-operation of witnesses. Any party to an action can require the attendance of any person as a witness by having that person served with a specific document of the court, generally known as a "subpoena," or a "summons to a witness." Any person receiving such a document is obliged to appear at the indicated time and place, and bring with him any documents mentioned in the subpoena provided he has them. If the person fails to attend, the judge may order that the witness be brought to court by the police or the sheriff, and further the witness may be fined or sentenced to jail for contempt of court for failing to attend. Invariably the threat of these sanctions is enough to prompt witnesses to attend.

Attending court as a witness is often a frustrating process, and invariably involves more time waiting in corridors than actually appearing in court. Busy professional people are often reluctant to be witnesses, but they are nevertheless obliged to respond to a subpoena. It is sometimes possible to arrange with the party who subpoenaed a witness that the witness will attend at a specific time, rather than waiting outside the court-room all day.

A witness is entitled to be paid a "witness fee," the amount of which is set by law, but usually this is not sufficient to compensate a witness for the loss of time involved. It is possible for an expert witness who is attending in the course of his professional work to be paid an additional "expert witness fee." For example, a psychologist may conduct an assessment of a child for the C.A.S., and then be subpoenaed to court to testify at a wardship hearing. If he is paid by the Society on a hourly basis, he is entitled to be compensated not only for the time he spends in his office doing the assessment, but also for the time spent at court. The psychologist cannot refuse to testify if he does not receive this additional fee, but he may refuse to be a consultant for the Society in the future, and arguably could sue the Society for the additional fee in a civil action. It is important to realize that the expert's entitlement to this fee does not arise out of the fact that he is a busy man whose time is valuable and who is forced to come to court, but rather out of the nature of the contractual relationship he has with the Society, in which the Society agreed to pay him for services rendered, services which included testifying in court. If the same psychologist happened to witness a motor vehicle accident and was subpoenaed to come to court in regard to that matter, he would only be entitled to the ordinary witness fee, a fee which is invariably only a fraction of the expert witness fee.

2. Privilege

A witness who is subpoenaed to court must not only attend, he must, as a general rule, answer all questions put to him. The refusal to answer a question will constitute contempt of court, and the presiding judge may order the witness fined or imprisoned. A witness may be ordered imprisoned until he answers the questions put to him, or he may simply receive a definite term of imprisonment or a fine. While it is recognized that if the court is to discover the truth in a case, witnesses must answer questions which are put to them, it is also recognized that there are other conflicting social goals which may require that certain types of witnesses not be compelled to testify, and that certain types of communication not be disclosed. The term "privilege" is used to describe a right which a person may have to prevent the court from hearing certain types of evidence. Some of the more important rules regarding privilege will be considered here.

A. Self-Incrimination

The privilege against self-incrimination has a history dating back to the Court of the Star Chamber. According to the rule, as it is now formulated, no person in a criminal proceeding can be required to testify against himself. It originally developed because of the abuses and torture which arose when the accused could be required to testify. It has come to be an accepted tenet of our criminal justice system that the prosecution should be able to prove its case, beyond a reasonable doubt, without relying on the testimony of the accused. The accused may, of course, testify on his behalf, and he then becomes subject to complete cross-examination. Further, if the accused has elected not to testify at a criminal trial at which he is charged with an offense, he can then be ordered by the court to testify; various statutory provisions, such as s. 5 of the *Canada Evidence Act*, specify that if a witness testifies in this situation, the answers given by him cannot be used in subsequent criminal proceedings. Also, the privilege does not apply to proceedings which are not criminal trials. Thus, at a wardship hearing, when the C.A.S. is alleging child abuse, the Society may call the mother as a witness and ask her whether she assaulted her child. An affirmative answer could open the mother to a criminal prosecution. She can make use of the protection offered by the *Canada Evidence Act* by objecting to answering such a question on the ground that it may tend to incriminate her, and the judge may then order her to testify under the protection of the Act. It is important to note that the protection offered by the *Canada Evidence Act* only comes into force if there is a specific objection by a witness to answering a question, and an order from the judge to answer under the protection of the Act.

B. Spousal Privilege

Another old common-law rule is that one spouse cannot be called by the prosecution to give evidence against the other in a criminal proceeding. The rationale for this rule is that forcing one spouse to testify would tend to weaken and disrupt families, and that preserving families is as important as discovering the truth. This rule does not apply to common-law spouses. Further, it does not apply if the spouse who is testifying is the victim of the offense, or if the offense is one of a number of statutorily specified offenses, mainly of a sexual or immoral nature.[36] A spouse of the accused may still be called as a witness by the defense in a criminal prosecution. There is no privilege concerning spousal testimony in trials not involving criminal charges.

The desire to promote marital harmony has also led to other types of spousal privileges. Thus, in any type of proceeding, whether it is criminal or civil, one spouse cannot be required to reveal communication received from the other.[37] In a child protection proceeding involving alleged child abuse by the mother, the father can be required to testify for the C.A.S., but he cannot be required to reveal what his wife told him; for example, he cannot be required to testify that his wife admitted to him that she beat the child. The spouse who is testifying may choose not to exercise this privilege and testify about the communication.

C. Professional Privileges

The notion that communication between a lawyer and his client must not be revealed has its origins in ancient Roman law, and has come to be embodied in our rules concerning "solicitor–client privilege." The rationale for the existence of this privilege is that without an assurance of complete confidentiality the effectiveness of the legal system, and the legal profession, would be greatly impaired. The privilege covers statements made by both the lawyer and the client. It also extends to the notes and records kept by a lawyer concerning a case, and to reports produced for the lawyer in preparation for litigation. In preparing for a custody trial, a lawyer may send his client to a psychiatrist to obtain a report on his client's capacity to care for a child. Neither the psychiatrist nor the lawyer can be compelled to reveal the contents of the report.

The solicitor–client privilege is sometimes described as the client's privilege. It is only the client who can decide to testify in court about matters governed by this rule, or instruct his lawyer to testify. The lawyer cannot, of his own volition, decide to waive this privilege. The privilege cannot be raised to cover otherwise admissible testimony simply because the information was also the subject of solicitor–client communication. If the accused chooses to testify in a murder trial, he cannot refuse to answer a question asking whether he was at the scene of the crime simply by stating that the information is privileged since he gave the information to his lawyer. On the other hand, the lawyer cannot be called upon to testify what the client admitted to him.

The relationship of a lawyer and his client is not the only relationship based on confidentiality. Other relationships include priest and penitent, doctor and patient, and social worker and client. There are ethical and legal rules protecting these relationships and preventing the disclosure of information gained in confidence. But in Canada,[38] these relationships are not afforded an absolute legal privilege which prevents disclosure of communication if one of the parties is subpoenaed to testify in a trial.

The situation in which this most often arises is when a party to an action has made some sort of an admission to a professional person, and the professional person is then subpoenaed to testify to relate that admission to the court. The professional person may be reluctant to reveal the nature of the communication because it will jeopardize the relationship of trust which the professional wants to establish, not only with the party concerned, but with all those with whom he interacts. For example, a father may admit to his doctor or his priest that he sexually abuses his daughter. As was discussed in Chapter 4, such a person will have a duty to report this information to child protection authorities. The person may also be required to come to court and testify about such admissions.

It is possible for a witness who wishes to protect a confidential relationship to tell the judge that he would prefer not to answer as this would disrupt the relationship. Although there is no absolute privilege, the judge has a discretion to allow a witness to keep his confidentiality if this should appear to be in the public interest. In *Cronkwright v. Cronkwright*,[39] an Anglican clergyman had been counselling two spouses; the clergyman objected to answering questions about the counselling. The judge noted that he had a discretionary power to grant a privilege and did not order the minister to answer. The judge remarked:

> "It is my personal opinion that it is the position that ought to be taken by all persons who, by their profession or in the work in which they are engaged, find themselves in a position of confidence. I think that professional people and people enjoying confidence of this kind, by reason of their office or special work, have a duty to endeavour to preserve that confidence as much and as far as is open to them.
>
> "As far as the Court is concerned, I do not recognize any of these as privileges or points of view that should prevail, in proper cases, against the overpowering necessity in our society for the fair and open administration of justice."

In somewhat similar situations, judges have allowed doctors and psychiatrists to refrain from answering questions.[40] The courts have seemed particularly prepared to respect the need for confidentiality when testimony relates to what transpired during an attempted reconciliation of spouses. However, if the welfare of a child may be affected by the refusal to testify, the courts are particularly apt to order a witness to answer questions.[41]

It is, of course, always open to a witness to explain his position to the judge. The judge may then order the witness to answer, but the witness may still refuse to respond, and, if it is a matter of firm belief, indicate that he is prepared to go to jail rather than testify. Faced with this form of conscientious objection and a carefully explained position, most judges will be very reluctant to send a respected professional person to jail for contempt of court.[42]

3. Refreshing the Memory of a Witness

A witness at a trial will be testifying about events which occurred in the past, sometimes several weeks previous, but more usually several months, or even years in the past. It is hardly surprising that witnesses frequently do not recall all the details of an event, or perhaps do not even recall the event itself. Problems of recollection of past events are especially acute for a witness who is testifying about a matter connected with the ordinary course of his employment, as frequently many similar events occur which are difficult to distinguish. For example, if a motorist decides to fight his speeding ticket at court, a trial will usually be held many weeks after the event. This may have been the only occasion on which the motorist has been stopped by a policeman, and he will doubtless remember this unique event in vivid detail. The policeman, however, will probably have stopped several hundred motorists for speeding since this ticket was issued, and he may not even remember meeting this motorist. It is hardly surprising that rules have been developed to allow witnesses to refresh their memory before or during testimony. Most frequently, a witness will be using his own notes to assist his memory.

The general rule is that a witness may use a written document to assist him in testifying, if one of two conditions is satisfied:
(1) The document was made by the witness at or near the time of the occurrence of the event or matter recorded; or
(2) The document was made by a person other than the witness, recording events or matters observed by the witness, and the witness verified that the document was accurate, while the facts were still fresh in his memory.
It is important to realize that it is only if one of these two conditions is satisfied that a witness can refer to notes or written documents while testifying.

The effect of this is that many professional witnesses will not have notes or files which they will be permitted to use to assist them while testifying. This rule of evidence is not satisfied if a witness dictates notes which are typed by a secretary, unless the witness checks the accuracy of the typing while the events are fresh in his mind. It is, similarly, not sufficient for a witness to review a file and make notes from the file prior to testifying, and then expect to use the notes recently made. As with any other rule of evidence, the parties may agree not to strictly enforce this rule, and there is a tendency to be notably lax when a witness is giving expert opinion evidence; however, witnesses must always be aware of the strict dictates of the law. Frequently, witnesses who intend to rely on notes or other writings which are not technically permissible are rendered ineffective witnesses when they find these aids to the memory withdrawn.

If a witness wishes to refer to a written record for the purpose of refreshing his memory, the judge's permission should be asked, and the judge should be satisfied that the conditions for doing so have been met. Counsel for the opposite party is entitled to inspect the document, and to cross-examine the witness as to its contents. There is authority for the proposition that counsel can demand the production of documents used to refresh a witness's memory prior to testifying, even if they are not used on the stand.[43] Thus if a witness has been using his notes selectively to pick out facts which support his current view of the situation, he may be confronted with some other facts referred to in the notes which are not as consistent.

Prior to testifying, a witness may refresh his memory by referring to any type of memory aid, including any type of documents, or photographs, provided the witness is indeed simply bringing his memory back into sharper focus. If, however, the witness has no independent recollection of the events in question and must rely totally on the record available, then the only record which the witness should refer to, even prior to testifying, is one which could be used while testifying, and which satisfies the two conditions outlined above;[44] failure to do so may result in judicial censure and seriously affect the weight given to the testimony.

In recent years, witnesses have been making use of more exotic memory aids than written documents. In *R. v. Pitt*,[45] a woman was charged with the attempted murder of her husband and wished to testify on her own behalf. She had difficulty in recalling the events at the crucial time. The judge allowed a psychiatrist to hypnotize her in open court to assist her in remembering the details. After she was assisted in recalling the events through hypnosis, she took the stand and testified in the usual way. It was left for the jury to decide whether the hypnosis actually revived her repressed memory. In some American cases, use has been made of sodium Pentothal, a so-called "truth serum," to assist a witness in recalling past events.

4. Exclusion of Witnesses

In earlier chapters there was a discussion of the fact that public access to certain proceedings involving children is strictly limited. These include child protection, adoption, and delinquency hearings. In any type of hearing, the judge has an inherent power[46] to exclude people who are going to be called to testify as witnesses, except that the parties themselves can virtually never be excluded. The purpose of giving a judge this power is so that he can ensure that one witness is not influenced by another. Also, a witness may have an advantage in preparing for his own examination and cross-examination by listening to the questioning of other witnesses. The order for the exclusion of witnesses will generally be made if requested by a party.

FOOTNOTES

1. Two good Canadian legal texts on the laws of evidence are, John Sopinka and Sidney Lederman, *The Law of Evidence in Civil Cases* (Toronto, 1974); and Peter McWilliams, *Canadian Criminal Evidence* (Toronto, 1974)
2. The *Canada Evidence Act*, s. 14; and, for example, the Ontario *Evidence Act*, s. 17. Other provinces have similar provisions.
3. *R. v. Ah Wooey* (1902), 8 C.C.C. 25
4. The *Criminal Code*, s. 120
5. See Rupert Cross, *Evidence*, 4th ed. (London, 1974), at p. 10
6. See *Re A.M.* (1976), 22 R.F.L. 78
7. (1838), 168 E.R. 1136 at p. 1137
8. *R. v. Cooper* (1977), 74 D.L.R. (3d) 731
9. *Montreal Tramways Co. v. Leveille*, [1938] S.C.R. 456 at p. 475
10. Sir James F. Stephen, *A Digest of the Law of Evidence*, 12th ed. (London, 1948), at p. 4
11. See *MacDonald v. MacDonald* (1976), 21 R.F.L. 42
12. Rupert Cross, *Evidence*, 4th ed. (London, 1974), at p. 6
13. [1956] 1 W.L.R. 965
14. (1976), 28 R.F.L. 181
15. *Supra*, at p. 182
16. The *Criminal Code*, s. 122
17. See, for example, the *Child Welfare Act, 1978*, s. 28(5). See also *Battah v. Battah* (1978), 5 R.F.L. (2d) 383
18. *Re Maloney* (1971), 12 R.F.L. 167
19. *Kapulica v. Dumancic*, [1968] 2 O.R. 438
20. (1970), 10 D.L.R. (3d) 432. See also *C.A.S. of Sarnia v. Brander* (1978), 8 R.F.L. (2d) 58
21. See *de Genova v. de Genova* (1971), 20 D.L.R. (3d) 264
22. *Ibrahim v. The King*, [1914] A.C. 599 at p. 609
23. The Evidence Acts of the various provinces and the federal government have all limited the effect of the hearsay rule. The Law Reform Commission of Canada, Report on Evidence (Ottawa, 1975), recommends further restrictions on the rule. See also *Ares v. Venner*, [1970] S.C.R. 608
24. Charles T. McCormick, *Handbook on the Law of Evidence*, 2nd ed. (St. Paul, 1972), at pp. 23-24
25. *Wilband v. The Queen*, [1967] S.C.R. 14 at p. 21

26. For somewhat contrasting views in the Ontario Court of Appeal, see *R. v. Rosik* (1971), 2 C.C.C. (2d) 351; and *R.v. Swietlinski* (1978), 5 C.R. (3d) 324

27. (1912), 27 O.L.R. 410 at p. 413

28. (1978), unreported ruling, Judge Goulard (Ont. Prov. Ct. (Fam. Div.))

29. "Family Courts Are No Place for Psychiatrists, Two Doctors Say," *The Globe & Mail*, June 17, 1978

30. See *R. v. Anderson* (1914), 16 D.L.R. 203

31. For a discussion of the cross-examination of expert witnesses, see the 1969 *Special Lectures* of the Law Society of Upper Canada

32. [1969] 2 C.C.C. 141 at pp. 145-46

33. (1978), 1 R.F.L. (2d) 46

34. *Supra*, at pp. 51-52

35. For a description of the *Vicky Ellis* case, see Peter Silverman, *Who Speaks for the Children? The Plight of the Battered Child* (Toronto, 1978), Chapter 1

36. The *Canada Evidence Act*, s. 4

37. The *Canada Evidence Act*, s. 4(3); and the Ontario *Evidence Act*, s. 11

38. The American legislatures have tended to be much more protective of such relationships. See Jeff Rosley, "Child Abuse and the Social Worker: Rights of Parents," 1 Fam. L. Rev. 247 (1978); and Charles T. McCormick, *Handbook on the Law of Evidence,* 2nd ed. (St. Paul, 1972), Chapter 11.

39. (1970), 2 R.F.L. 241 at p. 243. The *Newfoundland Evidence Act*, s. 6, and the Quebec *Code of Civil Procedure*, art. 308, grant absolute privilege to clergymen.

40. See *Dembie v. Dembie* (1963), 21 R.F.L. 46; and *Shakotko v. Shakotko* (1976), 27 R.F.L. 1. Quebec has legislation granting privilege to doctors; the *Medical Act*, s. 60(2).

41. *Robson v. Robson*, [1969] 2 O.R. 857

42. See Haymen, "Psychoanalyst Subpoenaed," *The Lancet* (England, October 16, 1965), at p. 785

43. *R. v. Lewis*, [1969] 3 C.C.C. 235, but see *R. v. Kerenko*, [1965] 3 C.C.C. 52, for a different point of view

44. *R. v. Hubands* (1973), 24 C.R.N.S. 188

45. *R. v. Pitt*, [1968] 3 C.C.C. 342. See a note on this decision at 11 Crim. L.Q. 120 (1969)

46. There is often a statutory power: see, for example, the Ontario Rules of Practice, Rule 253. *Moore v. Lambeth County Court Registrar*, [1969] 1 W.L.R. 141, suggests that there is an inherent power in a trial judge to make such an order.

Chapter 9

The Child and the Professional

A. MEDICAL TREATMENT

1. General

Consider the following scenario: a 16-year-old girl is engaging in sexual relations with her boyfriend. Concerned about the possibility of pregnancy, she visits a physician to discuss various means of contraception. During the course of her consultation, the girl requests that her visit, and the reason therefor, be kept confidential—specifically, she is concerned about her parents.

This fact situation raises two issues. Can the doctor treat the girl without parental knowledge and consent and, assuming the answer is in the affirmative, can he subsquently maintain a policy of confidentiality and not advise the girl's parents of the nature of her consultation.

The answers to these questions place a physician treating a child patient in a precarious legal position. Historically, as discussed in the preceding chapters, a child is without legal capacity to act on his own behalf in many circumstances relating to his day-to-day affairs. As a consequence, often the child must involve an adult, usually his parents, in order to obtain certain services. The issue of medical treatment is no different and a special set of rules apply to children seeking medical advice.

If a physician administers treatment to a child, and if the child's consent is held to be invalid,, he may be liable in tort law (negligence) through the mechanism of a "tortious" assault.

Concerning the matter of a tortious assault, the classic statement of the law is found in Salmond, *The Law of Torts*:[1]

> The application of force, to the person of another without lawful justification
> amounts to the wrong of battery. This is so, however trivial the amount
> or nature of the force may be, and even though it neither does nor is
> intended nor is likely nor is able to do any manner of harm. Even to touch
> a person without his consent or some other lawful reason is actionable.

For instance, if an intra uterine device is inserted without valid consent, an assault may have occurred. Even prescribing a birth control pill may amount to a "technical'' assault since the intention is to bring an object (the pill) into contact with another person.[2]

Other cases have considered the question of whether, by prescribing birth control devices, a physician has in effect contributed to the delinquency of his child patient. The issue of delinquency was canvassed in Chapter 6 and it was noted there that it is necessary to establish some causal connection between the act complained of and any subsequent delinquency engaged in by the child. Applying this logic to the question of contraceptives, it would be necessary to establish a causal connection between the act of providing access to contraceptives and any subsequent sexual immorality (a delinquency) indulged in by the female patient. On this point, most authorities are agreed that sexual activity on the part of children is not dependent on the availabilty of contraceptives. One American writer who explored this issue noted that a wide variety of contraceptive devices are already available to a child "in the know." Therefore, he concluded that a physician who makes oral contraceptives or intra uterine devices available:[3]

> . . . is not providing a contraceptive service that would otherwise be wholly
> unavailable, he is only increasing the degree of protection already
> obtainable. To convict a physician of contributing to a minor's delinquency
> it would therefore be necessary to prove that it was the extra increase
> of birth protection that encouraged the minor to become sexually active.

It is highly unlikely that a Canadian court would be prepared to attach criminal liability to a physician prescribing contraceptives to a child patient.

However, the physician still faces the dilemma of so advising such patients because of his potential civil liability, that is, the possibility of being negligent in accepting an invalid consent. On the one hand, the doctor has a young girl engaging in sexual intercourse facing the risk of an unwanted pregnancy; on the other hand, he faces the possibility of incurring liability. There is unfortunately, at least at present, no statutory authority to guide him in his treatment of children independent of parental consent. The common law is very confusing in this sensitive area. A "composite" profile of what may be described as the "emancipated child" may be put together from the cases[4] which have discussed treatment of children without parental consent. A child so described *may* give a valid consent to most forms of medical treatment, including requesting advice on contraception. If a child meets the following criteria (derived from the case-law), a physician may essentially treat the child as if he were an adult patient:

(1) the treatment must benefit the child;
(2) the child must be sufficiently mature to understand the nature and consequences of the treatment;
(3) the degree of the child's withdrawal from parental influence must be considered.

Other factors implicit in the above considerations must also be weighed, including the age of the child, the purposes for and the complexity of the treatment. It should be noted that these criteria apply to any form of treatment and not just the prescription of contraceptive devices.

From the foregoing, it may be concluded that the younger the child the more difficult the decision facing the physician.

Returning to the scenario described at the outset of the chapter, assume the girl (16 years old) is living at home with her parents. She is a grade 11 student and is doing well in school. Should her physician prescribe a contraceptive device independent of parental knowledge and consent? Would your answer change if the girl had moved out of the family home and was living with her boyfriend? What if the girl was only 15 and still living at home? It is probable that a 16-year-old girl living with her boyfriend could give a valid consent. On the other hand, the girl living at home, be she 15 or 16 years old, presents a more difficult situation. However, it is probable that if she is of sufficient maturity to understand the nature and consequences of the use of contraceptives, her physician would be protected from civil liability in prescribing a contraceptive device.

The Canadian Foundation for Children and the Law Incorporated, mentioned briefly in Chapter 1, has prepared a brief on the medical consent of children.[5] The Foundation recommends statutory guidelines to assist physicians and other health care officials in determining situations in which a valid consent may be given by a child. The issue of consent would be decided according to the following criteria:

1. (i) Any person may give a valid consent to health care treatment if they have the capacity to give an informed consent.
    (ii) An informed consent exists if:
        (a) the person has been fully informed of the proposed procedures;
        (b) the person understands the nature and consequences of the prodedures;
        (c) consent is freely given.

2. Without limiting the generality of the foregoing, health care providers should consider the following criteria in the determination of competence:
    (i) any person aged 16 years or more or emancipated shall be presumed to have capacity to give an informed consent as if she/he had attained the age of majority;
    (ii) the minor's own recognition of his health needs;
    (iii) the minor's maturity;
    (iv) the minor's intellectual functioning;
    (v) the minor's ability to assess possible options;
    (vi) the complexity of the health services contemplated;
    (vii) any danger to the life and functioning of the minor.

3. Where the minor has capacity to consent to treatment, no further consent should be required, except in circumstances in which "major" surgery may be involved.

It has been said by health care authorities that the incidence of venereal disease in young people has reached epidemic proportions. As a consequence, special legislation exists in most provinces with respect to venereal disease. In Ontario, the *Venereal Diseases Prevention Act* directs that any notices or orders (treatments) for the purpose of treating and containing venereal diseases must be given to the parents of an afflicted child under the age of 16. Thus it would appear that a physician is under a legal obligation to advise the parents of a child he is treating for a venereal disease. The Canadian Foundation for Children and the Law Incorporated are at odds with this legislative position. Given the sensitive and intimate nature of such a medical problem, the Foundation advocates that *any* child (regardless of age) should have an absolute right to treatment independent of parental knowledge and consent. The Foundation applies the same "emancipated" philosophy to the issues of contraception, abortion, and alcohol or drug abuse.

These issues, because of their sensitive and personal nature, must be examined with the utmost discretion by those involved in the treatment and counselling of children so affected. At issue is the privacy and integrity of the child's self-image. The State's intervention in such personal issues must be handled with extreme caution at the risk of denying a child a basic human right—the invasion of privacy.

What about the issue of confidentiality? It would appear that a physician may treat his child patient in confidence provided the child could be considered as "emancipated" and, therefore, could validly consent to treatment. In such circumstances, only upon the consent of the child could a physician disclose confidential medical information to the child's parents.

What are the possible consequences if a physician fails to advise the parents of certain medical treatments administered by him to a child patient who is not described as "emancipated"? In *Re D. and Council of College of Physicians and Surgeons of British Columbia*,[6] British Columbia Supreme Court dismissed an appeal from a ruling of the British Columbia Council of Physicians and Surgeons wherein a doctor had been found guilty of "infamous or unprofessional conduct" when he inserted an intra uterine device in a 15-year-old female patient without parental consent and knowledge. Thus, a physician may be guilty of malpractice according to the rules of the professional body regulating his practice of medicine. He may also be found to be negligent in failing to obtain parental consent and/or not advising parents of treatments if his child patient's consent is held to be invalid. The above case underlines the need for the physician to discuss fully any treatments he may be administering to his patient child and to ensure that his young patient has the maturity to comprehend the nature and consequence of the treatment. If the physician is in doubt as to the issue of maturity then he would be wise to discuss the matter with the child's parents.

2. Admission to Treatment Centres

As a general rule, before a child can be admitted to a treatment facility such as a hospital or a mental health clinic, the consent of a parent must be obtained. However, some facilities will allow an "emancipated" child to sign himself in. More particularly, these institutions allow the emancipated child to consent to treatments, while he is resident in the institution. This issue is more troublesome when one is dealing with a child suffering from a mental health problem such as an emotional or other behavioural disturbance. This is because the treatment may involve controversial techniques such as segregation, physical restraint, shock treatments, and medication. In such circumstances, treatment officials are very reluctant to commence procedures without parental or guardian approval.

However, perhaps the most troublesome issue involving children and mental health centres is that parents may have their child committed without a hearing. In general, adult admissions to such centres may be described as either voluntary or involuntary. An involuntary committal of an adult cannot be accomplished without a hearing before a competent medical committee. As noted above, this right (the purpose of which is to ensure that involuntary committals are screened, thus avoiding unwarranted committals which could otherwise occur) is not extended to a child. Consequently, a parent, whether *bona fide* or not, can have a child committed without a hearing. Needless to say, this casual procedure is of grave concern to those interested in protecting the rights of children. A number of the provinces are investigating a legislative remedy whereby the committal of children to mental health centres would be subject to scrutiny at a proper hearing.

B. COUNSELLING

Counselling by those in the child care field (other than physicians) is best distinguished from medical treatment. Physicians are subject to "policing" by the professional organization to which they belong. On the other hand, there are many types of professionals in the field of child care—psychologists, social workers and child care workers—who are essentially unfettered in the sense of an absence of legislative regulations governing the conduct of their profession. Therefore, those who provide what may be generically described as counselling services are subject to a different standard of care from the medical practitioner. In addition; a counsellor apparently has more latitude in advising children independent of parental knowledge and consent. This perhaps mostly due to the intangible nature of the process of counselling as opposed to the physical character of usual medical treatment. None the less, a counsellor may be found liable in civil law and also in criminal law if he trespasses in certain specified areas. For instance, a counsellor may not interfere with a parent's right to "possession" of a child under the age of 14 found in a youth hostel. Thus, if such a child seeks refuge in a hostel and a counsellor employed in that establishment counsels the child to disobey a parental command to return to the family home, that counsellor may be in jeopardy of breaching the criminal law and being found guilty of the offense of harbouring. In such circumstances, therefore, it is essential and incumbent upon the counsellor to ensure the child is seeking advice of his own free will; and that further, the counsellor is not advising the child to disobey the lawful demand of a parent.

A counsellor must also be on the alert not to provide accommodation (even in a hostel or group home) or act in such a way that he "takes or causes to be taken" a female child under the age of 16 out of the possession of and *against the will* of the parent. It is not a defence to the counsellor that the child came of her own free will. Two things should be noted both with respect to "harbouring," the situation described above concerning a child under the age of 14, and "abduction," taking a female child away from her parents. First, there is no onus on the counsellor to notify the parents of the child's whereabouts; secondly, if the child is in effect "living on the streets," giving such a child shelter will almost certainly not be construed as either harbouring or abduction.

In addition to the criminal liability described above, a counsellor may be liable in the law of negligence if, as a result of his actions, he caused the child to suffer some form of harm. Either the child or the parents could sue the counsellor for financial compensation.

Lastly, it should be noted that both the medical practitioner and the counsellor, in certain jurisdictions (Ontario, for instance), is under a legal obligation to report any suspected incidents of child abuse. Failure to so report may result in the counsellor/physician being subject to a penal sanction including a fine. This issue was discussed in detail in Chapter 4.

In conclusion then, physicians and other child care professionals must tight-rope walk the thin line between administering medical treatment or giving advice without parental consent and the risk of incurring legal liability if the consent is found to be invalid. The law is obscure in this area. There are common-law guidelines, but of course, few health care professionals know the common law and are prone to denying services out of an overabundance of caution. Legislative intervention is apparently required and indeed some provinces such as British Columbia and Ontario are moving to define criteria in which valid consents may be given by children to medical treatment and to counselling.

FOOTNOTES

1. 15th ed. (London: Sweet and Maxwell, 1969), at p. 157
2. See Lord Nathan, *Medical Negligence* (London: Butterworth, 1957)
3. Richard Gilborn, "Legal Problems Involved in the Prescription of Contraceptives to Unmarried Minors in Alberta," 12 Alta. Law Rev. 359 (1974)
4. See *Younts v. St. Francis Hospital and School of Nursing Inc.* (1970), 469 P. 2d 330; *Booth v. Toronto General Hospital* (1910), 170 W.R. 118; and *Johnson v. Wellesley Hospital*, [1971] 2 O.R. 103
5. See paper published by Justice for Children (Canadian Foundation for Children and the Law Inc., Toronto, Ontario), "Brief on Medical Consent of Minors," February 18, 1980
6. (1970), 11 D.L.R. (3d) 570

Appendix

Finding the Law*

A. SOURCES OF LAW

Though it is generally not very difficult for a trained person to discover what the law says about a particular matter, sometimes it can be a trying task even for a skilled and patient mind. Much of our law is found in various pieces of legislation, or statutes, passed by the different levels of government. Some of the law is found in the decisions of judges, often referrred to as "cases" or "judgements." These cases may interpret the statutes, or expound on the common law. The most important cases are collected into "law reports" and published, though sometimes "unreported decisions," decisions which are not found in any law reports, may be of interest. The concepts of statutory law and common law, and the significance of cases, were discussed in Chapter 2.

There are also a number of "secondary sources" which assist one in discovering the law, including legal periodicals, textbooks, and case-books. Legal periodicals contain articles discussing various points of law and are often published by law schools, such as the *Osgoode Hall Law Journal*, or they may deal with a particular subject-matter, such as the *Canadian Journal of Family Law*. Textbooks are written by authors who explain and interpret areas of law, often interrelating statutes and case-law. Case-books are frequently used in law schools and generally contain collections of cases from different courts dealing with a particular area of law. There are also various legal encyclopaedias, digests and indexes which help one locate cases dealing with particular issues.

All Canadian law schools have large libraries to which the public can obtain limited access. Many of the larger public libraries have at least a few law books, generally some statutes and textbooks, particularly texts such as this which are written for the layman. In most county towns and court-houses there is a law library which would contain most of the materials referred to in this book. Access to these libraries is generally restricted to lawyers and judges, but it is sometimes possible for a member of the public to obtain special permission to make use of such a library.

B. STATUTE LAW

After a statute is passed by either Parliament or a provincial legislature, it is

---

*This appendix is partially based on *Criminal Law and the Canadian Criminal Code*, Kenneth L. Clarke *et al.* (Toronto: McGraw-Hill Ryerson, 1977) at pp. 6-8.

published by the official government press. Usually all the statutes (or Acts) passed in one legislative session are contained in one volume. About every 10 years, all the statutes are revised and consolidated into one set of volumes. Parliament then repeals the former statutes and enacts as law the newly revised ones. Revisions are necessary mainly to correct any errors in the original statutes and to incorporate into each any subsequent amendments. The last revision of the federal statutes occurred in 1970. So, a law first passed in 1965 can be found in the 1970 revised statutes. Here, each Act is given a separate chapter number and is listed alphabetically. A statute passed in 1976 will be found in the sessional volume for that year. These are usually listed in order of enactment. At the back of each sessional volume is a Table of Public Statutes which lists the Acts by title or subject-matter. These tables are very useful for locating statutes and checking for amendments.

The titles of the volumes are often referred to in abbreviated form. Revised statutes are abbreviated as "R.S." followed by the initial of the province or a "C." for Canada. If a sessional volume is referred to the "R." is dropped. Next the year of enactment is given. Thus, R.S.C. 1970 stands for Revised Statutes of Canada enacted in 1970. If a particular statute is mentioned its chapter number is given after the year. Statutes are divided into sections. If a section is referred to, a lower case "s" followed by the section number is written after the chapter number. For example: *Juvenile Delinquents Act*, R.S.C. 1970, c. J-3, s. 9.

C. CASE-LAW

There are many different series of case reports including national, regional, provincial and topical series. Some of these are official publications, while others are printed by private publishing companies. Only the more important cases are contained in these reports. The cases which would typically be reported would be the decisions in cases that have been appealed, cases which set precedents, and cases involving unclear areas of law. Not everything that has occurred in a case is reported. Usually, only the judge's written decision, which may often include a recital of the facts, and the reasons for his decision is reported. If more than one judge has heard the case (an appeal court frequently has more than one judge sitting) and there is a dissenting opinion, this will often be included in the report. A dissenting opinion results when the judges who have heard the case fail to reach a unanimous decision. In this situation the decision agreed to by a majority of the judges becomes the official decision of the court. The decision of the minority becomes the dissenting opinion. The court's decision is often referred to as the "holding" in the case. Similarly, a reference may be made to what the judge (or court) "held" in a case.

At the beginning of each case there will be a brief summary of the case known as a "headnote."

To locate a case it is important to understand case citation, which is a particular form of citation and abbreviation that is used by the legal profession. The glossary following this appendix gives a complete list of the names and accepted abbreviations for the various series used in this text.[1]

The following chart indicates the form used for citing cases most frequently used and the meaning of each element of the citation.

READING A CASE CITATION

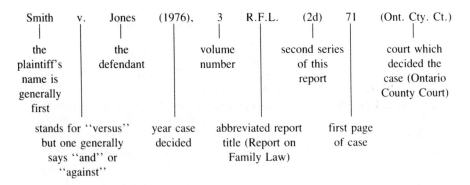

If a case involved a criminal prosecution, the case will often be cited as *R. v. Jones*; "R." stands for Rex (King), or Regina (Queen), depending on who was on the throne at the time the case arose. In a civil case, the first name will generally be that of the person bringing the matter to court, who may be referred to as the plaintiff, the petitioner, or the applicant, while the second will be respectively known as the defendant or the respondent. If the decision reported is that of an appeal court, usually the name of the appellant (the party appealing) is given first, followed by name of the respondent (the party responding to the appeal).

A case involving a child may, for example, be referred to as *Re Danny T.* "Re" is Latin for "in the matter of." Cases involving children often refer to the parties involved by their first names or initials to preserve their anonymity.

FOOTNOTES

1. For further assistance see J.A. Yogis *et al.*, *Legal Writing and Research Manual* (Toronto, 1974)

Glossary

Abbreviations for Case Reports and Periodicals
(Unless indicated references are Canadian)

A.	Atlantic Reporter (American)
A.C.	Law Reports Appeal Cases (English)
A.C.W.S.	All Canada Weekly Summaries
All E.R.	All England Law Reports (English)
ALR	American Law Reports (American)
Alta. Law Rev.	Alberta Law Review
Amer. Crim. Law Rev.	American Criminal Law Review (American)
A.P.R.	Atlantic Provinces Reports
Can. Bar Rev.	Canadian Bar Review
Can. J. Crim.	Canadian Journal of Criminology
Can. J. Crim. & Corr.	Canadian Journal of Criminology and Corrections
Can. J. Fam. L.	Canadian Journal of Family Law
C.A.S. Jo.	Children's Aid Society Journal
C.C.C.	Canadian Criminal Cases
Ch.	Law Reports Chancery Division (English)
Chitty's L.J.	Chitty's Law Journal
Cox's C.C.	Cox's Criminal Cases (English)
C.R.	Criminal Reports (English)
Crim. L.Q.	Criminal Law Quarterly
C.R.N.S.	Criminal Reports, New Series
D.L.R.	Dominion Law Reports
Duquesne Law Rev.	Duquesne Law Review (American)
E.R.	English Reports (English)
Fam. L. Rev.	Family Law Review
F.L.R.R.	Family Law Reform Reporter
L.M.Q.	Legal Medical Quarterly
Man. L.J.	Manitoba Law Journal
N.B.R.	New Brunswick Reports
N.E.	North Eastern Reporter (American)
Nfld. & P.E.I.R.	Newfoundland and Prince Edward Island Reports
N.S.W.R.	New South Wales Reports (Australian)
N.W.	North Western Reporter (American)
O.L.R.	Ontario Law Reports
Ontario Medical Rev.	Ontario Medical Review
O.R.	Ontario Reports
Osgoode Hall L.J.	Osgoode Hall Law Journal
O.W.N.	Ontario Weekly Notes

P.	Pacific Reporter (American)
Q.B.	Law Reports Queen's Bench (English)
R.F.L.	Reports of Family Law
San Diego Law Rev.	San Diego Law Review (American)
S.C.R.	Supreme Court Reports
S. Ct.	Supreme Court Reporter (American)
Sol. J.	Solicitors' Journal (English)
S.R. (N.S.W.)	State Reports (New South Wales) (Australian)
U.S.	United States Reports (American)
U.T.L.J.	University of Toronto Law Journal
Vil. Law Rev.	Villanova Law Review (American)
W.L.R.	Weekly Law Reports (English)
W.N.	Weekly Notes (Australian)
W.R.	Weekly Reports (English)
W.W.D.	Western Weekly Digest
W.W.R.	Western Weekly Reports

Index